FOREIGN LANGUAGE TEACHING

An Anthology

FOREIGN LANGUAGE TEACHING

An Anthology

JOSEPH MICHEL

University of Texas

THE MACMILLAN COMPANY, NEW YORK

COLLIER-MACMILLAN LIMITED, LONDON

First Printing

Library of Congress catalog card number: 67–13620

THE MACMILLAN COMPANY, NEW YORK
COLLIER-MACMILLAN CANADA, LTD., TORONTO, ONTARIO

PRINTED IN THE UNITED STATES OF AMERICA

ACKNOWLEDGMENTS

The editor wishes to thank the following for their kind permission to use the material reprinted in this volume.

American Association of Collegiate Registrars and Admissions Officers: The selection by William R. Parker from *College and University,* Winter, 1957. Reprinted by permission of the publisher.

American Psychological Association, Inc.: The selection by Elizabeth Peal and Wallace E. Lambert from *Psychological Monographs,* Vol. 76, No. 27, Whole No. 546, 1962. Reprinted by permission of the authors and the American Psychological Association.

Dwight L. Bolinger: The selection by Dwight L. Bolinger from a "Work Paper for Seminar on Language Teacher Training" given at the University of Washington, 1962. Used by permission of the author.

College Entrance Examination Board: The selection by Howard Lee Nostrand from *Curricular Change in the Foreign Languages,* 1963. Reprinted by per-

019686

PREFACE

Never before in the history of American education have foreign languages held the eminent place they hold today. Never before have the programs, aims, and methods of foreign language teaching been examined and evaluated as in the last three decades. Several factors are responsible for this, not only the leadership of the United States in world affairs, increased world trade, and the National Defense Education Act of 1958, but also the development of linguistics and the increased interest of psychologists in language.

If foreign language teaching is to keep its prominent place and to intensify the effectiveness of its methods, the teacher should be thoroughly prepared. Many colleges and universities have programs for preparing foreign language teachers, though these programs in some cases have not been designed to fit current thinking and demands. The NDEA foreign language institutes have done tremendous work in giving teachers further professional and subject-matter preparation. They have also succeeded in kindling the spark of enthusiasm. Modern technology has contributed the language laboratory and numerous audio-visual materials which are invaluable tools of instruction, nor has the textbook field lagged. However, much of the current thinking in foreign language teaching is published in diverse periodicals and journals and hence of difficult access, even in the better libraries.

It was in order to put some of these materials into the hands of students that this book was conceived. It is intended as a supplement, not as a text; there are already some excellent texts, such as those by Nelson Brooks and Robert Lado.

In order to stimulate the student to do his own thinking, evaluating, and synthesizing, essays were assembled to demonstrate different points of view. They are meant to provoke questioning and further investigation, to provide a framework for the future teacher to solve problems and determine methods and practices. They need not be read in order of appearance, because they are grouped topically, not logically. The difficulty of the essays varies, but I have found them to be quite within the grasp of the average undergraduate student.

This volume does not subscribe to any given methodology, because to acknowledge one method as the ultimate is to engender stagnation. The thinker may theorize and the scientist hypothesize, but the procedure to be used in a concrete situation can only be determined by the teacher himself. Hence it is imperative that he be given the background necessary to make intelligent decisions.

Some articles in this anthology are classics in the field, outstanding because of their historical importance or their contribution to the body of thought relating to foreign language teaching. Discussions of the theory of language and language teaching, as well as some of the more practical aspects of language teaching, are included. Essays were also chosen to represent themes that are basic to foreign language teaching: the nature of language, language and its relation to linguistics, literature, culture, physiology, and psychology. Thus the history, theory, and practice are treated so that the future teacher can evolve his own approach to the teaching of language in consonance with the nature of language and the scientific principles of language teaching. In each instance an expert opinion was selected. Thus we have a philosophical approach from Susanne Langer and a neurological one from Wilder Penfield. The thinking of university professors, administrators, high-school teachers, and experimenters is expressed, adding to the variety of viewpoints.

As in all anthologies there will be disagreement with inclusions and disappointment over omissions. The editor accepts this responsibility but would remind you that the ideas expressed are those of the individual authors.

Although specific acknowledgments appear with each article, I wish to thank the authors represented in this book, the publishers, and the journals for their generous permission to reprint these works. My thanks also to my students, the seeding ground of my ideas, and to my wife, Mary Virginia, whose critical sense and endless patience were indispensable.

J. M.

CONTENTS

PART 1

Some Theoretical Aspects of Language

LANGUAGE

SUSANNE K. LANGER

This fascinating chapter by Susanne Langer is taken from her book Philosophy in a New Key. *It contains a stimulating discussion of the nature of language. Its influence has been far-reaching and the title gave rise to the expression "language teaching in the new key." Few philosophical treatises on language are as well documented scientifically or as cogently and as interestingly presented as this. It is necessary for the teacher to know the nature of what he teaches; from this follows the importance of this essay. Of particular interest is the treatment of language as the acquired ability to symbolize.*

Language is, without a doubt, the most momentous and at the same time the most mysterious product of the human mind. Between the clearest animal call of love or warning or anger, and a man's least, trivial *word*, there lies a whole day of Creation—or in modern phrase, a whole chapter of evolution. In language we have the free, accomplished use of symbolism, the record of articulate conceptual thinking; without language there seems to be nothing like explicit thought whatever. All races of men—even the scattered, primitive denizens of the deep jungle, and brutish cannibals who have lived for centuries on world-removed islands—have their complete and articulate language. There seem to be no simple, amorphous, or imperfect languages, such as one would naturally expect to find in conjunction with the lowest cultures. People who have not invented textiles, who live under roofs of pleated branches, need no privacy and mind no filth and roast their enemies for

Reprinted by permission of the publishers from Susanne K. Langer, *Philosophy in a New Key*, Cambridge, Massachusetts: Harvard University Press Copyright 1942, 1951, 1957, by the President and Fellows of Harvard College.

dinner, will yet converse over their bestial feasts in a tongue as grammatical as Greek, and as fluent as French.[1]

Animals, on the other hand, are one and all without speech. They communicate, of course; but not by any method that can be likened to speaking. They express their emotions and indicate their wishes and control one another's behavior by suggestion. One ape will take another by the hand and drag him into a game or to his

[1] There are several statements in philological and psychological literature to the effect that certain primitive races have but a rudimentary language, and depend on gesture to supplement their speech. All such statements that I have found, however, can be traced back to one common source, namely Mary H. Kingsley's *Travels in West Africa* (1897). This writer enjoyed so high a reputation in other fields than philology that her casual and apparently erroneous observations of native languages have been accepted rather uncritically by men as learned as Sir Richard Paget, Professor G. F. Stout, and Dr. Israel Latif. Yet Miss Kingsley's testimony is very shaky. She tells us (p. 504) that "the inhabitants of Fernando Po, the Bubis, are quite unable to converse with each other unless they have sufficient light to see the accompanying gestures of the conversation." But in an earlier part of the book she writes, "I know nothing of it [the Bubi language] myself save that it is harsh in sound," and refers the reader to the work of Dr. Baumann for information about its words and structure; Baumann gives a vocabulary and grammar that would certainly suffice a European to carry on any ordinary conversation in the dark. (See O. Baumann, "Beiträge zur Kentniss der Bubesprache auf Fernando Póo," *Zeitschrift für afrikanische Sprachen*, I, 1888, 138–155.) It seems plausible, therefore, that the Bubis find such conversation personally or socially "impossible" for some other reason. Her other example is no surer. "When I was with the Fans they frequently said, 'We will go to the fire so we can see what they say,' when any question had to be decided after dark . . ." (p. 504). It is strange that a language in which one can make, in the dark, so complex a statement as: "We will go to the fire so we can see what they say," should require gesture to complete other propositions; moreover, where there is a question to decide, it might be awkward for the most civilized congress to take a majority vote without switching on the lights.

I am inclined, therefore, to credit the statement of Edward Sapir, that "the gift of speech and a well-ordered language are characteristic of every known group of human beings. No tribe has ever been found which is without language and all statements to the contrary may be dismissed as mere folklore." After repudiating specifically the stories just related, he concludes: "The truth of the matter is that language is an essentially perfect means of expression and communication among every known people." (From article "Language," in *Encyclopedia of the Social Sciences*, by permission of The Macmillan Company, publishers. Cf. Otto Jespersen, *Language: Its Nature, Development and Origin* [1922], p. 413.)

bed; he will hold out his hand to beg for food, and will sometimes receive it. But even the highest apes give no indication of speech. Careful studies have been made of the sounds they emit, but all systematic observers agree that none of these are denotative, i.e., none of them are rudimentary words.[2] Furness, for instance, says: "If these animals have a language it is restricted to a very few sounds of a general emotional signification. Articulate speech they have none and communication with one another is accomplished by vocal sounds to no greater extent than it is by dogs, with a growl, a whine, or a bark."[3] Mr. and Mrs. Yerkes, who are very reluctant to abandon the search for prehuman speech functions in simians, come to the conclusion that "although evidence of use of the voice and of definite word-like sounds to symbolize feelings, and possibly also ideas, becomes increasingly abundant from lemur to ape, no one of the infra-human primates exhibits a systematization of vocal symbols which may approximately be described as speech."[4]

If the apes really used "definite word-like sounds to *symbolize* feelings and possibly also ideas," it would be hard to deny their power of speech. But all descriptions of their behavior indicate that they use such sounds only to *signify* their feelings, perhaps their desires. Their vocal expressions of love are *symptoms* of an emotion, not the name of it, nor any other symbol that represents it (like the heart on a Valentine). And true language begins only when a sound keeps its reference beyond the situation of its instinctive utterance, e.g., when an individual can say not only: "My love, my love!" but also: "He loves me—he loves me not." Even though Professor Yerkes' young apes, Chim and Panzee, met their food with exclamations like "Kha!" or "Nga!" these are like a cry of "Yum-yum!" rather than: "Banana, today." They are sounds of enthusiastic assent, of a very specialized emotional reaction; *they cannot be used between meals to talk over the merits of the feast.*

[2] In 1892 R. L. Garner published a book, *The Speech of Monkeys*, which aroused considerable interest, for he claimed to have learned a monkey vocabulary of about forty words. The book, however, is so fanciful and unscientific, and its interpretations so extravagant, that I think it must be discounted *in toto*, especially as more careful observations of later scientists belie its findings.

[3] W. H. Furness, "Observations on the Mentality of Chimpanzees and Orang-Utans," *Proceedings of the American Philosophical Society*, LV (1916), 281–290.

[4] R. M. Yerkes and A. W. Yerkes, *The Great Apes* (1929), p. 569.

Undoubtedly one reason for the lack of language in apes is their lack of any tendency to babble. Professor and Mrs. Kellogg, who brought up a little chimpanzee, Gua, for nine months exactly as they were bringing up their own child, observed that even in an environment of speaking persons "there was no attempt on Gua's part to use her lips, tongue, teeth and mouth-cavity in the production of new utterances; while in the case of the human subject a continuous vocalized play was apparent from the earliest months. . . . There were no 'random' noises to compare with the baby's prattle or the spontaneous chatter of many birds. On the whole, it may be said she never vocalized without some definite provocation, that is, without a clearly discernible external stimulus or cause. And in most cases this stimulus was obviously of an emotional character."[5] She had, indeed, what they called her "food-bark," and a pathetic "Ooo-oo" of fear; the bark was extended to signify assent in general, the "Ooo-oo" to express dissent. That is as near as she came to language. The child, too, used only a few words before the comparative experiment ended, but it is noteworthy that they were not "yes" and "no," but were *denotative words*—"din-din," "Gya" (Gua), and "Daddy." The use of true vocables for "yes" and "no" is apt to be late in children. Their interest in words centers on *names* for things and actions.

If we find no prototype of language in our nearest simian relatives, the apes, how can we conceive of a beginning for this all-important human function? We might suppose that speech is man's distinguishing instinct, that man is by nature the linguistic primate. Horatio Hale expressed this view in a presidential address to a learned society, many years ago.[6] He was deeply impressed with a phenomenon that occurs every so often—the invention of a spontaneous, individual language by a child or a pair of children, a language unrelated to the tongue spoken in the household. Some children will persist up to school age, or even a little beyond it, in this vagary. Such observations led him to believe that man is by

---

[5] W. N. Kellogg and L. A. Kellogg, *The Ape and the Child* (1933), p. 281. This passage and those from the same book quoted on the following pages are reproduced by permission of the McGraw-Hill Book Co., publishers.

[6] The Origin of Languages and the Antiquity of Speaking Man," *Proceedings of the American Association for the Advancement of Science*, XXXV (1887), 279–323.

nature a language-making creature, and learns his "mother tongue" merely by the overwhelming force of suggestion, when he hears a ready-made language from earliest infancy. Under the primitive conditions of nomadic family life, he thought, it might well happen that a group of young children would be orphaned, alone in the wilderness; and where the climate was warm and food abundant, such a little company might survive. The younger children's language would become the idiom of the family. Rather ingeniously he develops this notion as an explanation of the many utterly unrelated languages in the world, their distribution, and the mystery of their origin. But the interesting content of his paper in the present connection is his underlying assumption that man makes languages instinctively.

"The plain conclusion," he says, "to which all examples point with irresistible force is, that the origin of linguistic stocks is to be found in what may be termed the language-making instinct of very young children."[7]

After citing a case of two children who constructed an entirely original language, he comments: "There is nothing in the example which clearly proves that the children in question would have spoken at all if they had not heard their parents and others about them communicating by oral sounds—*though we may, on good grounds* (as will be shown), *believe that they would have done so*."[8]

The last part of his statement embodies the "instinct theory"; and that, so far as we know, is—*mere* theory. What do we know of children who, without being deaf and therefore unaware even of their own voices, have grown up without the example of people using speech around them? We know very little, but that little serves here to give us pause.

There are a few well-authenticated cases on record of so-called "wild children," waifs from infancy in the wilderness, who have managed to survive by their own precocious efforts or the motherly care of some large animal. In regions where it was (or is) customary to expose undesired infants, babes in the wood are not a nine days' wonder. Of course they usually die of neglect very soon, or are

---

[7] *Ibid.*, p. 285.
[8] *Ibid.*, p. 286. Italics mine.

devoured; but on a few known occasions the maternal instinct of a bear or a wolf has held the foundling more sacred than did man's moral law, and a child has grown up, at least to preadolescence, without human influence.

The only well-attested cases are Peter the Wild Boy, found in the fields near Hanover in 1723;[9] Victor, known as "the Savage of Aveyron," captured in that district of Southern France in 1799;[10] and two little girls, Amala and Kamala, taken in the vicinity of Midnapur, India, in 1920.[11] Several other "wild children" have been reported, but all accounts of them require considerable sifting, and some—like Lukas the Baboon Boy—prove to be spurious. Even of the ones here mentioned, only Victor has been scientifically studied and described. One thing, however, we know definitely about all of them: *none of these children could speak in any tongue, remembered or invented.* A child without human companions would, of course, find no response to his chattering; but if speech were a genuine instinct, this should make little difference. Civilized children talk to the cat without knowing that they are soliloquizing, and a dog that answers with a bark is a good audience; moreover, Amala and Kamala had each other. Yet they did not talk. Where, then, is "the language-making instinct of very young children?"

It probably does not exist at all. Language, though normally learned in infancy without any compulsion or formal training, is none the less a product of sheer learning, an art handed down from generation to generation, and where there is no teacher there is no accomplishment. Despite the caprices of the children cited by Professor Hale, it is fairly certain that these little inventors would *not* have talked at all if they had not heard their elders speaking. Whatever talent it is that helps a baby to learn a language with three or four times (or any number of times!) the ease of an adult, this talent is apparently not a "speech instinct." We have no birthright to vocabularies and syntaxes.

This throws us back upon an old and mystifying problem. If we

[9] See Henry Wilson, *Wonderful Characters*, 2 vols. (1821), vol. II; also J. Burnett, Lord Monboddo, *Of the Origin and Progress of Language*, 6 vols. (1773), vol. I.

[10] See E. M. Itard, *The Savage of Aveyron* (English translation, 1802).

[11] See Arnold Gesell, "The Biography of a Wolf-Child," *Harper's Magazine*, January, 1941.

find no prototype of speech in the highest animals, and man will not say even the first word by instinct, then how did all his tribes acquire their various languages? Who began the art which now we all have to learn? And why is it not restricted to the cultured races, but possessed by every primitive family, from darkest Africa to the loneliness of the polar ice? Even the simplest of practical arts, such as clothing, cooking, or pottery, is found wanting in one human group or another, or at least found to be very rudimentary. Language is neither absent nor archaic in any of them.

The problem is so baffling that it is no longer considered respectable. There is a paragraph of Sapir's in the *Encyclopedia of Social Sciences*, repudiating it on excellent grounds. But in the very passage that warrants the despair of the philologists, he justifies the present philosophical study in its hopefulness, so I quote his words for their peculiar relevance:

Many attempts have been made to unravel the origin of language but most of these are hardly more than exercises of the speculative imagination. Linguists as a whole have lost interest in the problem and this for two reasons. In the first place, it has come to be realized that there exist no truly primitive languages in a psychological sense. . . . In the second place, our knowledge of psychology, particularly of the symbolic process in general, is not felt to be sound enough to help materially with the problem of the emergence of speech. It is probable that the origin of language is not a problem that can be solved out of the resources of linguistics alone but that it is essentially a particular case of a much wider problem of the genesis of symbolic behavior and of the specialization of such behavior in the laryngeal region which may be presumed to have had only an expressive function to begin with. . . .
The primary function of language is generally said to be communication. . . . The autistic speech of children seems to show that the purely communicative aspect of language has been exaggerated. It is best to admit that language is primarily a vocal actualization of the tendency to see reality symbolically, that it is precisely this quality which renders it a fit instrument for communication and that it is in the actual give and take of social intercourse that it has been complicated and refined into the form in which it is known today.[12]

If it is true that "the tendency to see reality symbolically" is the real keynote of language, then most researches into the roots of the

[12] From Sapir, article "Language," p. 159. By permission of The Macmillan Company, publishers.

speech function have been misdirected. Communication by sound is what we have looked for among the apes; a *pragmatic use of vocables* is the only sign of word conception that we have interpreted to their credit, the only thing we have tried to inspire in them, and in the "wild children," to pave their way toward language. What we should look for is *the first indication of symbolic behavior*, which is not likely to be anything as specialized, conscious, or rational as the *use* of semantic. Language is a very high form of symbolism; presentational forms are much lower than discursive, and the appreciation of meaning probably earlier than its expression. The earliest manifestation of any symbol-making tendency, therefore, is likely to be a mere *sense of significance* attached to certain objects, certain forms or sounds, a vague emotional arrest of the mind by something that is neither dangerous nor useful in reality. The beginnings of symbolic transformation in the cortex must be elusive and disturbing experiences, perhaps thrilling, but very useless, and hard on the whole nervous system. It is absurd to suppose that the earliest symbols could be *invented;* they are merely *Gestalten* furnished to the senses of a creature ready to give them some diffuse meaning. But even in such rudimentary new behavior lies the first break with the world of pure signs. Aesthetic attraction, mysterious fear, are probably the first manifestations of that mental function which in man becomes a peculiar "tendency to see reality symbolically," and which issues in the *power of conception*, and the life-long habit of speech.

Something very much like an aesthetic sense of import is occasionally displayed by the anthropoid apes. It is like a dawn of superstition—a forerunner of fetishes and demons, perhaps. Especially in chimpanzees has this unrealistic attitude been observed by the most careful investigators, such as Yerkes, Kellogg, and Köhler. Gua, the little chimpanzee who was given the benefits of a human nursery, showed some very remarkable reactions to objects that certainly had no direct associations with her past experiences. For instance, the experimenters report that she stood in mortal fear of toadstools. She would run from them, screaming, or if cornered, hide her face as though to escape the sight of them. This behavior proved to be elicited by all kinds of toadstools, and to be based on no warning smell that might betray their poisonous properties (if, indeed, they are poisonous to apes. Some animals, e.g. squirrels, seem to eat all kinds with impunity). Once the experimenters wrapped some toadstools lightly in paper and handed her the package which, of course, smelled of the fungi, and watched her reception of it.

She accepts it without the slightest show of diffidence, and even starts to chew some of the paper. But when the package is unwrapped before her, she backs away apprehensively and will thereafter have none of the paper or its contents. Apparently she is stimulated only visually by toadstools.[13]

By way of comparison, toadstools were then offered to the thirteen apes at the experimental station near by. Only four of the subjects showed a similar fear, which they did not show toward pinecones, sticks, etc. These four were two adult females and two "children" three years old. Since the reaction was not universal the observers concluded that it was merely due to the chimpanzee's natural fear of the unknown. But surely pinecones are just as strange as toadstools to a caged chimpanzee. Moreover, they say (in the very same paragraph) that "Gua herself avoids both plucked and growing toadstools 2½ months after her original fright—or as long as any specimens can be found in the woods. It is quite likely that her reactions would have remained essentially the same throughout the entire period of the reseach."[14] Certainly the plants cannot have frightened her by their novelty all summer long!

The reaction on the part of the apes, limited as it was to about one subject in every three or four, has just that character of being common, yet individual, that belongs to aesthetic experiences. Some are sensitive to the sight, and the rest are not; to some of them *it seems to convey something*—to others it is just a thing, a toadstool or what you will.

Gua had other objects of unreasonable fear: a pair of blue trousers, of which she was afraid the first time she saw them and ever after; a pair of leather gloves; a flat and rusty tin can which she herself had found during her play outdoors. "It is difficult," say

[13] Kellogg, *The Ape and the Child*, p. 177.
[14] *Ibid.*, p. 178.

her observers, "to reconcile behavior of this sort with the ape's obvious preference for new toys."[15]

Yerkes and Learned have recorded similar oddities of simian behavior.

The causes of fear or apprehension in the chimpanzees were various, and sometimes difficult to understand. Thus Panzee stood in dread of a large burlap bag filled with hay, which she was obliged to pass frequently. She would meet the situation bravely, however, holding her head high, stamping her feet, and raising her fur, as she passed with an air of injured dignity.[16]

Remembering some of the strange inanimate objects in the world of early childhood, one may wonder what sort of expression the burlap bag was showing to Panzee.

The best account of what may be termed "aesthetic frights" is given by Wolfgang Köhler, who tells, in *The Mentality of Apes*, how he showed his chimpanzees

some primitive stuffed toys, on wooden frames, fastened to a stand, and padded with straw sewn inside cloth covers, with black buttons for eyes. They were about thirty-five centimeters in height, and could in extremity be taken for oxen and asses, though most drolly unnatural. It was totally impossible to get Sultan, who at that time could be led by the hand outside, near these small objects, which had so little real resemblance to any kind of creature. . . . One day I entered their room with one of these toys under my arm. Their reaction-times may be very short; for in a moment a blacker cluster, consisting of the whole group of chimpanzees, hung suspended to the farthest corner of the wire roofing; each individual tried to thrust the others aside and bury his head deep among them.[17]

His comment on these events is simple and cogent.

It is too facile an explanation of these reactions to assume that everything new and unknown appears terrible to these creatures. . . . New things are not necessarily frightful to a chimpanzee, any more than to a human child; certain inherent qualities are requisite to produce this special effect. But, as the examples cited above prove, any marked resemblance to the living foes of their species does not seem at all es-

[15] *Ibid.*, p. 179.
[16] R. M. Yerkes and B. Learned, *Chimpanzee Intelligence and its Vocal Expression* (1925), p. 143.
[17] Wolfgang Köhler, *The Mentality of Apes*, p. 333.

sential, and it almost seems as though the immediate impression of something exceptionally frightful could be conveyed in an even higher degree by *constructing* something frightful, than by any living animal (with the possible exception of snakes). For us human beings as well, many ghost-forms and specters, with which no terrible *experience* can be individually connected, are much more uncanny than certain very substantial dangers which we may easily have encountered in daily life.[18]

Not only fear, but also delight or comfort may be inspired in these animals by objects that have no biological significance for them; thus Gua, who was so attached to Mr. Kellogg that she went into tantrums of terror and grief whenever he left the house, could be comforted by being given his pair of coveralls.

This she would drag around with her, as a fetish of protection until his return. . . . Occasionally, if it was necessary for him to go away, the leave-taking could be accomplished without emotional display on the part of Gua if the coveralls were given her before the time of departure.[19]

Here certainly is a case where the object is *significant*. Superficially it reminds one of a dog's recognition of his master's clothes. But whereas a dog is prompted to the action of seeking the possessor of them, Gua let the possessor go out and contented herself with the proxy. Therein lies the difference. Gua was using the coveralls even in his presence as a help to her imagination, which kept him near whether he went out or not.

Köhler describes how the chimpanzees will hoard perfectly useless objects and carry them between the lower abdomen and the upper thigh, a sort of natural trouser pocket, for days on end. Thus Tschego, an adult female, treasured a stone that the sea had rounded and polished. "On no pretext," he says, "could you get the stone away, and in the evening the animal took it with it to its room and its nest."[20]

No one knows what made the stones so valuable to Tschego; we cannot say that it was *significant*, as we can in the case of Gua's keepsake. But certainly an object which is aesthetically satisfying or horrifying is a good candidate for the office of fetish or bogie, as

18 Köhler, *Ibid.*, p. 334.
19 Kellogg, *op. cit.*, p. 160.
20 Köhler, *op. cit.*, p. 99.

the case may be. An ape that can transfer the sense of her master's presence to a memento of him, and that reacts with specific emotions to the sheer quality of a perception, certainly is nervously organized above the level of purely realistic conditioned response. It is not altogether surprising, therefore, to find even more definite traces of symbolic behavior in the chimpanzee—this time a real preparation for the function of *denotation*, which is the essence of language.

This behavior is the performance of symbolic acts—acts that really seem to epitomize the creature's apprehension of a state of affairs, rather than to be just a symptom of emotion. The difference between a symbolic and a symptomatic act may be illustrated by contrasting the intentional genuflexion of a suppliant with the emotional quaver of his voice. There is a convention about the former, but not about the latter. And the *conventional expression* of a feeling, an attitude, etc., is the first, the lowest form of *denotation*. In a conventional attitude, something is summed up, understood, and consciously conveyed. So it is deeply interesting that both Köhler and Kellogg have observed in their apes quite unmistakable cases of symbolic (not signific) gesture. Köhler reports that when a young chimpanzee would greet Tschego, it would put its hand into her lap.

If the movement of the arm will not go so far, Tschego, when in a good mood . . . will take the hand of the other animal, press it to her lap, or else pat it amicably. . . . She will press our hand to just that spot between her upper thigh and lower abdomen where she keeps her precious objects. She herself, as a greeting, will put her huge hand to the other animal's lap or between their legs and she is inclined to extend this greeting even to men.[21]

Here we certainly have the dawn of a conventional expression of good will. But a still more clearly significant act is described by the Kelloggs in their account of Gua: that is the kiss of forgiveness. Kissing is a natural demonstration on the part of chimpanzees, and has an emotional value for them. In her human surroundings the little ape soon employed it in an unequivocally conscious way.

She would kiss and offer her lips in recompense for small errors many times a day. . . . Thereafter she could be put down again and would play, but unless the ritual had been satisfactorily completed she would

---

[21] *Loc. cit., infra.*

not be quiet or turn away until it had, or until some other climax superseded it.[22]

The upshot of all these considerations is that the tendency to a symbolic transformation of experience, the primary requisite for speech, is not entirely wanting in the ape, though it is as rudimentary as the rest of his higher functions—his perception of causal relations, for instance. If we take symbolic representation, rather than communication, as the criterion of a creature's capacity for language, we see that the chimpanzee, at least, is in some measure prepared; he has a rudimentary capacity for it.[23] Yet he definitely has no speech. He makes no stumbling attempts at words, as he does at using tools, decorating his body, dancing and parading, and other primitive pursuits. He is conceptually not far from the supreme human achievement, yet never crosses the line. What has placed this absolute barrier between his race and ours?

Chiefly, I think, one difference of natural proclivities. The ape has no instinctive desire to babble in babyhood. He does not play with his mouth and his breath as human infants do; there is no crowing and cooing, no "goo-goo" and "ba-ba" and "do-de-da" in his otherwise uproarious nursery. Consequently there are no sounds and syllables that please or frighten him by their sheer aesthetic character, as he is pleased, frightened, or comforted by purely phenomenal sights. Oddly enough, it is just because all his utterances have *signification*—all are pragmatic or emotional—that none of them ever acquire *significance*. He does not even imitate sounds for fun, as he imitates gestures, and gravely mimics practices that have no utility for him.

This mutism of the great apes has been little realized by people who have not actually studied their habits; in fact, our satirists have made much of the supposedly simian trait of constant unsolicited chatter. "Heavens, what a genius for tongues these simians have!" said Clarence Day in one of his clever books. And assuming that we are descended from such arboreal geniuses, he comments on our political problems: "The best government for simians seems

---

[22] Kellogg, *op. cit.*, p. 172.

[23] For a detailed study of chimpanzee behavior, see Köhler, *op. cit., passim;* for a general evaluation of the findings, the appendix, pp. 281–342, "Some Contributions to the Psychology of Chimpanzees."

to be based on a parliament: a talk-room, where endless vague thoughts can be warmly expressed. This is the natural child of those primeval sessions that gave pleasure to apes."[24] And even Kipling, who has lived in a land where monkeys and apes are wild, did not observe that their chatter (when they do chatter) is no more imitative than the "ch-ch-ch-chee" of an angry squirrel; if he had, we might be the poorer by missing that delightful parody on human loquacity, the council scene in "Cold Lairs."

A genuine symbol can most readily originate where some object, sound, or act is provided which has no *practical* meaning, yet tends to elicit an emotional response, and thus hold one's undivided attention. Certain objects and gestures appear to have this phenomenological, dissociated character for some apes, as well as for man; sounds have it for man alone. They annoy or please him even when they are not signs of anything further; they have an inherently interesting character. Add to this the fact that man spontaneously produces random syllables in infancy, whereas the ape does not, and it is immediately apparent that verbal symbols are easily available to the one and very remote and unnatural to the other. Man, though undoubtedly a simian, must trace his descent from a vocalizing race—a genus of ape, perhaps, in which the rudiments of symbolic conception, that apparently are dawning in the chimpanzee, were coupled with an instinctive tendency to produce sounds, to play with the vocal apparatus.

Furness succeeded in teaching a young orangutan two words, which it certainly appeared to use intelligently. Unfortunately for science, as well as for the ape, it died five months after this achievement, so we do not know how much further it might have gone on the road to Parnassus. But the experimenter had little confidence, despite his success. His chief obstacle was not the subject's lack of understanding, but of instinctive response, of any tendency to imitate his mouthings and articulations. Its lips had to be moved by hand instead of by example. Once it learned the trick, it soon had the words; but *the trick was something it would never in the world have thought of by itself.*[25] For this reason, if for no other, it is unlikely that the descendants of our great apes, ten thousand years

[24] *This Simian World* (1920), p. 69.

[25] Furness' own account of this training is worth repeating here. His own estimate of his success seems to me too modest, considering the difference in

hence, will hold parliaments (the prognosis is better for World Fairs). The apes will not evolve verbal symbolism because they do not instinctively supply themselves with verbal material, interesting little phonetic items that can acquire conventional meanings because they carry no natural messages.

The notion that the essence of language is the formulation and expression of conceptions rather than the communication of natural

---

learning-time of the first word and the second. For he says: "It seems wellnigh incredible that in animals otherwise so close to us physically there should not be a rudimentary speech-center in the brain which only needed developing. I have made an earnest endeavor and am still endeavoring, but I cannot say that I am encouraged.

"In teaching articulate speech I found the first difficulty to be overcome in both the orang and the chimpanzee is their lack of use of lips or tongue in making their natural emotional cries.

". . . In the case of the orang-utan it took at least six months to teach her to say 'Papa.' This word was selected not only because it is a very primitive sound, but also because it combined two elements of vocalization to which orang-utans and chimpanzees are . . . unaccustomed, namely: the use of lips and an expired vowel. . . ."

Presumably, this latter fact precluded the occurrence of the "word" by accident, and the danger of interpreting as a "word" some mere natural sound. The teacher manipulated the ape's lips, and also made the motions and sounds for her with his own mouth.

"At the end of six months, one day of her own accord, out of lesson time, she said 'Papa' quite distinctly and repeated it on command. . . . She never forgot it after that and finally recognized it as my name. When asked 'Where is Papa?' she would at once point to me or pat me on the shoulder."

Once, while being carried into the water, "she was panic-stricken; she clung with her arms about my neck; kissed me again and again and kept saying 'Papa! Papa! Papa!' Of course, I went no further after that pathetic appeal."

Her next word was "cup." The greatest art was needed to teach her the purely physical trick of pronouncing *k* with an open vowel, *ka;* but once this was learned, "after a few lessons when I showed her the cup and asked 'What is this?' she would say 'cup' very plainly. Once when ill at night she leaned out of her hammock and said 'cup, cup, cup,' which I naturally understood to mean that she was thirsty and which proved to be the case. I think this showed fairly conclusively that there was a glimmering idea of the connection of the word with the object of her desire." (Furness, *Observations on the Mentality of Chimpanzees and Orang-Utans,* pp. 281–284.)

Once *the idea of the spoken word* was awakened in the ape, which awakening took all of six months, the learning of a second word was chiefly a matter of conquering the unnaturalness of the physical process. Who knows how far this development might have gone if the subject had lived?

wants (the essence of pantomime) opens a new vista upon the mysterious problem of origins. For its beginnings are not natural adjustments, ways to means; they are purposeless lalling instincts, primitive aesthetic reactions, and dreamlike associations of ideas that fasten on such material. The preparations for language are much lower in the rational scale than word uses; they can be found below the evolutionary level of any communication by sounds.

Moreover, this originally impractical, or better, *conceptual,* use of speech is borne out by the fact that all attempts to teach apes or the speechless "wild children" to talk, by the method of making them ask for something, have failed; whereas all cases where the use of language has dawned on an individual, simian or human, under such difficult circumstances, have been independent of the practical use of the word at the moment. After all the efforts of Helen Keller's teacher in formal daily lessons to make the child *use* words like "cup" and "doll" to obtain the denoted objects, the significance of the word "water" suddenly burst upon her, not when she needed water, but when the stream gushed over her hand! Likewise, Yerkes' efforts to make Chim use an articulate syllable to ask for a piece of banana all failed; he articulated no "word" resembling the speech of man, nor did he seem to establish a relation between the sound and any particular object.[26] Furness, on the other hand, carefully kept all practical interests out of his experiment. He tried only to associate an impression, a visual experience, with a word, so that by constant association the two should fuse, not as sign and result, but as name and image; and he has had the greatest success on record so far as I know.[27]

But the most decisive and, at the same time, pathetic evidence that the utilitarian view of language is a mistake, may be found in

[26] See Yerkes and Learned, *op. cit.,* p. 56: "The experimenter succeeded in training him to speak for food as a dog may readily be taught to do. This he did, however, not in imitation of the trainer but to secure the food."

[27] See Furness, *op. cit.,* p. 285: "As to a comprehension of the connection of spoken words with objects and actions both the orang-utan and the chimpanzee, I think, exceed any of our domestic animals; both of my anthropoids have been able to understand what I said to them, more intelligently than any professionally trained animals I have ever seen. In their education the enticement of food has never been used as an incentive to action, and praise and petting have been the only rewards. In other words my object has been to endeavor to make them show signs of thought rather than a perfunctory performance of tricks."

the story of Victor, the Savage of Aveyron, written by the young doctor who undertook to study and educate him. Since the boy always took notice when anyone exclaimed "Oh!" and even imitated the sound, Dr. Itard undertook to make him use the word *"eau"* as a *sign* when he wanted water; but this attempt failed because he used every sign *but* the vocal one, and water could not be indefinitely withheld to force the issue. So a second attempt was made with the word *"lait,"* of which Itard gives the following account:

The fourth day of this, my second experiment, I succeeded to the utmost of my wishes; I heard Victor pronounce distinctly, in a manner, it must be confessed, rather harsh, the word *lait*, which he repeated almost incessantly; it was the first time that an articulate sound has escaped his lips, and of course I did not hear it without the most lively satisfaction. I nevertheless made afterwards an observation, which deduced very much from the advantage which it was reasonable to expect from the first instance of success. It was not till the moment, when, despairing of a happy result, I actually poured the milk into the cup which he presented to me, the word *lait* escaped him again, with evident demonstrations of joy; and it was not till after I had poured it out a second time, by way of reward, that he repeated the expression. It is evident from hence, that the result of the experiment was far from accomplishing my intentions; the word pronounced, instead of being the sign of a want, it appeared, from the time in which it was articulated, to be merely an exclamation of joy. If this word had been uttered before the thing that he desired had been granted, my object would have been nearly accomplished: then the true sense of speech would have been soon acquired by Victor; a point of communication would have been established between him and me, and the most rapid progress must necessarily have ensued. Instead of this I had obtained only an expression of the pleasure which he felt, insignificant as it related to himself, and useless to us both. . . . It was generally only during the enjoyment of the thing, that the word *lait* was pronounced. Sometimes he happened to utter it before, and at other times a little after, but always without having any view in the use of it. I do not attach any more importance to his spontaneous repetition of it, when he happens to wake during the course of the night.[28]

Another word which Victor acquired quite spontaneously was "Li," which Itard identifies as the name of a young girl, Julie, who

[28] *The Savage of Aveyron*, pp. 93–96.

stayed at the house for several weeks, to Victor's great delight; but this word he uttered to himself, all the time, and "even during the night, at those moments when there is reason to believe that he is in a profound sleep," so no importance was attached to it as a sign of reason.

Unfortunately, the young doctor was such a faithful disciple of Locke and Condillac that after his "failure" with the word *"lait"* he gave up the attempt to teach the Wild Boy spoken language, and tried to instruct him in the deaf-mutes' alphabet instead. Victor picked up a few spoken words, subsequently, by himself; but as he merely said them when he contemplated their objects with joy or sorrow, not when he *lacked* anything, no one paid much attention to these "mere exclamations" or made response to them.

Young children learn to speak, after the fashion of Victor, by constantly using words to bring things *into their minds,* not *into their hands.* They learn it fully whether their parents consciously teach them by wrong methods or right or not at all. Why did Victor not defy the doctor's utilitarian theories and learn language by the babbling method?

Because he was already about twelve years old, and the lalling-impulse of early childhood was all but completely outgrown. The tendency to constant vocalization seems to be a passing phase of our instinctive life. If language is not developed during this period, the individual is handicapped—like the apes—by a lack of *spontaneous phonetic material* to facilitate his speech experiments. The production of sounds is conscious then, and is used economically instead of prodigally. Victor did not articulate to amuse himself; his first word had to be stimulated. Wild Peter, we are told, never babbled to himself, though he sang a great deal; Kamala, the surviving little "wolf-girl" found at Midnapur, had learned about forty words at the end of six years in human surroundings, and formed sentences of two or three words; but even with this vocabulary, which would serve a three-year-old to carry on incessant conversations, Kamala *never talked unless she was spoken to.*[29] The impulse to chatter had been outgrown without being exploited for the acquisition of language.

[29] The most trustworthy, because contemporary, accounts of the Midnapur children are probably the brief notes published in the *American Journal of*

In a social environment, the vocalizing and articulating instinct of babyhood is fostered by response, and as the sounds become symbols their use becomes a dominant habit. Yet the passing of the *instinctive phase* is marked by the fact that a great many phonemes which do not meet with response are completely lost.[30] Undoubtedly that is why children, who have not entirely lost the impulse to make random sounds which their mother tongue does not require, can so easily learn a foreign language and even master several at once, like many English youngsters born in India, who learn not only one vernacular, but speak with every native servant in whatever happens to be his dialect. A British psychologist, J. W. Tomb, has called attention to this phenomenon and concluded from it that children have a *linguistic intuition* which is lost later in life.[31]

But *intuition* is a slippery word, which has to cover, in this case, understanding, reproduction, and use—i.e., independent, analogous application—of words. It is hard to imagine any "intuition" that would bestow so many powers. It is better, perhaps, to say that there is an *optimum period of learning*, and this is a stage of mental development in which several impulses and interests happen to coincide: the lalling instinct, the imitative impulse, a natural interest in distinctive sounds, *and a great sensitivity to "expressiveness" of any sort*. Where any one of these characteristics is absent or is not synchronized with the others, the "linguistic intuition" miscarries.

The last requirement here mentioned is really the "higher function" of the mind that shines forth so conspicuously in human

---

Psychology by Kellogg and Squires. See P. C. Squires, " 'Wolf-Children' of India," XXXVIII (1927), 313–315; W. N. Kellogg, "More About the 'Wolf-Children' of India," XLII (1931), 508–509, and "A Further Note on the 'Wolf-Children' of India," XLV (1934), 149–150.

[30] Thus Israel Latif, speaking of the "lalling stage" of babyhood, says: "Many more sounds are produced by the infant during this period than are later used, at least in its own language. . . ." (To this effect he cites many authorities—Stern, Lorimer, K. C. More, Stanley Hall, Preyer, and Conradi.) "Now, out of this astonishingly rich and varied repertoire of sounds, those which are used by the child's elders are reinforced, and become habitual; the others cease to be uttered."—"The Physiological Basis of Linguistic Development and the Ontogeny of Meaning," *Psychological Review*, XLI (1934), 55–85, 153–176, 246–264. See esp. p. 60.

[31] See his article "On the Intuitive Capacity of Children to Understand Spoken Language," *British Journal of Psychology*, XVI (1925–1926), 53–55.

intercourse; yet it is the one that linguists and psychologists either overlook entirely, or certainly do not credit to early childhood. The peculiar impressionability of childhood is usually treated under the rubric of attention to exact colors, sounds, etc.; but what is much more important, I think, is the child's tendency to read a vague sort of *meaning* into pure visual and auditory forms. Childhood is the great period of synaesthesia; sounds and colors and temperatures, forms and feelings, may have certain characters in common, by which a vowel may "be" of a certain color, a tone may "be" large or small, low or high, bright or dark, etc. There is a strong tendency to form associations among sensa that are not practically fixed in the world, even to confuse such random impressions. Most of all, the overactive feelings fasten upon such flotsam material. Fear lives in pure *Gestalten*, warning or friendliness emanates from objects that have no faces and no voices, no heads or hands; for they all have "expression" for the child, though not—as adults often suppose—anthropomorphic form. One of my earliest recollections is that chairs and tables *always kept the same look*, in a way that people did not, and that I was awed by the sameness of that appearance. They *symbolized* such-and-such a mood; even as a little child I would not have judged that they *felt* it (if any one had raised such a silly question). There was just such-and-such a look —dignity, indifference, or ominousness—about them. They continued to convey that silent message no matter what you did to them.

A mind to which the stern character of an armchair is more immediately apparent than its use or its position in the room, is oversensitive to expressive forms. It grasps analogies that a riper experience would reject as absurd. It fuses sensa that practical thinking must keep apart. Yet it is just this crazy play of associations, this uncritical fusion of impressions, that exercises the powers of symbolic transformation. To project feelings into outer objects is the first way of symbolizing, and thus of *conceiving* those feelings. This activity belongs to about the earliest period of childhood that memory can recover. The conception of "self," which is usually thought to mark the beginning of actual memory, may possibly depend on this process of symbolically epitomizing our feelings.

From this dawn of memory, where we needs must begin any firsthand record, to adolescence, there is a constant decrease in such dreamlike experience, a growing shift from subjective, symbolic, to practical associations. Sense data now keep to their categories, and signify further events. Percepts become less weighted with irrelevant feeling and fantasy, and are more readily ranged in an objective order. But if in theory we count backward over the span which none of us recollect, and which covers the period of learning language—is it likely that the mind was realistic in its earlier phase? Is it not probable that association was even more trivial, more ready, and that the senses fused more completely in yielding impressions? No experience belongs to any class as yet, in this primitive phase. Consider, now, that the vocal play of the infant fills his world with *audible actions*, the nearest and most completely absorbing stimuli, because they are both inner and outer, autonomously produced yet unexpected, inviting that *repetition* of accidental motions which William James deemed the source of all voluntary acts; intriguing, endlessly variable noises mysteriously connected with the child himself! For a while, at least, his idle experiments in vocalization probably fill his world.

If, now, his audible acts wake echoes in his surroundings—that is to say, if his elders reply to them—there is a growth of experience; for the baby appears to recognize, gradually, that the sound which happens there and comes to him, is the *same* as his lalling. This is a rudimentary abstraction; by that sameness he becomes aware of the tone, the product of his activity, which absorbs his interest. He repeats that sound rather than another. His ear has made its first judgment. A sound (such as "da-da," or "ma-ma," probably) has been *conceived*, and his diffuse awareness of vocalizing gives way to an apparently delightful awareness of a vocable.

It is doubtful whether a child who never heard any articulate sounds but his own would ever become conscious of different phonemes. Voice and uttered syllable and the feeling of utterance would probably remain one experience to him; the babbling period might come and go without his recognizing any *product* of his own activity. If this guess is correct, it is easy to understand why Victor and Wild Peter did not invent language, and were nearly, if not entirely, past the hope of acquiring it when they were socialized.

A new vocable is an understanding *Gestalt*. It is a possession, too, because it may be had at will, and this itself makes it very interesting. Itard tells us that when Victor pronounced his first word he re-

peated it "almost incessantly"; as does every baby who has learned a
new syllable. Moreover, an articulate sound is an entirely *unattached*
item, a purely phenomenal experience without externally fixed relations; it lies wide open to imaginative and emotional uses, syn-
aesthetic identifications, chance associations. It is the readiest thing
in the world to become a symbol when a symbol is wanted. The
next sharp and emotional arrest of consciousness, the next deeply
interesting experience that coincides with hearing or uttering the
vocable, becomes fixed by association with that one already distinct
item; it may be the personality of the mother, the concrete character of the bottle, or what not, that becomes thus identified with the
recognizable, producible sound; whatever it is, the baby's mind has
hold of it through the word, and can invoke a conception of it by
uttering the word, which has thus become the *name* of the thing.

For a considerable time, playing with conceptions seems to be
the main interest and aim in speaking. To name things is a thrilling
experience, a tremendous satisfaction. Helen Keller bears witness to
the sense of power it bestows. Word and conception become fused
in that early period wherein both grow up together, so that even
in later life they are hard to separate. In a sense, language is conception, and conception is the frame of perception; or, as Sapir has
put it,

Language is heuristic . . . in that its forms predetermine for us certain
modes of observation and interpretation. . . . While it may be looked
upon as a symbolic system which reports or refers or otherwise substitutes for direct experience, it does not as a matter of actual behavior
stand apart from or run parallel to direct experience but completely
interpenetrates with it. This is indicated by the widespread feeling,
particularly among primitive people, of that virtual identity or close
correspondence of word and thing which leads to the magic of spells.
. . . Many lovers of nature, for instance, do not feel that they are truly
in touch with it until they have mastered the names of a great many
flowers and trees, as though the primary world of reality were a verbal
one and as though one could not get close to nature unless one first
mastered the terminology which somehow magically expresses it.[32]

The fact is that our primary world of reality *is* a verbal one.
Without words our imagination cannot retain distinct objects and

[32] From Sapir, Article "Language," p. 157, by permission of The Macmillan
Company, publishers.

their relations, but out of sight is out of mind. Perhaps that is why Köhler's apes could use a stick to reach a banana outside the cage so long as the banana and the stick could be seen in one glance, but not if they had to turn their eyes away from the banana to see the stick. Apparently they could not look at the one and *think of* the other.[33] A child who had as much practical initiative as the apes, turning away from the coveted object, yet still murmuring "banana," would have seen the stick in its instrumental capacity at once.

The transformation of experience into concepts, not the elaboration of signals and symptoms, is the motive of language. Speech is through and through symbolic; and only sometimes signific. Any attempt to trace it back entirely to the need of communication, neglecting the formulative, abstractive experience at the root of it, must land us in the sort of enigma that the problem of linguistic origins has long presented. I have tried, instead, to trace it to the characteristic human activity, symbolic transformation and abstraction, of which prehuman beginnings may perhaps be attributed to the highest apes. Yet we have not found the commencement of language anywhere between their state and ours. Even in man, who has all its prerequisites, it depends on education not only for its full development, but for its very inception. How, then, did it ever arise? And why do all men possess it?

It could only have arisen in a race in which the lower forms of symbolistic thinking—dream, ritual, superstitious fancy—were already highly developed, i.e., where the process of symbolization, though primitive, was very active. Communal life in such a group would be characterized by vigorous indulgence in purely expressive acts, in ritual gestures, dances, etc., and probably by a strong tendency to fantastic terrors and joys. The liberation from practical interests that is already marked in the apes would make rapid progress in a species with a definitely symbolistic turn of mind; conventional meanings would gradually imbue every originally random act, so that the group life as a whole would have an exciting, vaguely transcendental tinge, without any definable or communicable body of ideas to cling to. A wealth of dance forms and antics, poses and manoeuvres might flourish in a society that was somewhat above the apes' in nonpractical interests, and rested on a slightly higher

[33] Köhler, *op. cit.*, p. 37.

development of the symbolific brain functions. There are quite articulated play forms, verging on dance forms, in the natural repertoire of the chimpanzees;[34] with but a little further elaboration, these would become most obvious material for symbolic expression. It is not at all impossible that *ritual*, solemn and significant, antedates the evolution of language.

In a vocalizing animal, such actions would undoubtedly be accompanied by purely fanciful sounds—wavering tones, strings of syllables, echoing shouts. Voice play, which as an instinct is lost after infancy, would be perpetuated in a group by the constant stimulation of response, as it is with us when we learn to speak. It is easy enough to imagine that young human beings would excite each other to shout, as two apes excite one another to jump, rotate, and strike poses; and the shouting would soon be formalized into song. Once the vocal habits are utilized, as in speech or song, we know that they do not become lost but are fixed as a lifelong activity. In a social group, the infantile lalling instinct would be constantly reinforced, and instead of being outgrown, would become conventionalized in social play forms. "Never a nomadic horde in the wil-

[34] Even at the risk of letting Köhler's apes steal the show in this chapter, I must quote his account of these plays. Tschego and Grande developed a game of spinning round and round like dervishes, which found favor with all the others. "Any game of two together," says Köhler, "was apt to turn into this 'spinning-top' play, which appeared to express a climax of friendly and amicable *joie de vivre*. The resemblance to a human dance became truly striking when the rotations were rapid, or when Tschego, for instance, stretched her arms out horizontally as she spun round. Tschego and Chica—whose favorite fashion during 1916 was this 'spinning'—sometimes combined a forward movement with the rotations, and so they revolved slowly round their own axes and along the playground.

The whole *group* of chimpanzees sometimes combined in more elaborate *motion-patterns*. For instance, two would wrestle and tumble near a post; soon their movements would become more regular and tend to describe a circle round the post as a center. One after another, the rest of the group approach, join the two, and finally march in an orderly fashion round and round the post. The character of their movements changes; they no longer walk, they trot, and as a rule with special emphasis on one foot, while the other steps lightly; thus a rough approximate rhythm develops, and they tend to 'keep time' with one another. . . .

It seems to me extraordinary that there should arise quite spontaneously, among chimpanzees, anything that so strongly suggests the dancing of some primitive tribes." (*op. cit.*, pp. 326–327.)

derness, but must already have had its songs," says Wilhelm von Humboldt, "for man as a species is a singing creature. . . ."[35] Song, the formalization of voice play, probably preceded speech.

Jespersen, who is certainly one of our great authorities on language, suggests that speech and song may well have sprung from the same source (as Herder and Rousseau, without really scientific foundation, imagined long ago). "Word-tones were originally frequent, but meaningless," he observes; "afterwards they were dropped in some languages, while in others they were utilized for sense-distinguishing purposes."[36] Furthermore, he points out that in passionate speech the voice still tends to fluctuate, that civilization only reduces this effect by reducing passionate utterance, and that savages still use a sing-song manner of speaking; and in fine, he declares, "These facts and considerations all point to the conclusion that there was once a time when all speech was song, or rather when these two actions were not yet differentiated. . . ."[37]

Yet it is hard to believe that song was ever an essential form of communication. How, then, was language derived from it? He does not tell us; but the difficulty of tracing an instrument like language to a free exercise like song is minimized in his sagacious reflection: "Although we now regard the communication of thought as the main object of speaking, there is no reason for thinking that this has always been the case."[38]

Strangely enough, Professor Jespersen seems to be unacquainted with an essay by J. Donovan, "The Festal Origin of Human Speech," which appeared in the form of two articles in *Mind* as long ago as 1891–1892,[39] and which develops, quite fully and logically, the very idea he advances. Probably the fact that it appeared in a philosophical journal caused it to escape the notice of philologists. Its thesis, however, is so well corroborated by Jespersen's more recent and perhaps more reliable findings, that I present it here as a very suggestive and arresting hypothesis; the sort of idea that throws light at least on the problem of human articulateness, once we ac-

---

[35] *Die sprachphilosophischen Werke Wilhelm von Humboldts*, ed. Steinthal (1884), p. 289.

[36] *Language*, p. 418, n.

[37] *Ibid.*, p. 420.

[38] *Ibid.*, p. 437.

[39] Vol. XVI (O. S.), pp. 498–506, and vol. XVII, pp. 325–339.

cept the *Leitmotif* of symbolic activity, rather than intelligent signaling, as the key to language.

Donovan's theory is, in brief, that sound is peculiarly well adapted to become symbolic because our attention to it requires no utilitarian motive.

The passivity of the ear allowed auditory impressions to force themselves into consciousness in season and out of season, when they were interesting to the dominant desires of the animal and when they were not. These impressions got further into consciousness, so to speak, before desire could examine their right of entrance, than was possible for impressions which could be annihilated by a wink or a turn of the head.[40]

Since noises have this intrinsic and commanding interest, and the ear cannot be closed, they were peculiarly well suited to become "free" items where they had no biological value, and to be utilized by the imagination in sheer play. Especially in the "play-excitement" following successful communal enterprise (one is reminded of the apes' outburst of pure *joie de vivre* culminating in a dervish-like spin), such noises as rhythmic beating and handclapping were used to emphasize the playmood and keep it steady—for this primeval man was probably, like the ape, incredibly distractible. The voice could be used, like the drum, to attract attention and accentuate rhythm; and thus the force of a change of pitch to make some notes stand out (one in four, etc.) was naturally discovered. Being more variable than the drum, voices soon made patterns, and the long wandering melodies of primitive song became an integral part of communal celebration.

First the actions of the "dance" would tend to become pantomimic, reminiscent of what had caused the great excitement. They would become ritualized, and hold the mind to the celebrated event. In other words, there would be conventional modes of dancing appropriate to certain occasions, so intimately associated with *that kind of occasion* that they would presently uphold and embody the concept of it—in other words, there would emerge *symbolic gestures*.

The voice, used to accompany such ritual acts, would elaborate its own conventions; and in a babbling species, certain syllables

[40] Donovan, "The Festal Origin of Human Speech," part I, p. 499.

would find favor above others and would give color to festal plays.

Now, the centering of certain festivities round particular individuals, human or other—death dances round a corpse, triumph dances round a captive female, a bear, a treasure, or a chief—would presently cause the articulate noises peculiar to such situations to become associated with that central figure, so that the sight of it would stimulate people to utter those syllables, or more likely *rhythmic groups of syllables,* even outside the total festive situation.

And every moment during which such objects, connected as they are with the natural appetites of the animal, could be dominated by the emotional strength of festal play, and kept, however dimly, in consciousness, without firing the train of passions natural to them (e.g. to food, females), would mean the melting away of a link in the chain which held the animals below the possibility of human development.[41]

In the early history of articulate sounds they could make no meaning themselves, but they preserved and got intimately associated with the peculiar feelings and perceptions that came most prominently into the minds of the festal players during their excitement. Articulate sounds . . . could only wait while they entered into the order imposed on them by the players' wild imitations of actions, and then preserve them in that order.[42]

Without the vestige of a conscious intention behind it, this impulse (the play) induced the players to dwell on some sort of an image of an individual in relation to the actions imitated, whilst rhythmic and

[41] *Ibid.,* part II, p. 330. The importance here given to the festal as opposed to the impulsive spirit in the origination of speech stands in striking contrast to the opinion expressed by Markey, who also recognizes the probability of an emotional, perhaps ritual, source; in *The Symbolic Process* Markey writes: "Symbols must have developed only after long association had conditioned instinctive cries or sounds to specific behavior in which two or more individuals were involved. In order that the mnesic traces become sufficiently vivid and consistent to result in the necessary integration, a highly emotional state was probably necessary. While the festive group occasion of song and dance may have served as a background, it is probable that definite sex behaviour furnished the relatively similar, recurrent, and specific activity necessary for the conditioning process associated with a highly emotional facilitating state. Specific sounds being associated with this type of behavior, would furnish a similar stimulus which could be produced and interchanged by each person" (p. 159). But specific sex behavior is just the sort of *overt* expression that obviates the need of imaginative consciousness and its symbolic expression.

[42] Donovan, *op. cit.,* part II, p. 332.

articulate utterances were absorbing ear and mind, and, at the same time, getting fixed upon the perceptions which they were associated with repeatedly.

Thus a rhythmic group of syllables conventionally associated with the object or central figure of a certain type of celebration—say, with a certain warrior—"would become its vocal mark, and be uttered when any objects of nature gave impressions which could, however faintly, touch the springs of the latent mass of sensations belonging to the festal imagining of the destroying warrior."[43]

This passage is interesting for two reasons: (1) because it assumes that the original use of language lies in *naming, fixating, conceiving* objects, so that the communicative use of words is only a secondary one, a practical application of something that has already been developed at a deeper psychological level; and (2) because it suggests the very early, very primitive operation of *metaphor* in the evolution of speech. The nature of metaphor is another topic which cannot be properly understood without a symbolistic rather than a signalistic view of language; but to this matter we will presently return.

When particular syllables got fixed upon particular actions, they would be brought up with them, and here two chief interests of the festal excitement would begin to clash, the interest of significance, and that belonging to the impulse to make the vocal apparatus produce the easiest possible enticements to the ear. . . . In the familiar observation of travellers about the "unmeaning interjections scattered here and there to assist the metre" of savage songs, as well as in the most polished alliterations, assonances, rhymes, refrains and burthens, there can be no doubt that we behold the demands for aural absorption trying to make their way among syllables which have been fixed by significance.[44]

Recent anthropological literature has certainly borne out the observations of the travelers he cites; we need only turn to Boas' statement, quoted by Jespersen,[45] that Indian song may be carried on purely rhythmic nonsense syllables, or

consist largely of such syllables, with a few interspersed words suggesting certain ideas and feelings; or it may rise to the expression of emo-

---

[43] *Ibid.*, part II, pp. 334–335.
[44] *Ibid.*, part II, p. 337.
[45] Jespersen, *Language*, p. 437.

tions connected with warlike deeds, with religious feeling, love, or even to the praises of the beauties of nature.[46]

The first symbolic value of words is probably purely connotative, like that of ritual; a certain string of syllables, just like a rite, embodies a concept, as "hallelujah" embodies much of the concept expressed in the Easter service. But "hallelujah" is not the name of any thing, act, or property; it is neither noun, verb, adjective, nor any other syntactical part of speech. So long as articulate sound serves only in the capacity of "hallelujah" or "alack-a-day," it cannot fairly be called language; for although it has connotation, it has no denotation. But denotation is the essence of language, because it frees the symbol from its original instinctive utterance and marks its deliberate *use*, outside of the total situation that gave it birth. A denotative word is related at once to a conception, which may be ever so vague, and to a *thing* (or event, quality, person, etc.) which is realistic and public; so it weans the conception away from the purely momentary and personal experience and fastens it on a permanent element which may enter into all sorts of situations. Thus the definiteness of sticks and stones, persons and acts and places, creeps into the recollection and the anticipation of experience, as its symbols, with their whole load of imagery and feeling, gradually become anchored to real objects.

The utterance of conception-laden sounds, at the sight of things that exemplify one or another of the conceptions which those sounds carry, is first a purely expressive reaction; only long habit can fix an association so securely that the word and the object are felt to belong together, so that the one is always a reminder of the other.

---

[46] The purely phonetic origin of song texts survives in our "hey-nonny-nonny" and "tralala"; Donovan remarks that such nonsense syllables have been relegated entirely to the choruses of our songs, and are no longer mixed with genuinely verbal elements; but in purely festal songs, such as drinking and cheering songs, we still find such conglomerations of words and babble as:

> "With a veevo, with a vivo,
> With a veevo-vivo-vum,
> Vum get a rat-trap bigger than a cat-trap,
> Vum get a cat-trap bigger than a rat-trap,
> Cannibal, cannibal, sizz-boom-bah,
> (College, college), rah rah rah!"

Nothing in the savages' repertoire could answer better to Boas' description, "nonsense syllables with a few interspersed words."

But when this point is reached, the humanoid creature will undoubtedly utter the sound in sport, and thus move the object into nearer and clearer prominence in his mind, until he may be said to *grasp* a conception of it by means of the sound; and *now the sound is a word*.

In a sociable species this game would presumably become a joint affair almost at once. The word uttered by one pre-Adamite would evoke a fuzzy, individual conception in another; but if the word, besides stimulating that conception, were tied up to the same *object* for the hearer as it was for the speaker, the word would have a common meaning for them both. The hearer, thinking his own thought of the object, would be moved thereby to say the word, too. The two creatures would look at one another with a light of understanding dawning under their great brow ridges, and would say some more words, and grin at some more objects. Perhaps they would join hands and chant words together. Undoubtedly such a wonderful "fashion" would become immensely popular.

Thus in a genuinely prehuman manner, and not by social contract or practical forethought, articulate sounds with a festal expressive value may have become *representative*. Of course this is pure speculation; but all theory is merely speculation in the light of significant facts. Linguists have avowedly given it up, in this case, for lack of such facts; a general study of symbolism may supply them, and yield at least a plausible theory in place of the very unsatisfactory current conviction that language simply *cannot* have begun in any thinkable way.

But another mystery remains. Given the word, and the thought of a thing through the word, how did language rise from a sheer atomic conglomeration of symbols to the state of a complex relational structure, a logical edifice, such as it is among all tribes and nations on earth? For language is much more than a set of symbols. It is essentially an organic, functioning *system,* of which the primary elements as well as the constructed products are symbols. Its forms do not stand alone, like so many monoliths each marking its one isolated grave; but instead, they tend to integrate, to make complex patterns, and thus to point out equally complex *relationships* in the world, the realm of their meanings.

This tendency is comprehensible enough if we consider the preeminence which a named element holds in the kaleidoscopic flow of sheer sense and feeling. For as soon as an object is denoted, it can be *held*, so that anything else that is experienced at the same time, instead of crowding it out, exists *with* it, in contrast or in unison or in some other definite way. If the ape who wants a banana beyond his cage could only keep "banana, banana," in his head while he looks behind him at the convenient bamboo, he could use the rod to fetch his lunch. But without language, relations are either taken for granted in action—as by a dog, for instance, who looks hopefully *inside* the garbage pail, or takes shelter from punishment *under* the sofa—or they cannot be experienced at all. The ape simply knew nothing about the relation of stick and fruit when their copresence was not visible.

This phenomenon of *holding on to the object* by means of its symbol is so elementary that language has grown up on it. A word fixes something in experience, and makes it the nucleus of memory, an available conception. Other impressions group themselves round the denoted thing and are associatively recalled when it is named. A whole occasion may be retained in thought by the name of an object or a person that was its center. The one word "river" may bring back the excitement of a dangerous crossing, a flood, a rescue, or the thought of building a house at the water's edge. The name of a person, we all know, brings to mind any number of events in which he figured. That is to say, a mnemonic word establishes a *context* in which it occurs to us; and in a state of innocence we use it in the expectation that it will be understood with its context. A baby who says "cookie" means, and trusts his nurse to know, that he sees, or wants, or has a cookie; if he says "out" he may mean that he is going out, that someone has gone out, that the dog wants to go out, etc., and he confidently expects his utterance to be understood with its tacit context.

Carl Bühler has called this elementary stage the "empractic" use of language.[47] The context is the situation of the speaker in a setting visible to the hearer; at the point where their thinking is to converge, a word is used, to fix the crucial concept. The word is *built into* the speaker's action or situation, in a diacritical capacity, settling a doubt, deciding a response.[48]

---

[47] See Bühler, *Sprachtheorie*, chap. iii, *passim*.

[48] Where a diacritical verbal sign is built into the action, it frequently needs no surrounding framework or other verbal indicators. For in place of such

The distinction between the novel predication in a statement and the merely qualifying situation, given by visible and demonstrable circumstance (Bühler calls it *das Zeigfeld*), or verbally by exposition (*das Symbolfeld*), was recognized fifty years ago by Philip Wegener; in a little book called *Untersuchungen über die Grundfragen des Sprachlebens* Wegener expounded the growth of explicit statement from such a matrix, such communication by mere key words, eked out by pointing and by their setting in an obvious state of affairs. He recognized two general principles of linguistic development: *emendation*, which begets syntactical forms of speech, and *metaphor*, the source of generality. The first principle serves to solve the problem of structure, so I will briefly set it forth.

Since a word, in the elementary social use which babies and foreigners make of it, and which probably represents a primitive stage of its communicative function, is meant to convey a concept not of a mere object, but also of the part played by that object in a situation which is supposed to be "understood," such a single word is really, in meaning, a *one-word sentence*. But it requires a certain amount of good will and like-mindedness to understand the speaker of a one-word sentence. We always assume that our own attitude toward things is shared by our fellows, and needs only the "empractic" use of a vocable to designate our particular thought in that setting, until we find ourselves *misunderstood*. Then we supplement the lone verb or noun with demonstratives—little words like "da!" "his!" From such syllables, added as supplements to the one-word sentence, arise inflections, which indicate more specifically what the word-sentence asserts about the expressed concept. Wegener has traced interesting parallels between inflections and demonstratives. More and more vocables are needed to *modify* the original expression, and to accompany and emphasize gestures and attitudes; so the grammatical structure evolves by emendation of an ambiguous expression, and naturally follows quite closely the relational pattern of

---

substitute it is surrounded by that for which they are proxy, and is supported by it. That the patron of a restaurant intends to consume something . . . is thoroughly understood by his partner (the waiter). The customer uses a verbal sign . . . only at the moot point in his otherwise tacit, intelligible behavior, as a diacritical sign. He inserts it, and the ambiguity is removed; that is the *empractic* use of language. *Ibid.*, p. 158.

the situation that evokes it. In this way, the context of the primitive word-sentence is more and more adequately expressed in verbal terms. At first modifiers and identifiers follow the crucial word that expressed the required *predication* in too great haste. "Appositives and relative clauses are subsequent corrections of our deficient presentations."[49] Hence the cognate nature of relative and interrogative, or relative and demonstrative pronouns. All these auxiliary utterances Wegener calls the "exposition" of the original word, which contains the real "novelty" to be asserted. This exposition finally becomes the *verbal context* in which the assertion is made. When the speaker is fully aware of the context and the need of stating it, his speech is full-fledged. As Wegener puts it, "Only the development of speech as an art and a science finally impresses on us the duty of rendering the exposition before the novel predication."[50]

Since language is grafted on a vocalizing tendency in immature humans and is kept up only by becoming habit, linguistic forms very easily become fixed, because they are habitual responses. The trick of accompanying all communication with words quickly becomes an ingrained custom; so that words without important meanings creep in simply to fill gaps in the vocal pattern, and utterances become *sentences* of certain standard forms. At the highest development of these language-making functions, the resultant systems are immensely inflected. Then separate items, or "roots," become conventionally attached to very bare items of conception, abstractable from the articulated whole; and the logic of language, which appears to us in our awareness of syntax, emerges as an amazing intellectual structure.

The significant feature of Wegener's theory is that it derives grammatical structure from the undifferentiated content of the one-word sentence, and the literal, fixed denotation of separate words from the total assertion by gradual crystallization, instead of trying to build the complexities of discursive speech out of supposed primitive "words" with distinctly substantive or distinctly relational connotations. No savage society of unintellectual hunters and squaws could ever *build* a language; they could only produce it by some

[49] Wegener, *Untersuchungen*, p. 34.
[50] *Ibid.*, p. 40.

such unconscious process as endless misunderstanding, modification, reduplication for emphasis (as we reduplicate baby words—"goody-goody," "naughty-naughty," "bye-bye," etc.) and "filling in" by force of a formal feeling based on habits.

The structure of language may, indeed, have grown up by gradual emendation, but not so its other essential value, *generality*. Even a contextual language is still primarily specific as long as the verbal exposition merely replaces the situation of an "empractically" used word, and the word is a *name*. Here we encounter the second, and I think more vital, principle of language (and perhaps of all symbolism): metaphor.

Here again Wegener's study shows us a natural process, born of practical exigencies, effecting what ultimately proves to be an incomparable achievement. But to follow his reasoning it is necessary to go back to his conception of the nature of communication.

All discourse involves two elements, which may be called, respectively, the context (verbal or practical) and the novelty. The novelty is what the speaker is trying to point out or to express. For this purpose he will use any word that serves him. The word may be apt, or it may be ambiguous, or even new; the context, seen or stated, modifies it and determines just what it means.

Where a precise word is lacking to designate the novelty which the speaker would point out, he resorts to the powers of *logical analogy,* and uses a word denoting something else that is a presentational symbol for the thing he means; the context makes it clear that he cannot mean the thing literally denoted, and must mean something else symbolically. For instance, he might say of a fire: "It flares up," and be clearly understood to refer to the action of the fire. But if he says: "The king's anger flares up," we know from the context that "flaring up" cannot refer to the sudden appearance of a physical flame; it must connote the idea of "flaring up" as a *symbol* for what the king's anger is doing. We conceive the literal meaning of the term that is usually used in connection with a fire, but this concept serves us here as proxy for another which is nameless. The expression "to flare up" has acquired a wider meaning than its original use, to describe the behavior of a flame; it can be used metaphorically to describe whatever its *meaning* can symbolize. Whether it is to be taken in a literal or a metaphorical sense has to be determined by the context.

In a genuine metaphor, an image of the literal meaning is our symbol for the figurative meaning, the thing that has no name of its own. If we say that a brook is laughing in the sunlight, an idea of laughter intervenes to symbolize the spontaneous, vivid activity of the brook. But if a metaphor is used very often, we learn to accept the word in its metaphorical context as though it had a literal meaning there. If we say: "The brook runs swiftly," the word "runs" does not connote any leg action, but a shallow rippling flow. If we say that a rumor runs through the town, we think neither of leg action nor of ripples; or if a fence is said to run round the barnyard there is not even a connotation of changing place. Originally these were probably all metaphors but one (though it is hard to say which was the primitive literal sense). Now we take the word itself to mean *that which all its applications have in common,* namely *describing a course.* The great extent and frequency of its metaphorical services have made us aware of the basic concept by virtue of which it can function as a symbol in so many contexts; constant figurative use has generalized its sense.

Wegener calls such a word a "faded metaphor," and shows, in an argument too long and elaborate to be reproduced here, that all general words are probably derived from specific appellations, by metaphorical use; so that our literal language is a very repository of "faded metaphors."

Since the *context* of an expression tells us what is its sense— whether we shall take it literally or figuratively, and how, in the latter case, it is to be interpreted—it follows that the context itself must always be expressed literally, because it has not, in turn, a context to supplement and define its sense. Only the novel predication can be metaphorical. A discourse divorced from physical situations, i.e., a discourse in which the context is entirely expressed and not bound to "empractic" utterances, is not possible until some words have acquired fixed, general connotations, so that they may serve in a conventional, literal fashion, to render the *exposition* of the crucial assertion.

All words, therefore, which may be logical subjects (of predications) and hence expository, have acquired this capacity only by virtue of their "fading" in predicational use. And before language had any faded words to denote logical subjects, it could not render a situation by any other means than a demonstrative indication of it in present experience. So

the process of fading which we have here adduced represents the bridge
from the first (one-word) . . . phase of language to the developed
phase of a discursive exposition.[51]

Metaphor is our most striking evidence of *abstractive seeing,* of
the power of human minds to use presentational symbols. Every new
experience, or new idea about things, evokes first of all some metaphorical expression. As the idea becomes familiar, this expression
"fades" to a new literal use of the once metaphorical predicate, a
more general use than it had before. It is in this elementary, presentational mode that our first adventures in conscious abstraction
occur. The spontaneous similes of language are our first record of
similarities perceived. The fact that poverty of language, need of
emphasis, or need of circumlocution for any reason whatever,[52]
leads us at once to seize upon a metaphorical word, shows how
natural the perception of common form is, and how easily one and
the same concept is conveyed through words that represent a wide
variety of conceptions. The use of metaphor can hardly be called a
conscious device. It is the power whereby language, even with a
small vocabulary, manages to embrace a multimillion things;
whereby new words are born and merely analogical meanings become stereotyped into literal definitions. (Slang is almost entirely
far-fetched metaphor. Although much of it is conscious and humorous in intent, there is always a certain amount of peculiarly apt
and expressive slang which is ultimately taken into the literary
language as "good usage.")

One might say that, if ritual is the cradle of language, metaphor
is the law of its life. It is the force that makes it essentially *relational,* intellectual, forever showing up new, abstractable *forms* in
reality, forever laying down a deposit of old, abstracted concepts in
an increasing treasure of general words.

The intellectual vocabulary grows with the progress of conceptual
thinking and civilized living. Technical advances make demands
on our language which are met by the elaboration of mathematical,
logical, and scientific terminologies. Anthropomorphic metaphors are

---

[51] Wegener, *Untersuchungen,* p. 54.

[52] For detailed studies of motives governing the use of metaphor, see Heinz
Werner, *Die Ursprünge der Metapher* (1919); Hermann Paul, *Principles of
the History of Language* (1888; German 1880); Alfred Biese, *Die Philosophie
des Metaphorischen* (1893).

banned, and the philological laws of word change become almost
all-important in the production of further nomenclatures and usages.
Meanings become more and more precise; wherefore, as Jespersen
says, "The evolution of language shows a progressive tendency from
inseparable conglomerations to freely and regularly combinable
short elements."[53] Speech becomes increasingly discursive, practical,
prosaic, until human beings can actually believe that it was invented
as a utility, and was later embellished with metaphors for the sake
of a cultural product called poetry.

One more problem invites our speculation: Why do all men
possess language? The answer, I think, is that all men possess it
because they all have the same psychological nature, which has
reached, in the entire human race, a stage of development where
symbol using and symbol making are dominant activities. Whether
there were many beginnings of language or few, or even only one,
we cannot tell; but wherever the first stage of speaking, the use
of any denotative symbol, was attained, there the development of
speech probably occurred with phenomenal speed. For the notion
of giving something a *name* is the vastest generative idea that ever
was conceived; its influence might well transform the entire mode
of living and feeling, in the whole species, within a few generations. We ourselves have seen how such a notion as the power
engine can alter the world, how other inventions, discoveries, and
adaptations crowd in its wake. We have watched human industry
change from handicraft to mass production in every phase of life,
within the memory of individuals. So with the advent of language,
save that it must have been more revolutionary. Once the spark was
struck, the light of reason was lit; an epoch of phenomenal novelty,
mutation, perhaps even cerebral evolution, was initiated, as Man
succeeded to the futile simian that had been himself. Once there
were speaking men on earth it would take utter isolation to keep
any tribe from speaking. And unless there have been many cradles
of mankind, such total isolation of a society, from prehuman aeons
to historic times, is hard to imagine.

The general theory of symbolism here set forth, which distin-
guishes between two symbolic modes rather than restricting intelligence to discursive forms and relegating all other conception to

53 *Op. cit.*, p. 429.

some irrational realm of feeling and instinct, has the great advantage of assimilating all mental activity to reason, instead of grafting that strange product upon a fundamentally unintellectual organism. It accounts for imagination and dream, myth and ritual, as well as for practical intelligence. Discursive thought gives rise to science, and a theory of knowledge restricted to its products culminates in the critique of science; but the recognition of nondiscursive thought makes it just as possible to construct a theory of *understanding* that naturally culminates in a critique of art. The parent stock of both conceptual types, of verbal and nonverbal formulation, is the basic human act of symbolic transformation. The root is the same, only the flower is different.

Bibliography

Cassirer, Ernst. *Language and Myth.* New York: Harper & Row, Publishers, Inc., 1946.

Jespersen, Otto. *Language: Its Nature, Development and Origin.* Holt, Rinehart, and Winston, Inc., 1922.

Kellogg, W. N. and L. A. Kellogg. *The Ape and the Child.* McGraw-Hill Book Co., 1933.

Köhler, Wolfgang. *The Mentality of Apes.* Harcourt, Brace & World, Inc., 1926.

Urban, W. M. *Language and Reality; the Philosophy of Language and the Principles of Symbolism.* The Macmillan Company, 1939.

THE FUNCTIONS OF LANGUAGE

JAMES L. KINNEAVY

The uses and functions of language are in close correspondence. Their relationship to each other and the implications for foreign language teaching are discussed with clarity in the following essay. To the teacher reading the essay will come the realization that one's teaching techniques must also change according to which function of language is stressed. The writer of foreign-language textbooks could also consider some of the theories expressed. A knowledge of linguistics, literature, philosophy, and culture makes possible a broad and comprehensive view of the functions of language from a multi-discipline viewpoint. The teacher should be as aware of the functions of language as of the four skills. A student knows a language only when he can apply the four skills to the five functions set forth in this essay.

Some persons undertaking the learning of a foreign language have fairly concrete purposes in mind—they may be interested in the information available only in that language's scientific publications, they may wish to explore a new culture, they may wish to market new products or old religions, or they may be interested in new literary universes, etc. Others dutifully enter the mastery of a new tongue with some vague suspicion that there will be a liberalizing feedback at some time in their educational career. Others, of course, have foreign languages thrust upon them by geography, college curricula, etc.

Yet aside from a few perfunctory offerings in, say, technical German, much foreign-language teaching fails to take into account the aims of the learners. And, even in such cases, it is questionable if such a narrow restriction is really a proper introduction to any-

41

thing more than passing the formality of a predoctoral language requirement.

Foreign language teachers are not alone in their neglect of a consideration of the aims of language, however. Grammarians and historical, descriptive, and comparative linguists have generally little or nothing to say about the functions of language. Doubtless the nineteenth-century historical fixation with fact, and the twentieth-century fear of "meaning" contamination have been at least contributory factors to this neglect. More specifically, an application of the functions of language—even by those who talk about such things—has not been made with a concrete orientation to foreign language learning and teaching.

A common view of the "functions" of foreign language teaching at present takes function to mean the *ability* to perform adequately in speaking and listening situations; these are viewed as fundamentally more important than the ability to read or write the language. The language laboratory is an attempt to achieve this concept of function.

But no one speaks just to speak; he speaks for a purpose. And one can view "function" as meaning the *purpose* for which one listens, speaks, reads, or writes. This is the usual sense the word "function" has for the philosopher of language.

Thirdly, function can also mean *reference*, the kind of thing referred to by the language. And language certainly functions in this sense also.

An example may clarify these various functions. "The train is coming" is a statement in English. It can be written, read, spoken, or listened to; the foreign language student can achieve each of these mechanical art skills. The statement also functions as *reference;* it refers to a happening in the universe; it is a narrative statement, not an evaluative, or definitional, or simple descriptive statement. Finally, however, the statement functions as *aim;* it can simply inform, or (with a certain intonation or punctuation) it can question (explore), or warn (persuade), or entertain (as the punch line of a joke), or merely express astonishment that the event is actually happening (expression).

These three concepts of function should be carefully distinguished. Often they are not. Of the three different notions of function, the arts and the reference forms of a language are actually only means to the aims. To build a program on mere speaking and listening skills, for example, would be equivalent to buying a train ticket to nowhere in particular. Yet this is common practice in foreign-language programing.

Possibly the most important distinction that must be kept in mind in approaching the problem of the functions of language is a determination of the unit of analysis. This is a basic problem in any science. What unit of language is minimally necessary to enable the analyst to determine how language is functioning, i.e., what aim is being achieved?

Considerable debate has gone into a discussion of the unit or units of linguistics. Are they sounds, words, sentences, etc.? It seems clear from the example of the train given above that the function of a sentence (its aim) cannot be achieved in a strictly grammatical framework. Some sort of context is required. Nor can even the paragraph (or its verse equivalent, the stanza, etc.) be determinative.

It seems that the full verbal text of the language act must be required to determine function. Maybe even the situational context in which the verbal text occurs is needed. Possibly the total cultural context is required to determine the fundamental intended and/or achieved aim of a linguistic act. In other words, the analyst of the functions of language cannot be molecular in his approach to language. He must approach a language act as a totality and then analyze the parts in their relationship to the whole.

This principle is important for the teaching of both the native and the foreign language. The general procedure has been to move from the part to the whole. A typical high-school textbook in English or a foreign language usually moves from word to sentence to paragraph and finally to full "text" composition. Function is largely ignored in such a synthetic approach.

Language teachers have come more and more to recognize the sterility of a purely grammatical approach to the teaching of a language. In English teaching, the inadequacy of formal grammar taught divorced from actual composition or speech situations is almost axiomatic in modern treatments of the problem. In foreign language teaching, this movement has taken the direction of an insistence on actual speaking situations rather than formal grammatical emphases.

If one is to view the functions of language intelligently some divisions are necessary. There should be a consideration of: the *text* (the entire verbal process—whole poem, twenty-minute conversation, text of a sermon, etc.); the *situation* in which the text is delivered; and the elements of the *cultural context* which are necessary to give significance to the text in the given situation.

The importance of this principle for foreign language learning can scarcely be overemphasized. A foreign language text that is really concerned with the aims of language should incorporate small but complete samples of language uses and accompany these samples with the necessary situational and cultural annotations to make the texts meaningful to the learner alien to the new language. Otherwise one teaches only skills, not the language as a purposive instrument. The language laboratory itself can, because of its novelty and basic design, fail to take purpose into account. It is only a tool, nothing more.

A survey of various theories of the purposes of language reveals a striking persistence of certain basic functions. The problem has been the concern of many different disciplines. People concerned with the evolutionary development of language functions—whether it be in prehistory or in the primitive or in the child or in a specific historical culture—sign theorists, communication and information theorists, logical positivists, semanticists, educators, metaphysicians, expressionists, and comparative philologists all have representatives who have devoted some consideration to the issue. Though there are important divergences, the basic uses of language are repeated again and again in different contexts. The use of language to express emotion, the use of language to refer to known reality, the questioning use of language to explore unknown reality, the persuasive use of language in propaganda and rhetoric, and the entertaining use of language in literature and song are functions which are repeatedly mentioned.[1]

The purposes to which anything can be directed are necessarily restricted by the structure of the object or process. The structure of a cup allows it to be adapted to certain functions and obviously rules out other functions. Can not a view of the structure of the

---

[1] The editor regrets that limitations of space did not permit the inclusion of the comprehensive survey of theories which was a part of the original manuscript.

language process point out the functions to which it can be adapted? Many theories implicitly or explicitly have taken the components of the structure of the language process into consideration, but it has not been made sufficiently clear that a stress on one component of the language process rather than on another produces a specifically different function of language. A systematic survey of the possibilities can be shown by means of the accompanying diagram.

The components of a language process are the expressor, the receptor, the language, and the universe.

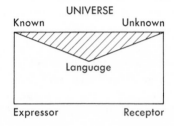

Language can be used to refer to known reality or to explore for reality that is unknown. The two uses of language are very different and are subject to different logics, different organizational patterns, different styles, etc. Consequently the universe is broken down here into the known universe and that aspect of reality which is suspected, though unknown. Any language's view of reality is conditioned by the linguistic and cultural axioms of the particular civilization, and for that reason the screen is interposed between the universe and its linguistic expression.

First, it is clear that language can be used for simple expression. Curse words, exclamations, etc., are simple examples of this use. Language, which has emotive potential, can be the vehicle of an emotional discharge. In a very real sense, all language has an "expressive" component, for all language is motivated by some instinct, drive, emotion. Some uses of language, however, seem preponderantly expressive. Certain conversational uses ("I just wanted to talk to you"), cathartic interviews in psychology, some religious and political credos or manifestoes, myths of primitive or sophisticated societies, value systems, etc., are often primarily expressive uses of language whereby an individual or a group expresses its intuitions and emotional aspirations. The expressor dominates the process.

Second, language can be an instrument to inform the receptor about the expressor's concept of reality. This is a reference to what is viewed as "known" about reality. This use of language gives informative discourse, at varying levels of sophistication. In this use the other components of the language process are subordinate to the "reality."

Third, language can be used as an instrument to explore the unknown. Seminars, discussion groups, essays, etc., are exploratory uses of language. This is dominated by the hypothesized reality.

Fourth, language can be used as an instrument to convince the receptor to feel a certain way, to do a certain thing, to think in a certain fashion. The success or failure of the linguistic instrument will be judged by his acceptance or rejection of the proposed alternative. Examples of such uses are propaganda, advertising, preaching, etc. Universe, expressor, and language are subordinate to the receptor, to the extent that reality may be distorted, crassly misrepresented, or certain aspects of it ignored. The expressor may purposely create a false image of himself; and language must be subordinated to what the receptor will accept, not to accuracy of representation or beauty of form.

Finally, language can be used to call attention to itself, to its own structure, not as references to reality or as expressions of personal aspirations or as exploratory devices, or as instruments of persuasion, but as a structure worthy of contemplation for delight in its own right. This is a literary use of language. And, at least in more advanced cultures, such instances of this use abound. In this situation, language itself dominates the linguistic process and the other components are subordinate. Language can be compared to a windowpane. You may throw bricks at it to vent your feelings, you may use it to view or explore reality, you may use a piece of its glass to chase away an intruder, but you can also use a windowpane to call attention to itself (as a stained-glass window). This is the windowpane as art.

An analysis of the components of the structure of the linguistic process reveals five basic uses of language: expression, information, exploration, persuasion, and entertainment. Because all of the elements are components of the linguistic process, it is immediately evident that there can be no "pure" expression, or information, or exploration, or persuasion, or literature. All uses of language must necessarily contain some elements of the expressionistic—for example, even the most scientific style reveals something of the intuitions, interests, values, etc., of the writer. Literature, to give another example, because it uses words that refer to reality, has even been viewed as essentially mimetic in essence; for a similar reason, because it embodies expressed aspirations, it has been viewed as essentially expressionistic in character; again, because it explores for values or attempts to inculcate them as "themes," it has been viewed as exploratory or pragmatic in nature. In general, any use of language must usually incorporate all the components, but one component will normally dominate.

Such an approach does not give priority to any one use of language and look with deprecatory condescension on the others. Rhetoric, as a use of language, is as valid as science or literature, for example.

A corollary of such a tolerant view of the various functions of language is that the variant logics, organizational patterns, styles, etc., that are effective in one function are assets for that function, though they may well be liabilities in another. Thus, verbal ambiguity is a vice in science, but a necessity in dialectic, a useful tool in rhetoric, often valuable in literature, and frequently irrelevant in expression. Again, emotional language is out of place in science, tolerated occasionally in dialectic, but quite pertinent in literature, rhetoric, and expression.

The application of the functions of language to foreign language learning must be done under the umbrella of a protective principle that respects the linguistic and cultural relativity of the native and the target language. Concretely, this means that the fundamenal expressionistic aspirations, scientific judgments, exploratory dialectics, persuasive techniques, and literary forms of one linguistic culture cannot be naively assumed to be neatly transferable into another linguistic culture.

It is generally accepted by most logical analysts of the structures of languages that the components of a language (its phonemic, morphemic, and syntactic structures) are *intuitive formalities* that enable the users of a given language to picture the world. In a manner quite parallel to a given physics (say Newton's), they *impose* a form on the world. Russell, Wittgenstein, and others generally agree that the structure of the language must have something in common with the structure of the reality which it represents,[2] but the possibilities of different structural similarities are probably infinite.

The potential of a language to interpret reality (or to perform other functions) is thus restricted by its own intuitive structures. For this reason, as Wittgenstein says, "The limits of my language mean the limits of my world."[3]

These different structural principles of a language give rise to a basic "world view" in a given linguistic culture. And the translation ability of a language depends upon its adaptability to render one world view into another. But adaptation always involves some distortion. Thus linguistic relativism becomes part of a larger cultural relativism. Specifically, as Carroll says, one has to understand the Navaho tongue to understand the Navaho mind.[4] The converse is also true, and Whorf has said, "A change in language can transform our appreciation of the Cosmos."[5] This, incidentally, is certainly one of the major reasons that justify the study of a foreign language.

It is possible and desirable for a culture to be approached, understood, and sympathized with *on its own terms*. To investigate a culture from within, with what might be called an empathy, is to investigate it from an emic standpoint, to use Pike's term.[6] On the contrary, to approach a culture with generalizations formed from outside (though possibly similar) behavior systems is to approach a culture from an *etic* standpoint.

Naturally, one cannot be other than alien in first approaching a

---

[2] Cf. Ludwig Wittgenstein, *Tractatus Logico-Philosophicus*, trans. D. F. Pears and B. F. McGuinness (New York: The Humanities Press, 1961), pp. 16, 37, 51, 55, 135–138.

[3] *Ibid*, p. 115.

[4] John B. Carroll, "Introduction" to Benjamin Lee Whorf, *Language, Thought and Reality* (New York: Wiley, 1956), p. 28.

[5] Benjamin Lee Whorf, *Language, Thought and Reality* (New York: Wiley, 1956), p. vii.

[6] Kenneth L. Pike, *Language, In Relation to a Unified Theory of the Structure of Human Behavior* (Glendale, California: Summer Institute of Linguistics, 1954), pp. 8 ff.

new culture. Consequently, one's first approaches as an outsider must be etic; only slowly can one take on the emic attitude. There is the existential problem of learning each individual language and appropriating another culture to oneself. There is no one cultural passkey, there are only keys to separate chambers, each of which has its own treasures.

It may be said that three main pillars have been established to serve as supports for a superstructure which will consider the functions of language in a specific application to foreign language learning and teaching. (1) One must view function as recognizable only in a "text"—a complete act of speech; function is not taught by reading or speaking isolated words, sentences, or even small paragraphs. (2) The basic functions of language are five: expression, information, exploration, persuasion, and entertainment. (3) The principle of cultural relativism demands that we approach each individual language in terms of its own expressed aspirations, scientific outlooks, exploratory methods, persuasive techniques, and literary forms; otherwise there is no real communication. Once communication is established and the speaker and listener can come to appreciate and understand each other's views, then there may be mutual enrichment. This may involve discarding some emic approaches and taking on others on the part of either side.

To be able to "think" in a foreign language one must understand the expressionistic aspect of a culture, both in its linguistic and non-linguistic manifestations. These are the fundamental aspirations, intuitions, feelings, values—in a word, the emotions of a culture.

There are two types of sources one can immerse oneself in to probe for the expressionistic dimensions of a culture. First there are the fairly overt and near-pure expressionistic uses of the language itself. Its myths, its religious credos, its political manifestoes are largely expressionistic. Diaries, journals, autobiographies, and much informal conversation are also highly expressive in nature. Curiously, for instance, there is a strong trend of blasphemy in French curse words, of obscenity in Spanish curse words, and of a concern with hell and damnation in English curse words.

But much of the expressionistic dimension of a culture can only be ferreted out by examining implicit embodiments in other uses of the language. Its other uses of language reflect its interests and aspirations. Anthropologists are making significant attempts to study various cultures in terms of their internal values. Content analyses of mass media can furnish valuable expressionistic guide lines.

Just as with a person, a culture's emotional expressions are peculiarly individual. A foreign language teacher (or text) who does not take into account the emotional context of a language and the fundamental aspirations of a culture is almost necessarily doomed to turn out aliens to the culture. And this cannot be remedied by an appendix that abstractly presents a cultural survey of the given civilization. There is no substitute for primary sources—actual texts embodying these values.

The use of language to interpret reality, with this *reference* dominating the language framework, can be as naive as some magical and superstitious interpretations of reality found in some cultures, as informal as the report of a train wreck by a Long Island commuter to his wife, or as scholarly as a mathematical treatise. To be prepared to discourse scientifically, therefore, with the natives of a culture, the foreigner must have some insight into the native "world perspective." There may be almost abysmal differences separating the two views of reality, or there may be what may appear as only slight distinctions. In the former case, communication will involve a good deal more than mere usage of verbal or syntactic equivalents.

Just as it may be argued in expressionistic usage that the fundamental aspirations of mankind are the same, so it has been argued that there is a unity of logic behind all languages. Yet the fundamental human aspirations find expression in quite divergent value systems. Similarly, the scientific view of the universe is very dissimilar in some cultures. The necessity, therefore, of an internal, empathic approach to a culture's science is obvious. Pike remarks,

People of one nation sometimes appear to be "illogical" or "stupid" or incomprehensible simply because the observer is over a long period of time taking an alien standpoint from which to view their activity, instead of seeking to learn their emic patterns of overt and covert behavior.[7]

Scientific discourse, despite its problems, is not as difficult as expressionistic or rhetorical. In fact, of the basic aims of language, the scientific may well be the easiest to achieve in translation. Yet many

[7] Pike, *Ibid,* I, p. 17.

foreign language texts include no scientific material in their sample readings. This is a shortcoming which could easily be remedied.

Exploratory discourse has much in common with informative discourse, for what is viewed as known is determined by the methods one has used in approaching the unknown. And, since different aspects of reality interest different cultures, the modes of exploration have been quite dissimilar.

For the Platonic and medieval mind the best approach to a problem was to sit down and turn it over in a conversation that would incorporate something like the Socratic method. The Renaissance mind preferred, as a logic of discovery, an experimental methodology. This was refined by Mill into his canons of inquiry and by modern statistical research methodologies into more sophisticated treatments of variable possibilities and degrees of probability.

The facile and invalid assumption that a Western dialectic can be assumed as readily acceptable immediately to other cultures is much more amplified when there is a question of more primitive and/or non-Indo-European civilizations. Careful analysis of typical and complete texts in the foreign language is the only really protective assurance for a sympathetic understanding of the emic methods of exploration by the culture in question. Curiously enough these are rarely represented in foreign language texts, which usually have a heavy orientation to the mere conversational or the literary. Yet to establish the necessary reciprocal communicative sympathy, this sort of text would seem to be called for, even as a preliminary to the scientific. For the exploration of the possibilities of the reciprocal transfer of the two "scientific" world views is a necessary prerequisite to the mutual scientific enrichment or even to a one-way enrichment.

One of the better etic approaches to a science of persuasion still seems to be the various kinds of persuasive proofs outlined in Aristotle's *Rhetoric*. Of course, Madison Avenue motivational analysis, the Institute for Propaganda Analysis, much of the invaluable work done by the semanticists, propaganda analysis of the Lasswell-Smith type, and the work by other ancillary disciplines have given breadth, depth, and edge to the sometimes provincial, sometimes superficial, and sometimes blunt positions of Aristotle. Many speech departments in colleges still work within the Aristotelian framework.

It is, in fact, not too far removed from the skeleton of analysis suggested by the famous Lasswell-Smith formula for propaganda analysis, "Who says what to whom, how, why, and with what effect?" But the application of this formula to particular cultures is still in its infancy as a technology.

When one extends the problem to the achievement of persuasive effectiveness in *any* culture, the dimensions of rhetorical communication become staggering. Of course, the kinds of message that will effectively convince will heavily reflect the expressionistic aspect of a culture more than any other, though the view of reality and the problem-solving methodologies will also be relevant.

As with the science of a given culture, there is no cultural passkey; each persuasive situation is unique. The inclusion of "domestic" rhetorical samples in foreign language texts is, again, a practice that is generally neglected. Yet an emic approach seems the only answer.

The final use of language is the use of language to delight, and it varies in scale from the humble joke to the grand tragedy, from the popular soap opera to Shakespeare, from the ballad to the epic.

Literary texts, possibly more than others, have been common vehicles in the teaching of foreign languages from the high school through the university. Foreign language departments at the upper class levels usually tend almost totally to the literary uses of the language, as do their English counterparts.

Yet comparative literature, like comparative rhetoric, is a discipline almost in its infancy. Literary pieces, leaning so heavily on the internal structure of the language, and often preponderantly on the phonemic structures of the language, defy translation maybe even more than do expressionistic pieces. The Italian proverb that to translate is to betray (and the phonemic parallelism is lost in translation) and the Spanish proverb that translations are like women, the beautiful are seldom true and the true are seldom beautiful, reflect this difficulty.

Literature, whether humorous or tragic, whether lyric or dramatic or epic, etc., also demands an inner sympathetic approach. And anyone who has tried to foist a Spanish joke on a Frenchman knows this. Drama is one thing in classic Greece, another thing in nineteenth-century Sweden, and quite another in Japan.

If we believe Cassirer's statement, the problem of translation presided at and determined the birth of Western civilization.[8] And, though it has been with us ever since, its intensity has reached fearful dimensions in our present shrinking world where we are more and more brought into daily contact with peoples from all over the globe—and beyond lies space.

The birth of a "world civilization" must likewise be presided over by the problem of translation—an international language might remove some of the superficial problems, but obviously not all.

The problem of learning a foreign language must take into consideration, with a scope it has hitherto ignored, the functions of language. Function, as has been shown, can mean the aim of the language act, the reference of the language act, and the language art itself. These aims, forms of composition (resulting from reference), and language arts are only fully appreciated in a study of complete "texts" not in isolated grammatical or paragraph units.

Further, these complete texts can ultimately only be understood by standing within a culture and viewing the texts with in-culture sympathy.

Consequently, a full program of foreign language should incorporate texts exemplifying all of these basic uses of the language by the natives, accompanied by the usual phonemic, morphemic, and syntactic analyses, but also accompanied by an analysis studying underlying logics, structures, views of reality involved, fundamental aspirations implied, etc.

A full program should likewise take into account the functions of a language considered as language arts. A person knows the language from this point of view when he can listen to, speak, read, and write the language with ease and rapidity.

Finally, the texts should also exemplify "function" viewed as reference. Here the in-cultural traditional forms of composition should be illustrated.

Obviously, the approach here recommended considerably enlarges the duties of the foreign language teacher. He cannot afford to live in a linguistic vacuum. He must take language out of dictionaries, grammars, and laboratory tapes and teach his students to *use* the language. The product of such an approach will not be just a phonemic or syntactic robot, but a person who can think and feel in a new dimension.

[8] Ernst Cassirer, *An Essay on Man* (New Haven: Yale, 1944), p. 134.

Bibliography

Cassirer, Ernst. *An Essay on Man.* New Haven, Conn.: Yale University Press, 1944.

Croce, Benedetto. *Aesthetic,* trans. Douglas Ainslie. New York: The Macmillan Company, 1922.

Hayakawa, S. I. *Language in Thought and Action.* New York: Harcourt, Brace & World, Inc., 1949.

LaDrière, J. C. "Rhetoric and a 'Merely Verbal Art'." *English Institute Essays, 1948,* (ed.) D. A. Robertson, Jr. New York: Columbia University Press, 1949.

Malinowski, Bronislaw. *Coral Gardens and Their Magic.* New York: American Book Company, 1935.

Miller, George A. *Language and Communication.* New York: McGraw-Hill Book Company, 1951.

Morris, C. W. *Signs, Language and Behavior.* New York: G. Braziller, 1955.

Ogden, C. K. and I. A. Richards. *The Meaning of Meaning.* London: K. Paul, Trench, Trubner & Co., Ltd., 1945.

Pike, Kenneth L. *Language, in Relation to a Unified Theory of the Structure of Human Behavior.* Glendale, California: Summer Institute of Linguistics, 1954.

Russell, Bertrand. *Human Knowledge, Its Scope and Limits.* New York: Simon and Schuster, Inc., 1948.

Slama-Cazacu, Tatiana. *Langage et Contexte.* 's Gravenhage: Mouton, 1961.

Whatmough, Joshua. *Language, A Modern Synthesis.* New York: New American Library, 1957.

Whorf, Benjamin Lee. *Language, Thought and Reality.* New York: John Wiley & Sons, Inc., 1956.

Wittgenstein, Ludwig. *Tractatus Logico-Philosophicus,* trans. D. F. Fears and B. F. McGuinness. New York: Humanities Press, 1961.

WHY A FOREIGN LANGUAGE REQUIREMENT?

WILLIAM R. PARKER

The foreign language teacher will often hear from students the question: "Why do we have to study foreign languages?" An academic answer to this question is provided in this article written by a former secretary of the Modern Language Association who is currently professor of English at the University of Indiana. In his discussion the reasons for foreign language study are analyzed and evaluated and the inclusion of foreign languages in the liberal arts curriculum examined. The rationale arrived at is entirely applicable to the high school which must clearly determine its own specific aims and goals for including foreign language instruction in its curriculum.

This essay concerns a situation in more than eight hundred liberal arts colleges, though some of its points apply elsewhere in American education. The question posed—why a foreign language requirement?—has fresh relevance because the 1930–1950 trend of dropping this requirement for the Bachelor of Arts degree has very recently been reversed.

The question implies a larger question which had better be confronted first. Why *any* specific requirements in a degree program? In many institutions a qualified person may enroll as a "special student" and take such courses as he pleases; but degrees are universally, and not unreasonably, awarded only to those who complete a certain *kind* of program that has been designed by "experts" to achieve certain educational objectives. That many persons want the degree for reasons irrelevant to the objectives is no reason for altering the objectives or making the degree more easily

Reprinted by permission of the American Association of Collegiate Registrars and Admissions Officers from *College and University*, Winter, 1957.

obtained. That some seekers of the degree disapprove the program or its objectives is likewise irrelevant. No liberal arts faculty can escape the responsibility of defining what it considers the proper ingredients of a "liberal education." It can be wrong, but it must decide; its degree signifies its collective recognition, not of hours spent or grades received, but of satisfactory completion of a program collectively approved.

Any such program will involve requirements. They may be many or few. The present tendency, in reaction to results of the elective system, is to make them many. This may change, but some requirements there must be. They fall generally into two categories: specific learning considered basic and indispensable to liberal education (e.g., skill in the use of one's native language); and some experience of certain broad areas of learning, to be achieved by satisfactory work in one or several courses out of various possibilities in each area (e.g., experience of scientific method).

Does foreign language study fall into either of these categories? In answering this question one must distinguish carefully between educational values in general (which presumably *all* academic subjects offer) and values *indispensable to liberal education*. The question, in other words, must be answered only in reference to explicit definition of liberal education. Unfortunately, it is too often discussed in reference to other matters, such as the problem of exceptions, vocational considerations, the relevance of foreign language skills to the work of specific departments, the practice of other institutions, and educational trends.

EDUCATIONAL TRENDS

A college or university faculty should, of course, be interested in educational trends, both new and old. Former trends are revealing of passing enthusiasms, or changes in basic educational philosophy, or significant social forces at work. New trends invite a healthy re-examination of conscious or long-forgotten conclusions. Because trends may be good or bad, no college or university should make changes merely because others are doing so. A trend is not itself an argument for altering established practice. Eighty-four percent of all accredited liberal arts colleges in the United States resisted the prolonged trend of dropping the language requirement for the B.A. degree.[1]

Since 1952 there has been a trend toward *restoration* (or institution) of the foreign language requirement for the B.A. At least fifteen colleges or universities in eleven states have taken this step;[2] at least four have restored the foreign language *entrance* requirement;[3] still other places, notably Cornell and Michigan, have recently strengthened or extended their former degree requirement. But these developments, however interesting, are not in themselves an argument for restoring or instituting requirements elsewhere, despite the fact that in earlier years some institutions were clearly influenced by a contrary trend. On the other hand, the new trend *is* an argument—and a strong one—for reconsideration of current practice. Such reconsideration may result in deciding the trend unwise, but unwillingness to reconsider is certainly unwise, for it implies that past decisions are sacrosanct despite any degree of social change.

PRACTICE ELSEWHERE

Most institutions of higher education normally compete for good students with other institutions in their class, often within certain geographical limits. Thus, of sixty-three accredited liberal arts colleges in New England, only two, American International and Bennington, lack a foreign language degree requirement, and the former has a language requirement for entrance. In Arizona, Mississippi, South Carolina, Utah, Virginia, and Wisconsin—to mention

[1] The statistics and some of the other facts in this essay are drawn from the fourth revision of "Foreign Language Entrance and Degree Requirements," *Publications of the Modern Language Association (PMLA)*, LXXI, Sept., 1956, Part 2, 49–70.

[2] Arkansas State College, Chatham College (Pennsylvania), Detroit Institute of Technology, Fairmont State College (West Virginia), Mary Manse College (Ohio), Norwich University (Vermont), Middlebury College (Vermont), University of Minnesota and its Duluth Branch, Ohio Northern University, University of Redlands (California), Stetson University (Florida; but see n. 5, below), Stillman College (Alabama), Virginia State College, and Williams College (Massachusetts).

[3] Calvin College (Michigan), Middlebury College (Vermont), Pacific Union College (California), and Stanford University (California).

states in other areas—*all* colleges granting the B.A. require foreign languages for the degree, as does the one accredited institution of higher learning in Delaware, Nevada, and Wyoming. There are ten other states (plus the District of Columbia), with a total of 181 liberal arts colleges, in each of which only a single accredited institution lacks a language requirement for the B.A.: District of Columbia (American University), Georgia (Oglethorpe), Illinois (Aurora College), Indiana (St. Joseph's), Michigan (State University), Nebraska (Wesleyan), North Dakota (Teachers College at Mayville), Oregon (Cascade), South Dakota (Wesleyan University),[4] and Texas (Texas Western College).

On the other hand, the State Board of Education in California has decreed, since April 1951, that no foreign language shall be required by a state college as a condition to graduation, a ruling that directly affects nine institutions granting the B.A. degree. In general, the mountain states and those on the Pacific coast have the largest proportion of colleges without a language requirement, with the eleven West Central states next in regarding language study as unessential to a liberal arts program for the students they enroll.

RELEVANCY

"It's of no value to *us*," members of some departments may say flatly to any suggested requirement. "Our students *have* to have languages," the scientist or art historian may reply. But the relevance of foreign language learning to the work of a given department or departments is quite beside the point, and arguments raising this issue should therefore be quickly recognized and dismissed. The value of language learning to, say, psychologists or students of American literature is no more pertinent to a discussion of the place of foreign languages *in a liberal arts program* than would be examination of the value of history to psychologists or the value of physical education to students of American literature. Any who say, "It's of no value to us," are identifying the aims of a total program with limited departmental objectives. The discussion must stay on the subject, which is the nature of liberal educa-

---

[4] The Wesleyan institutions in Connecticut, Georgia, Illinois, and Texas all require languages for the B.A.; those in Iowa, Kentucky, Nebraska, Ohio, South Dakota, and West Virginia do not.

tion, not the need—or lack of need—of any department for language as a tool.[5]

Foreign languages are, of course, a cultural and professional tool, and any department has the right to require German or Latin or some other language of all its majors. This is another problem, outside the scope of this essay—as it should be outside the scope of faculty discussion of foreign languages in a liberal arts program, despite the inevitable faculty member who shamelessly exhibits his own ignorance by announcing, "Everything of any importance is available in English" or "I've forgotten all the French and German I ever learned, and I've got along all right." There is not much to be said to end the embarrassed silence or nervous titters that such confessions usually produce. Blind men "get along" too, but the difference is that one can admire their triumph over handicap. Nothing is to be gained by pointing out to this protester the untranslated books or journals in foreign languages that he should have read and has not. Nothing is to be gained by arguing that faulty products of liberal education are dubious moulders of its future. The best course is to end the silence by getting back to the subject.

VOCATIONAL CONSIDERATIONS

A college student may elect to major in one liberal arts subject rather than another because of its presumed vocational value to him, but no subject is included among the liberal arts because it trains one directly to earn a living. This point is as important as it is confusing. It is confusing because all departments in a liberal arts program lead two lives: in greatly varying degrees they do, in fact, provide training toward a profession or occupation, and they also contribute to a liberal education. A student in a philosophy

[5] In some institutions (e.g., St. Benedict's College, Kansas) foreign languages are required of all candidates for the B.A. except physical education majors. In some other institutions (e.g., Stetson University, Florida) education majors are solely excepted. In still others (e.g., Texas Western College) both education and physical education majors are exempted. When the U.S. Air Force Academy opened in July 1955 it was announced that cadets would have a choice between a foreign language and a course in aircraft design, but in March 1956 it was decided to require an intensive course in French or Spanish of all cadets.

class may eventually become a teacher of philosophy—or a chemist. A student in a chemistry class may eventually become a chemist or a teacher of philosophy. It so happens that a department of philosophy has much less direct effect on future vocations than does a department of chemistry, but it has, nevertheless, equal importance as a contributor to liberal education.

In any consideration of degree requirements, therefore, vocational values are irrelevant. They may be otherwise very relevant to the prosperity of the department, for today's students are often vocationally minded even in a liberal arts program; but vocational values have no bearing upon faculty discussions of such a program and, if introduced, should be quickly recognized and dismissed.

Because of recent and revolutionary advances in transportation and in communication media, produced by science and technology, modern foreign language teachers are likely to stress the increasingly important vocational values of their subject. Such talk—or any counter argument ("Very few Americans will ever need a second language")—is quite irrelevant to discussion of whether or not foreign languages should be required as part of a B.A. program. The answer to this question depends solely upon the contribution that learning a second language can make to a nonvocational, liberalizing education. Language teachers (or their critics) should be held strictly to this issue.

THE PROBLEM OF EXCEPTIONS

Requirements are formal expressions of collective standards and judgment. Efficient administration demands that they be definitely stated, widely publicized, and wisely enforced. Enforcement is not a purely clerical matter, but becomes such from the moment that a college faculty loses interest or completely delegates responsibility. When it becomes a purely clerical matter, the spirit and intent of requirements get forgotten, and the routine imposition of them begins to arouse resentments.

There is probably not a single requirement in connection with college or university work for which *unpublicized* exceptions should not occasionally be made by wise and responsible persons. It is not merely that the physically handicapped should be excused from the usual physical training, or the blind be given unorthodox examinations; an institution of higher learning should also be a place where the occasional aberrations of brilliance are understandingly dealt with, and where clearly superior students are not unduly penalized for inadequate preparation beyond their control. On the other hand, part of sound education is the discovery of one's limitations and mistakes—not the pleasure of having them coddled. Exceptions to requirements should be made only by persons who thoroughly understand the spirit and intent of the requirements.

A persistent argument against requiring foreign languages for a degree is that there are good students who simply do not "get" languages. The number of such persons is not known; the nature of their difficulty has never been analyzed; and their names are rarely if ever made a part of the argument. There probably are such persons; doubtless intellectual as well as physical allergies exist, and doubtless human emotions play an occasional part in both. A well-known American scientist who learned to master a number of foreign languages confesses that he could never "get" French. It should, of course, be remembered that this kind of inhibition or mental block does not limit its operation to language study. Wise administrators know what to do about it in the case of a really exceptional student. It is not a relevant argument against requiring any particular subject.

THE MATTER OF ALTERNATIVES

Inattention to the basic concept of liberal education is liable to result in a bookkeeping attitude toward requirements—an arbitrary, sometimes politically minded disposition to sanction "alternatives," not in terms of comparable educational values, but rather in terms of comparable "pressures" or nuisance values. Vigorously pressed departmental claims, when they cannot be allowed as valid, may thus, in certain situations, be recognized through compromise as acceptable alternatives to the claims of other departments.

The device of allowing formal alternatives is not unknown as a stratagem for eventually abandoning requirements. Thus, if a faculty concludes that elementary science courses are not really providing the broad introduction to scientific method indispensable to liberal education, it may not actually discard the "science requirement," but, rather, allow the student seeking a liberal education to choose between science courses and courses in Speech (both of which, the faculty may then assure itself hopefully, will develop "clear thinking"). This illustration, although hypothetical, is not an exaggeration of what has often happened when a political, bookkeeping attitude has affected the liberal arts program.

Student choice between or among alternatives is not necessarily harmful to a program of liberal education; it may add meaning to the word "liberal." What is harmful is providing alternatives that are educationally indefensible—forcing choices between learning experiences that are not truly comparable, despite their balance in the scale of academic politics or the "tie" they drew in a race for a single slot in the curriculum.

Alternatives cannot be justified in a program of liberal education unless they represent *closely similar experiences of nearly equal value*. The bookkeeping attitude congratulates itself on having discovered "nearly equal value," but shuts its mind to the subtler problem of discovering "closely similar experiences." Science and speech, English and economics, foreign languages and mathematics have, let us say, nearly equal educational values, but do not represent the kind of similar experiences that must be distinguished in formulating a pattern of liberal education. In terms of basic principles and methods of inquiry, they do not offer true or even approximate alternatives as an educational experience, compared, say, with history and political science, sociology and economics, botany and zoölogy, physics and chemistry.

A faculty fulfilling its unavoidable obligation to define liberal education must try to steer a course between glib categorizing and strictly departmental fragmentation of learning. Mounting enrollments, and the consequent emphasis upon departmental organization, have made this course increasingly difficult to steer. It is not merely that departments compete with one another; worse, departmental programs may even compete with the total liberal arts program, or "strong" departments may exhibit their strength by requesting a larger share of the liberal arts program. Every faculty member, however, has at least two duties: one is to his department, the other is to his college. As a member of a college his duty is to rise above departmental thinking, to think as one responsible for a total program of liberal education. In this latter role, he should not approve alternatives unless they represent closely similar experiences of nearly equal value in view of the objectives agreed upon by a majority of his colleagues.

Modern foreign language teachers may make this decision confusing for others by claiming for their subject a number of *secondary values.* Some, for example, may urge the study of languages as a means of knowing foreign cultures and civilizations, a claim that immediately suggests the pairing of foreign languages with courses that more directly and easily (because they are in English) pursue this objective. Still others may urge the study of languages as a gateway to foreign literature, a claim that might suggest pairing with courses in English literature or, worse, suggest foreign literature in translation as an alternative to the originals.

Study of any liberal arts subject may, and usually does, have secondary values. These assume importance to the extent—and only to the extent—that they are made conscious objectives by the individual teacher and are intelligently striven for in the classroom. Thus, foreign language study, under the direction of a given instructor, may concentrate on a foreign civilization rather than on its literature, or may stress belles lettres at the expense of history, social customs, and other broadly cultural matters.

It follows that a reasonable alternative to foreign language study in liberal education—if one exists—must be one that provides an experience *like in kind* to the *primary and essential* values of acquiring a second language as a means of communication and a means of learning. Mathematics, for example, meets part of these conditions: it is a specialized means of communication and learning.[6] But it does not liberate one from monolingualism; mastering it does not teach that human beings in other cultures use sounds and symbols to express concepts which may find no real equivalents in English.

THE CASE FOR LANGUAGE STUDY

Although tradition or social change may influence decisions, the faculty of each individual institution must determine the objectives of its own program of liberal education. This essay, therefore, will

---

[6] B.A. degree candidates must choose between mathematics and foreign languages at Hamline University (language requirement dropped 1950) and Princeton University (dropped 1947).

not try to argue what these should be, though it has inadvertently been implying some on previous pages, and it can hardly ignore further what is almost universally agreed upon.

If, for example, liberal education means broadening and training the mind by pursuing knowledge for its own sake, it should not be forgotten that mind training is largely *verbal* training—and most "experts" in the liberal arts have signified their conviction that a single language just does not provide a sufficient range of verbal perceptiveness for a liberally educated person. Such a person, let us say, should be logical; but what is the validity of any "logic" *based on language patterns* that do not have universal validity? Ask the best of our scientists. It would seem that learning a foreign language is a "liberalizing" experience because, among other things, it teaches the limitations that the speech patterns of any single language impose upon individual thinking processes or even upon national attitudes and assumptions. (The Spanish have no word for "honest"—only "honorable." What does a Russian mean by "democratic"? A German by "du"? In France a "liberal" is what we should call a reactionary, a "radical socialist" is a conservative, and "free enterprise" means freedom from competition. Of what value are English translations if language behaves, as it forever does, so "unreasonably"?)

There is much popular misunderstanding about the aims and methods of foreign language study, and even professional literature on these subjects is confusing in its multiplicity and its partisanship. Until very recently, faced with falling enrollments and dropped requirements, most language teachers have tended to be defensive in outlook, and not a few of them have published exaggerated claims as a result. Perhaps more than other professionals, they have quarreled among themselves about objectives and methods of achieving them. It is not easy to find a clear, succinct statement that limits itself to the appropriate role of foreign language study in liberal education for American students.[7]

One way of clarifying the role of language study—and of testing its merits as a requirement—is to reverse the usual approach and define what will be true of all students with *no* experience of learn-

[7] A more or less official statement on "Values of Foreign Language Study" appears in *PMLA*, LXXI, Sept. 1956, Part 2, xiv.

ing a modern foreign language. We can begin—inviting the academic modernist to scoff—with the simple fact that a student with no knowledge of a second language has missed an intellectual experience which has been integral to the humanistic tradition in universities of the Western world from their remotest beginnings. A second fact may explain the first. The person who has never comprehended, spoken, read, or written a language other than his mother tongue has little or no perspective on his own language, particularly its unique structure, and, more important, he has never penetrated the rich areas of learning and experience lying beyond monolingual communication. His linguistic horizon is fixed. Though he may have acquired insights into other cultures through music or art, though he may even have traveled widely in other lands, he has never experienced directly a different culture in terms of the spoken and written symbols with which it uniquely reveals itself. Born a citizen of a multilingual world, he is, among the educated of that world, conspicuous in his limitations. If he does travel, he cannot help advertising his single-culture orientation. His interests may be wide, his international outlook generous, but abroad he must either hope to meet with people better educated than himself or else communicate lamely through interpreters; and at home, if he wishes to learn about other cultures, he must depend always upon translations (when they exist) or knowledge at second hand.

So much for summary of the negative approach, which implies, of course, what may be said positively about the values of language learning. Much more can be said positively, but should not be said without stipulated conditions regarding (1) *time* and (2) the *content and method* of the language courses. For language study is both a progressive experience and a progressive acquisition of a skill. Limit the time allowed for these and you limit the results.[8] It takes only a few weeks to teach social amenities and practical phrases that will be at least comprehensible to a foreigner; but new accents and intonations demand long practice (and new habits), and the acquisition of active vocabulary proceeds (as with the mother tongue) slowly and haltingly. Consider the vocabulary and command of idiom essential to any serious conversation *in English* with an educated person, or the amount essential to enjoy in

[8] See "The Problem of Time," *PMLA*, LXXI, Sept. 1956, Part 2, xviii–xix.

English a book with some stylistic distinction, and it should be obvious that attainment of an equivalent knowledge of any foreign language is not the work of a year or two divided with other studies. On the other hand, granted time sufficient to achieve a minimum functional proficiency, appreciable results in communication skills and, through them, knowledge of another culture can be reasonably assured.

What form this knowledge of another culture will take depends, not only upon time, but also upon the content and method of the language courses. Only nonsense syllables can be taught without *content;* the words of a living language must mean *something,* and what they convey of subject matter the instructor decides. It is therefore foolish to talk about language study conveying direct knowledge of a foreign literature if the instructor is making it convey, instead, direct knowledge of nonliterary aspects of a foreign civilization. It is, moreover, idle to talk about language study developing communication skills if the instructor is chiefly making it develop skill in reading. Language study is not a uniform activity; its content is not inevitable. It follows, therefore, that if a faculty wants foreign languages to achieve certain results in a liberal arts program, it had better make its desires clearly known—and had better allow time sufficient to achieve these results. Any other course is unrealistic, indulges wishful thinking, and invites eventual disillusion.

This is not to say that a comparatively limited experience of learning a foreign language is worthless in terms of a liberal education. To be sure, some will feel that the result, to justify itself, must be thoroughly functional and that the time necessary to this not inconsiderable achievement is simply unavailable in a crowded curriculum. Thus, ideals clash with practicalities, and there will be those who will refuse bread because they can have, not a loaf, but only a slice. On the other hand, depending upon how a faculty defines the objectives of liberal education (and the degree to which this definition recognizes both a smaller world and America's larger role in it), the briefest experience of breaking the barriers of a single language and a single culture may well seem one of the most liberalizing adventures that a liberal arts college can offer today.

AMERICAN EDUCATION: ONE WORLD?

Requirements of any sort imply standards, and the complex problem of standards in American education *at any level* is comprehensible only with recognition of the phenomenal growth of student population at all levels, and with recognition of the *history* of each level's effort to cope with a changing situation—on its own terms. One of the important facts in this history is that, at the college and the precollege levels, two very different groups of people, acting independently rather than cooperatively, have sought solutions. Until recently, each group seems to have miscalculated the significance of statistics that influenced its actions, and made the mistake of thinking the other group's concerns different and therefore remote from its own.

For example, although college entrance requirements are theoretically determined by college faculties after learned discussion, they have in fact been a product of the relationship between secondary education and higher education in a given region or in the nation as a whole.[9] During the last forty years or so, the substance or quantitative aspect of entrance requirements has generally reflected the dominant curriculum in public secondary education, which has been a product, not of relationships with colleges, but rather of efforts by "professional educators" to provide a suitable *terminal* education for an ever-increasing secondary school population.

With few exceptions, public secondary schools have developed their curricula without regard to what college faculties consider adequate preparation for college work, and the extent to which individual colleges have been able to apply their announced criteria for admission has therefore depended on applicant supply and demand. Institutions that have had more qualified applicants than they can accommodate have maintained their standard of college work and have continued to require specific preparation to meet that standard. Other institutions, the great majority, have either abandoned their former entrance requirements, or modified them

[9] In what follows I am indebted to a very sensible and illuminating article by Frank H. Bowles, "The Past, Present, and Future of Admission Requirements," *College and University*, XXXI, Spring, 1956, 309–327.

as pressure dictated, or worded them ambiguously enough to permit unembarrassed shifts from rigor to laxity with rising or lessening pressures from applicants.

Time was when almost every college and university in America required a certain amount of foreign language study for entrance,[10] thus making possible the *use* of foreign languages as a tool in liberal or scientific studies. However, as more and more students entered our secondary schools, and as a growing body of professionally trained administrators coped with the new problem of education for all American youth, these educators decided—usually without consulting the colleges—that foreign language study has less relevance for mass-democratic education than have other, more "practical" subjects. Behind this decision may have been some personal disillusion with the results of language learning (irregular verbs— "I couldn't order a meal"); behind it, certainly, was a spirit of political and cultural isolationism not peculiar to this group. Behind it also was the *assumption*—once warranted but no longer warranted by the facts—that high school would be the end of formal education for almost all our youth, with college education accessible to only the privileged few.

Thus, after World War I, foreign language study was steadily deemphasized in the public secondary schools. Whereas one out of every two pupils was once enrolled in a foreign language class (still true of the schools of New York City, but of few public high schools elsewhere), today 56 percent of all our public high schools do not even *offer* instruction in modern foreign languages, and only about 14 percent of all public high school students are enrolled in any kind of modern foreign language class.[11] It is no coincidence that only 31 percent of the accredited liberal arts colleges in the United States still require foreign languages for entrance—and, by doing so, discourage some intelligent and otherwise well prepared students from applying.[12] Nor is it coincidence that in many of the

[10] In 1913, out of 306 institutions studied, 89 percent had a modern foreign language entrance requirement; in 1922, out of 517, it was 70 percent.

[11] For the situation state by state see *PMLA*, LXX, Sept. 1955, Part 2, 52–56.

[12] Most of them will, actually, permit promising students to enter with a "deficiency" to be made up in college, sometimes without credit. There are

remaining 69 percent of our institutions of higher education the language requirement for the bachelor's degree (or for graduate degrees) has been peculiarly susceptible to criticism. Recognized or not, it is a fact that changes in secondary school education have influenced faculty views of what a *college* education should be.

To be sure, of the 69 percent of B.A.-granting colleges that have abandoned the foreign language entrance requirement in their catalogues, a considerable number actually, when applicants are numerous, admit few or no students who have failed to study languages in high school.[13] The ambiguity of their policy (foreign language study "recommended" but not "required") has not, of course, encouraged any high schools to stress or revive language instruction, and these colleges have therefore been defeating their own purposes.

Where do all these developments lead? It is today a fact—though it seems as yet to be little recognized—that *almost half* (48.7 percent in 1955) *of all high school graduates are going on to college.*[14] The unprecedented enrollments that have wrought such radical changes in elementary and secondary education in America are reaching the college level. The curve is upward, and a drastic reconsideration of basic assumptions is demanded *all along the line.*

Should not college teachers and administrators, as enrollments mount, make a new and sympathetic effort to understand the thinking of professional educators who have long had to meet this problem on other levels? To what extent have their ideas about curricula been warranted by events? To what extent have these ideas now been invalidated by the inclusion of college in the grand pattern of education for the majority? Should college education hereafter be conceived of as a "third stage" in popular education, to be thoughtfully coordinated with the other two through a series of

---

twelve institutions that have no formal language requirement for the degree but do require languages for entrance.

[13] Examples are Bryn Mawr, Goucher, Skidmore, Sweet Briar, Wellesley, Cornell, Johns Hopkins, and Yale. Of 217 institutions lacking an entrance requirement, and queried in 1954, one fourth replied that *at least* 78 percent of their freshmen offered two or more high school units in foreign language.

[14] In 1955 there were 1,399,300 graduates of public and private secondary schools in the continental U.S., and 682,639 first-time college freshmen (U.S. Office of Education statistics). The percentage for 1954 was 46.9.

mutual adjustments in curriculum planning? Will postgraduate training in some form eventually become a fourth stage?

Should not professional educators, facing the prospect of more than half of our high school graduates going on to college, readjust their thinking to recognize their responsibility to this hitherto neglected group? Are they not confronted with a new and somewhat staggering fact, with college training becoming part of the total pattern of American education? Herold C. Hunt, Under Secretary of Health, Education and Welfare, put it this way on April 15, 1956:

Surely the time has come, then, for some shift in emphasis—for high schools to devote more student time to preparation for college. Graduates of the future . . . will need more of the broader training associated with the liberal arts. More of it during the final years in high school would spur the incentive to go on to college and enable students to do better in college in the first year or so when so many of them fail their courses—possibly because of inadequate preparation in high school.

Many leaders among professional educators have recently called for new emphasis on foreign language study.[15] Calling for it is one thing; achieving it is another. As a means of achieving it, should not colleges now discuss with elementary and secondary school administrators, at least in their own area, the desirability of reinstating or strengthening the foreign language entrance requirement? The problem we have been outlining is, of course, much larger than that of the future of language study, but we must begin *somewhere* the major readjustment that is bound to come as informed liberal arts people and informed professional educators get together, in a spirit of good will, to discuss the future of American education in its complex and interdependent totality.

We began this essay with a question about the foreign language requirement for the B.A. degree, and found a requirement warranted only when a faculty considers some knowledge of a second language an essential part of liberal education in the second half of the twentieth century. The allied question of a language requirement for admission to college led us to facts demanding nothing

[15] Among them John Bartky, W. W. Brickman, Marion L. Brooks, Oliver J. Caldwell, Hollis L. Caswell, Herbert G. Espy, Paul R. Hanna, I. L. Kandel, Earl J. McGrath, Robert Ulich.

less than readjustment of educational standards and curricula all the way from kindergarten to graduate school. This larger perspective reminds us, finally, of another recent development in American education, the nearly 300,000 small children who are today studying foreign languages in our public elementary schools. The number of communities trying this fascinating experiment increased from 89 in 1952 to 357 in 1955. Will the number continue to grow? Have we at long last put the experience of second language learning, and the awareness of different cultures, at the level where they make the deepest impression and where the acquiring of accent and vocabulary is not only easiest but also most enjoyable? If so, the time may eventually come when language requirements for college entrance or for college degrees will be little more than paper reminders of a myopic and monolingual past. Meanwhile there is a language curtain still to be lifted, and there are intellectual borders still to be crossed, in this multicompartmentalized world of American education which we are just beginning to discover is really one world.

HOW CAN MODERN LANGUAGE
TEACHING PROMOTE
INTERNATIONAL UNDERSTANDING?[1]

MARJORIE C. JOHNSTON

In her essay Dr. Johnston, who is with the U.S. Office of Education, stresses the cultural contributions of foreign language learning to the enrichment of the student as a person. She points out one of the reasons for the government's great preoccupation and interest in the teaching of foreign languages in the high school. The author possesses an intimate knowledge of foreign language teaching in the American school. In her discussion she considers how curriculum planning should take the cultural values of language into account and how these values can be taught in a foreign language class. Although the relationship between language and culture is the subject of another essay in this volume, you will note the author indicates here how the social and cultural outcomes of language learning can be imparted. The needs of the foreign language teaching profession, which form the conclusion of this article, merit special consideration.

Experience in direct communication through speech or writing, imaginative identification with the people whose language is used, a feeling of personal involvement, induction into a different thought process and cultural medium—these are the ways in which modern

Reprinted by permission of the author and the National Association of Secondary-School Principals from the *Bulletin of the National Association of Secondary-School Principals,* December, 1956. Copyright: Washington, D.C.

[1] The first draft of this chapter was written after consultation with the following persons, who later made valuable suggestions for the final draft:

foreign language study can make a significant and indispensable contribution toward international understanding.

Although understanding of other peoples must rest on information, factual knowledge alone does not bring understanding; therefore, to collect all sorts of facts *about* a people, to learn a great deal about their language, their history, political system, social practices, art, and other cultural elements, does not substitute for the experience of learning to react *in* the language and thus actually to *participate* in a different culture. Without a working knowledge of their language one is insulated from other people.

Effective language teaching is characterized by an awareness that language is itself an integral part of the behavior system of a people and at the same time a means for the expression and summing up of this system or culture. Every stage of foreign language learning must relate in some manner to the life and civilization of the people because the linguistic forms belong in a frame of reference that is different from that of the learner. Early in the beginning course, even the first day, the student should begin to realize that the new words and language forms symbolize experiences, attitudes, and points of view unlike those that give meaning and connotations to corresponding forms in English. The more skill he develops in the use of the language, the greater his progress should be toward a real understanding of the foreign people. This is why a course in general language, although useful, is not enough, and why constructed languages such as Esperanto, not being rooted in any culture, can never go beyond the code function of language.

There has not been a time, presumably, in the history of modern language teaching in the United States when secondary school courses of study did not state or imply that one of the objectives of the program was to foster understanding of the people whose language was being studied. Until recently this objective was seldom clearly defined, and more often than not it was regarded in practice as something quite incidental to the main purpose of the instruction. Language teachers generally consider it self-evident that certain cultural insights can be gained only through active experience

---

Theodore Andersson, Emma H. Birkmaier, Esther M. Eaton, Frederick D. Eddy, Otto G. Graf, Kenneth Mildenberger, William R. Parker, and Emilie Margaret White.

with the foreign language, but they have found it extremely difficult to explain this outcome or to tell what they do to achieve it.

A questionnaire study[2] sought to find out how language teachers define the cultural objective, how important they consider it to be in introductory courses, and whether they feel that they are adequately achieving this purpose. All shades of opinion were expressed, but a striking thing about the results is that high school teachers, public and private, tend to rate nearly all aspects of the cultural objective as more important than do college teachers. A possible explanation is the high school teachers' greater concern with general education and the realization that, since few secondary schools offer advanced foreign language classes, introductory courses provide virtually their own opportunity to foster cultural understanding through the language. The most highly valued aspects of the objective were "appreciation of how ideas are differently expressed in a foreign language, with recognition of the inherent difficulties of translation" and "an increased respect and tolerance for the ideas, values, and achievements of a foreign culture."

It has also seemed obvious to language teachers that direct communication establishes a rapport that is utterly lacking in interpretation even when simultaneous, but they have frequently defeated their own purposes in this aspect of language teaching by requiring students to work with a set of abstract grammatical rules before they have acquired an ability to communicate in the language. Since in the past, teachers generally made no sustained effort to achieve the cultural objective and too often traveled circuitous routes in the development of functional skills, many students—far too many—in language classes ended their study with the same naive assumptions they started out with: that learning a new language is simply a matter of recoding one's own, that languages are alike except for the words, that thought and ideas are universal and can be put into words by all languages in much the same way. They never gained, therefore, the basic concept that language and culture are inextricably interwoven, that speakers of different languages see relationships and interpret experiences in very different ways, that language not only conveys thought, but also shapes it,

[2] John B. Carroll, *et al.*, "The Place of Culture and Civilization in Foreign Language Teaching," *Reports of the Working Committees,* 1956 Northeast Conference on the Teaching of Foreign Languages, 1956.

that a foreign language leads the learner into an entirely new world of tradition and thought and feeling.

DEFINITION OF OBJECTIVES

Language teachers, along with those in other fields, are rethinking their objectives and trying to devise effective ways of achieving them. In 1953 the Steering Committee of the Foreign Language Program of the Modern Language Association of America formulated some basic objectives. (see Chap. 18, p. 371)

Their statement has had wide acceptance by the various national and regional associations and conferences of language teachers. The ideas were amplified in a report by the Committee on Foreign Language Instruction in Secondary Schools at the 1956 Northeast Conference on the Teaching of Foreign Languages—a report prepared on the basis of the committee members' professional experience and that of teachers in thirty-five secondary schools cited by colleges and universities for the excellence of the language preparation given their students. This committee's recommendations emphasize the need for the five-fold objective of understanding the spoken language—speaking, reading, writing, and knowledge of the foreign civilization.

CURRICULUM PLANNING

How opportunities are utilized or, if need be, created, challenges the best thinking of any teaching and administrative staff. Even though the foreign language field is a "natural" for the cultivation of broad human understanding, and even though the complex of skills being developed provides an open door to accurate comprehension of other ways of thinking, language learning is an exceedingly complicated and many-sided process. The factors involved need to be carefully analyzed and reckoned with. To assure a reasonable chance of success, teachers and students alike must have a clear understanding of what the aim is, they must use effective materials and methods of teaching and learning, must apply themselves diligently to the task, and must have some means of evaluating the outcomes.

The same principles and many of the activities that have proved themselves in other learning experiences apply, of course, to a foreign language. Students learn to understand the spoken language by listening; to speak by speaking; to communicate in social situations by practice in communicating; to understand the nature of language and culture by firsthand acquaintance and experience with them; to know and appreciate more fully one's own language and culture by getting outside the familiar culture pattern, by seeing them in perspective from the vantage point of another language and culture. Unless these aims are a conscious, inherent part of the teaching process, the study of a foreign language does not *automatically* increase the ability to communicate successfully or to understand foreign cultures. This fact has been emphasized by various national and international groups seeking to determine the part that languages play in developing international understanding.

Much confusion exists about what foreign language study can and cannot do to foster international understanding. In order for schools to provide suitable curriculum experiences in a language other than the mother tongue, this confusion needs to be cleared up. There are certain broad elements of international understanding to which nearly all phases of the total school curriculum—including of course the teaching of a modern foreign language—can make valuable contributions: helping students obtain a realistic view of some of the world's problems; helping them see the United States in its relationship with other nations; helping them appreciate the contributions of all peoples to the world community; helping them value the services of international organizations devoted to better world understanding (*i.e.*, United Nations, Organization of American States), and the like. Then there are a number of specific contributions, some of them unique, which the teaching of a modern foreign language can make to an understanding of other people.

Working toward international understanding in a formal educational situation involves the cultivation of generous and informed attitudes through (1) factual knowledge of other peoples, (2) significant experience of other cultures, and (3) communication skills that increase knowledge and experience, and prepare for personal foreign contacts. The first two, factual knowledge and significant experience, are possible to a considerable extent without a foreign language. The obvious advantage of foreign language study as a part of a total program that has cultivation of international understanding as one of its objectives is that it provides a *skill* making possible direct communication with another people in a world in which more and more Americans are meeting foreigners. And the more facility a student gains in a second language, thereby readying himself for contact with one other people, the more he increases his readiness for quickly familiarizing himself with any additional foreign language or culture which he encounters in his life's work. The foreign language can also provide a *content* and an *experience* which contribute uniquely to that acquired through other fields. Since language learning is not possible without subject matter, an appropriate, if not the natural, subject matter of a foreign language class is material which reveals the foreign culture. And since the language is an essential element in the culture, foreign language learning broadens the mental horizon and constitutes significant experience of the foreign way of life.

In this connection, one of the greatest barriers to international understanding is the normal tendency of human nature to react against the strange and unfamiliar, and foreign language learning is probably the quickest and most direct method of making familiar what before was strange, by actually participating in and experiencing a different mode of thought. A person who can speak German, for example, may not like or admire the Germans, but he is no longer disliking them on instinctive grounds just because they sound queer.

The implications for curriculum planning are clear: (1) since language is a medium through which the value systems of a culture are expressed, the acquisition of language and of cultural understanding should be a simultaneous, not separate, process; (2) the language itself should be taught, not just information about the language; (3) it should be taught in cultural context, not as an exercise in abstract reasoning. Each language class should take the students, so to speak, on a brief excursion into another way of life. In other words, foreign language teaching in the high schools today must contribute as fully as possible to the general education of boys and girls and to their ability to adjust to life in the modern world. The primacy of the communication approach seems right for the high school. Students who may later specialize in one or more foreign languages will take up technical linguistic subjects as they continue their study.

Another point of confusion has to do with proper standards for language work. To adapt foreign language teaching to the interest, maturity, and psychological needs of high school students is not to lower the standards of achievement or to "water down" the subject matter. On the contrary, there is much evidence that high school students can do solid work and that they do it with zest when their goals are clear, when they can note progress toward those goals, and when they can see the usefulness of the assigned work in relation to the goals. By the age of five and a half years, every normal child has learned the complex system of his native language —its structure, gestures, tone, and intonation—and, as his experience grows, vocabulary is added with relative ease. Although individuals learn at different rates and exhibit varying degrees of aptitude in self-expression, the power of all of them to communicate adequately proves that the underlying patterns composing the language are acquired by everyone in the culture. There is no basis, therefore, for believing that a high school student cannot learn a second or a third language and no good theoretical reason to restrict foreign language study to the gifted. To pitch the level or the tempo of a course higher than is attainable by more than half the student body is not synonymous with high standards of achievement in terms of the stated objectives of modern foreign language teaching.

In the selection of curriculum experiences, then, teachers must see that students (1) undertake only as much as can be accomplished in the time available, (2) that they do well what they set out to do, (3) that they take stock frequently of their progress, (4) that they finish the course with a measure of satisfaction and, in addition, (5) carry with them an attractive vista of study to be continued or taken up again later. They will remember that language learning is a continuum and that no one should expect to "master" a second language in a few hours a week during the course of two or three years.

With the trend toward an earlier start in languages, many students upon entrance to the high school will have acquaintance with a second language and will have acquired varied abilities in speaking and understanding it. There is the greatest need to see that such pupils progress without starting over or waiting two or three years before they can continue their foreign language study. This means that the idea of "covering the course of study" each year, as often conceived, can no longer apply. It should be noted, too, that there is a growing inclination by college language departments to give entering students oral-aural and written placement tests. Obviously, the attempt to teach a complete course in formal grammar at the expense of practice in the use of the language must soon rate a low priority in the choice of learning activities. The exigencies of the situation seem certain to stimulate a type of curriculum planning more conducive to the attainment of the objectives as now defined.

LEARNING ACTIVITIES

What are some of the learning activities in foreign language that prove useful, both for communication skills and growth in international understanding? Many are conducted in the language classroom and laboratory, many in correlation with other departments in the school, others within the community or in larger relationships.

With Native Speakers

Real people in real situations requiring the use of the foreign language offer most stimulation, and even a few such occasions serve as powerful motivation for other less vitalizing experiences. In most schools it is becoming easier all the time to locate such visitors or people living in the community who can participate in foreign language classes or projects. Advance preparation through reading and discussion about the visitor's country and practice of essential phrases for greetings, questions, appreciation, and the like, as well as some follow-up lessons, will enhance the contribution of the native speaker.

In International Contacts

It would be ironic, however, in the matter of natural occasions for using the language and getting to know the people, to overlook the resources of the school's environment. Intercultural misunderstanding and friction frequently have international repercussions; thus, in a very immediate sense, the cultivation of international understanding begins in the home community. Since some twenty million Americans speak a language other than English as their mother tongue, most communities, whether in a cosmopolitan city or rural area, present unexcelled opportunities for cooperation with foreign language groups in civic and social programs. Many communities have foreign language radio broadcasts and foreign language newspapers. Intercultural understanding and an appreciation of the rich contributions made by people of foreign ancestry to the fabric of American life go hand in hand with the development of international understanding. Some school and community links in foreign language activities point to changed attitudes and behavior or to heightened awareness of cultural ties. The following experience might apply in numbers of communities of the Southwest:

I teach two classes in Spanish for Mexican-American children only. The purpose of these classes is to teach them to read and write Spanish and to improve their spoken Spanish. English vocabulary, spelling, pronunciation, and composition are emphasized as they relate to the Spanish language. It is a wonderful method of getting across American *mores* and of interesting these students in better scholastic achievement. I have spoken at a general faculty meeting about the nature of the Mexican-American student, some of his difficulties and needs. I suggested that teachers learn Spanish in order to bring about better rapport, and about forty members of our faculty are now taking an in-service course in Spanish given at our school. Many teachers and parents have come to me with problems about the Mexican-American children because I am a Spanish teacher and am interested in them.

Another teacher reported an incident involving discussion of a hilarious take-off of the foibles and exasperating traits of a different nationality. One of the language students injected a sobering remark, saying that he thought the book silly, that it used an easy form of humor and failed to give a true picture of the national characteristics. Others have noted that students become more tolerant of foreigners' mistakes in English because they see why certain mistakes are made. One story concerns the Italian shoemaker who always said things like "Your shoe, he is not ready" and "Close the door, she is open." A boy from the Italian class told the people in his neighborhood to stop laughing at him. Some teachers report recreational or seasonal activities in which language students collaborate with a foreign language group, as, for example, taking part in Christmas parties and choral singing of German societies in the community. In one town students attended church services conducted in Spanish for recently arrived Puerto Rican families. Even the most halting and imperfect attempts to speak generally go a long way to help bridge the chasm that divides person from person and group from group when they represent different languages and customs.

With Audio-Visual Materials

In the development of communication skills nothing can obviate the necessity for drill. But it is important, just as for other skills, that the practice be accurate, graded in difficulty, regularly scheduled, and interesting enough to hold the learner's attention and enlist his best effort. The classroom activities of listening to new sounds, imitating, memorizing, and trying to converse are greatly aided by the use of tape recordings, phonograph records, sound movies, slides and filmstrips, radio, and television. Mimeographed scripts and careful briefing are needed in the use of foreign language films and radio transcriptions.

Experiences of high schools that have introduced a language laboratory as part of the regular classwork reveals a decided upswing in oral-aural abilities, especially in the matter of helping students to make automatic responses in the language. The student takes a "Copernican step" and the day he realizes that, he is responding directly in the language without the intermediate process of translating expressions to or from English. Getting the feel of thinking in another language gives him a tremendous boost toward achievement in two ways: the power to communicate adequately, even if in very restricted situations, and the break across the boundaries of a single culture.

A well-planned variety of class and laboratory drills makes for such thorough learning of essential speech patterns that study of grammar rules then comes about naturally as an observation or generalization of what the student already does through habit. The use of tape recordings for practice is particularly helpful because it introduces students to a greater number of voices and personalities than would normally occur in class meetings, and time is allowed for recording his own imitation of the model. When he hears himself and compares what he said with the model, he is convinced of the need for improvement and is not satisfied until his effort approximates the native speech. This is a far cry from the teacher's perplexing admonition of "No, say it this way," followed by a repetition of the same error as before.

Through Role Playing

Singing, reciting poetry, reading aloud, writing from dictation, and participating in dramatic performances are also excellent ways of inducing direct responses in the foreign language. The rhythm and melody of songs, as well as the spirit and thought of the lyric, facilitate pronunciation, natural speed, and intonation, at the same time producing a pleasurable reaction to the people and the language. Memorizing and acting out parts in dialogues, skits, and plays are invaluable ways of acquiring confidence in speaking, for this activity also lends itself to overlearning without boredom and thereby aids the ability to respond somewhat automatically and in the role of the native speaker. Some teachers try to make all learning activities appear to take place in the country whose language is studied. They do this on the theory that students gain through play acting a better understanding of the psychology of the people and learn more about the cultural similarities and differences, since information about the foreign environment and tradition is associated with particular situations of a given time and place. Emotional connotations of words become clearer too.

In Foreign Atmosphere

Color and authentic atmosphere are brought to the classroom through the use of maps, railway posters, airline calendars, costumed figurines, foreign publications (textbooks, children's stories, games, cookbooks, service manuals for automotive mechanics, magazines, newspapers), exhibits (handicrafts, coins, flags, stamps, pictures of heroes, foreign place names in the United States, typical products, menu cards, theater programs, transportation networks, kodachrome views), and special bulletin board displays such as the following:

"Can you read the letter with the foreign stamp?"

"Now and later," featuring cartoons such as the student presently studying French and a soldier (later) interpreting for his buddies and the French washer-woman

"Don't miss these," announcing new travel books, foreign language movies, community programs, concerts

"The world beckons," illustrating need for foreign languages in transportation, trade, advertising, travel, industry, banking, social service, religious work, police services, librarianship, fine arts, engineering, *etc.*

Classes in larger cities sometimes borrow paintings of foreign artists from the art museum and exhibit them in the classroom, changing the picture several times a year in order to include portraits, landscapes, still life, and historical subjects. An idea that is popular in some schools is to arrange a corner of the classroom to represent a grocery store, using foreign labels for cans and other articles, and showing price lists in the currency of the country, the metric system of weights, and other features lending reality to the scene. Drills on numbers, articles, pronouns, and verbs are carried on in this setting through various kinds of conversational practice.

Through Current Events

Language departments sometimes have a news question box and devote a little time each week for students to draw and answer questions written in the language and having to do with current events pertinent to the subject; for example, the new record for flying time between New York and Buenos Aires, the return of Alberto Gainza Paz to *La Prensa,* the state visit of the president of Uruguay in Denver, lost missionaries in the jungle of Ecuador, student riots in Madrid, hurricane and floods in Tampico, earthquake in Peru, return of the swallows to Capistrano. Mispronunciations of proper names by radio announcers rarely escape the notice of these news-conscious pupils.

Another device is to put a headline in the foreign language on the blackboard every day with five or six key words, asking who can tell the news story. This activity develops the learners' power to utilize in a new context the phrases they know and to add meaningful items to their working vocabularies.

In Reading

A proverb or pithy saying placed on the board once or twice a week calls attention to an outlook on life and provokes comparisons with English maxims. Stories and other reading materials help develop a fellow feeling through allusions to ties of family and friends, love of country, the spirit of hospitality, anecdotes concerning animals, adventure, danger, *etc.* Biographies of national heroes or literary figures and episodes from history or literature can be dramatized following the plan of radio quiz programs and shows.

Through the departmental or school library, a good assortment of foreign language magazines and at least one newspaper, together with foreign editions of United States periodicals, should be provided for their intensely interesting content and illustrations of life in the countries being studied. Students pore over such publications as *Realités* and *France-Illustration* from Paris, *Mundo Hispánico* from Madrid, *Hispanoamericano* from Mexico, and *Frankfurter Illustrierte* from Germany.

Supplementary reading in English can include translations of foreign literary classics, historical fiction, and travel books dealing with the culture being studied. Such reading, while more appropriately assigned in correlation with classes in world literature,

English, or social studies, should be encouraged by foreign language teachers.

In Correlation with Other Subjects

Innumerable foreign language activities relate to other parts of the curriculum and can be carried out on a school-wide, city-wide, or larger basis. An intensive interest in one foreign culture is complementary to the whole field of social studies and touches every field in some way: art, music, dancing, sports, speech, world literature, English language, natural science, agriculture, home economics, business subjects, library. When, for example, students have units in social studies or English such as "Exploring New Worlds," "Friends from Other Lands," or "Hi, Neighbor!" the foreign languages have many points of contact. Individual projects utilizing special interests may originate in or coincide with language study.

A noteworthy illustration of a state-wide program in which schools participate under the leadership of Spanish departments is the Pan American Student Forum, sponsored by the Good Neighbor Commission in Texas. Forum chapters from schools throughout the state send delegations to a two-day annual convention and participate in programs and contests including the following: one-act plays, choral singing, poetry and essay writing, group and solo dancing, declamations, "Information Please," meetings with Latin American scholarship students from the state colleges, handicraft and art work, scrapbook judging, elections and business meetings, luncheons, addresses by Latin American officials, and a *fiesta*.

Even international activities are sometimes carried on through language departments. Schools in places having town affiliations with towns in other countries are in a specially favored position to correlate studies with real life outside the United States. Students of French in a city which is twinned with one in France through Le Monde Bilingue (Paris), for example, can participate widely in activities involving many people of both countries.

Groups such as the Experiment in International Living (Putney, Vermont), American Friends Service Committee (Philadelphia), Brethren Service Commission (New Windsor, Maryland), Girl Scouts of the U.S.A., International Division (New York), and American Youth Hostels (New York) encourage students to acquire a functional knowledge of a foreign language and help provide opportunities for high-school youngsters to live and study abroad.

These and other organizations, such as American Field Service International Scholarships (New York), Kiwanis International (Gainesville, Georgia), National Grange (Washington, D.C), and the New York Herald Tribune Forum for high schools, help arrange for foreign secondary-school students to live with families in the United States and attend the local high school. Teenage exchanges are sponsored in some instances also by local chapters of the Lions and Rotary clubs, the U.S. Junior Chamber of Commerce, and various church groups.

RESOURCES FOR TEACHERS

The information and services of broadest scope are those available through professional associations of language teachers and through newsletters or bulletins distributed in most cases gratis by committees on foreign language teaching in almost all of the forty-eight states. The Modern Language Association of America (4 Washington Place, New York 10003), through the Foreign Language Program, carries on a large volume of correspondence and maintains extensive files of research studies and other materials on important aspects of foreign language teaching in the United States. It participates in many national and international conferences and groups concerned with modern languages, and publishes the scholarly journal *PMLA* (Publication of the Modern Language Association).

Other national associations, devoted to the interests of particular languages, publish very useful journals, provide service centers and international correspondence bureaus, sponsor national contests and honor societies, exhibit textbooks of commercial publishers and audio-visual and other instructional materials at annual meetings, have affiliated local chapters, and set up working committees to study teaching problems. The names and addresses of these associations and their journals are as follows:

American Association of Teachers of French, *The French Review; Secretary,* 428 E. Preston St., Baltimore 2, Md.

American Association of Teachers of German, *The German Quarterly; Secretary,* Syracuse Univ., Syracuse 10, N.Y.

American Association of Teachers of Italian, *Italica; Secretary,* Northwestern Univ., Evanston, Ill.

American Association of Teachers of Slavic and East European Languages, *The AATSEEL Journal; Secretary,* Shiffman Hall, Brandeis Univ., Waltham 54, Mass.

American Association of Teachers of Spanish and Portuguese, *Hispania;*
Secretary, DePauw University, Greencastle, Ind.

The National Federation of Modern Language Teachers Association publishes *The Modern Language Journal,* largely pedagogical
in nature and of interest to all modern language teachers. Subscrip-
tions, eight issues a year, are available from the Business Manager,
13149 Cannes Drive, St. Louis, Mo. 63141. Other important publications are *Language Learning,* a journal of applied linguistics, English Language Institute, University of Michigan, Ann Arbor, and
the *Monograph Series on Languages and Linguistics,* School of
Foreign Service, Georgetown University, Washington, D.C.

Many items of importance to teachers of Spanish and Portuguese
are available from the Pan American Union. The various foreign
information offices in New York and many of the transportation
companies will send information and publications to teachers or
school officials. Consultative services, reference lists of sources of
teaching aids, and assistance in teacher exchanges are available
from the Office of Education, U.S. Department of Health, Education, and Welfare, Washington 25, D.C.

Travel and study opportunities are listed in the language journals
and in the following publications: *Handbook on International Study*
(Institute of International Education, New York); *Summer Study in
Latin America* (Pan American Union, Washington, D.C.); *Study
Abroad,* International Handbook published annually by Unesco;
and summer school brochures from United States colleges and universities announcing workshops, interdisciplinary seminars, foreign
study tours, and other programs pertinent to the teaching of modern
languages.

URGENT NEEDS

A consideration of modern language teaching as it is and as it
ought to be in American high schools can lead to only one conclusion: some encouraging progress is being made but several important improvements are of immediate urgency.

1. *More and better qualified teachers.* Unless teachers have the
ability to speak and understand the language and have firsthand
acquaintance with the people and country, how can they guide
their students toward the attitudes, skills, knowledge, understanding,
and significant experiences to which their study of a modern lan-

guage entitles them? The Foreign Language Program of the Modern Language Association has issued an official statement of qualifications for secondary-school teachers of modern foreign languages based on demonstrated abilities rather than course credits; it has received wide endorsement from leaders in foreign languages and professional education. A large-scale movement to permit residence and study abroad, both for pre-service and in-service teachers, is of the utmost importance. United States teachers need to get the feeling expressed recently by a visiting teacher from France:

> If I feel that my stay in the States has been profitable, it is because when I get back to France, I shall be in a position to pass on to my pupils such direct, vivid, or picturesque information as I have had the opportunity to gather here. This information may still be very partial and limited. Yet Ford's assembly line, the speedways and the drive-ins, the museums and the galleries, the drug-stores and jukeboxes, the American homes and their wife-saving gadgets, the lavishness of nature and the warm hospitality of men—all these have now taken for me a quality of concrete experience and actual reality that throws the mere bookish second-hand knowledge into the realm of bloodless shadows.

The preparation of modern language teachers should include a better background in American civilization and culture, including work in social psychology and cultural anthropology planned in correlation with linguistic studies. And, since our heritage is deeply rooted in Western European tradition, an introductory study of a language which is unrelated to the one taught would do much to overcome the undiscriminating enthusiasm sometimes exhibited by language teachers. Learning experience in the unrelated language would better prepare the teacher to convey the concept of how and why language shapes or governs thought. At least some knowledge of linguistic science is also a must. In other words, if teachers are ever to learn how to plan curriculum experiences in their field effectively and in collaboration with their colleagues in other fields, their own preparation must include some interdisciplinary experience.

Greater professional spirit is likewise a necessary element in the high-school language teacher's equipment. Much productive work and much inspiration would result from attendance at annual meetings of the state, regional, and national language associations. At present an infinitesimal number of high-school teachers go to national meetings, work on state committees, carry on experimental research, contribute articles to journals, work to achieve good articulation with the elementary school and the college, produce new instructional materials, learn language laboratory techniques, and otherwise demonstrate their sense of responsibility to the profession. Should not the local school board give some material encouragement to high-school teachers who are disposed to attend annual meetings of professional associations or serve on working committees?

2. *More schools offering modern languages.* The high-school years have been described as a linguistic wasteland for an alarming proportion of students, and with some justification. A study conducted in 1962 by the Modern Language Association reveals that 32 percent of our public high schools fail to offer any modern foreign language, that only 24.4 percent of the total high-school population is currently enrolled in a modern foreign language class (*PMLA*, September 1964). Along with measures to remedy this situation, it might be advisable for a few of the larger cities to provide a specialized high-school devoted to the teaching of foreign languages and cultures.

3. *A longer sequence of study.* Students with special interest and aptitude should be able to continue the language long enough to make real proficiency possible. The customary two-year high-school program in modern language is unsuited to the needs of students today.

4. *Opportunity to Study Asiatic, African, and East European languages.* Spanish and French are taught in all of the states for which enrollment figures are available; German is taught in thirty-two states, Italian in eight. Polish, Greek, Hebrew, Russian, Portuguese, Norse, Chinese, and Swedish are available to an extremely limited extent. Many secondary schools are known to have classes in Russian, for example, and some offer spoken Chinese. Many current problems in international relations center in Asia and other areas that are little known in the United States; they are likely to be long with us, and their solution will require an ability to reach a meeting of minds with peoples whose traditions and psychology are almost a complete blank to most Americans. Will the present high-school generation be better prepared than their parents to maintain amicable relations with these areas of the world?

5. *Instructional materials designed to develop skills in communication and cultural insights.* New texts, kinescopes, wall pictures, and many kinds of materials are needed, pooling the best thinking and experience of the profession. Language laboratory facilities are

another necessity. Recently one of our linguistic scientists stated: "The time is past when a school can boast of possessing language laboratory facilities. The time is at hand when those who are lacking such facilities will have to find some explanation."

6. *More interdepartmental planning.* In the interest of economy, efficiency, and meaningful, integrated content, modern language instruction needs to be closely meshed with that in other fields.

7. *More research and evaluative criteria.* There are many questions that remain unanswered in the field of language learning and tests and measurements. Some significant research in psycho-linguistics has already been done and more is in progress. Modern language teachers need to assimilate and disseminate the results of such research and try to apply the best information available to the construction of measures by which they can evaluate progress in such abilities as speaking and listening comprehension, desirable attitudes toward other cultural groups, and growth. Travel, for example, is believed to have some relation to better international understanding. Modern language study ought to motivate a student to travel, prepare him to profit more from the experience when the opportunity comes, and fit him to add his bit toward the creation of a more favorable attitude abroad toward the United States citizens. How, therefore, do we judge to what extent this is happening? In the absence of adequate measuring devices, teachers should keep better anecdotal records and collect more samples of student and community reaction to apparently successful modern language teaching.

In summary, modern languages for modern living are beginning to be taught in a new key—one attuned to an awareness of the ways in which language study can lead to cultural understanding—and the new key will be recognized more and more generally as greater numbers of teachers and students are prepared to feel at home in a second language. Clearer objectives and more direct ways of achieving them have been emerging in the wake of recent advances in linguistic science and with the trend toward interdepartmental or interdisciplinary approaches to language study. The improvements in progress and those remaining to be made coincide with the growing need for language proficiency in the national interest and with the widespread conviction that through language we get a personal view of peoples that we cannot get in any other way.

Bibliography

Caswell, Hollis L. "Modern Foreign Languages in a Modern Curriculum," *Education*, April 1955, pp. 489–493.

Chase, Stuart. "How Language Shapes Our Thoughts," *Harper's Magazine*, April 1954, pp. 76–82.

Kroeger, Ruth P. *et al.* "Foreign Language Instruction in Secondary Schools," *Reports of the Working Committees*, 1956 Northeast Conference on the Teaching of Foreign Languages, pp. 49–68. Available for $2.50 from Mr. Nelson Brooks, MAT Program, Yale University, New Haven, Conn.

McQuown, Norman A. *"Report of the United States Delegation to the United Nations Educational, Scientific and Cultural Organization International Seminar on the Teaching of Modern Languages,* Nuwara Eliya, Ceylon, August 3–28, 1953." Washington 25, D.C.: Department of State, 1954.

Marckwardt, Albert H. "Developing Cultural Understanding Through Foreign Language Study: "A Report of the MLA Interdisciplinary Seminar in Language and Culture," *PMLA*, December 1953, pp. 1196–1218.

Parker, William R. *The National Interest and Foreign Languages.* A Discussion Guide and Work Paper for Citizen Consultations initiated by the U.S. National Commission for UNESCO, Department of State, Washington 25, D.C.: U.S. Government Printing Office, 1954.

"Qualifications for Secondary-School Teachers of Modern Foreign Languages," published in various places, including *Bulletin of the National Association of Secondary-School Principals*, Vol. 39, November 1955, pp. 30–33.

Starr, Wilmarth H. *et al.* "The Role of Foreign Languages in American Life," *Reports of the Working Committees*, 1955 Northeast Conference on Teaching of Foreign Languages. Available for $2.50 from the French Department, Washington Square College, New York University, Washington Square, New York 3.

Strong, C. F. *Teaching for International Understanding.* An Examination of Methods and Materials. A Statement prepared for the United Kingdom National Commission for UNESCO. London, Her Majesty's Stationery Office, 1952. "Modern Languages," Chapter IV (4), pp. 49–55.

UNESCO. *The Teaching of Modern Languages.* Vol. X of the series Problems in Education. A volume of studies deriving from the International Seminar organized by the Secretariat of UNESCO at Nuwara Eliya, Ceylon, in August 1953. Paris: UNESCO. 1955.

LANGUAGE ANALYSIS AND
LANGUAGE TEACHING

ARCHIBALD A. HILL

In general, teachers have become aware only relatively recently of linguistics. In the following essay Professor Hill, of the University of Texas, masterfully sets forth the contributions that linguistics can make to foreign language teaching. In so doing he brings out the fact that the linguist is the ally of the foreign language teacher and can supply him with some of the rationale necessary to judge good and bad teaching practices. It is implicit in the article that a well-prepared foreign language teacher should have a good linguistic knowledge of both his own and the target language.

The foreign language teacher should know the functions and relationships of language, linguistics, and grammar. Few disciplines have contributed so much as has linguistics to the improvement of foreign language teaching; few disciplines are changing so rapidly. It is therefore imperative that the foreign language teacher keep informed of the progress of this science.

The pages which follow are based on the belief that language teachers have an important job to do, and are devoted to doing it. Consequently, if scientific analysis of language produces results which are of use to the language teacher, and if linguistic scientists can state them in a usable form, these results should sooner or later reach the classroom. Unfortunately, linguistics has an awesome terminology, an uncomfortably rigid technique, and a body of attitudes which sometimes run counter to those established by long

Reprinted by permission of the author and The Modern Language Association of America from *F. L. Bulletin No. 41* (Dec., 1955).

tradition and inculcated by much of our education. It is nonetheless possible to speak of linguistics with a minimum of special terminology, with presentation of results rather than exposition of techniques, and an avoidance of attitudes which would appear controversial to the reasonable nonlinguist. If the linguist wishes to bring his results to the classroom, he must write of his science in just this spirit, and with a humility which has not always been a part of his make-up.

The linguist's first statement about language is that it is made up of *sounds*. Other symbolic systems—writing, Morse Code, even hieroglyphics—are *secondary* representations, and are at best, substitutes for language. Even in our own literate community we learned to speak long before we learned to write, and we carry our daily affairs far more by means of speech than by writing. Yet, since writing enjoys prestige as a permanent record, as the vehicle of literature and as the basis of education, it is easy to forget its secondary position. Many people fall, therefore, into the attitude of regarding writing as the fundamental part of language which is only imperfectly and ephemerally represented by speech. As a result, many statements about language are really about writing.

Most language teachers realize that their first task is to train students to manipulate a set of sound symbols. Even if the aim is to teach the student to read and translate rather than speak, the student must have some means of responding to what he sees with something that he hears. If he can make no sounds at all, he has such a narrow field of stimulation that he will not learn the sequences of letters he is being taught. In some situations—a Latin class, for instance—his sounds do not have to be those of a native, but sounds he has to have, and they have to be arranged systematically enough so that he can make differing responses for all the differing items that make up the language. In a modern language, his set of sounds must be as nearly as possible those of a native, since on the very lowest level he must communicate orally, at least with his teacher, who presumably has such a native or near-native set.

Although it is easy to confuse writing and speech, in the language classroom it is disastrous to do so, since if sound and speech are to be taught and mastered, they must be clearly presented. Language teachers can do much to bring about the necessary clarity by exam-

ining textbooks to see how well they present the sounds of the
tongues they describe. Here are some simple rules by which a textbook can be judged. The rules take the form of descriptions of
typically bad presentation, followed by contrasting descriptions of
good presentation. The rules will be general and, it is hoped, applicable to the teaching of French, Spanish, German, or even
English as a foreign language.

A *bad* book covers the pronunciation of the foreign language in
no more than five or six pages. It presents its material in terms of
letters and their "values," a term that is enough in itself to make
the reader suspicious. A typical bad book presents in five and a half
pages the pronunciation of Provençal for speakers of French. Its
first statement reads as follows:

"The Provençal alphabet has twenty-three letters, five of which
are vowels, and eighteen of which are consonants, pronounced as
follows: 1) A, a, *a* preserve their alphabetic value." We have all
seen many such descriptions, not only of rarer languages like
Provençal, but of the great languages we are ordinarily called on
to teach. All such descriptions seriously confuse speech and writing,
and so make the teaching of speech more difficult.

A bad book, when it ventures to describe sounds at all, does so
in vague or confusing terms. This Provençal grammar says that one
sound "is pronounced *ts* or *tz* in a fashion intermediate between
Spanish *muchacho* and Italian *barbozza*." The statement explains
the unknown by the more unknown, since two other languages
besides French and Provençal are introduced, only to say that
Provençal is like neither of them. Sometimes the explanation can
be merely verbal, as in the following drawn from a text which has
been widely used in American classrooms. Of two sets of contrasting consonant types, one is called "soft and liquid," the other "hard
and dry." The explanation is merely an elaboration of the folk term
for one set, which is often called *soft*. If a text calls the vowels of a
continental language clearer and more musical than their English
equivalents, it is committing the same fault.

Even beyond the section on pronunciation, a bad book shows the
effects of confusion between letters and sounds. Far too many
grammars of English as a foreign language contain a statement we
can remember from our own days in the schoolroom—"the plural
of nouns is formed by adding -*s* or -*es*." Such a statement conceals

the fact that there are three regular plurals, that found in *dogs,* that in *cats,* that in *horses.* (Pronounce them.) Speakers of Spanish who have learned their English from such books, not unnaturally have difficulty in handling the distinction between *dogs* and *docks.* Not that spelling does not have its place in language instruction. A general principle, however, is that *spelling is useful only when the student knows what it is that is being spelled.* The quoted rule for the formation of the plural disregards this principle.

There is a second type which need not hold us long. Such books describe sounds, but in terms of the native language alone. They usually provide a system of spelling to indicate the pronunciation of words and phrases. The respelling, however, is not consistent and is meant to be read without special training, solely by means of the *native alphabetic tradition.* These books have their uses—for Latin they may be all that is needed. Most "phrase-books," telling the reader how to master French in six easy lessons, are prepared on this principle. Sometimes the respelling is remarkably ingenious, as in this from a phrase-book for GI's: "*Rheims* is pronounced like English *Rance.*" Yet ingenious or not, all such presentations are open to a serious objection. They reinforce the student's naïve belief that all languages are alike except for the words in them, and convince him that there is really little to learn.

In the paragraphs which follow, I shall try to say what a good book does about pronunciation. I should make it clear at the start, however, that I do not believe any description of sounds and how they are made can be a substitute for imitation of native or near-native speech. Furthermore, the younger the learner, the more reliance there should be on imitation, and the less on description. The purpose of description, and of drills based on description, is student's attention to exactly what he is trying to imitate, giving him some control of the mechanism of imitation, and organizing the drills so as to focus imitation on only a few features at a time, features which are then repeated until a habit is set up. Description of sounds, indeed, does not directly instruct the learner in how to produce them, and fails in any instance where the articulating organs are out of conscious control. Thus the *rr* of Spanish *perro* cannot be taught to an English speaker who does not have it, by describing the action of the tongue. The teacher has to start from one of the many practical devices which have long been used in the classroom, such as modification of the *brr* which in English means "I'm cold." Similarly the guttural *r* of some varieties of German can be taught by starting from a snore. On the other hand, in all instances where the articulation can be consciously controlled, description is an indispensable tool. A Spaniard can be most easily taught to pronounce an English final *m*, for instance, by being told to close his lips. The usefulness of a good description is not denied if we recognize the truism that no one can learn a good pronunciation by reading about it. It is usual for all books except those for the youngest students to give some sort of systematic account of pronunciation. Such accounts must be as accurate as possible, and must at least not actively confuse the learner.

What then does a *good* book do about pronunciation? First, it describes the sounds of the foreign language accurately and fully *in terms of articulation.* It tells the reader, for example, that the tip of the tongue is against the back surface of the teeth in pronouncing a French or Spanish *t*. When the description has been given, it invites the student and teacher to compare articulatory positions in the native and the foreign language, so as to verify the difference described, and give the student a means of self-criticism. It may even recommend the use of a mirror, or feeling with the fingers, to observe articulation. Typically, there will be comparison of English *two* and Spanish *tu*, or the like. The student will be given the opportunity to observe that the first English sound (the *t*) is articulated farther back than the Spanish, and to observe and learn to hear the acoustic difference which results.

Second, a good book uses *terminology* which is technical it is true, but accurate and fully explained. Thus in describing the *t*'s in *two* and *tu* it introduces the term *aspiration,* and explains that it means the puff of air which can be felt as part of the release of the *t* in *two,* but which is absent in *stew* and Spanish *tu*. It again invites student and teacher to verify by comparing the English and Spanish words. Such accurately defined terminology contrasts sharply with impressionistic names and descriptions. Students and teacher, one provided with the term aspiration, have a quick means of correction—the teacher can say, "Watch out, Mr. Jones, don't aspirate," and Mr. Jones knows what is meant and what to do about it. If the teacher can only say, "Make your *t* sharper and more metallic," the chances are Mr. Jones will go right on making an English *t* as he would have without any instruction at all.

A good book takes up matters of *accent* and *intonation*. If it is presenting English for the foreigner, it points out that *brief case* and *briefcase* are distinguished by their accents, a matter which speakers of a language with a different system of accentuation from our own, like Spanish or French, will slight unless they are warned to observe it. A good book will not stop with one or two examples, but will give a whole series of contrasting accent forms:

I saw him by the bank.	the greenhouse	light gray stone blocks
I saw him buy the bank.	the green house	light-gray stone blocks
	the Green house	light graystone blocks

The forms given are a few illustrations only from the many where distinctions in accent identify different utterances in English. The difference in accent should be presented, also, not merely for intellectual understanding, but as fundamental parts of the language, with copious drills. Intonation should be similarly treated, presenting the contrast between *John went home,* and *John went home?* for English, and furthermore, contrasting the intonation of the foreign language when it differs. Thus the intonation of some sentences of command differ in English and German. If an English sentence like "Mary, let's go home now," is contrasted with its literal equivalent in German, "Maria, lass uns jetzt nach Hause gehen," the German sentence shows a finality, a downward intonation, on the name Maria, like that we would give a word standing alone as a complete sentence. If we give the English sentence the same kind of treatment, "Mary. Let's go home now," we are being brusque or rude; in German, such treatment is merely normal and not associated with rudeness at all. The difference is not without social importance—we often react to German intonation patterns as if the German were being intentionally "Prussian." A good book presents all such matters of accent and intonation as parts of the language pattern, which differentiate utterances from one another, which vary from language to language, and which have to be learned by the student like the rest of the habits which make up the foreign tongue.

A good book is written from a thorough knowledge of the *structure* of both the native language and the foreign language. Its presentation of pronunciation is in terms of the similarities and differences between the two, and therefore recognizes that presentation of the same foreign language necessarily differs for two groups with differing native language. The description of Spanish for English students warns them that English diphthongizes the vowels in a phrase like "pay so" and that this is therefore not an equivalent of Spanish *peso.* Such a warning would be superfluous in a grammar designed for speakers of French or Italian. Again, in a grammar of Spanish for speakers of English, little attention need be given to the Castilian pronunciation of a word like *cinco* or *lápiz,* since English has a readily available equivalent or near-equivalent. For a speaker of French or German, such a sound would need careful description, and directions for its production.

A good book presents sounds not alone in terms of what they are, but *how they are arranged,* again with careful attention to similarities and differences between foreign language and native language. For instance, it is not enough to say that Spanish has sounds approximately like (though with differences of detail) the *d* of *den* and the *th* of *then.* A good book explains that in normal Spanish, the *d* sound occurs after most consonants and pause, the *th* sound between vowels. That is, *donde* has *d's,* but in the phrase *a donde,* the first *d* becomes a *th.* A part of the arrangement of sounds, also, are the transitions between them. In consequence, a good book for Spanish would say that in ordinary conversation the two sentences *Es un hombre?* and *Es su nombre?* would be indistinguishable. The kind of transitional pauses which an English speaker puts in to mark his word boundaries are often absent in Spanish—as many a student has found out to his sorrow when he hears natives speak the language he has painfully studied in school. Again, a part of arrangement of sounds is their sequences. Thus a good grammar of Spanish points out that the nasal consonants of *un padre* and *un tio* are different, since Spanish does not permit the sequence *np* without intervening pause. English does permit such sequences, so that the student must be warned against them.

The most important point yet mentioned is that a good book presents pronunciation in terms of contrasts, and of contrasts as they appear in normal and complete sentences. It is next to useless simply to list and describe English or French vowels. The sounds must be presented in words such as *ship* and *sheep* for English, *patte* and *pate* for French, and these contrasts then further placed in sentences such as "I saw a big ship," and "I saw a big sheep." Individual contrasts are not to be avoided; rather, once given, they should be illustrated from sentences which actually occur in speech.

A *good* book presents material on pronunciation, not only in its introductory chapters, but throughout the work, in terms of systematic *respelling, always together with ordinary orthography.* Since such systems may, however, be used in confusing and harmful ways, some explanation of their purpose is necessary. Even with the so-called phonetic language like Spanish and Finnish, the ordinary orthography does not record all of the language. The features of pause, much of accentuation, and intonation have to be supplied by the teacher. If they are also given by a system of respelling in the textbook, the teacher's task is greatly lightened. With a language like English the importance of the respelling is much greater. Not only does English make many distinctions like that between the initial sounds of *thy* and *thigh* which are not shown in spelling at all, but has sequences like *-ough* in *though, through, cough, enough,* and *bough* which have to be learned item by item. Time is therefore saved by a respelling which is consistent.

Respelling is no more than an aid to the learning of pronunciation, and secondarily an aid to learning the system by which pronunciation is partially recorded in orthography. If either book or teacher uses it otherwise, it is harmful. Damage was recently done unintentionally by a book prepared as a manual for writers of textbooks. The manual presented drills in respelling alone, leaving it to the textwriters to supply the orthographic version. When the book was unavoidably pressed into service as a textbook, students and teachers not unnaturally complained that they had to learn a "language of phonetics" and then learn English all over again after that. Again, as soon as a student or a class accomplishes the aims for which the respelling was devised, further attention to the system can be dropped. Yet since it is impossible for a textwriter to predict at exactly what point such mastery will be achieved, he provides the respelling throughout the book. If his student realizes that the respelling is provided as an aid, and not as something extra that must be mastered for itself, it is normally true that he will make good use of it. A not uncommon experience for teachers of English as a second language in classes which use some of the books now available in complete and systematic respelling, is to have members of the class correct an inadvertent misreading of intonation or accent.

It was stated above that the respelling should be used throughout the book. An instance of its usefulness in sections other than those on pronunciation would be that a good statement of English noun plurals would say that there are three regular endings, /-s/, /-z/, and /-iz/, using respelling to indicate their sound, and using it further to indicate the sounds after which each one occurs. Moreover, when instruction in spelling is given, the sounds are first presented in the already learned respelling, and then the way they are represented in ordinary orthography is systematically explained. A useful English spelling rule is that a single consonant letter between vowel letters is an indication that the first vowel letter represents a diphthong, while two consonant letters in the same situation indicate that the first vowel letter spells a simple vowel. The rule is useless unless the student knows a respelling which gives the first vowel of *liking* as a diphthong, and the first vowel of *licking* as a simple vowel. The respelling is used not only in the introductory chapters, in grammatical presentation, in the treatment of spelling, but throughout in the drills which should accompany each chapter.

In the preceding pages we have been working with a single explicit assumption, that language is sound. Yet there has been another assumption implicit in all that we have said. This is that *sounds make patterns of contrasts,* and that these patterns differ from language to language quite as much as do the sounds themselves. The different treatment of *d* and *th* sounds in Spanish and English is an instance of pattern difference more important than difference in sound entities. The notion of patterning extends not only to sound, but to all parts of language, to grammar, syntax, and even to vocabulary. It is important to make the student recognize that when he has learned a vocabulary correspondence like *hand-mano* he has not yet learned all that is necessary, since Spanish employs *mano* where we would use *coat* in a *coat of varnish, una mano de barniz.* The patterning of grammar and vocabulary items is as important, and as unpredictable, as the patterning of sounds.

A third related assumption is that it is the formal differences in sound which make the differences in larger items, and so in turn make the differences in meaning possible. Differences in meaning are therefore best arrived at through study of the formal differences. The contrary assumption is that differences of meaning impose the formal differences, which are therefore secondary and unimportant. Yet the formal differences are the signals to which we respond, and which give us our knowledge of the meaning differences. If the reader says the two sentences, "They didn't have money to eat," and "They didn't have bread to eat," he will of course recognize that the phrase "to eat" has a different function in the two. If he compares his pronunciation of both, he should be able to recognize that *eat* gets a stronger accent in the first than in the second. Now let him try the first sentence with a nonsense word in place of money, "They didn't have *cadsov* to EAT." Pronounced in this way it is clear that *cadsov* is the same kind of thing as money, and is not something edible like bread.

How does this assumption work out in the presentation of grammatical material? First, a good book presents drills designed to give the student habitual mastery of formal patterns; it does not present formal or even semantic principles as sole and sufficient guides. Thus for a Chinese student of English, sentences like "It's a nice day," must be drilled until they become an easily manipulated model into which other utterances like "It's raining," "It's hot," and so on, can be fitted. Only if this mastery is given, will accompanying explanation of the use of the fictitious pronoun subject be fully useful.

Yet since books for more mature students find it useful to present systematic grammatical description as a supplement to drill, the assumption given necessarily affects this systematic reference material also. A bad book presents its account of grammatical classes *primarily in terms of meaning. A good book* presents them first *in terms of their formal characteristics,* with descriptions of meaning only after the formal characteristics have been used to isolate and identify the entities described. A typical bad presentation is one that we all remember—"A pronoun is a word used instead of a noun." The definition does not define, since if a pronoun is a noun used for another noun, the definition is not needed. If on the other hand, a pronoun is not a noun, we are left to wonder what it is. A typically good presentation—and fortunately there are many such—begins by giving the inflectional forms of pronouns and, since the class is not large, listing the words that share them. Only thereafter does such a book go on to say that pronouns are used as noun substitutes, and to give the conditions under which the substitution takes place. In dealing with nouns, a good presentation begins by saying that English nouns have two cases and two numbers, and can be preceded by articles and adjectives in the same phrase. When such characteristics have been given, it may go on to say that nouns correspond fairly well with the category of things in the real world. A good presentation will, however, never use a category of "thingness" to define such a word as *whiteness* or *penetration* as a noun. Definition, in short, should precede description. If the class of nouns has first been isolated so that the student knows what words belong in the class, description of the class is genuinely useful, though of course its value is in contributing to the intellectual understanding of language structure, not to the learning of language habits. To draw a parallel, one would not attempt to decide that a particular living being was a man or an ape by describing all the important accomplishments of mankind; it would be far more useful to stick to the anthropologists' defining differential, "man alone has an opposed thumb."

The attitude that it is better to work through the formal characteristics to arrive at functions and meanings affects the presentation of language material in other ways also. In general, a book is to be condemned if it sets up classes for which there are no formal differentiating characteristics, or which conflict with them. Usually the reason for setting up such classes is an introduction of history at a point where it is confusing, or an attempt to fit all languages into a classic mold. Thus, for instance, it is defensible to talk about uses of the verb in English which correspond to subjunctive forms in other languages. Such forms as "if this be treason" can then be called subjunctive uses. It is certainly wasteful to set up a complete paradigm for a subjunctive mood in English, however, since all the forms which occur in subjunctive uses occur elsewhere in the verb inflection, and there are no special subjunctive endings. Again, in the treatment of English verb forms for the learner of the language it is confusing to list the forms according to their various Old English classes, as at least one grammar does. In the presentation of German, the historical origin of the umlaut vowels can easily be pressed beyond the point of usefulness. Yet a simple structural parallel between the umlaut plurals of *man* and *Mann* may well interest the student and act as a worthwhile mnemonic device.

The presentation of grammatical material, syntatic patterns, even of vocabulary differences, like the presentation of sounds, proceeds from a thorough knowledge of both the native and the foreign language. Such a knowledge is not merely the ability to speak both languages fluently, but is much more an analysis of both structures, and the resultant ability to describe both similarities and differences. A good book wastes little time, however, with the similarities, and directs its attention instead to the differences. A Spanish grammar for speakers of English need not list all the uses of the Spanish definite article, since many are similar to English. An instance of what should be pointed out is the Spanish use of the definite article with parts of the body and intimate possessions, where we use a pronoun possessive. That is, Spanish says "he bumped the head," where we say "his head." If on the other hand, Spanish is being presented for speakers of a Slavic tongue, the treatment of the definite article will have to be full and detailed. Once more, the problem is different for each language group.

Next, a good book provides *drills* for all phases of the material presented. So indeed, do many bad books, though with a difference. A *bad book presents a set of sentences to be laboriously translated,* employing many different constructions in any one of which the student can make a mistake. We all remember the sets of Latin sentences, employing ablative absolutes, gerunds and gerundives, accusatives of extent of time, and so on, through which we struggled. Such sentences could be solved only like crossword puzzles, and for most of us they never led to any fluency in Latin. Drills which present the student with the whole of the language at once always make him stop and think and search his memory for the right form. Yet to talk we have to be so habituated to the proper form that it comes out automatically. If we have to search for it, the conversation has left us long before we arrive at the proper answer. Drills which consist solely of paradigms may be a hindrance, since students often cannot bring out the proper form without running over the whole set first. A familiar example of this sort of fault is the student who cannot name the day of the week without starting with Monday.

A *well-constructed drill turns on a single contrast,* and asks the student only to supply the proper form A or form B, always within a single frame. A proper drill for English might turn on this simple sentence frame:

I ——————— go to the bank, this morning.

The blank should be filled with normal verbs like *want, hope, plan,* and so on, all of which must be followed by *to,* and then by *can, may, will* and *shall* which omit the *to.* The drill should give ample opportunity for oral practice, until the student acquires a habit, much in the fashion that an American child acquires the habit of using or dropping *to* in this construction, before he is five years old. *Can go* and *want to go* represent a basically formal and arbitrary difference, and here as often in language no semantic or historical discussion is very helpful. The learner of English does not need to know the intricacies of preteritive-present verbs in Germanic; he needs only the habit of saying *can go.*

A good approach to such a Spanish problem as order in adjectives will similarly be based on drill, and, as we have been trying to suggest, the drill will be split into separate sets, each involving a small point in structure. A good drill can be made on nothing more than Spanish *todos* and *ambos. Todos* has many of the same order characteristics as English *all,* and there is one-for-one correspondence between *todos los hombres* and *all the men.* But *ambos* does not go with *todos* in the same way that *both* goes with *all.* That is, we can say *all the men,* or *both the men:* in Spanish, on the other hand, we can say only *todos los hombres,* not *ambos los hombres.* Subsequent drills, based on accurate surveys of Spanish habits, would then be devoted to adjectives which occur before and after the noun, those which occur in both positions with change of meaning, those which occur in both positions with change of form, and so on.

A good book does not present a language as a set of contrasts in a vacuum, but rather as a system which is intimately connected with other human activities, habits, and values. Indeed, it is ultimately this connection that we are talking about when we say that language has meaning, and which gives language its transcendent importance in our daily lives. A presentation of German should give the conditions under which a German addresses another as *du,* and will compare these with the conditions under which an American uses a first name. Not the least value of such an approach is that it brings into the student's awareness some of his own cultural habits, which he has probably taken for granted as instinctive. The German book should also pay some attention to the body movements which accompany speech, pointing out that Germans of different social status stand slightly farther from each other in talking than do speakers of similar status in English. This kind of information should then be related to the description of the use of *du*. There should also be some mention of levels of usage, realistically described in terms of the social responses that variant forms call forth. It should be emphasized that all such correlation with other habits and with social values is not a mere "talking about the language," of the sort rightly condemned as a turning aside from learning it. It is rather the necessary flesh and blood which makes a skeleton structure a living body.

The mention of the correlation of language with a community's set of values brings us inevitably to the subject of literature and reading in the language classroom. The emphasis so far given has been on language as speech, so that a false impression may have been inadvertently created. Literature is of the greatest importance in language training, and is often enough the student's real aim in study. But before such reading can be profitable, a good deal of preliminary training is necessary. The great works of literature abroad, as at home, are often considerably removed from contemporary speech. Such works as *Don Quixote* or *Hamlet* can be meaningfully read only when the student has gained some command of the patterns of the language. Since we cannot carry on conversation in Spanish of the Golden Age, or in Elizabethan English, the only way in which the student can be drilled in language patterns is through practice in living speech. The aim of those who want to read literature has then to be the same in the beginning stages as for those who want to learn the language so as to get a job abroad—for that matter, the same as those who merely want to meet a language requirement. All must be given skill in handling patterns of speech. Specialization must come later.

For these reasons, the classics do not belong in the beginning class. Most of us have seen the results of premature literary study in the foreigner who has been dragged through a Shakespeare play but is unable to communicate in any recognizable form of English.

In the beginning class, the place of the classics might well be taken by carefully graded readers whose content is the normal habits and beliefs of the foreign community—for instance, Spanish habits of dress. For lack of such training on both sides of the language barrier, American tourists often give offense by dressing in shorts on the street, and Latins all too often have an impression of immorality in American life based on just this American ignorance of foreign ways.

The content of the reader should be presented in a structurally organized fashion. That is, each section should make use of a single type of grammatical contrast. Happily there is at least one such reader for English, in which home life in an average American town is so described. Each chapter deals with some such structural point as "it is raining now" in contrast with "it rains every day." The language should be simplified in two ways. There should not be much strange vocabulary. The new words and phrases should be given at a constant rate, and with constant reemployment. The vocabulary should be carefully scrutinized to make sure that new items do not slip in carelessly. An otherwise excellent reader contains a schoolgirl's question, "Where's my English book?" The phrase evidently slipped by the compiler without his realizing that it is a special construction, "book for a class in English literature or composition," not the more predictable phrase "book from England."

The second sense in which the language should be simplified is in the number of grammatical constructions used. If the simplification is in vocabulary alone, the result is to throw complicated constructions at the student before he is ready for them. A horrifying example of such simplification of vocabulary without simplification of constructions is this sentence brought to me by a Japanese student of English from the first chapter of her reader: "It is thinking that makes what we read our own." Often in readers where the vocabulary has been thus simplified, it is easy to discover an underlying confusion between the adult foreigner and the native child. One whole series of English readers for foreigners is organized around keeping the vocabulary monosyllabic. The simplified language must be strictly natural. Often enough it is quaint and unpredictable, as in this sentence from an English reader in use in Italy—"What does Miss Blackhead bid?" (Miss Blackhead is a teacher of English, not a bridge player.) A slightly less repulsive example is this from a reader widely used in America—"After she had powdered her face . . ." (American girls usually powder their noses.) More importantly, grammatical simplification may be done so as to do violence to structure. In a set of English materials used in the Orient, all verbs are used in the simple present ("It rains now,") in the early chapters, because the "is raining" construction is regarded as too difficult.

Up to this point we have been talking about how the language teacher can select already prepared material. Far more important is what he does in his own classroom. Much of what will be said on this subject is application of the same principles which govern the compilation of a good text. Much more is confirmation of what has been practiced in language classes by good teachers at any time. The linguistic scientists' recommendations are not new or revolutionary doctrine, but simply recommendations of what those linguists who are also practical language teachers have found to be effective.

Many language teachers are now provided with books which use the type of respelling described earlier. Such a text puts a burden on the teacher, since he must learn to read it in a consistent fashion, giving the sounds, accent, and intonation that the respelling calls for. The task, however, is not as heavy as the unfamiliarity of the symbols would suggest. The teacher already has command of the language, so that if he pronounces a sentence at all, it will be in a possible form. The respelling is consistent, so that when sound and symbol are correlated, they are learned once and for all. Any such text will provide descriptions of acceptable dialect variants, and direct the teacher to use his natural form when there is such an alternative. The respelling does not direct him to learn a new kind of speech, since he already speaks in an acceptable fashion. If he pronounces Spanish *cinco* with an *s* or *beard* without an *r,* he need do no more than call the attention of his class to a dialect variant. When it is once possible to read the respelling consistently, the teacher is repaid in the speed and accuracy with which he can make distinctions and corrections. He can also lead his class to pronounce sentences so that they sound like natural and expressive language, not like separate and meaningless words.

The teacher will often be called on to design oral drills supplementing those he takes from his text. All that has been said about good and bad drills applies as well to those the teacher designs as to those he merely adopts. In pronunciation, the first drills should be in recognition of the foreign distinctions, with the student responding by number or some other device which does not involve producing the foreign sounds. Ability to recognize by no means guarantees ability to produce, but a student has no chance of producing a distinction until he has learned to hear it.

At later stages, reading aloud is useful. The first reading should be of texts already learned from a version in the respelling, read without reference to the respelling except for correction. When the students advance to reading without the respelling aid, the aim should be to see that they recognize the correlation, imperfect though it may be, between punctuation and the expressive properties—accent, intonation, pause—of speech. It is a minor point, but one worth making, that it is by no means always necessary to make a student translate a passage to determine whether he has understood it. If he reads the passage expressively, this is often evidence enough of understanding. After reading exercises have been introduced, dictation can be employed, again with the same aim, that of drilling on the correlation between punctuation and the expressive qualities of speech. Dictation should never be given in the form "John went home question mark," but naturally, leaving the student to recognize that the sentence is a question from the way it sounds.

Drills should be as nearly as possible at normal speed, allowing the student to catch up by pauses placed at normal breaks in the sentence. It is important to recognize that slow speech is often— if not usually—distorted speech. If the teacher is able to train himself to slow speech which is not distorted, slow speech becomes very valuable indeed, but such training is difficult. Speakers, at least of the literate Western languages, have long been trained in a bookish formal style used when speaking slowly, and which differs greatly from the forms of conversation. When a speaker of a Western language slows his speech, he automatically falls into the bookish style. A sentence like "Don't you want a cup of coffee?" employs forms like "doncha" and "cuppa" in all normal conversation, though it is difficult to represent such forms in ordinary spelling without creating a false impression of illiteracy, which is a heritage of dialect writing. The reader should compare a slow and a rapid pronunciation of the sentence. In slow speech he will use separate and distinct consonants for *don't* and the following pronoun, a clearly pronounced *t* in *want,* and an equally clearly pronounced *v* (not *f* of course) in *of*. In rapid speech all these features are slurred, by both educated and uneducated speakers. It is not here argued that the conversational style is best for all purposes; rather it is maintained that the conversational style is a normal and necessary part of the language, and not a mark of carelessness or lack of education.

If the teacher can produce slow speech only in the bookish style, his only chance of introducing students to the conversational style that they must master if they are to use the language, is to talk at conversational tempo. If the teacher is enough of a virtuoso to be able to say "doncha" at half speed and without distortion, then he has at his disposal one of the most effective teaching devices there is. The distorting effect of the bookish style is amply born out by classroom experience. With learners of English, one of the first tasks is to convince them that Americans really say things like "I'm going," or "I'll go," instead of the formal "I am going" and "I will go." They have seen the formal style in books and think of it as normal, so that they have great difficulty with even such simple conversational sentences as those given.

What the teacher does in his classroom can be seriously affected, for good or bad, by his ideas of usage. The teacher should use as good and as educated a form of speech as he can, but if his speech is not that of some body of native speakers, he is a bad model. I have known at least one teacher of German who regularly pronounced all *h*'s, even that of *gehen,* a pronunciation as unreal as insisting on the first *d* in *Wednesday.* A markedly formal pronunciation, if genuine even though uncommon, like the stage pronunciation of German, can be objected to only if it is the only type to which the student is exposed. If he gets some practice in a more conversational style, but himself adopts the stage pronunciation, he should be able to understand and to talk, both acceptably.

All good teachers are aware of differences in rapid and slow style, and informal and formal speech, and all attempt to deal with them in some fashion. Yet a common solution to the problem is to try to produce a compromise style suitable for all occasions. Standard languages serve a part of this purpose, and should always be taught to the exclusion of local dialects, or speech without social prestige. Yet the attempt to construct a single form of speech for all class purposes is open to some objections. The matter of speed of utterance can be controlled, but the effects of speed cannot. If the sentence used is "Don't you want a cup of coffee?" there comes a point in any series of utterances graded by speed, at which there is a dividing line between the bookish and the colloquial forms. The only way in which a compromise form could be set up would be to give, say, the bookish form for *don't you,* and the colloquial form for *cup of.* Since such compromise forms are therefore apt either not to be genuine compromises, or to be unreal mixtures, it is simpler and more accurate to expose the student systematically to more than one type of speech, of the sorts that he is likely to encounter.

Far more serious than an unreal type of speech is confusion between native mistakes and those the foreigner is prone to. The native mistakes are the use of a form belonging to a definite social level on another level of higher prestige, which makes the form inappropriate. The foreigner's mistakes are carry-overs from his native language, so that the form produced is not English at all. The confusion has been very frequent in classes of English for foreigners, since until recently teachers of such classes usually had a background solely in instruction of native speakers. Thus an English class for speakers of Polish at least once spent a whole session on the proper use of *shall* and *will,* and I know of a book for speakers of Chinese which warns very carefully against splitting infinitives. Both of these mistakes would be committed only by a native. A foreigner who actually splits an infinitive is making progress toward some form of colloquial English, perhaps not just what we would choose for him, but progress none the less. In short, a teacher should produce an acceptable variety of the foreign language, and not worry too much over whether he speaks exactly like his colleagues. If they too produce an acceptable variety, it is to the student's advantage to become acquainted with more than one normal type. Again, the teacher should examine his list of errors to be avoided, and make sure that they are errors the foreigner is prone to. If they are native errors, he can well dismiss them from his mind. For speakers of Spanish a genuine error is failure to distinguish *no* and *not;* an occasional form like *he don't* can be dismissed with no more than passing mention.

Two matters can conclude this discussion. The first is the "direct method," still used, though no longer without modification, in most schools. Throughout these pages it has been said, in as many ways as possible, that language is pattern—patterns of sound, of words, of phrases and sentences. The native speaker moves through these patterns, making expansions, substitutions, and contractions without thinking about them, without real awareness. The patterns have become habits so deeply embedded in the early years of his adjustment to his community that they seem to him almost instinctive. There is no way in which an adult can acquire a new set of such habits except by initial intellectual understanding, backed by drill which transforms the understanding into automatic response. The intellectual understanding is of great value to the adult, but without the following drill it is useless. *The direct method, rigidly followed, gives no initial understanding of the patterns, since it rules out communication in the known tongue.* Similarly, it gives drill, it is true, but seldom in the systematic form which is most helpful.

In its history, the direct method was a healthy revolt against overcomplicated grammatical analysis, and against the translation approach. It has the virtue of exposing the student to large amounts of the foreign tongue, and *succeeds better than any method which does not do so.* It is a truism that one cannot learn French by talking about it; one learn French by talking French. In practice, however, *the direct method assumes that the adult learner is exactly like the native child, unsophisticated in any language* and with five years or more in which to do nothing but learn to talk. The amount of time the direct method can waste is, to say the least, discouraging. A teacher who begins with a sentence like "los libros están en la mesa," without some reference to translation, gets a collection of random guesses like "made of wood," "in English," "in front of you," and so on.

A sensible plan, instead of the direct method, is *initial explanation, as accurate and simple as possible, in the native language, followed by drill* aimed at the acquisition of patterns. Each sentence learned should be a frame for expansion and substitution, so that the student begins to talk controlled and minimal bits of the language. Such a Spanish sentence as that given above should be followed by substitution drill using such words as *silla, sala,* to be followed by others with change of gender or number. The aim of all such drill can be summed up by saying its purpose is to teach a little of the language at a time very well, rather than a lot of the language at once and badly.

The last matter is the vexed question of the native or nonnative teacher. The native teacher often enjoys a prestige which his American colleagues do not reach. Yet to say that only a native can teach a language is nearly equivalent to saying that no one can learn a second language. It is true that an adult almost never learns a new tongue without slight trace of a foreign accent, so that it is always important that students hear considerable native speech as a model. But except for this, there is little to choose between native and well-trained American. Granted that the American commands the language, his excellence as a teacher depends on his professional competence as a classroom teacher, as explainer of language forms, and as designer of effective drills. If the teacher is a native, his excellence depends on the same qualifications, plus the fact that what he gains in command of the language to be learned he may lose in command of English.

In many schools, however, no native speaker is available, so that American teachers have no one to consult if they wish to investigate a point of usage, and the students have no perfect model for pronunciation. In such a situation much can yet be done. One modern solution is extensive use of recordings. Another is a determined search for a native, not to act as a member of the faculty, but as an assistant whose job it is to talk, so that he can be observed and imitated. In all large cities and even in many small ones such native models are available, sometimes on a volunteer basis. One native can enormously improve the teaching situation by making recordings, or by coming to class at intervals and talking long enough to convince the students that what they are studying is a genuine and living vehicle of human communication.

In closing I return to my starting point. Language teachers have an important job, and they are devoted to doing it. Linguistic scientists also have an important job, to which they are also devoted. Their results are fragmentary—as are those of all science—but important, and growing in importance. It is unthinkable that the enormous task of unlocking the language barrier will not be one in which teacher and investigator cooperate in friendly fashion. All that the investigator can tell the teacher about the system of language, and how to exploit it in presentation, will benefit the classroom. All that the teacher can tell the investigator about students' responses, failures, and successes will benefit the investigation of how language works.

A SECOND CULTURE: NEW IMPERATIVE FOR AMERICAN EDUCATION

HOWARD LEE NOSTRAND

The relationship of language and culture, in the liberal arts sense, has been traditionally recognized and language has been taught with the intent of imparting the culture of the nation whose language is being studied. Unfortunately much thinking on this subject, particularly from the educational point of view, has been nebulous. In this scholarly essay Professor Nostrand, of the University of Washington, gives teachers a framework that can well serve to determine how much culture and what in the culture can be conveyed as one teaches the foreign language. Inherent is the distinction between culture in the liberal arts sense of the word and culture in the anthropological sense. It is the latter which should be more the concern of the foreign language teacher, the textbook author, and the curriculum planner when considering content. Dr. Nostrand likewise makes clear that the social sciences should be just as ancillary to the foreign language teacher as linguistics and psychology. A true and deep cross-cultural understanding can be achieved only through a thorough knowledge of a people's language.

The question of what Americans really need to comprehend about foreign cultures is an unsolved problem, the occasion for an adventure of inquiry and not for a paper that lays down a prescriptive answer. I believe we are ready for a fresh attack on the whole cross-

Reprinted by permission of the author and the College Entrance Examination Board from *Curricular Change in the Foreign Languages*, 1963.

cultural aspect of the curriculum, an attack which can result both in a consensus on the kinds of things that should be taught, and in a research effort to provide systematic descriptions of cultures.

Even those curriculum specialists who earnestly question any value in learning a foreign language believe that the general curricular goals of respect for persons, empathic understanding, and cooperativeness should apply to international as well as to domestic human relations. Some even recognize a specific goal of "better communication" among peoples.[1]

Many modern language teachers have broadened their professional aims to include a responsibility for teaching the sociocultural context of foreign languages. This concern was prominent in all the papers presented in 1962 at the Modern Language Association's annual review of its Foreign Language Program. The Language Development Program of the United States Office of Education is enabling me, with help from social scientists, to prepare a handbook for use in describing and teaching literate cultures.

Social scientists can be counted upon to develop part of the needed descriptive knowledge. Anthropologists, geographers, and sociologists have established committees in their national associations to study curricular problems.[2]

THE IDEAL OF AN INTERNATIONAL COMMUNITY

Let me try to make explicit the values I believe we have in common that bear on what should be taught in our schools about the outside world. Some half dozen major American values prove

[1] Elizabeth Engle Thompson and Arthur E. Hamalainen, *Foreign Language Teaching in Elementary Schools; an Examination of Current Practices* (Washington, D.C.: Association for Supervision and Curriculum Development, National Education Association, 1958), p. 9.

[2] American Anthropological Association, Anthropology Curriculum Study Project: Mrs. Malcolm Collier, Director, 5632 Kimbark Avenue, Chicago 37, Ill.

Joint Committee on Education, Association of American Geographers and National Council for Geographic Education: William D. Pattison, Director, Study on the Improvement of High School Geography, Department of Geography, University of California at Los Angeles, Los Angeles 24, Calif.

American Sociological Association, Committee on the Social Studies in the Secondary Curriculum: Neal Gross, Chairman, Harvard University Graduate School of Education, Cambridge 38, Mass.

relevant, and central among them is the relatively young ideal of an international community of peoples.

The President's Commission on National Goals referred to essentially the same ideal of international community when it named "helping to build an open and peaceful world" as the first of its "goals abroad."[3] This ideal belongs to our conception of a good society, but it is also related to our conception of good self-fulfillment of the individual.

In our ideal of society, international community is one of the conditions that we believe would provide the individual with the best opportunity for the kind of inner life we value. Other conditions, I suggest, are the social freedoms that favor the inner freedom of the individual; social justice; a certain cultural solidarity within the nation; and relationships of community in all the groups we participate in, ranging from our families and immediate associates to the nation.

Politically, we mean by international community a community of peoples dominated by none, in which all individuals have representation through their governments. We do not mean, for the foreseeable future, a world government beyond the decentralized pattern of intergovernmental agencies, with specified powers, which has been developing. Our ambition is rather to live harmoniously in domestic, religious, and political communities which are related one to another by peaceful interchange, understanding, and healthy rivalry.

In economics, we mean a community based on persuasion and not on coercion, a community in which everyone is as free as possible to trade or not, according to his best interest as he sees it.

Culturally, we want the fewest possible barriers to the free interchange of ideas, scientific knowledge, technological advances, and artistic innovations. We want every culture to be left intact and to change only through voluntary reinterpretation and adjustment. At the same time, "community" means the possessing of something in common that is deeper than the conventionalities of politeness and legal agreements. The sort of tolerance we choose requires a consciousness of common problems and purposes. Voluntary community

[3] *Goals for Americans,* President's Commission on National Goals (Englewood Cliffs, N.J.: Prentice-Hall, 1960), p. 17.

calls for a higher degree of mutual understanding than does a coercive structure.

If I am right in contending that the principle of persuasion is basic to the political, economic, and cultural environment we must strive for, I am introducing a new imperative into the canons that guide our international behavior. We who have enjoyed unparalleled power must now learn to persuade with the voice of a minority group. In international trade, we now have to sell our automobiles and refrigerators in competition with other exporting countries. In international politics, the whole Caucasian contingent has become a minority, and we must persuade Asians and Africans, as well as Europeans, that their interests and ours coincide. And the time is coming when we shall control only a minor fraction of the world's military power.

Our superior wealth has aroused envy and resentment, and we face a new problem of winning friends and persuading people. It is proverbial that the American abroad gives the impression of acting as if he didn't care who owned the place. We must learn to show genuine respect for our hosts, appreciation for their culture, and an understanding of their interests, aspirations, and ways of doing things. We have no assurance that we can succeed, even if we educate in the best way we know, against the odds of human selfishness, narrowness, and opposition to change.[4]

---

[4] At the Colloquium, Edward D. Sullivan of Princeton University questioned whether it is possible, as I am supposing, to teach values by precept and example. He doubted the connection, therefore, between my effort here to define values to be taught and the curricular proposals presented later.

It seems clear from the studies of socialization in dissimilar societies that young children do learn values partly by precept and example, but this does not prove what I am assuming—that the curriculum at later stages of life can exert a strong influence. Some evidence is accumulating, however, that substantial changes in values and personality, not necessarily desirable, take place as late as the undergraduate period. (See Mervin B. Freedman, *Impact of College*. New Dimensions in Higher Education, No. 4. Washington, D.C.: Government Printing Office, 1960; and Nevitt Sanford (ed.), *The American College; Psychological and Social Interpretation of the Higher Learning*. Prepared by the Society for the Psychological Study of Social Issues. New York: Wiley, 1962). Students in one college estimate that the influence of courses and teachers accounts for a fourth of the significant changes they believe they have undergone in four college years. They rate the curriculum as the most powerful force, followed closely by work experience, "just growing up," fellow

INDIVIDUAL SELF-FULFILLMENT RELATED TO
INTERNATIONAL COMMUNITY

Now let us look into the values that form our ideal of individual self-fulfillment. Here a sense of international community extends the scope of four values in particular: purposefulness, balance or perspective, respect for persons, and intelligent love.

Purposefulness appears in individuals in widely varying ways, but civic responsibility is one element of it that every individual must learn. Society is designed to serve the individual, but we expect every individual in return to help build a good society.[5]

Perspective must in our century be cross-cultural. Our ideal, I think, is to combine an active, empathic understanding of other faiths and ways of life with convictions of one's own, reasonably but firmly held. We have faced essentially the same problem in reconstructing the past: we grow more broadly human by projecting ourselves as far as possible into the mentality and feelings of those who have lived in another age. But we are firmly rooted in our own time, and we thus gain a historical perspective that our ancestors

---

students, a faculty member, and the atmosphere of the college (*Antioch College Reports, 4; Effecting Change in the College Student* . . . Yellow Springs, Ohio: Office of Educational Research, Antioch College, 1963). I would maintain that the curriculum has a good chance of influencing values, and that the influence can be improved by refining our purposes and means, even if the means of transmitting values consist largely of implicit or indirect teaching.

[5] Local Association Activities Leaflet No. 12" (Washington, D.C.: National Education Association, 1962) includes a resolution passed by the chairmen of international committees of eighteen NEA departments: "Good U.S. citizenship includes knowledge and understanding of the world's econimic and political systems and cultures, as well as the economic, political, and cultural traditions of the United States. . . ." The leaflet then sketches out the personal qualities that education should consequently develop in all citizens: adaptability, cultural empathy, ideological clarity, patience, knowledge of the world, and responsibility.

William L. Langer, in an essay on "The United States Role in the World," written for the President's Commission on National Goals (see footnote 3), says: "Only breadth of outlook, readiness to recognize the need for change, and ability to adjust to novel conditions will enable even the greatest nations to keep pace with developments and aid statesmen in charting their course through the incredible complexities of international living."

could not have. Failures in cross-cultural perspective are punished more sharply than failures in historical perspective, however, and our ancestors cannot throw us off balance or on the defensive, as our contemporaries do when they question our values and beliefs.

Cross-cultural perspective does not allow the individual the freedom to choose whatever assortment of mores appeals to him, for cultures are functional wholes whose parts have to fit together.

Respect for persons or human dignity, which constantly figures in current definitions of world civic spirit, I take to mean fairness to every human being whether we like him or not. This principle is important, especially when the spirit of love gives way to indignation or annoyance. If the principle is to be extended to our remotest human relations, it must be learned as a habit, not just an idea.

Respect, however, is cold and often humiliating to a sensitive person, unless there goes with it the love that the great religions talked about long before the idea of respect for all human beings entered our value system. To free the great concept of love from the taint of Romantic sentimentality, I suggest the term "intelligent love,"[6] meaning a love that realistically and reasonably seeks the well-being of its object rather than indulging in self-satisfaction. To achieve the intelligent love necessary for a sense of international community, we must radically strengthen the education we give, on both the intellectual side and the emotional or "cathectic" side. Certainly none of us has enough time to identify himself with all the world's peoples, but I believe that each of us, as a part of his education, should pick one foreign culture and internalize certain aspects of it.

The social skills needed for the development of cross-cultural understanding fall in the categories of communication and self-confidence or poise, which are related to values I have already mentioned. Among the main resources of self-confidence and the ability to communicate are purposefulness, perspective, respect for the other person, intelligent love, and whatever other qualities make up the individual's general social adequacy.

We can perhaps agree on two points about the communication

[6] This term is gratefully borrowed from the Jesuit professors who contributed to one of the discussion groups at the twenty-second session of the American Assembly, October 1962.

skills. First, it is imperative that all our young people outgrow the limitations of parochial minds so that they can express themselves and understand others, to the extent of their abilities, within the framework of the values we have been considering. Second, it is desirable that all who can afford the time should learn to communicate in at least one language besides their own. We cannot afford to be misled by the short-sighted tactic, "Let 'em learn English." At a recent meeting of microbiologists in Rome, the Italians, Germans, French, and Russians all could speak English, with some effort; only one of the Americans spoke any second language, and he could sense the underlying resentment at the fact that every conversation participated in by the Americans had to be held in English.

The self-confidence to be oneself in any human situation is decidedly important in cross-cultural give-and-take. For we have all seen how embarrassment can make the most knowledgeable person do the wrong thing in spite of himself.

BOTH KNOWLEDGE AND EXPERIENCE REQUIRED

From this working draft of common values, I want to draw one cardinal inference for the curriculum. It is that understanding requires two ingredients: *knowledge about* and *experience of*. If the knowledge is lacking or misleading, experience will be forgotten or misapplied. We may spend our full time experiencing our own culture, after all, and still come out with little understanding of it that we can express or apply, unless we use knowledge to select and organize what is significant in the experience. On the other hand, the organizing knowledge becomes merely academic, empty of vital meaning, if its verbalizations allude to experience that simply isn't there. Neither experience nor knowledge can be so excellent as to make up for deficiencies in the other, and the understanding we seek to bring about will be mediocre unless we achieve excellence in both components and in their interaction to form an organized whole.

We want to help design a curriculum that will bring about a fruitful interplay between experience of and knowledge about the values we have been considering. We may distinguish two large provinces of needed knowledge: generalized propositions about cultures and societies, and descriptive knowledge of specific socio-cultural areas. When we come to the experiential side of understanding, we shall not be able to make this distinction. For the generalized concepts are abstractions from the abstractions about specific ways of life. Experience, always concrete, can vivify directly only the lower-level abstractions drawn directly from it; by bringing these to life, it gives life indirectly to the abstractions of the second order. This will mean that experience of specific societies and cultures must do double duty and will take on a double importance, if generalized concepts are really needed.

A person needs to comprehend at least three aspects of cultures and societies in general: what sort of thing they are; their mode of existence and of being transmitted; and their principal parts. I shall sketch out only enough of these three aspects to show that their proper understanding requires some revision of school and college curriculums.

First, then, all human cultures and societies are, by nature, highly patterned complexes of shared behavior; and their parts are sufficiently interdependent to form a functional whole. It seems essential for cross-cultural perspective to appreciate what it means that a person's thought process, emotional reactions, even his perception of reality, are all constituted in ways that vary from one culture to another. It is essential also to understand that cultures and societies function as wholes. We cannot always expect other peoples to adopt our individualism and free enterprise, our conception of achievement, our majority rule and voting procedures, however successful we find these patterns to be at home.

Insight into the nature of culture and society requires understanding of why they change and how they are transmitted. A. L. Kroeber's remark has often been repeated that "perhaps *how it comes to be* is really more distinctive of culture than what it *is*."[7] Culture "comes to be" through adaptive changes and internal readjustments as the patterns interact with new conditions, including the changing personality structures in new generations of learners; for culture is learned behavior. The same is true of the patterns that make up social institutions. Most of us have very scant insight

---

[7] *Anthropology* (New York: Harcourt, Brace, 1948), p. 253.

into the process of learning. We all have rich experience of the process, yet for lack of enlightening knowledge to go with it, our personal experience sheds little light on the contrasts between cultures.

Are we not inconsistent in omitting the field of learning theory from our curriculums, while we rightly include the study of heredity on the ground that one should know what one can about the biological part of our inheritance? A grasp of learning theory would bring understanding and attract interest to other important areas besides that of cultures and societies. In the student's own learning it would make the difference between guiding himself and being excessively controlled by others, particularly when he comes to programed self-instruction. One can imagine that a proper knowledge of learning and of "socialization"—the processes by which one internalizes the approved behavior patterns of a society—could lead to more active interest in child development, which would be a boon indeed to many children who are now reared with cruel ineptitude.[8]

The third general aspect of cultures and societies—their principal parts—I shall treat here simply by grouping the parts into large categories,[9] for two purposes: to give an idea of the knowledge one needs in order to have a feeling for the similarities and differences among cultures; and to provide an inventory of the descriptive knowledge one must have in order to understand the inner workings of a specific sociocultural system.

It is useful to distinguish four levels of organization, even though they interpenetrate. The bottom level comprises the biological and psychological integration of the human organism and its interaction with the environment, without the intervention of consciousness. The second level is that of the personality structure, including its conscious thought, feeling, and volition.

The third level represents the organization of society. It comprises the shared norms of behavior which form the social roles and the institutions of a society. The top level consists of the shared patterns

[8] Wallace E. Lambert, "Psychological Approaches to the Study of Language. Part I: On Learning, Thinking and Human Abilities," *Modern Language Journal,* February, 1963, pp. 51–62.

[9] The principal parts are listed on page 129.

of meaning which together are called a culture.[10] The chief patterns of this sort are a system of values, including some that shape the methods of seeking truth, of solving problems, and so on; basic premises not subject to proof, concerning the nature of man and the world; empirical knowledge; and systems of expressive forms: language, the accompanying systems of paralanguage and kinesics,[11] humor, and art forms, from the simplest folk art to the most elaborate types of imaginative literature, music, and visual art.

[10] This conceptualization of four levels follows Talcott Parsons. See particularly his introductory chapters in Talcott Parsons, Edward Shils, Kaspar D. Naegele, and Jesse R. Pitts (eds.), *Theories of Society; Foundations of Modern Sociological Theory* (New York: The Free Press, 1961), two volumes. Of the top two levels he writes: "The social-system focus is on the conditions involved in the interaction of actual human individuals who constitute concrete collectivities with determinate membership. The cultural-system focus, on the other hand, is on 'patterns' of meaning, e.g., of values, of norms, of organized knowledge and beliefs, of expressive 'form.' The basic concept for the integration and interpenetration of the two is institutionalization. . . ." (Vol. I, p. 34).

Julian Steward goes less far than Talcott Parsons toward organizing the cultural level as a system distinct from social structure. Steward finds that in western Europe the culture consists of international patterns that do not form a system but contribute to a sociocultural system within each nation. See his "Area Research; Theory and Practice," *Social Science Research Council Bulletin 63*, pp. 151–152. Even so, Steward agrees that culture and society must be visualized separately since they vary independently, for example in their degree of stability: a Hopi or an Amish community may have a rigid culture while their populations disintegrate by emigration; a certain Iowa farming community has a stable society and a rapidly changing culture.

[11] For paralanguage (for example, tone of voice, stress) and kinesics (gestures and body motions), see Edward T. Hall's *The Silent Language* (Garden City, N.Y.: Doubleday, 1959). Hall plans to publish further research on "proxemics," the spatial distance between conversing persons, which varies according to society and status. A conference on paralinguistics and kinesics was held at Indiana University in May 1962, with support from the U.S. Office of Education. The proceedings are to appear late in 1963 in Thomas A. Sebeak, Alfred S. Hayes, and Mary Catherine Bateson (eds.), *Approaches to Semiotics* (The Hague Mouton). The volume will include five papers by scholars representing psychiatry, cultural anthropology, linguistics, and education, as well as an overview paper by Margaret Mead. Plans are under way for an eight-week seminar on semiotics (now redefined as total communication via all modalities, including touch, taste, and smell) to be held in the summer of 1964 under the direction of Alfred S. Hayes and Mary Catherine Bateson.

Awareness of all these aspects of cultures, societies, and the persons who transmit them are essential if one is to have a feeling for the similarities and differences among ways of life. The abstract categories I have listed are the universals. Within the universal categories one must learn to expect surprises and accept the immense variation among the specific systems of values, beliefs, expressive forms, social institutions, personality structures, and even among the conditioned forms of the biological processes.

UNDERSTANDING A SINGLE CULTURE AND SOCIETY

If we turn now to the problem of understanding a single culture and society, the inventory just reviewed shows what a formidable quantity of descriptive knowledge it takes to understand a socio-cultural whole in more than a superficial way. What is worse, the problem extends beyond this inventory in at least three directions.

In the first place, the inventory is concerned with regularities, with what is usual. Even if we express the usual patterns as ranges of variation, one must still add to these a knowledge of the unusual in the culture—for example, the exceptional achievements of great figures, in which the whole population takes pride.

Second, both the regularities and the exceptional achievements have a historical dimension which is an essential part of their significance. Cross-cultural inventories concentrate upon a synchronic tableau, but it would be false to regard the tableau as static. Some selective knowledge of the past is essential for understanding the drives and stresses in the momentary situation, which make it essentially dynamic.

In the third place, the inventory that fits all cultures and societies is not the best organization of data to express the unique flavor of life in a given culture area. Useful as the inventory's cross-cultural categories are as a checklist for both descriptive and comparative purposes, one needs also to know the major themes of a culture, its large, motivating principles, usually about ten or twelve in number, which permeate and color the structures of personality, institutions, and ethos—themes such as our American conception of personal achievement, the French concern for perfect craftsmanship, the Hispanic theme expressed in the adage, "If you work in order to live, why work yourself to death?" Such themes always have a value component uppermost in them, for they carry the strongest emotional charge at the point at which they imply what one ought to do or ought to be; but each theme is likely also to include elements of factual belief, intellectual method, expressive form, and social behavior.

Our national ideals of individual self-fulfillment and a good society require, then, a certain understanding of cultures and societies, and this understanding depends on coupling knowledge with experience. But the universal concepts about cultures and societies are abstractions of a second order, drawn from generalizations about particular sociocultural areas. Understanding of both orders of ideas must draw its basic experiential ingredient, therefore, from experience of one or more particular ways of life.

The conclusion seems inescapable that some delimitable experience of a second culture is essential for a modern education. A comparative approach to at least two culture areas is needed. A person must compare at least two systems in order to comprehend the generalities about the ways cultures and societies differ from one another, and to appreciate how the universals are derived. And he must compare the systems as wholes, in order to grasp that they differ not only in their anatomical parts but in the functional relationships among the more or less analogous parts. Granting that the first of the two systems selected may be the learner's own culture and that he already has the needed experience of it, the second culture poses the problem of assimilating both the descriptive knowledge and the essential experience to go with it.

Margaret Mead convinces me that in teaching about a second culture we need to refer also to a third culture, in order to avoid the naïve contrast of "We do this, they do that." The learner "is still in a box," as she observes. Yet I hope it will suffice to refer continually to parts of diverse cultures to serve this purpose, rather than to any third culture studied as a whole.

Since the end of World War II dissatisfaction with our success in the teaching of world-mindedness has brought about a change in curricular thinking in America.

In 1945 the National Education Association Committee on International Relations and two NEA departments joined in preparing a volume in which they defined at length "the world-minded American."[12] In a sanguine foreword the United States Representative to the United Nations, Warren Austin, urged exuberantly that "Children ought to grow up with intimate feelings of association with people of every culture and condition." The book recommends nothing less comprehensive than a knowledge of "the customs and habits of people in all parts of the world; and the economic, social, political, and religious environment in which they live."

In retrospect, however, this great blueprint seems unrealistic in its hope of how much territory could be covered. How time has chastened our expectations since the time of that pioneering volume is illustrated by three publications of 1962.

The National Council for the Social Studies and the American Council of Learned Societies sponsored a book of essays by distinguished specialists in history, geography, political science, economics, cultural anthropology, sociology, psychology, and area study of Asia and of Russia and Eastern Europe. Gordon Turner of the ACLS reports in the foreword that the authors and the representatives of the two sponsoring councils, in a preliminary meeting, reached three decisions: that the authors would discuss the important educational contributions of their fields; that the resulting content should be proposed as important for all who finish high school; and that "students should have an understanding of at least one culture other than their own. . . ."[13]

A second illustration comes from the Anthropology Curriculum Study Project, whose director enters these cautions in her report on the project to the Fellows of the American Anthropological Association:

> We must make it very clear that a course or unit is not anthropology just because it is about American Indians or other preliterate groups. It must be about them in a particular way. It must be about whole societies, be comparative, be inductive. We also insist on sufficient quantities of data to be meaningful and not just enough to be illustrative. . . .
>
> Another general caution is for people who expect anthropology to save

[12] National Education Association, Association for Supervision and Curriculum Development, and National Council for the Social Studies, *Education for International Understanding in American Schools; Suggestions and Recommendations* (Washington, D.C.: National Education Association, 1948).

[13] *The Social Studies and the Social Sciences* (New York: Harcourt, Brace, 1962), pp. vii–viii.

the world and promote the peace by developing "understanding through familiarity." If we can help students take the first steps away from an ethnocentric view of the world, the contribution will be important, but over-expectation of quick, practical results can only lead to disillusionment.[14]

A third example of the present more realistic attack is the report of a conference convened by the United States Office of Education, on the ideals of American freedom and the international dimension of education.[15] The five prominent persons who served as chairmen of the working committees make a series of statements, one of which is particularly pertinent here: "Current citizenship competencies require a more comprehensive knowledge of the societies and cultures of other peoples than heretofore."[16] A paragraph developing the statement begins, "The ways and means of communication are so changed as to require a new approach to teaching about other societies." The new approach involves selection of illustrative sociocultural areas, for the paragraph points out that "Area studies are a promising vehicle which has only begun to be tested." Another statement recommends concentration on one culture area as a vehicle of understanding: "The international dimensions of education and the contracting political environment require the rapid extension of instruction in the languages of other peoples, beginning with the elementary grades." The ensuing explanatory paragraph proposes that experimental elementary and secondary schools "offer a second language in every grade, and perhaps a third in the upper grades, with emphasis on conversational skill and cultural understanding, with systematic programming, continuity, and competent teachers. . . ."

It is prudent, finally, to see that each learner experiences two cultures in some depth. Verbal constructs are bad masters unless

[14] Mrs. Malcolm Collier, "Report on the Anthropology Curriculum Study Project," *Fellow Newsletter, American Anthropological Association,* November, 1962, pp. 2–4.

[15] *Education for Freedom and World Understanding: A Report of the Working Committees of the Conference on the Ideals of American Freedom and the International Dimensions of Education, March 26–28, 1961,* United States Department of Health, Education, and Welfare, Office of Education (Washington, D.C.: U.S. Government Printing Office, 1962).

[16] *Ibid.,* p. 14.

they are used by a person who has a feeling for how far to trust them, and nothing but concrete experience can reveal how much of an actual phenomenon a verbal approximation fails to capture. Ambassador Hu Shih said, "The mark of the educated mind is that it does not take generalizations literally."

Some non-Western thinkers, among them the Senegalese poet and statesman, Léopold Senghor, contrast the whole analytical and synthetic approach toward understanding, which we Westerners take for granted, with their own approach through "participating" in a phenomenon. Our Western approach needs no apology; non-Western societies are borrowing advantageously its science and its technologies of medicine, agriculture, and industry. But at its best, our approach uses conceptual knowledge only in conjunction with experience of its referent; and this experience is essentially the same self-projection that Asian and African traditions refer to as "participating" in the undifferentiated continuum of reality, perceiving it aesthetically before imposing constructs upon it.

Should every American's second culture be non-Western? Tentatively, I think not. The advantage every person might thus gain toward his self-fulfillment seems to me less than the advantages he would gain both in enrichment of his personal life and through the improvement of his nation's effectiveness, by living in a society in which every contemporary culture is the hobby of some persons, and in which some persons are assimilating the cultures of the great extinct societies.

Any culture more remote from us than those of the British Commonwealth seems to offer sufficient culture shock, provided we project ourselves into it experientially, to bring about the Copernican step from an ethnocentric to a comparative view. French culture, for example, despite our heavy borrowings from its ideology of liberty, equality, and community, can still shock our more dogmatic attitudes toward political heresy and toward individual deviations in mores. And when French children are brought vividly into a group of our children, as happens when an authentic film is shown in the classroom, the shock to ethnocentrism sparks from a hundred unexpected details. In one unit of the filmed course "Parlons Français"[17] two French girl scouts arrive at the top of a

[17] Produced by the Modern Language Project (Robert W. Cannaday, Jr., director of the French Project). Published by Heath deRochemont Corp., 6

hill and decide to sit down there and eat their lunch while they enjoy the view and cool off after the warm climb—a situation as universal, in the abstract, as the proposition that children are the same the world over. Yet in the concrete it provokes a derisive twitter among fifth-graders because the French girls wear odd scout uniforms and have an odd way of exclaiming about the heat. The teacher can of course modify this reaction by appealing beforehand to the children's broad-mindedness. Indeed, good teachers can use such episodes to develop in their students an active interest in conquering intercultural barriers.

CHANGING THE CURRICULUM

The problem of bringing the requisite experience and accompanying knowledge into an already brimful curriculum is difficult but no cause for defeatism. After all, the curriculum has been brimful before, yet logically necessary changes have been brought about. We shall simply have to add sparingly and change not so much by discarding as by suffusing the old with new meaning. If we can decide first what parts of a foreign sociocultural system really need to be experienced, we shall be able to examine how the parts might be fitted into the curriculum.

What the learner needs to experience depends on our educational purposes. We can discover empirically what a given group of learners finds hard to understand or to get along with in the target culture and society, and we can logically inquire what major parts of the sociocultural whole one must comprehend in order to deal intelligently with any one part.

Among the many reasons for studying foreign cultures and societies, I think the curriculum can concentrate on two: cross-cultural understanding and communication. The understanding we mean calls for experience that will support a cross-cultural perspective on oneself, and insight into the nature of cultures and societies in general, as well as a comprehension of two sociocultural systems. The ability to grasp meanings that depend on the context of one's second culture is a part of this comprehension.

Newbury Street, Boston 16, Mass., 1959. Distributed by the National Educational Television and Radio Center, Ann Arbor, Mich.

The cross-cultural communication we mean calls for the further ability to use a foreign language and to participate in the target society—not as a facsimile of a native, but rather as a welcome outsider.

At this point we should list—however diffidently—the parts of a sociocultural whole that need to be experienced for the purpose of cross-cultural understanding. It is useful to list in a parallel column the additional items required for the ability to communicate. The items can be stated briefly by including only their knowledge component. One must imagine the interacting experience in the form of multiple concrete examples. Experience must be presented selectively—for example, through books or films—to make real the fact of social and cultural change. One must also take into account variations by geographical regions, socioeconomic groups, age groups; contrasts between urban and rural subcultures; and discrepancies between professed principles and behavioral practices. A draft of the two lists is given on the following page.

Surprisingly, the items needed for understanding a sociocultural system turn out to be much bulkier than those needed additionally for communicating with its members, even though the latter column includes the active use of a second language. The value system and social structure, however they are presented, would each make the equivalent of a year-long project, comparable to a year of language study, if one undertakes to combine the descriptive knowledge with experience and to put them in historical and cross-cultural perspective. The literature and folklore of a people, whether experienced directly or indirectly through translations, would fill a third such unit. The geography of the area, whether expounded as such or integrated into projects, would add at least half of a fourth unit.

It will doubtless become possible to reduce somewhat the experience implied in the first column, when we have empirical research to show that some points can safely be omitted. It will certainly be possible to make the materials easier to assimilate by organizing the interdisciplinary knowledge involved, and by identifying main themes in a culture so that a single situation can provide experience of a value, its related factual assumptions, and its impact on social institutions and on individuals. If literature is read in the original, it can combine a tremendous variety of experience into a single encounter. Nevertheless, in order to acquire a near-adult perspective, a learner must somehow experience, through multiple examples, most of what is summarized in that long column.

Needed for understanding and for communication	*Needed additionally for communication*
1. All the culture-wide values (Parsons' motivational or consummatory subsystem[18]), including the method-shaping values.	
2. The key assumptions about reality (Parsons' "ground of meaning" subsystem). Historic achievements of the people in philosophy and religion.	
3. Any empirical beliefs (Parsons' cognitive subsystems) whose substance or functional relationships will differ from the learner's expectation. Historic achievements in the sciences and mathematics.	
4. Enough of the language for a sense of what it has in common with other languages, what makes it unique: structures that express key assumptions, words and phrases that express values, disvalues, sentiments, proprieties, intergroup attitudes, and so forth.	1. Active use of all common structures and vocabulary of the language.
5. Enough of the paralanguage and kinesics to know all types of expressiveness indicative of the culture.	2. Active use of the few main types of paralinguistic expression. Kinesics probably not needed for active use.
6. Humor: common types, topics, and proprieties.	
7. Art forms (Parsons' "expressive symbolization" subsystem). Examples of all common types, especially of literature (which could	

[18] Talcott Parsons, "The Functional Differentiation of Cultural Systems," in Talcott Parsons, Edward Shils, Kaspar D. Naegele, and Jesse R. Pitts (eds.), *Theories of Society; Foundations of Modern Sociological Theory, op. cit.,* Vol. II, pp. 982–984.

Needed for understanding and for communication	*Needed additionally for communication*
best be understood in the original). The main historic masterworks in the arts.	
8. The social institutions: familial (including socialization), religious, educational, economic-occupational, political and judicial, intellectual-aesthetic, recreational. Analysis of these institutions into their main component roles; and the norms of behavior approved, permissible, or disapproved in relation to each role. The processes of pattern maintenance and of social change.	3. Assimilation of the behavior patterns acceptable from a foreign guest.
9. The society's adaptation to geography and climate. The people's main achievements in technology.	
10. The prevalent types or characteristics of personality, and any indicative behavior patterns at the organismic level. The processes by which the characteristic patterns are internalized.	

We can delimit more explicity how much we mean by "multiple examples" of the regularities in the culture and the social structure. A regularity in the behavior of an individual—for example, the submissiveness of a child to parental authority—is most accurately represented not as a point, but as a range of variation. The child is not uniformly submissive on all occasions, nor on all issues. The same regularity in a whole society will cover a wider range of variation, which will include the individual case. In order to understand a feature of one or more societies in cross-cultural perspective, we can place their ranges of variation against the total range of all known societies, and also—since more extreme cultures may be discovered—against an absolute scale ranging from, for example, the most extreme imaginable degree of child submissiveness to the extreme of independence. To express the relationships graphically, we could mark off gradations on the absolute scale and place the partial ranges accordingly:

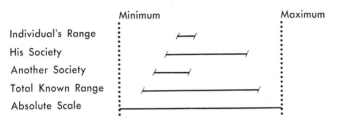

What is the place of the language in the left-hand column of the list at the top of this page? Alternatives for complex, untranslatable value terms of a people would amount to ineffectual resymbolizing in substitute terms. The same applies to the role relationships in a social structure, expressed in terms of address or by pronouns that distinguish between familiarity and formality, or between power and deference. How can such distinctions be experienced, as contrasted with merely knowing that they exist as "strange customs in foreign lands"? Experience appears to mean observing the distinctions, or using them, until they no longer seem alien.

The learning of a language can make several other contributions toward the learner's development, apart from his understanding of a second culture. It can teach how much we are demanding of others if we expect them to learn our language. It can make us more language-conscious, more attentive to the phenomenon of language and its functions in our life—a blind spot in the self-understanding of most bearers of our American culture, which results in most of us proving to be poor craftsmen when we are forced to organize words consciously. And a language rightly learned gives us a method and the self-confidence to learn whatever we need or want of other languages in later life—an ability that certainly would strengthen what is now a weak point in our culture.

The need for a second culture in our young people's development seems bound to become greater. Meanwhile, applied psychology and linguistics are steadily increasing the efficiency of language learning. At some point, the time seems bound to come when the most economical approach to a culture will include enough of the language for at least simple communication and the reading of representative literature.

In my judgment, that time has now arrived.

NEED FOR CULTURAL SYNTHESIS

How can the curriculum enable the learner to assimilate what he needs—just for the purpose of cross-cultural understanding—of a foreign sociocultural system including whatever of its language, literature, and history will serve economically toward that purpose? Let us answer this question as far as possible on the plane of practical devices, assuming that the understanding that we contrive to impart exists, or will exist, in a usable state.

We need to be able to assume that we have at our disposal a synthesis of the understanding an adult should have concerning cultures and societies in general, his own and his second sociocultural system. I suggest choosing the end of college education, rather than of secondary schooling, as the target point for completion of the cycle. The objective most worth formulating is an adult understanding, and this is the objective that scholars and scientists are competent to define. A cultural synthesis would define the curriculum's long-range objective, in terms of content essential for understanding at an adult level. But childhood and adolescence are not only a preparation for adulthood; they should have their own fulfillment and satisfactions. The long-range objectives and the more immediate objectives have to be reconciled, in the devices we use to make the requisite content assimilable into the process of the learner's life.[19]

The first step toward applying a cultural synthesis is to assign each of its items to the earliest age level at which the item can be grasped. The National Council for the Social Studies, in its Curriculum Series, has produced excellent examples of the needed kind of working syllabus, within the limitations of the synthesis that was

[19] I am assuming that the culture of an individual, and also of an epoch, is an interplay between process and content—the universally human activity of thought and sensitivity to feeling, interacting with the dated and localized content of a particular "culture" and social structure. I have examined this assumption in "Toward Agreement on Cultural Essentials," *Journal of General Education,* January, 1958, pp. 7–27.

available.[20] At this step, the central role devolves on those expert in the learner's growth and development. But the specialists in the materials to be taught can be very useful in their accessory roles. They know what knowledge and experience in their fields can arouse interest and motivate initiative at each age level.

In general, the experience of and knowledge about a given item should probably both be assigned to the same age level; but exceptions and complications are inevitable. The child who enjoys learning a nursery rhyme, or learning to exchange amenities with a foreigner, can have significant knowledge of what he is doing, yet at a later age he will be able to build the same experience into a much more general understanding. It is also possible, at least after childhood, for ideas to precede their realization in experience. John Dewey once mentioned that some of his ideas had first come to him wholly by logical inference and it was only later that they were confirmed experientially.

After the essential content has been arranged by age levels we can organize the items into meaningful sequences so that the successive stages will coincide with the developing interests of the learner. In this complex step lies the hope of improving our crowded curriculum. If we skillfully organize the sequences, approaching old topics from new directions, we can achieve much of our cross-cultural objective by showing new relationships instead of by adding new substance; and we can make some old content so much more exciting that ideas we now teach over and over again—as in the case of grammar and good usage—will be grasped more quickly. Energy will thus be freed for whatever new content is selected. It is a heartening sign that the director of the Anthropology Curriculum Study Project believes that an introductory course in anthropology may be unnecessary for the purpose of adding her discipline's large contribution to the curriculum; she considers that we might gain more by incorporating the needed content into other sequences, from kindergarten on.[21]

PROPOSED CURRICULAR SEQUENCE

Now let me try to picture a model sequence designed to carry out the learner's essential purpose of experiencing empathically how

[20] See Nos. 4 (1956) through 11 (1961).
[21] See footnote 14.

"life" feels and how "reality" is pictured in his second culture. I shall postulate that if we draw into this sequence all the essential experience of the culture and social structure that can be given most efficiently through the culture's language, the time required for a modest, active competence in the language can be justified as a means of gaining cross-cultural understanding, without considering the other benefits to the learner. The interacting knowledge about the culture and social structure would meanwhile be given partly in parallel sequences dealing with the general nature of societies and cultures, but the language sequence would apply the general knowledge, elaborate the descriptive knowledge of the target culture, and compare that system with the learner's mother culture.

The model would begin in the lowest grades with songs that are sung by children of the same age in the foreign country, simple poems, stories, and proverbs, selected for the cultural themes or social behavior they can be used to exemplify. The selections should have artistic merit besides illustrating some feature of the foreign culture or society. (They will of course be easier for the learner if they are chosen from those already borrowed into his own culture.) Ideal for introducing French, German, or Danish culture, for example, are the fables and fairy tales that have been given their classic form in those languages; for these literary genres yield immediately, even to young children, a part of the attitudes and values they embody, and they store up in the learner's mind a vivid experience of the culture, which will interact with his broadening knowledge as he grows.

Filmed episodes would be used, in which children of the foreign country would "model" the social patterns to be learned. The classroom teacher would add some comment, conveying whatever insights have been assigned to this age level: perhaps, for example, an observation on the common humanity of all children and the relative unimportance of surface differences. Expressions for greetings, for "please," for "thank you," etc., would likewise be introduced from the beginning, as short "situational dialogues" presented on film and film strip, with comment on the universality of kindness and thoughtfulness, and the necessity of using the proprieties customary in the culture. At this early age, children should acquire a "feeling" for the language and for what it expresses, along with correct pronunciation, intonation, and syntax. Comment which would include descriptive generalizations about the foreign society and culture would come later at the fourth-grade level.

From the third or fourth grade through the sixth, situational dialogues can be learned and acted out. These are best presented through a coordinated use of films, film strips, and tapes. The audio-visual presentation enables the pupils to understand the meaning of the dialogue without the interference of English. The comment should now be preceded by first-hand observation: the films and film strips will show surface manifestations of the culture, whether the films are staged from controlled script, as here, or taken from real life, as later exhibits would be. But the learner is dependent on the descriptive comment, which has been neglected, for an understanding of the generalized ideas that confer significance on the illustrative details. It can be an absorbing game for a class to sleuth out social and cultural details observable in authentic models: how children act toward grown-ups, how close the people stand to one another in conversing, what their facial expressions and tone of voice mean, and so on.[22] Soon the children will be ready to be taught some of the regularities in the target system: descriptive knowledge will be meaningful and easy to remember because it summarizes what they have observed. And since they have also participated momentarily in the culture, by acting out and living what they have observed, their knowledge will be on its way toward freedom from the egocentric "Gee whiz" attitude toward "foreign customs."

In order to present needed generalizations before a class is able to discuss them in the foreign language, and still avoid spending contact time speaking English, the students can be given brief formulations to take home, after they have been motivated in class to read these with curiosity. The curiosity aroused can also motivate children to look into encyclopedias and read source books in English. But students are ready surprisingly soon to carry on class discussions in the language, asking simple questions and grasping more complicated answers, provided the instructional methods and ma-

---

[22] Nelson Brooks, in his *Language and Language Learning; Theory and Practice* (New York: Harcourt, Brace and Co. 1960) lists 23 key questions an anthropologist is likely to pose in observing a culture (pp. 83–84). He then adapts the list to the interests of young foreign learners, with the result of a very useful inventory of 64 items (pp. 87–92).

terials conduce to a "coordinate system" of language acquisition instead of a "compound system," as these terms are used by Nelson Brooks in *Language and Language Learning*, (Harcourt, Brace and World, Second Edition, 1964, pp. 48 and 267).

For seventh- and eighth-grade students, it becomes increasingly important to avoid monotony by interspersing the situational dialogues with stories and poems, which from the start can be works of literary merit. Some junior-high students, with the help of a gifted teacher, have created authentic Guignol puppet shows in the classroom, making their own puppets and scenery and writing the scripts. Later a class can watch a motion picture to see what values and behavior patterns it reveals. Students find it fun to try out their knowledge of the culture by guessing and discussing, halfway through a film, how they expect the story to end.

In senior high school, after several years of instruction in the language, literature can be introduced to give experience of just about any feature of a society or culture one may wish: its greatness or its regularities (once they are established), its present or its past, its conscious thought or unconscious assumptions, its critically examined ideas and its vague expressions such as our "the American way," which pass unchallenged because the culture-bearers consider the referents self-evident.

Literature read in the original can give a many-sided experience that the reader of translations cannot suspect. To him one may explain that Racine achieves miracles of sublimity by combining simple, everyday words with a subtle elegance that gives a feeling of greatness; but such descriptions mean little if they allude to experience that is not there.

Literature and the documentary approach need not be kept separate. Juan Marichal of Harvard arranges for his advanced students, on a tour of Spain, to interview a contemporary author they have studied. Authors cannot oblige all foreign students this way, to be sure. But how inspiring a film of such an interview might be for thousands of students interested in Spanish culture, provided they have a modest competence in Spanish.

The language gives access to newspapers and magazines, radio broadcasts and television, with their interpretations of current affairs. Students can make clippings files on their personal interests, and they can collect theme expressions from the writings and behavior of the culture bearers they observe and have the satisfaction of building their own account of themes in the culture; without the language, they would be restricted and dependent. This freedom of approach makes it possible to penetrate more effectively into the history of the culture, with individual excursions into any period or field.

Whatever a student's central interest, the language will free him to follow it into his second culture. The high school or college student of mathematics who has chosen French culture, for example, would be fascinated not only by classical writings in that field from Descartes to Poincaré, but also by some of the essays still being produced by the authors of the *Traité d' Analyse* who write under the fictitious name of Bourbaki.

If one can eventually visit a foreign country, kowledge of the language frees him to converse with people in various sectors of the society. A person who has learned about a second culture in the manner we have been considering would make such a purposeful tourist that a dull moment would be difficult for him and his hosts as well.

If one never visits the country, the new media now can give vivid experience of its life. A filmed course such as "Parlons Français"[23] needs only to combine the rich experience it already offers with equally authentic descriptive knowledge—which awaits the process of synthesis. The new media will not stop where they now are, however. Museums are developing vivid new presentations of a people's everyday life as well as its exceptional achievements; and these concentrated exhibits can at least be filmed if they cannot travel about. Most striking of all, perhaps, is the proposal by F. Rand Morton of the University of Michigan that the language-laboratory booth and the teaching machine be transformed into a multisensory "acculturation chamber," which might educate the learner to respond to cultural situations much as a jet pilot is trained to react to the conditions of supersonic flight.[24] This product of his creative imagination may be no more impractical than his once visionary idea of a language laboratory in which the student would be able to dial minimal-step exercises at his own pace—a

[23] See footnote 17.

[24] "The Language Laboratory as a Teaching Machine," *International Journal of American Linguistics*, October, 1960, p. 165.

decidedly practical idea, since the "Dialog" laboratory, made by Chester Electronics, is now in operation in scores of schools and colleges.

Short of an optimum sequence such as the one I have sketched, it is still possible to use the foreign language effectively in giving experience of the second culture. In the intermediate grades, many of the items summarized in the column of 10 essentials could be presented in situational films simpler than the candid documentaries that the students in the model sequence would be able to handle by that time. At the high school and college levels literature can be studied, though less freely than with students who are more at home in the language. Other promising devices are syllabi and courses designed to add the experiential side to the study of expository materials, which are steadily improving.[25]

The syllabus approach would enable a student, with the help of his language teacher and other teachers, to take initiative in extending his experience of his second culture in accord with his personal interests. By making very selective suggestions, the syllabus could save him a great deal of hunting in the library. By spreading out the possible fields and activities, the device can broaden his view of his own interests. The nearest approximation thus far to such a *vade mecum* is probably the set of "Guides for Majors" recently produced by the several associations of language teachers at the suggestion of the Modern Language Association.[26]

One type of high school or college course designed to give experience of a culture is evolving from the old "civilization course," in much the same way that modern cultural museums are present-

[25] For example, Clyde and Florence Kluckhohn's worthwhile and readable exposition of cultural values and social structure will be published in the fall of 1963, somewhat shortened, as "Unit I: Man, Society, and Social Order" in Donald H. Riddle (ed.), *Problems and Promise of American Democracy* (New York: McGraw-Hill Inc., 1963), which is a high school text. See also footnotes 2, 13, and 14.

[26] Richard M. Chadbourne and Edward J. Geary, "A Program of French Studies: A Guide for the College Student," *French Review*, December, 1961, pp. 221–251.

Gardiner H. London and Robert G. Mead, Jr., "A Program of Hispanic Studies for the College Student," *Hispania*, May, 1961, pp. 383–406.

Olga Ragusa, "A Program of Italian Studies (Suggestions for the College Student)," *Italica*, June, 1961, pp. 161–173.

ing the ordinary life of significant groups in a society as well as the society's exceptional achievements. Another type of course, soon to be tried at the University of Washington on the graduate level, will start from the behavior and ideas of a population and give practice in organizing the data into intelligible wholes such as cultural "themes" or Parsonian "subsystems."

In one way or another, then, the curriculum can give every learner some understanding of a second culture. The learner's understanding must be expected to vary according to the thoroughness with which we in education organize and coordinate the sequences that make up the curriculum.

CULTURAL SYNTHESIS PREREQUISITE TO CURRICULAR CHANGE

This brings us to the last and most difficult problem of our inquiry, the practical steps to be taken on the plane of synthesis.

We first need a synthesis of enlightening knowledge about societies and cultures, to be arranged by the experts in human development according to the age level at which each item becomes understandable. The items of knowledge must then be organized, with experiences to vivify them in logical sequences.

Our need cannot be met by a series of departmental syntheses, nor even by three or four large partial integrations. The super-departments called divisions of knowledge are still disruptive and destructive of the coherence we must strive for if our objective is wisdom rather than a set of museum exhibits showing what one would think to be wisdom if one saw only this or that or the other side of the whole. The academic structure of departments and divisions, useful as it is, fails conspicuously when we build curricular sequences of a new type, illustrated by an interdivisional approach to civic education or to the understanding of rational method.[27]

The disruptive effect operates in subtler ways, moreover. If in

---

[27] I have urged in an earlier paper the need to sustain progress on four levels of inquiry: practical application, synthesis of knowledge, critique of the synthesis in use—and free inquiry, which differs from the three lower levels in not having to be relevant to accepted ideas but is necessary, since without it the three other levels become bankrupt of fresh ideas ("The Agenda for a New Generation," *Journal of General Education,* October, 1957, pp. 190–204). See also footnote 19.

teaching the humanities we use a reading book about Indians, about "foreign lands," or about American society, which misinforms the learner from the standpoint of the social sciences, we are missing a precious opportunity for economizing our efforts. What is worse, we are confusing the learner and wasting his time, which is more valuable than ours since he is younger and more impressionable and will probably retain what he learns after we have forgotten and been forgotten. Whatever sort of sequences we use, we must improve our success in making their internal details corroborate, not contradict, what is taught in other sequences.

In short, interdisciplinary coordination between curricular sequences necessitates the same coordination inside them. Whether or not our applied sequences teach in separate compartments about our culture and other cultures, or about science, social science, and humanities, we cannot escape the need for truly interdisciplinary coherence of outlook and for cooperation of specialists.

The appalling difficulty of culture-wide synthesis in our complex modern cultures arises from several sources. The fundamental source is our diversity of ultimate "grounds of meaning," or ultimate interpretations of reality. Two psychologists, for example, may disagree fundamentally on the meaning of an experimental event and the inferences that can be drawn from it. Another source of the difficulty is the fact that synthesis requires collaboration, and our individualistic society rewards achievements that can be signed individually. Still another source is our increasing "overspecialization" —by which we mean not excessive knowledge of a specialty but deficient understanding of other sectors in a culture-wide synthesis.

Our national culture has gradually become fragmented. The process has advanced in cycles that closely follow the thirty-year spans called "generations"[28]—a pattern that suggests an interesting implication for the present moment.

In the generation whose policies took shape about 1850, the college curriculum was broken into departmental specialties on the supposition, then valid, that essentially the same "ground of meaning" would be assumed in every discipline. The generation of 1880

[28] I have presented the evidence to support this contention in "La Evolución de la cultura académica en los Estado Unidos de 1760 a 1940," *Pensamiento Peruano,* November–December, 1945, pp. 11–18, January–February, 1926, pp. 21–28.

introduced the elective system, which extended the decentralization from academic fields to individual learners.

Then began the attempts to reverse the trend. The generation of 1910 tried to assure that our intellectual leadership would possess a culture-wide understanding by requiring the distribution of elective courses in the several divisions of knowledge, assuming that the samples would be mutually alternative, which they proved not to be.

The next generation, whose achievement culminated about 1940, endeavored to replace the alternative fragments with survey courses. This was "the general education movement" in higher education, paralleled by the movement of "integration" in high-school curriculums. Now that we can look back on that movement as a thing of the past, I think one can see that its tragic flaw was to attempt the organization of human understanding at the applied level of the curriculum.

The lesson we would have to learn, in order to better the modest success of that generation, is that coordination at the applied level depends on a deliberate, interdisciplinary endeavor on the plane of culture-wide synthesis. If the thirty-year cycles continue, as I believe they have since 1760, the success or failure of our generation will depend on how we use our energies between now and about 1970.

Given the interest of various professional groups, public support, and available research funds, precisely what can we do that would be adequate to our opportunity and to the danger that we may pile up one more comparative failure?

I suggest a program of synthesis organized separately from that of educational application, so that we cannot mistake success at the applied level, where we Americans excel, for success at the level of synthesis. Separate organization would mean that separate centers should provide the clearing-house service necessary, at both levels, for an informal, nonregimenting sort of leadership.

While the applied psychologists, curriculum designers, and teachers and educational administrators would take the lead on the applied plane, the research scholars needed on the synthesis plane might be brought together by organizations in the social sciences and humanities for the synthesizing of general knowledge about societies and cultures; and by the language, literature, and area-study specialists for the descriptive knowledge of specific sociocultural systems, including our own. Morris Opler, currently president of the American Anthropological Association, and the foremost developer of the thematic description of cultures, has remarked that while anthropologists tend to go from one culture to another, the specialists in a foreign language and literature tend to stay with one culture, so that these specialists may well be the proper persons to take a central responsibility in the study of the foreign cultures whose languages we teach. Margaret Mead has added the pertinent observation that the study of a culture should be undertaken by teams representing three or more cultural groups: natives to the culture and representatives of at least two outside cultures.

This suggests that foreign language teachers, and their professional associations and journals, should lead in describing as well as teaching foreign cultures. The teachers should carry on research in areas of personal competence. The associations could establish contact with other researchers on the same culture, both within its territory and in any other parts of the world. The journals could organize sets of status studies so that all may keep track of the rapid progress we need to make.

As we build a framework for cultivating the neglected level of synthesis, however, we must bear in mind above all that contributions added up end to end, from one discipline at a time, are not enough. Each of us, and each of our professional organizations, faces the almost impossible task of fitting a specialized contribution into a synthesis which alone can endow the contribution with its true meaning and usefulness.

[Note: An extended version of Dr. Nostrand's paper is available by interlibrary loan from the University of Washington Library, Seattle 5, Washington.]

THE RELATION OF BILINGUALISM
TO INTELLIGENCE[1]

ELIZABETH PEAL AND
WALLACE E. LAMBERT

The supposed adverse effect of bilingualism on learning has often been an argument against teaching a foreign language in the elementary grades. In their study of this problem Professors Peal and Lambert of McGill University evaluate previous experiments and then report on one of their own which was designed to avoid earlier inaccuracies. Their findings fully vindicate foreign language teaching at an early age and make bilingualism a desirable goal. In reporting their research many of the facets and factors of bilingualism are touched upon and briefly examined. This monograph is a detached and wholly scientific treatment of the subject.

Psychologists and linguists have wondered whether bilingualism affects intellectual functioning since as early as the 1920s when Saer (1923) and Smith (1923) reported research on the topic. Numerous studies since then have attempted to determine whether monolingual and bilingual young people differ in intelligence as measured

Reprinted by permission of the authors and the American Psychological Association from *Psychological Monographs*, Vol. 76, No. 27, Whole No. 546, 1962.

[1] This research was carried out with the financial support of the Carnegie Corporation of New York, through a subvention to W. E. Lambert. The authors are grateful to G. Barbeau and T. Boulanger of the Catholic School Commission of Montreal and to the principals and teachers of the six schools used in this study for their assistance and cooperation during the testing programs in their schools. Special thanks are expressed to Irene Vachon-Spilka for her assistance in translation and administration of the tests. The writer is indebted to R. C.

143

by standard tests. A large proportion of investigators have concluded from their studies that bilingualism has a detrimental effect on intellectual functioning. The bilingual child is described as being hampered in his performance on intelligence tests in comparison with the monolingual child. A smaller proportion of the investigations have found little or no influence of bilingualism on intelligence, in that no significant difference between bilinguals and monolinguals on tests of intelligence was apparent. Only two empirical studies were encountered which suggest that bilingualism may have favorable intellectual consequences.

An attempt will be made to understand these seemingly contradictory findings by critically reviewing representative studies reporting each type of effect. The studies will be evaluated mainly in terms of how well other relevant variables were controlled, particularly certain personal characteristics which are known to be related to intelligence and which should be taken into account when the effect of bilingualism on intelligence is examined.

In the design typically used, where two groups of subjects are being compared on intelligence, it is necessary to match the groups on as many features known or suspected to correlate with intelligence as possible so that the difference between the groups, if any, may be attributed to linguality itself. This model requires a clear definition of monolingualism and bilingualism in order that the two can be objectively determined without risk of overlap or confusion. Socioeconomic status has been repeatedly found to be related to intelligence and linguistic development (Jones, 1960; McCarthy, 1954). McCarthy states that "there is considerable evidence in the literature to indicate that there exists a marked relationship between socioeconomic status of the family and the child's linguistic development" (p. 586). From past research it is well established that girls are more advanced than boys in language development, especially in the early years. They have a larger vocabulary and are more skilled in the use of words. Since most intelligence tests draw heavily on verbal skills, it would be ad-

Gardner (McGill) and R. M. Olton (McGill) for writing the necessary programs for the IBM 650 computer, without which the statistical analysis would not have been possible. Thanks are also due to G. A. Ferguson (McGill) for his advice on statistical matters.

visable to have approximately equal numbers of boys and girls in the groups to be compared. Furthermore, groups should also be matched for age. The educational background of children may also affect their performance on standardized tests of intelligence. This variable could be approximately controlled by using subjects from the same schools or school system. The intelligence tests should be constructed and standardized on a population similar to the one being tested, especially with respect to language. A translation of a test from one language to another, without standardization, might bias the results for or against one group. Also, the tests should be given in the language in which the bilinguals are most proficient.

Studies Supporting the Detrimental Effects of Bilingualism on Intelligence

The studies in this category may be arbitrarily divided into two subgroups. The first of these consists of those which found that monolingual groups performed better than bilingual on *both* verbal and nonverbal intelligence tests. Can the depressed scores of the bilinguals be attributed to bilingualism itself, or were there uncontrolled variables which might account for the obtained differences between groups?

After testing 1,400 children in Wales, Saer (1923) reported a statistically significant inferiority of rural bilingual children when compared with rural monolingual children on the Stanford-Binet scale. This inferiority became consistently greater in degree with each year from seven to eleven years of age. Saer attempted to explain this trend in terms of the "mental confusion" encountered by the bilingual children. When urban children only were compared he found no significant difference between monolinguals and bilinguals. It should be noted that socioeconomic class was not controlled in this research and that a Welsh translation of the Stanford-Binet test was used.

Pintner (1932) administered the Pintner Language and Non-language tests to monolingual and bilingual groups in each of three schools in New York City. The results obtained are inconclusive in the sense that in one school monolinguals were superior on both tests while in another they were inferior and in the third, there was no difference between the groups. There was no control for socioeconomic class in this study and bilingualism was determined by looking at the child's name!

The most important study in this grouping was the one by Jones and Stewart (1951). After surveying the studies done prior to 1951 in Wales, they concluded that bilingual and monolingual groups differed little in nonverbal intelligence tests and that monolingual groups were usually superior to billingual groups in verbal tests. The design of their experiment was based on these conclusions. A verbal test and a nonverbal test were given to monolingual and bilingual groups in rural districts. The children were between ten years six months and eleven years six months of age. The monolinguals were found to score significantly higher on both types of tests. The two groups were equated statistically, by the analysis of covariance, on nonverbal IQ and the differences between them on verbal IQ were then noted. "It was therefore concluded that the bilingual children were significantly inferior to the monolingual children, even after full allowance has been made for the initial difference in the nonverbal intelligence tests" (Jones & Stewart, 1951). It could be argued that the bilinguals may have encountered greater difficulties because for them the tests were translated into Welsh, their vernacular, but not standardized in the Welsh culture. This may have lowered their scores on the verbal test. However, this would not account for the original difference in nonverbal IQ. After further investigations, Jones later conceded that the significant difference in nonverbal test scores observed in all his studies may have arisen from occupational rather than linguistic variations between the groups. Thus the complete work of Jones and his collaborators has, according to James (1960), "drawn attention to the influence of socioeconomic factors in comparisons between groups of monolingual and bilingual children and has emphasized the importance of such factors in the correct interpretation of test results."

In his most recent article, Jones (1960) criticized a study published by Lewis (1959) for the inadequate treatment given to socioeconomic class. Lewis had reported a statistically significant difference in favor of the monolinguals corresponding to about eight IQ points on a nonverbal intelligence test. Apart from his failure to control socioeconomic class, his method of selecting his groups was an improvement over previous studies. He assessed the linguistic background of ten-year-old children by means of a language questionnaire and attempted to make each group as homogeneous as possible.

Several studies (Graham, 1925; Mead, 1927; Rigg, 1928; Wang, 1926) have found that monolingual American groups performed better than children with various foreign backgrounds on intelligence tests. All these studies lacked controls for age and socioeconomic class, and in some bilingualism was not adequately measured.

The second subdivision of studies showing the unfavorable effect of bilingualism encompasses those which reported that monolinguals scored better than bilinguals on verbal tests, but the bilinguals scored better or as well as monolinguals on performance or nonverbal tests.

A rather well-controlled study by Seidl (1937) found that monolinguals were superior to bilinguals on all verbal tests, but bilinguals were superior to monolinguals on performance measures. The 1916 Stanford-Binet scale and the Arthur Point Scale of Performance were the tests used. The two groups of subjects, whose linguality was determined by a questionnaire, were matched on sex and age. However, the mean occupational level of the monolinguals' parents was in the laboring class while the bilinguals' was semiskilled labor. This difference in social class may partly account for the results. Seidl, however, concluded that the language handicap of the bilinguals interfered with their verbal IQ scores.

Pintner and Keller (1922) gave the Stanford-Binet and the Pintner Nonlanguage Group Test to two groups, one English-speaking and the other of foreign background, and found that the latter group received lower scores on the Stanford-Binet than on tests in which a minimum of English was required. The authors concluded that these children were penalized because the Stanford-Binet was used. However, no measures of bilingualism were used and no mention was made of the social status of the children's families.

Darcy (1946) reported on research carried out with 212 American preschool children of Italian parentage. In this study, the relevant variables were quite well controlled. The subjects were classified as bilingual or monolingual by a rating scale; the groups were matched for age, sex, and social class. The Stanford-Binet

(1937 Revision) was used as the verbal measure, and the Atkins Object-Fitting Test as the nonverbal. Darcy found that the monolingual group scored significantly higher than the bilingual on the Stanford-Binet, but lower on the Atkins test. She concluded that the bilingual subjects of her investigation suffered from a language handicap in their performance on the Stanford-Binet scale. However, the subjects were so young (from 2–6 to 4–6 years) that it would not be advisable to draw any general conclusions from this study. Even if the bilinguals suffered from a language handicap at this age, they might overcome it later. Also the intelligence of infants and preschool children is known to be somewhat difficult to determine accurately and depends more on performance items than on verbal.

Another study from which generalizations should not be drawn is that by Altus (1953) since both groups used were "dull" school children. They may have been classed as dull for various reasons. The groups were equated on age, sex, and the Performance IQ of the Wechsler Intelligence Scale for Children (WISC). Differences in IQ on the Verbal scale averaged seventeen points in favor of the monolingual group. Altus suggests that linguistic difficulties interfered with normal functioning in the bilingual group.

An important technique for objectively measuring bilingualism was introduced by Johnson (1953). His Reaction Time Test, derived from the earlier work of Saer (1931), was a measure of linguistic balance obtained by dividing the number of words produced in English in five minutes, by the number of words produced in Spanish in five minutes. The subjects for his experiment were thirty Spanish-English bilingual boys in the United States between the ages of nine and twelve years. The Goodenough IQ for these children was about average for the total population, but the Otis IQ was considerably below average. Johnson's Test of Bilingualism was found to correlate negatively with the Otis (a verbal test) and positively with the Goodenough Draw-a-Man Test (a performance test). The more bilingual the subjects were the better they did on a performance test and the poorer on a verbal test.

Levinson (1959) tested American-born Jewish preschool monolingual and bilingual children of similar socioeconomic level and found them to perform alike on the Goodenough test and most subscales of the WISC. However, on the Stanford-Binet and the

WISC Arithmetic, Vocabulary, and Picture Arrangement subtests the monolinguals scored higher.

Many of these studies of the detrimental effects of bilingualism lacked important controls. Taking this into account, the weight of evidence so far presented seems to support the contention that there is no significant difference between monolinguals and bilinguals on nonverbal intelligence, but the bilinguals are likely to be handicapped on verbal intelligence measures. The need for further research with more complete controls becomes evident.

Studies Supporting the Favorable Effects of Bilingualism on Intelligence

The paucity of studies that have found a favorable intellectual effect accruing from bilingualism would seem to suggest that bilingualism may not be as advantageous as has been thought by many language teachers and educators. In a study conducted in London, England, Davies and Hughes (1927) reported the superiority of Jewish over non-Jewish children in arithmetic, English, and general intelligence. However, no measure of bilingualism was used and the Jewish children were assumed to be bilingual. Other controls such as age, sex, and social class were notably absent, as they were in the study by Stark (1940), who found that at ten and eleven years of age, bilinguals were superior to monolinguals on one form of a test. At a later age, this trend was reversed, but the measurement was made on a different form of the test. Stark concluded that children of "innate verbal facility" may find early bilingualism an asset to their mental development.

Studies Finding No Effect of Bilingualism on Intelligence[2]

From his study of Japanese and American children, Darsie (1926) concluded that the differences in general mental capacity between the two groups were slight. On some tests, the Japanese subjects were inferior while on others the Americans were inferior. However, the social class of these two groups was not comparable and no measure of bilingualism was employed.

[2] Several studies (Arthur, 1937; Bere, 1924; Feingold, 1924; Hirsch, 1926) which have reported that bilingualism has no effect on intelligence lack too many important controls to be worth considering in detail here.

The best controlled study in this category is that of Hill (1936) with Italian-American children. Bilingualism was determined by a questionnaire and on the basis of language background. The two groups were matched on sex, age, IQ, socioeconomic class, and mental age. No reliable differences were found in scores on verbal, nonverbal, and performance tests between monolinguals and bilinguals. However, it should be kept in mind that since the two groups were matched on mental age and IQ, only minor differences between them could be expected on intelligence subtests. Thus, there may have been a selection of brighter Italian-American children in this instance.

Pintner and Arsenian (1937) gave the Hoffman Bilingual Schedule to 459 Jewish children in New York City; all the children were Yiddish-English bilinguals. The 20 percent receiving the highest scores on the Hoffman test constituted a high bilingual group, and the 20 percent receiving the lowest scores, a low bilingual group. The mean verbal and nonverbal IQs of these two bilingual groups were compared, and no difference was found between them. The authors concluded that the relationship between intelligence and bilingualism is "practically zero" ($r = -.059$).

Spoerl (1944) tested all the bilingual freshmen enrolled at an American college. These were matched with a group of monolingual freshmen for sex, age, intelligence, and social class. A student was considered bilingual if he had learned two languages before school entrance. No differences were found between monolinguals and bilinguals on the 1937 Stanford-Binet or Purdue Placement Test. A slight inferiority was shown by the bilingual students on five of the verbal items of the Stanford-Binet scale. It is interesting to note, however, that the bilinguals had done consistently better in school work than the monolinguals even though their IQs did not differ significantly. Spoerl mentioned that a compensatory drive arising from a feeling of environmental insecurity may have been a contributing cause of the superiority of the bilinguals in academic achievement.

Arsenian's (1937) experiments with American-born Italian and American-born Jewish children were well controlled from the point of view of age, sex, socioeconomic class, and measurement of bilingualism. However, Darcy (1953) questions the adequacy of the tests used (Pintner Nonlanguage Test, and the Spearman Visual

Perception Test) as measures of intelligence. The Spearman test was not even standardized. Furthermore, there were no tests of verbal intelligence. Several different combinations of subjects were used in the analysis; and in the comparison between bilinguals and monolinguals, the number of subjects (thirty-eight of each group) was too small to permit definite conclusions. The findings are nevertheless of interest and of some importance. The extent of bilingualism did not vary from nine to fourteen years. There was only a very slight relation between intelligence and socioeconomic class. There was no difference between the two language groups as to intelligence or age-grade status. Arsenian concluded: "it may be stated that . . . there was discovered no retardation or acceleration in the mental development of children from ages nine to fourteen in the groups studied, which might be attributable to bilingualism as such" (p. 120).

In summary, it becomes apparent that it is necessary to control certain variables in this type of study before any conclusions can be drawn. The important variables to control seem to be socioeconomic class, sex, degree of bilinguality, age, and the actual tests used. In view of the weaknesses of the studies reviewed, the best general conclusion is that there is little evidence to suggest that bilinguals differ from monolinguals on nonverbal intelligence, but that there may be differences in verbal intelligence as measured by intelligence tests. At a certain stage in the learning of the second language, a bilingual may suffer from a "language handicap."

Theoretical Considerations

Theoretically, what would be the expected effects of bilingualism on intelligence or mental development? Few of the psychologists who have studied this problem have attempted any explanation beyond rather vague references to a "language handicap" or "mental confusion."

An inquiry into the effects of the learning of two languages on mental development demands a serious consideration of the broader question of the relation between language and thought, and modern psychology has generally eschewed this question. The apparent belief of many is that at least partial answers to the broad question may appear from the study of the interrelation of language and intelligence. Arsenian (1937), after examining various theories of language and thought, hypothesized that language and intelligence are not identical. In line with this hypothesis, he maintained that:

the influence of bilingualism, whatever for the moment we may suppose it to be, does not extend to the whole area of thinking or intelligence, but to that particular section where linguistic symbolism and schemata are involved in the thinking process.

Susanne Langer (1942) made a distinction between speech and thought. She argued that "It [speech] is the normal terminus of thought. . . . But in fact, speech is the natural outcome of only one kind of symbolic process" (p. 45). Assuming then, that language and thought are not isomorphic, how would the learning of two languages influence scores on intelligence tests, which obviously require thought?

Several writers, assuming a lack of identity between language and thought, suggest that the learning of two languages from childhood has favorable effects on the thinking process. Two writers in particular have made this point. Leopold (1949), after extensive observations of the mental development of his own child, felt that the bilingual child learns early to separate the sound of a word from its referent. He writes:

I attribute this attitude of detachment from words confidently to the bilingualism. Constantly hearing the same things referred to by different words from two languages, she had her attention drawn to essentials, to content instead of form (p. 188).[3]

S. J. Evans of Wales (1953) also argues that the:

teaching of Welsh along with English does what the efficient study of any two languages must do: it frees the mind from the tyranny of words. It is extremely difficult for a monoglot to dissociate thought from words, but he who can express his ideas in two languages is emancipated (p. 43).

These arguments, suggesting that a bilingual has an intellectual advantage over a monolingual because his thinking is not restricted by language, give support to those few studies which found favorable effects of bilingualism on intelligence and mental development.

[3] From W. F. Leopold, *Speech Development of a Bilingual Child,* Vol. 3 (Chicago: Northwestern University Press, 1949). Used by permission. Copyright 1949.

In view of these arguments, it also seems possible that the type of benefit that comes from bilingualism might not become apparent on standard intelligence tests. It could be argued that the studies finding no difference or a deficit for bilinguals were simply using inappropriate measures.

O'Doherty (1958) suggests that it is necessary in any consideration of the influence of bilingualism on intelligence to distinguish between two types of bilinguals for whom the effects may differ— the pseudobilingual and the genuine bilingual. The pseudobilingual knows one language much better than the other and does not use his second language in communication. The true bilingual masters both at an early age and has facility with both as means of communication. O'Doherty states that there can be no question that bilingualism of the genuine kind is an intellectual advantage. "The pseudobilingual is the real problem, since very often he fails to master either language, while the bilingual by definition has mastered both" (p. 285). Thus, O'Doherty's writings lend additional support to the notion that "genuine" bilingualism may be an asset.

Can we find any theoretical support for the detrimental effects of bilingualism on intelligence? Weinreich (1953) makes the point that any individual who speaks two or more languages will experience interference due to the contact between them. That is, a bilingual's speech in each language will be different than it would have been had he only learned one language. The extent of the interference in any particular case will depend in part on certain linguistic differences between the two language systems.

The more numerous the mutually exclusive forms and patterns in each, the greater is the learning problem and the potential area of interference. But the mechanisms of interference . . . would appear to be the same whether the contact is between Chinese and French or between two subvarieties of English (pp. 1–2).

The language handicap reported for bilinguals could thus be attributed to interlingual interference. The effect of this interference would show up on verbal tests, but could be expected to influence performance on nonverbal tests only in so far as these depend on verbal skills.

It could be hypothesized that bilingualism might affect the very structure of intellect. Such a hypothesis could be developed from a current conceptualization of intellect as consisting of factors. Guilford (1956) and others propose that intelligence is composed of a general factor and many different specific factors, each of which may be isolated by factor analytic methods. Ferguson (1954) has put forth the thesis that human abilities are learned. Stated another way, a large proportion of an individual's intellectual ability is acquired through experience and its transfer from one situation to another. The "factors of intellect" are gradually developed through a series of learning situations. This learning process may proceed in different ways for different individuals depending on their experiences. Thus the structure of intellect will very likely vary from one individual to another. The developmental process for monolinguals and bilinguals is certainly different in respect to language, and the learning of abilities depends greatly on language. Bilinguals could have different and more complex contexts for learning than monolinguals. Arsenian (1937) states that, "The two different words in two different language systems for the same referent may carry different connotations and put the bilingual person in contact with two worlds of experience." We could, therefore, hypothesize that the structure of the intellect of monolinguals and bilinguals might differ in various aspects. Guilford (1956) states: "to the extent that factors [of intellect] are developed by experience, they would appear at such ages as the effects of experience have sufficiently crystallized" (p. 287). That is, the emergence of an intellectual factor is dependent on the accumulation of experiences. From this notion, it seems reasonable to propose that such factors would appear at different ages in monolinguals and bilinguals, since their linguistic and cultural experiences are quite different. It may therefore be important to discover the nature of the effects of bilingualism on intellectual functioning.

Some recent studies have emphasized the importance, for second language learning, of an individual's attitude toward the second-language community. Using a language involves personal participation in a second culture. Christophersen (1948) has made the point that a bilingual person belongs to two different communities and possesses two personalities which may be in conflict if the two language communities are in social conflict. Changes in the bilingual's attitude toward a language community may account for the variation in his efficiency in the use of that language which could even affect his performance on intelligence tests. Arsenian (1937) mentions that, "National, religious, and political sympathies or antipathies determine the affective tone or the *attitude* of a bilinguist toward the second language, and they introduce, therefore, important differences among bilinguists." The studies of Lambert, Hodgson, Gardner, and Fillenbaum (1960), and Anisfeld, Bogo, and Lambert (1961) suggest that certain community-wide negative stereotypes toward speakers of a particular language may have a negative influence on a bilingual who uses that language. He may be aware, for example, of the ridicule coming from others when he uses that language and this may constitute an intellectual interference in that language for him. This could have a detrimental effect for a bilingual when functioning in one of his languages if he had associations of inferiority or shame with that language. However, a bilingual even in Montreal's bicultural community could have favorable attitudes toward the use of both his own and the other language. The fact that an individual becomes bilingual in a bicultural community may be attributable to a favorable disposition toward both the linguistic communities, whereas the monolingual may be retarded in his acquisition of a second language because of his unfavorable attitudes toward both the other culture and its language.

STATEMENT OF THE PROBLEM

The present research was designed to examine more extensively the effects of bilingualism on the intellectual functioning of children and to explore the relations between bilingualism, school achievement, and students' attitudes to the second language community.

In line with previous findings, it was predicted that two groups of subjects, one monolingual and the other bilingual, should not differ significantly on nonverbal IQ, but might differ on verbal IQ as measured by intelligence tests standardized in the native language of both the monolinguals and bilinguals. The monolinguals were expected to perform significantly better than the bilinguals on the verbal tests. The groups were matched on socioeconomic class, sex, and age. They were selected from the same school system and where possible the same school. Several measures of degree of bilingualism were employed to determine objectively the bilingualism of each subject.

It was further predicted that the attitudes of the monolinguals would likely be less favorable to the other language group than those of the bilinguals, and that individual differences in these attitudes would be related to school achievement in the second language. For this purpose, several measures of attitude were used.

It was also thought that a relationship might be found between bilingualism and school grade. This idea stemmed from the work of Morrison (1958) who found that bilinguals were as much as 1½ years behind their age norms in school.

In line with the hypothesis that the structure of intellect might be different for the two groups of subjects, we used a wide variety of measures of different types of intelligence. It was predicted that bilinguals and monolinguals would perform differently on various types of subtests of intelligence. This is, in effect, an attempt to investigate the *nature* of the effect of bilingualism on intelligence.

METHOD

Subjects

The subjects were ten-year-old school children from six French schools under the jurisdiction of the Catholic School Commission of Montreal. Three of these schools were located in the western region of Montreal, and the remainder in the extreme eastern region of the island. All were roughly classified as middle class schools by the School Commission. In each school all the ten-year-olds available were tested, regardless of school grade.

Procedure

The testing took place in the classroom and was divided into five sessions of one hour each, spaced about a week apart. All instructions to the children were given in French by native speakers of French, except for the test of English vocabulary which was administered by a native speaker of English.

In the first session, all the ten-year-olds were administered a questionnaire and several tests to determine degree of bilingualism. The questionnaire sought general information about the child and his family, specific information about his language history, and details about his father's occupation. Three tests were used to determine whether the child was a *balanced bilingual,* that is, equally skilled in French and English, or whether he was a monolingual. His own self-ratings of his ability in English were also taken into account.

Criteria for Selection of Subjects

Word Association Test. The first test of bilingualism was based on an association fluency technique developed by Lambert (1956). Modifications were introduced to make the technique appropriate for use with children in a group setting. French and English words were presented alternately and the children were asked to write down as many words as they could think of in the same language as the stimulus which seemed to "go with" or "belong with" that word. An interval of sixty seconds was allowed for association to each word. For each subject the sum of the associations to all the French words was calculated (NF). The same was done for the associations to the English words (NE). These two sums were used to form a balance score:

$$\text{Balance} = \frac{\text{NF} - \text{NE}}{\text{NF} + \text{NE}} \times 100$$

A zero score indicates perfect balance between the two languages, a plus score means French dominance, and a minus score English dominance.

Word Detection Test. This test was also a modification of one developed by Lambert, Havelka, and Gardner (1959). It was postulated that bilingualism would express itself in the facility of finding short embedded English and French words in a series of letters such as *dansonodend.* The subjects were given four such series and allowed 1½ minutes to work on each. Approximately equal numbers of English and French words were embedded in each group of letters. A balance score was obtained here, similar to the one described above.

Peabody Picture Vocabulary Test. This test, derived from Dunn (1959), was used because it made possible a distinction between oral and graphic language skills. It was thought that there might be bilinguals who were not able to read or write English, but who would nevertheless be balanced bilinguals in the oral sense. Such bilinguals might be at a disadvantage on the two previous tests which required some knowledge of written English. The test consists of a series of plates, each of which has four pictures of objects or actions numbered 1–4. The examiner says one English word aloud and the subject has to point to the picture corresponding to the word. To adapt this for use with a group, we flashed each plate on a screen by means of an epidiascope, and an examiner pronounced the word in English. The children wrote down the number of the picture which corresponded to the English word pronounced. In this way, no graphic skills in English were required of the subjects. Twenty-one plates of increasing difficulty were presented. A score of the number of correct responses out of twenty-one was obtained for each child.

Subjective Self-Rating Score. The subjects were asked to rate their ability to speak, read, write, and understand English on four-point scales ranging from "not at all" (scored 1) to "very fluently" (scored four). For each subject an oral self-rating score was obtained by summing his weights on "speak" and "understand," and a graphic score by doing the same on "read" and "write." The maximum possible score was eight on each (oral and graphic scores).

On the basis of these tests, the entire sample of 364 subjects originally contacted was divided into three groups: one group composed of monolinguals, a second group of bilinguals, and a third group which could not be unambiguously classified as either monolingual or bilingual. Only the first two of these groups were further tested. The third group was not used again.

The criteria used in the classification of subjects were as follows: (a) Monolinguals—Word Association Test, a balance score of at least + 75; Word Detection Test, a balance score of at least + 75; Peabody Picture Vocabulary, a score of not more than 6; Subjective Self-Rating, a score of not more than 7 in oral and graphic skill in English (combined). (b) Bilinguals—Word Association Test, a balance score of 0 ± 30; Word Detection Test, a balance score of 0 ± 30; Peabody Vocabulary, a score of at least 15 out of 21; Subjective Self-Rating, a score of at least 13 out of a possible 16 in oral and graphic English (combined).

Two judges consulted on the classification of each subject. In some cases where the different criteria were in disagreement, more weight was given to the Vocabulary score than to the others.

Our selected sample was composed of 164 subjects: 75 monolinguals and 89 bilinguals; 96 boys and 68 girls. These subjects were tested four additional times.

Measures of Intelligence[4, 5]

Lavoie-Laurendeau (*1960*) *Group Test of General Intelligence* (*Variables 6–9; Variables 16–23*). Previous studies pointed to the importance of using a test of intelligence standardized in the native language of the subject and preferably prepared for use in that language community. The Lavoie-Laurendeau test, standardized by psychologists at the University of Montreal on a Montreal French-speaking school population, seemed to meet these requirements. It is based on several other well-developed tests (Wechsler-Bellevue, WISC, Barbeau-Pinard) using those sections which could best be adapted for group testing. The nonverbal and verbal sections of this test were administered to each group. Nonverbal, verbal, and total IQ scores were calculated for each subject. A ratio score was obtained by dividing the verbal IQ by the nonverbal IQ and multiplying by one-hundred.

Raven (*1956*) *Progressive Matrices Test* (*Variable 10*). The colored form of this (Sets A, Ab, and B) was administered as a group test. This was included as a measure of basic intelligence (pure "g"). A total raw score was obtained for each subject (maximum thirty-six).

Thurstone (*1954*) *Primary Mental Abilities* (*Variables 11–15*). An attempt was made to select those subtests from the Primary Mental Abilities which draw least directly on verbal skills. The following five were chosen and administered in French: Space, Figure-

----

[4] Appendices A–D have been deposited with the American Documentation Institute. Order Document No. 7308, from ADI Auxiliary Publications Project, Photoduplication Service, Library of Congress; Washington 25, D.C., remitting in advance $2.25 for microfilm or $5.00 for photocopies. Make checks payable to: Chief, Photoduplication Service, Library of Congress.

[5] The numbering in the following sections refers to the number assigned to that variable for the analysis and is consistent throughout the rest of the paper. For names and numbering of subtests of intelligence, see Appendix B.

Grouping, Perception, Number, and Verbal Meaning. This test was translated by a linguist at McGill.

Measures of Attitude

In the final testing session, the children were given a booklet containing a number of different measures of attitude. The complete versions of these are presented in Appendix C.

Attitude-to-English Scale (Variable 33); Attitude-to-French Scale (Variable 34). The first measure was an attitude questionnaire, devised especially for use with children in the Montreal setting, answers to which purportedly reflect social attitudes toward either English Canadians or French Canadians. Two scales were derived from this questionnaire. Each question was defined as belonging either to the Attitude-to-English scale or to the Attitude-to-French scale. Responses to each question were scored on a three-point scale, from favorable to unfavorable. All the responses to the questionnaire belonging to the Attitude-to-French scale were scored and summed, a high score indicating a favorable attitude to French and a low score an unfavorable attitude. The Attitude-to-English scale was scored in the same manner.

Parents' Attitudes to English Canadians (Variable 38); Parents' Attitudes to French Canadians (Variable 39). The questionnaire contained items relating to the parents' attitudes toward the French and the English communities. These were scored in the same way as Variables 33 and 34.

Evaluation of Moi (Me) (Variable 35); Evaluation of French Canadians (Variable 36); Evaluation of English Canadians (Variable 37). A second series of measures made use of the Semantic Differential (Osgood, 1957) as a technique for determining the subject's attitudes to various groups. The subjects rated several concepts on eighteen bipolar scales, each with seven points. The concepts used in the analysis of the data were: Me, *les canadiens français,* and *les canadiens anglais.*

Variables 35, 36, and 37 were obtained by summing the ratings assigned by a given subject to each of the concepts on all eighteen scales. A high score on these variables indicates a high evaluation of the concept and a low score a low evaluation.

Differential Evaluation of French Canadians (Variable 40); Differential Evaluation of French Canadians and English Canadians

(*Variable 41*); *Differential Evaluation of Me and English Canadians* (*Variable 42*). This measure was obtained by subtracting the evaluation of the concept listed second from the evaluation of that listed first. A high score indicates the first concept was evaluated more unfavorably than the second. A low score shows the opposite. A differential evaluation score was calculated between French Canadians and Me (Variable 40), between French Canadians and English Canadians (Variable 41), and between Me and English Canadians (Variable 42).

Identification of French Canadians and Me (*Variable 43*); *Identification of French Canadians and English Canadians* (*Variable 44*); *Identification of Me and English Canadians* (*Variable 45*). Osgood Ds were calculated between the subject's ratings of each pair of concepts. These constitute scores on Variables 43, 44, and 45. A high score (D) indicates greater semantic distance between the two concepts or less similarity between them. A low score shows closer identification of the two concepts as discussed by Lazowick (1955).

Voice Study (*Variable 46*). In an attempt to get at stereotypes which the subjects might hold about French Canadians and English Canadians, a study was carried out using tape recordings of the voices of children reading a passage in French and an English translation of the same passage—an adaptation of a study by Lambert et al. (1960). There were four speakers, each one reading twice, once in each language. The subjects were unaware that they were rating the personality characteristics of only four speakers who were perfectly bilingual. English and French voices were presented alternately, the two voices of any one speaker being maximally separated on the tape. The subjects were asked to rate what they thought each speaker must be like as a person from the sound of her voice. The ratings were made on fifteen traits, each one having a five-point scale. For each subject on each of the traits, the sum of his ratings for all the English voices was subtracted from the sum of his ratings for all the French voices, yielding a measure (D) of the direction of the difference between his ratings of the two. In this case a constant of five was added to all scores. A score of five would mean there was no difference perceived between the two guises. A score greater than five would mean that the English were perceived more favorably than the French and a score lower than five would indicate that the French were perceived more favorably than the English.

Achievement Measures

From the teachers, ratings were obtained of how well each child did in school in relation to the others in his class. The teacher rated each child along a five-point scale in terms of his achievement in general (Variable 24), in French (Variable 25), and in English (Variable 26) if this happened to be one of his subjects. We also obtained the marks in French that each subject received in *dictée* (Variable 27), *lecture* (Variable 28), and *composition* (Variable 29) at midterm.

The following measures were based on information from the original questionnaire filled out by each subject.

Sex (Variable 1); School Grade (Variable 4); Number of Years Speaking English (Variable 5); French Skills of Parents (Variable 30). Each subject rated the ability of his father and mother to speak, read, write, and understand French. These were scored in the same manner as his self-ratings of his English ability. The scores for mother and father were summed.

English Skill of Parents (Variable 31). This variable was derived in the same way as above, using the items about English in place of those about French.

Balance between English and French Skills of Parents (Variable 32). The score on Variable 30 was subtracted from the score on Variable 31 and a constant of one hundred added. A score of one hundred on this variable indicates that the parents are equally skilled in French and English. A score of less than one hundred means that the parents are more skilled in English than in French, and vice versa.

Socioeconomic Class (Variable 3). Realizing the relevance of socioeconomic class to language learning, we decided to investigate its role in detail. On the basis of information received from the child, the school records, the school principal, and the parents themselves when necessary, we placed each child into one of the seven categories outlined by Warner, Meeker, and Eells (1949). A small sample of 110 children was selected from the large sample so that there were equal numbers of bilinguals and monolinguals in each of the seven classes.

RESULTS AND DISCUSSION

Comparisons were made between the performance of the monolinguals and bilinguals on the various measures employed. Table 1
presents the means, t values, and associated probability levels for
each comparison for the entire sample of subjects (large sample).
The original statement of the problem required that the two groups
be matched for socioeconomic class since previous studies had indicated the importance of this variable. Although the subjects in
both groups were drawn from the same school system and in many
cases the same school, all of which were considered middle class
by the school commission, there was a significant difference between
the two groups on socioeconomic level (Table 1, Variable 3). Be-

TABLE 1

MEANS, t VALUES, AND PROBABILITY LEVELS FOR
MONOLINGUAL AND BILINGUAL GROUPS ON
ALL MEASURES, LARGE SAMPLE

Name of Variable	Bilingual M	Monolingual M	t value[a]
1. Sex	—	—	—
2. Linguality	—	—	—
3. Socioeconomic class	4.27	3.31	3.71***
4. School grade	4.86	4.42	5.61***
5. Number of years speaking English	5.68	.71	14.44***
6. Lavoie-Laurendeau (L-L) Nonverbal IQ	109.43	95.40	5.78***
7. L-L Verbal IQ	116.26	103.14	6.06***
8. L-L Total IQ	115.01	99.45	6.75***
9. L-L Ratio Score	106.60	110.34	−1.46
10. Raven Progressive Matrices	27.48	22.40	5.44***
11. Primary Mental Abilities (PMA) Verbal Meaning	26.91	24.94	3.13***

[a] Positive entries indicate that the mean for the bilingual group is higher
than the mean for the monolingual group. Negative entries indicate the reverse.
* $p < .05$.
** $p < .02$.
*** $p < .01$.

TABLE 1 (*cont.*)

Name of Variable	Bilingual M	Monolingual M	t value[a]
12. PMA Space	15.96	14.33	2.48**
13. PMA Figure-Grouping	19.21	17.49	2.62***
14. PMA Perception	22.32	20.19	2.07*
15. PMA Number	36.38	33.13	2.58**
16. L-L Picture Arrangement	8.55	6.19	4.80***
17. L-L Figure Manipulation	10.58	8.77	3.57***
18. L-L Dissimilarities	9.33	8.03	3.57***
19. L-L Picture Completion	10.10	8.43	3.58***
20. L-L Vocabulary	12.74	10.52	4.08***
21. L-L Comprehension	6.23	5.23	3.32***
22. L-L Similarities	9.08	7.70	3.93***
23. L-L Information	12.67	9.44	6.19***
24. Achievement in General	3.43	3.04	2.85***
25. Achievement in French	3.37	3.10	1.86
26. Achievement in English	4.16	2.63	7.61***
27. Marks in French *dictée*	73.65	71.14	1.02
28. Marks in French *lecture*	78.78	75.22	1.97
29. Marks in French *composition*	74.93	73.03	1.18
30. French skills of parents	22.15	23.26	−2.34*
31. English skills of parents	21.59	16.36	7.05***
32. Balance between Variables 30 and 31	100.74	106.92	−7.19***
33. Attitude-to-English scale	52.75	38.85	8.91***
34. Attitude-to-French scale	26.71	31.31	−5.46***

[a] Positive entries indicate that the mean for the bilingual group is higher than the mean for the monolingual group. Negative entries indicate the reverse.

* $p > .05$.

** $p > .02$.

*** $p > .01$.

TABLE 1 (*cont.*)

Name of Variable	Bilingual M	Monolingual M	t value[a]
35. Evaluation of self	111.18	105.12	2.11*
36. Evaluation of French Canadians (FC)	109.27	110.07	−.34
37. Evaluation of English Canadians (EC)	104.34	95.24	2.87***
38. Parents' attitude to EC	5.00	4.06	5.86***
39. Parents' attitude to FC	4.95	5.40	−2.92***
40. Differential Evaluation of FC—Me	511.58	485.25	2.36**
41. Differential Evaluation of FC—EC	477.75	425.80	2.83***
42. Differential Evaluation of Me—EC	466.55	441.26	1.38
43. Identification of FC and Me	37.55	39.40	−.23
44. Identification of FC and EC	56.63	82.75	−1.53
45. Identification of Me and EC	54.22	90.98	−2.06*
46. Voice Study	4.98	4.65	3.38***

[a]Positive entries indicate that the mean for the bilingual group is higher than the mean for the monolingual group. Negative entries indicate the reverse.

* $p > .05$.
** $p > .02$.
*** $p > .01$.

cause of this discrepancy, a small sample having equal numbers of bilinguals and monolinguals in each of seven socioeconomic status categories was analyzed separately. Table 2 shows the means, *t* values, and probability levels for this small sample. The general pattern of results for the two samples was highly similar.

For purposes of correlational analysis, thirty-eight out of the forty-eight variables were chosen and intercorrelated for the bilingual group and the monolingual separately. Thirty-one variables were selected on the basis of their appropriateness for factor analysis. That is, total IQ measures were eliminated and only subtests kept, ratio and balance scores were eliminated because they were composed of two other measures, and only two of the nine rating scales of attitudes were kept, to reduce the possibility of built-in correlations. Each thirty-one by thirty-one variable correlation matrix was factor analyzed by Thurstone's (1947) centroid solution and seven factors were extracted. The factors were rotated using the normal varimax rotation program developed at McGill.

The correlation matrices and factor matrices (centroid solution) are presented in Appendix A. The rotated factor matrices appear later in the Discussion section. In these analyses, the large sample was used, with socioeconomic status left free to vary in order that the extent of its influence could be determined.

TABLE 2

MEANS, t VALUES, PROBABILITY LEVELS FOR
MONOLINGUAL AND BILINGUAL GROUPS ON
ALL MEASURES, SMALL SAMPLE[a]

Name of Variable	Bilingual M	Monolingual M	t value[a]
1. Sex	—	—	—
2. Linguality	—	—	—
3. Socioeconomic class	3.80	3.83	.11
4. School grade	4.87	4.48	4.77***
5. Number of years speaking English	5.36	.72	11.24***
6. Lavoie-Laurendeau (L-L) Nonverbal IQ	110.26	95.85	4.84***
7. L-L Verbal IQ	114.98	104.43	4.08***
8. L-L Total IQ	114.62	100.60	5.11***
9. L-L Ratio Score	104.80	111.62	−2.13*
10. Raven Progressive Matrices	27.15	22.12	4.40***
11. Primary Mental Abilities (PMA) Verbal Meaning	26.94	25.35	2.23*
12. PMA Space	15.80	14.31	1.90
13. PMA Figure-Grouping	19.46	17.58	2.39**

[a] Equated for socioeconomic status.

[b] Positive entries indicate that the mean for the bilingual group is higher than the mean for the monolingual group. Negative entries indicate the reverse.

* $p > .05$.

** $p > .02$.

*** $p > .01$.

TABLE 2 (*cont.*)

Name of Variable	Bilingual M	Monolingual M	t value[a]
14. PMA Perception	22.06	20.33	1.29
15. PMA Number	35.92	33.29	1.65
16. L-L Picture Arrangement	8.50	6.15	4.00***
17. L-L Figure Manipulation	10.42	8.96	2.37**
18. L-L Dissimilarities	9.69	8.08	3.64***
19. L-L Picture Completion	10.35	8.50	3.21***
20. L-L Vocabulary	12.63	10.73	2.99***
21. L-L Comprehension	6.02	5.22	2.17*
22. L-L Similarities	8.77	7.80	2.21*
23. L-L Information	12.81	10.02	4.62***
24. Achievement in General	3.38	3.04	1.97
25. Achievement in French	3.35	3.11	1.29
26. Achievement in English	4.00	2.68	5.24***
27. Marks in French *dictée*	72.73	71.51	.40
28. Marks in French *lecture*	79.04	75.73	1.46
29. Marks in French *composition*	75.09	72.49	1.29
30. French skills of parents	22.50	23.10	−1.09
31. English skills of parents	21.13	17.08	4.27***
32. Balance between Variables 30 and 31	101.38	106.05	−4.75***
33. Attitude-to-English scale	51.76	38.85	7.12***

[a] Equated for socioeconomic status.

[b] Positive entries indicate that the mean for the bilingual group is higher than the mean for the monolingual group. Negative entries indicate the reverse.

* $p > .05$.

** $p > .02$.

*** $p > .01$.

TABLE 2 *(cont.)*

Name of Variable	Bilingual M	Monolingual M	t value[a]
34. Attitude-to-French scale	26.57	31.65	−5.00***
35. Evaluation of self	110.55	105.82	1.24
36. Evaluation of French Canadians (FC)	108.89	110.58	−.60
37. Evaluation of English Canadians (EC)	101.04	98.28	.76
38. Parents' attitude to EC	4.88	4.09	4.11***
39. Parents' attitude to FC	5.14	5.48	−2.03*
40. Differential Evaluation of FC—Me	510.04	492.42	1.24
41. Differential Evaluation of FC—EC	462.94	432.42	1.40
42. Differential Evaluation of Me—EC	453.26	439.66	.63
43. Identification of FC and Me	42.36	35.42	.74
44. Identification of FC and EC	70.64	64.98	.32
45. Identification of Me and EC	66.78	73.93	−.39
46. Voice Study	4.95	4.63	2.33*

[a] Equated for socioeconomic status.

[b] Positive entries indicate that the mean for the bilingual group is higher than the mean for the monolingual group. Negative entries indicate the reverse.

* $p > .05$.

** $p > .02$.

*** $p > .01$.

The main findings of the study will be presented in summary. Following this, each one will be examined separately in more detail. Finally, an attempt will be made to integrate all the findings.

The first hypothesis, that the two groups would not differ significantly on nonverbal IQ, was not supported. The results (Table 2) show that the bilingual group performed significantly better than the monolingual on the Raven Progressive Matrices, and the

Lavoie-Laurendeau Nonverbal IQ, and most of the subtests of the nonverbal type.

The finding that the bilinguals also scored significantly higher than the monolinguals on the Lavoie-Laurendeau Verbal IQ, and on all the verbal subtests, is in direct contradiction to the original prediction.

The monolingual and bilingual groups performed differentially on subtests of intelligence, as was expected. On certain subtests of the nonverbal type there were no significant differences between the groups, while on others, both nonverbal and verbal, the bilinguals performed better in differing amounts. However, on none of the subtests did the monolinguals exceed the bilinguals.

The predicted relation between attitudes to English and school achievement in English was found. For example, in the monolingual case, there is a significant correlation $(-.51)$ between achievement in English (Variable 26) and the degree of perceived similarity between Me and English Canadians (Variable 45).

Morrison's observation that bilinguals were often behind in school grade was not borne out in this study. Quite to the contrary, the results show that bilingual subjects who were of the same age as the monolinguals (ten years), were in a higher grade in school, even for the sample which was matched on socio-economic class.

The attitudes of the bilinguals toward English Canadians were significantly more favorable than those of the monolinguals, as indicated by the means on the Attitude-to-English scale. These attitudes appear to be related to the socioeconomic class, however, since in the larger sample where the bilinguals were of a higher social class, their favorable attitudes to English became evident on more variables measuring attitudes. It should also be noted that the monolinguals held more favorable attitudes to the French Canadians than the bilinguals.

No significant differences were found between the group means (small sample) for: achievement in general, achievement in French, evaluation of self, and most of the remaining attitude measures, although these do relate differentially to the other variables.

Performance on Nonverbal Intelligence Measures

The finding that a group of bilingual children scored higher on nonverbal intelligence tests than did a group of monolinguals runs counter to most previous findings in this area and to the original expectation of this study. It raises the question as to why the bilinguals scored higher on nonverbal tests.

This problem may be viewed from two perspectives. One may ask whether the more intelligent children, as measured by nonverbal intelligence tests, are the ones who become bilingual, or whether bilingualism itself has a favorable effect on nonverbal intelligence.

In support of the first notion, one could argue that the more intelligent child would be more able to pick up English from his playmates and his schooling than the less intelligent child, given the same opportunities. Previous studies have shown a correlation between intelligence and language aptitude (Garner & Lambert, 1959; Wittenborn & Larsen, 1944). When a frequency distribution is made of the scores obtained by the two groups on a nonverbal test (such as the Raven) we find that the distribution of bilinguals' scores is negatively skewed. That is, though there were some children of low intelligence who became bilingual, most of the bilinguals scored higher on this intelligence test. Also, there were a few monolinguals who did as well as the bilinguals on the test, but the majority was found near the middle or at the lower end of the distribution. This shape of distribution implies that at least some minimum level of intelligence is necessary to become a really balanced bilingual, at least to meet the requirements for bilingualism set in this study.

In a bilingual community such as Montreal, it is a very great asset and at times a necessity for French Canadians to know English. These advantages may be realized more fully by parents of higher intelligence who may be more inclined to encourage their children to learn English. Parents of higher intelligence may be expected to have more intelligent children. This notion is supported by the following facts. The bilinguals reported significantly more than the monolinguals that their parents encouraged them to learn to speak English and the parents themselves had more skill in English than did the parents of the monolingual children ($p < .01$) who apparently either failed to see the benefits of knowing English or reacted negatively to the English-Canadian community. The more intelligent children may themselves realize the value of knowing English and therefore seek opportunities to learn it. When they do show progress in learning English, one could predict that they would receive parental encouragement for so doing. Even if the less intelligent child should see the advantages, he might encounter difficulties in attempting to learn English and might give up more readily, being accustomed to failure in other areas. Furthermore, he does not receive encouragement from his parents. But for the bright child who is ahead in school, the opportunity to learn anything new may present a challenge, which he is capable of meeting.

An alternative explanation of these results is that bilingualism may in some way influence nonverbal intelligence. It may be that knowing two languages from an early age gives a child an advantage in his performance on nonverbal tests. If this is the case, why did the bilinguals not do better on *all* the different nonverbal subtests? In her chapter on Performance and Nonlanguage tests, Anastasi (1961) writes:

An important question to consider regarding non-language tests concerns the extent to which they depend upon spatial and perceptual functions, as contrasted to the symbolic manipulation of abstract relations, concepts, and factual information. The latter functions would seem to resemble more closely those required in the traditional verbal tests of "intelligence" . . . Some tests . . . stress spatial and perceptual factors almost to the exclusion of other functions . . . Other non-language tests employ a greater proportion of items calling for ideational or symbolic responses (p. 253).[6]

The nonverbal tests in this study can be subdivided conveniently into two groups in the fashion suggested by Anastasi. The Primary Mental Abilities Space and Perception tests both draw more on spatial and perceptual processes than on symbolic manipulation. The Number test of the Primary Mental Abilities is composed of simple addition questions which do not involve much mental "manipulation." Because this is a timed test, the important requirement is perceptual speed. In the Primary Mental Abilities Figure-Grouping, the Raven, and the Lavoie-Laurendeau Dissimilarities tests the subjects must form a concept or discover relations between elements which cannot be done without cognitive reorganizations.

[6] From Anne Anastasi, *Psychological Testing* (New York: Macmillan, 1961). Used by permission.

The Lavoie-Laurendeau Figure-Manipulation and the Lavoie-Laurendeau Picture Arrangement tests require reorganizations of relations and concepts. Thus, the different nonverbal tests do logically fall into two categories: (a) those with spatial-perceptual requirements: Primary Mental Abilities Space, Perception, and Number; and (b) those with symbolic reorganization requirements: Primary Mental Abilities Figure-Grouping, Raven Progressive Matrices, Lavoie-Laurendeau Dissimilarities, Figure-Manipulation, and Picture Arrangement. The Picture Completion test is difficult to categorize, a priori. Further support for the division of nonverbal or performance tests into two subtypes comes from an abstract of a study conducted by Ahmed (1954):

A factorial analysis study demonstrating that spatial visualization and mental manipulation are independent abilities . . . The author tentatively describes this ability as if it consisted of *mental flexibility* [italics added] which is involved in the process of mentally reorganzing the elements of a problem or situation.

Reference to Table 2 reveals that on the spatial-perceptual type of test, the two groups performed similarly whereas on the mental reorganization type there is a significant difference between them. The bilinguals therefore perform better only on the type of nonverbal tests involving concept-formation or symbolic "flexibility."

Several hypotheses will be proposed as to why bilinguals might have an advantage on these tests. People who learn to use two languages have two symbols for every object. From an early age, bilinguals may be forced to conceptualize environmental events in terms of their general properties without reliance on their linguistic symbols. This would be particularly relevant in the case of those bilinguals who are "compound" (Lambert, Havelka, & Crosby, 1958), that is, bilinguals who learned their two languages in the same setting and therefore have two words for the identical referent. Most of our bilinguals have learned both their languages in Montreal and would likely be compound. Leopold (see the introduction) noted that his bilingual child learned to separate the sound of the word from the thing itself. This ability to think in terms of abstract concepts and relations, independent of the actual word, apparently is required in the symbolic reorganization type tests. The monolinguals may never have been forced to form concepts or abstract ideas of things and may be more likely to think mainly in terms of concretes. They could not be expected, therefore, to be as agile at concept-formation as the bilinguals and they might appear handicapped comparatively. S. J. Evans (1953) implies that monolinguals may be at a disadvantage in that their thought is always subject to language. In summary, it is proposed that bilinguals, because of their training in two languages, have become more adept at concept formation and abstract thinking than the monolinguals, and that this accounts, in part, for their superiority on the symbolic reorganization type tests.

The second hypothesis is that bilinguals may have developed more flexibility in thinking. Compound bilinguals typically acquire experience in switching from one language to another, possibly trying to solve a problem while thinking in one language, and then, when blocked, switching to the other. This habit, if it were developed, could help them in their performance on tests requiring symbolic reorganization since they demand a readiness to drop one hypothesis or concept and try another. Morrison (1958) gives an example of a Gaelic-speaking boy of eleven, who had just taken the Raven Matrices test. When asked whether he had done his thinking in Gaelic or in English he replied, "Please, sir, I tried it in the English first, then I tried in the Gaelic to see would it be easier; but it wasn't, so I went back to the English" (p. 288). The monolinguals of course could not have developed a habit of alternating languages, and therefore, of making use of two different perspectives. One might thus expect them to be more rigid or less flexible than the bilinguals on certain tests. This might account for the significant difference between the two groups on these tests. This hypothesis could be more directly tested by giving groups of monolinguals and bilinguals tests of rigidity to see if rigidity-flexibility is a dimension on which they actually do differ.

Nonlanguage or performance tests depend, to a certain extent, on prior exposure to and familiarity with materials similar to those used in the test. The broader a child's experience, the higher the probability that he will have come into contact with the type of ideas and situations that will assist him in his performance. The bilingual child has been exposed to a wider range of experiences than the monolingual, because his experiences stem from two different cultures. This enriched environment may benefit him on nonverbal tests.

The bilingual's contact with the English culture should have put him in an advantageous position on the Primary Mental Abilities Test which is basically an English style test translated into French for present purposes. However, the fact that this was the test on which the bilinguals performed relatively the poorest would seem to justify our use of a translation; that is, it apparently did not give the bilinguals an advantage.

Performance on Verbal Intelligence Measures

The next finding to be discussed is that bilinguals also performed better on verbal tests. We had anticipated that the monolinguals would excel. Why this complete reversal? The superior performance of the bilinguals on the verbal tests may simply be a reflection of their overall superior intelligence. This seems to be the case for the small sample. An analysis of covariance (Table 3) showed that when the two groups were matched statistically on nonverbal intelligence, there was no significant difference between them on verbal intelligence. (The Lavoie-Laurendeau Nonverbal and Verbal IQs

TABLE 3

ANALYSIS OF COVARIANCE OF PERFORMANCE OF TWO GROUPS
OF SUBJECTS, SMALL SAMPLE

Source	df	X^2	XY	Y^2
Between groups	1	3998.51	3365.39	2832.52
Within groups	103	34207.89	21629.28	41040.82
Total	104	38206.40	24994.67	43873.34

| | *Analysis of Covariance* SS of errors of | | | |
Source	estimate	df	MS	F
Total	27521.80	103		
Within groups	27364.86	102	268.28	
Adjusted means	156.94	1	156.94	.584

Note.—Sums of squares and cross products for 2 groups of subjects (monolingual and bilingual) on Lavoie-Laurendeau Nonverbal IQ (X) and Lavoie-Laurendeau Verbal IQ (Y).

were used in this analysis.) For the large sample, this does not hold up (see Table 4). There is still a significant difference ($p = .01$) between the groups in favor of the bilinguals on verbal, even after they have been matched on nonverbal. Arguing from the large sample results, it appears that our bilinguals, instead of suffering from "mental confusion" or a "language handicap" are profiting from a "language asset." A partial explanation of this may lie in our method of choosing the bilingual sample. Those suffering from a handicap may unintentionally have been eliminated. We attempted to select bilinguals who were balanced, that is equally fluent in both languages. However, when the balance measures used did not give a clear indication of whether or not a given child was bilingual, more weight was attached to his score on the English vocabulary test. Thus some bilinguals who might be balanced, but whose vocabulary in English and French might be small, would be omitted from our sample. The less intelligent bilinguals, those who have not acquired as large an English vocabulary, would not be considered "bilingual" enough for our study.

TABLE 4

ANALYSIS OF COVARIANCE OF PERFORMANCE OF TWO GROUPS
OF SUBJECTS, LARGE SAMPLE

Source	df	X^2	XY	Y^2
Between groups	1	8284.89	6864.76	5687.94
Within groups	145	32361.41	14500.34	26389.26
Total	146	40646.30	21365.10	32077.20

| | Analysis of Covariance SS of errors of | | | |
Source	estimate	df	MS	F
Total	20847.00	145		
Within groups	198992.06	144	138.14	
Adjusted means	954.94	1	954.94	6.91*

Note.—Sums of squares and cross products for two groups of subjects (monolingual and bilingual) on Lavoie-Laurendeau Nonverbal IQ (X) and Lavoie-Laurendeau Verbal IQ (Y).

* Indicates significance at the 1 percent level of confidence.

In O'Doherty's terms, we may have included mainly genuine bilinguals, as opposed to pseudobilinguals. The genuine bilingual, having mastered both languages, is believed by O'Doherty (1958) to be clearly in an advantageous position intellectually. But this study does not include information about the other type of bilingual.

The superiority of the bilinguals on the verbal measures might be considered from another point of view. Bilinguals have a more extended total vocabulary than have monolinguals in the sense that they have learned both English and French symbols for most referents in their environment. The overlap of English and French vocabularies is considerable, so that an English-French bilingual may actually be helped when functioning in either language by the positive transfer derived from the other. The difference in the amount of overlap between two languages may, in part, explain the discrepancy between the results reported here and those reported previously from Wales. French and English have many more words derived from common roots than do Welsh and English. A Welsh-English bilingual would not benefit from as much positive transfer in vocabulary as would a French-English bilingual.

Differential Performance on Intelligence Measures

It was suggested in the introduction that bilinguals and monolinguals might be found to perform differently on various types of intelligence subtests and that this performance difference might somehow be related to a difference in the structure of the intellect of the typical students in the two groups. Reference to the factor analyses (Tables 5 and 6) shows that the bilinguals seem to have a greater number of separate or independent abilities on which to draw in completing these tests in contrast to the monolinguals who have fewer. That is, the bilinguals have more independent factors defined by intelligence variables than the monolinguals. For the bilinguals, Factor IV is clearly defined as a verbal intelligence factor. There are several nonverbal intelligence factors—III, V, VI, VII—which are defined by the intelligence measures, but also have loadings of achievement and attitude variables on them. Factor I also has some loadings of intelligence tests on it. For the monolinguals, on the other hand, most of the intelligence variables, both verbal and nonverbal, load together on Factor I which is clearly a general intelligence factor. Factor VI for the monolinguals is roughly equivalent to the verbal factor (IV) for the bilinguals, but it is not so pure and clear. Similarly, Factor VII (monolinguals) has high loadings of both intelligence and achievement in English. The remaining loadings of the intelligence variables on other factors do not play an important role for the monolinguals. Thus some support is given to the notion that bilinguals have developed more independent abilities and skills at an earlier age through their experiences and their learning of a second language. In summary, the structure of intellect of the bilinguals appears to be more diversified than that of the monolinguals. Thus, Guilford's (1956) belief that different experiences might cause different factors of intellect to appear at varying times for different individuals receives support here. Further research on this structure for monolinguals and bilinguals, including a greater number of different types of measures of intelligence, might prove extremely useful in current attempts to define the nature of intelligence. It would also be interesting to investigate whether the monolinguals eventually develop similar factors, or whether the basic structure remains different.

It is important to realize that it is not possible to ascertain from the present study whether the more diversified structure of intelligence of the bilinguals is attributable to their bilinguality or simply to the fact that they are more intelligent. Perhaps a higher degree of intelligence means more diversified abilities and aptitudes.

Attitudes to English and French

For all the measures of attitudes used, the means for the bilingual group were in the direction of being more favorable to English Canadians, while the means for the monolingual group were more favorable to the French Canadians. A comparison of Tables 1 and 2 shows that the differences between means reached significance on more of the relevant attitude variables for the large sample than for the small sample. These results present a clear picture of the bilingual group being more favorably disposed to English Canadians, and less to French Canadians than the monolingual group.

Several possible explanations of these findings come to mind. The greater contact which the bilinguals have with English Canadians and English culture may account in part for their more favorable attitudes. The very fact that they have succeeded in becoming bilingual indicates that getting to know the English and their language must have been a goal or value for them. This goal, which may have been engendered by parents (Gardner, 1960), led them to seek more contact with the English community. These contacts may well have been positively reinforcing thereby increasing the desire for further interactions. Support for the notion of the influence of the parents comes from our data. The bilingual children report that their parents' attitudes toward English Canadians are favorable. Their parents' skill in English is also significantly higher than that of the monolinguals' parents. The correlation (.48) between the bilinguals' attitudes to EC and the attitudes they reported that their parents held may indicate that the Parents' Attitude-to-English scale was just a reflection of how the children themselves feel. This in no way diminishes the importance of it as a measure. It is a child's *perception* of the attitudes his parents hold that to a great extent influences his behavior and thinking, whether or not this perception is in line with reality. For the monolinguals, the correlation between Attitude-to-English scale and the Parents' Attitude-to-English is lower (.27). Attitudes toward the English may not be salient for monolingual families and therefore less frequently discussed.

Because the bilinguals held more favorable attitudes toward English Canadians, does this necessarily mean they had to hold less favorable attitudes to French Canadians? The scales devised to measure these two attitudes were composed from the same questionnaire and had some overlapping items (e.g., My best friend is English Canadian? French Canadian? or other?) which might suggest that there is a built-in negative relation between the Attitude-to-English scale and the Attitude-to-French scale. If we examine the correlations between these two scales (Variables 33 and 34), we find that for the monolinguals the r is only $-.11$ which clearly suggests that the relation between attitudes to French and attitudes to English is not inherent in the nature of the scales. The correlation of $-.48$ for the bilinguals therefore needs some explanation. The fact that they have learned English indicates that they must have identified, to some extent at least, with the English Canadians. This tendency is reflected in the measure of Identification with English Canadians (Variable 45) on which the bilinguals identify with English Canadians more closely than do the monolinguals. It is psychologically difficult to belong to two communities at once, to identify to the same extent with two groups which are culturally different. It appears that the bilinguals have resolved this "conflict" by clearly identifying with the English Canadians rather than with the French Canadians. The closer identification with English Canadians is supported by the higher means for bilinguals on the Differential Evaluation measures where a higher score indicates that the second concept is evaluated more favorably than the first. This strong identification with the English seems to require the bilinguals to identify less with the French Canadians.

On the reactions to spoken language (Variable 46), the mean score for the bilinguals was 4.98, which suggests that the stereotypes they hold of French Canadians and English Canadians are of a similar degree of favorableness. This variable measures stereotypes and does not correlate with the attitude scores. The monolinguals' evaluations indicate that they hold more favorable stereotypes of the French Canadians than of the English Canadians.

Many of the monolinguals and bilinguals in our sample live in the same districts and have approximately the same opportunities to learn English. Why did the one group take advantage of these occasions for interaction while the other group did not? One could suggest that the less favorable attitudes of the monolinguals toward English Canadians and the lack of encouragement from their parents on this matter have had a powerful negative effect. This will be dealt with more fully in the following discussion of the relation between attitudes to English and achievement in English.

Attitude and English Achievement

If we examine the correlation and factor tables to determine which variables are related to achievement in English, we discover that the attitude variables are important for the monolinguals, but not for the bilinguals. The bilinguals as a group appear to have more clearly defined attitudes which are favorable to the English, and which have ceased to present a problem for them. To the extent that there is consensus among the bilinguals there would be less variance and less chance for correlation. For the bilinguals, Achievement in English is related more to intelligence than to attitude. The only significant relation for them between attitude and

TABLE 5

ROTATED FACTOR MATRIX FOR MONOLINGUALS

Variable	I	II	III	IV	V	VI	VII	h^2
3. Socioeconomic class	.03	−.04	.57	.20	.01	.25	.15	.46
4. School grade	.14	−.07	.51	.08	.04	.52	.09	.57
10. Raven Matrices	.71	.24	−.06	.20	−.02	.06	.19	.64
11. Primary Mental Abilities (PMA) Verbal Meaning	.47	.11	.08	.23	.28	.22	−.10	.43
12. PMA Space	.29	.06	−.01	.32	.15	.26	.40	.44
13. PMA Figure-Grouping	.40	.05	.06	−.04	.13	−.15	.58	.54
14. PMA Perception	.35	.20	−.06	.31	.09	.45	.33	.59
15. PMA Number	.04	.40	−.07	.25	−.05	.49	.16	.50
16. Lavoie-Laurendeau (L-L) Picture Arrangement	.74	.17	.09	.02	−.08	.06	.04	.59
17. L-L Figure Manipulation	.57	.22	.17	.21	.11	.16	.24	.54
18. L-L Dissimilarities	.13	.19	.09	.04	.34	.24	.46	.45
19. L-L Picture Completion	.64	.09	.15	−.17	−.01	.30	.21	.60
20. L-L Vocabulary	.50	−.07	.25	−.00	.20	.54	.02	.64
21. L-L Comprehension	.19	.19	.19	−.05	.29	.68	.10	.66

22. L-L Similarities	.38	.03	.28	−.05	.35	.11	.04	.37
23. L-L Information	.21	−.01	.30	.18	.08	.74	−.09	.73
24. Achievement in general	.26	.88	−.02	.14	.07	−.05	.08	.88
25. Achievement in French	.15	.87	.03	.09	.01	.12	.15	.82
26. Achievement in English	.11	.48	.08	.13	.79	.06	.32	.99
27. Marks in French *dictée*	.08	.85	.12	.01	.09	.14	.12	.78
28. Marks in French *lecture*	.15	.67	.03	−.07	.38	−.07	−.13	.65
29. Marks in French *composition*	.10	.74	−.15	−.28	.36	.11	.00	.80
30. French skills of parents	.12	.22	.25	.10	−.11	.09	.30	.24
31. English skills of parents	.12	−.04	.76	.15	.03	−.02	.21	.66
33. Attitude-to-English scale	−.03	.03	.42	−.35	.21	.17	.30	.47
34. Attitude-to-French scale	.10	−.08	.03	.52	.02	.13	−.04	.31
38. Parents' attitude to English Canadians (EC)	.09	.01	.34	−.05	.13	.07	−.02	.14
39. Parents' attitude to French Canadians (FC)	−.04	.09	.22	−.02	.24	.16	−.07	.14
43. Identification of FC and Me	−.00	−.14	−.12	−.63	−.19	−.03	−.19	.50
45. Identification of Me and EC	−.01	−.11	.02	−.14	−.58	−.10	−.12	.39
46. Voice Study	−.04	−.06	−.36	.04	.12	−.01	.19	.19

TABLE 6

ROTATED FACTOR MATRIX FOR BILINGUALS

Variable	I	II	III	IV	V	VI	VII	h^2
3. Socioeconomic class	-.05	.07	.07	-.06	-.05	.06	.47	.24
4. School grade	.14	.19	-.26	.58	.26	-.11	.08	.54
10. Raven Matrices	.32	.16	.54	.14	-.08	.39	.11	.61
11. Primary Mental Abilities (PMA) Verbal Meaning	.27	.03	.18	.75	.13	.09	-.01	.69
12. PMA Space	.09	.02	.24	.26	.41	.29	.40	.54
13. PMA Figure-Grouping	.18	.14	.41	.15	.06	.50	-.02	.50
14. PMA Perception	-.05	-.20	.11	.22	.56	.21	.02	.47
15. PMA Number	.22	.05	-.11	.07	.48	-.11	-.02	.32
16. Lavoie-Laurendeau (L-L) Picture Arrangement	.03	.12	.49	.31	.12	.06	.15	.40
17. L-L Figure Manipulation	.29	-.08	.32	.16	.10	.38	.32	.47
18. L-L Dissimilarities	.03	.08	-.02	-.05	.04	.60	.08	.38
19. L-L Picture Completion	-.17	-.14	.32	.43	.17	-.09	.15	.40
20. L-L Vocabulary	.21	-.20	.10	.68	.04	.11	.05	.58
21. L-L Comprehension	.11	-.08	.08	.41	-.02	.08	-.13	.22

22. L-L Similarities	-.02	-.05	.15	.36	-.02	.40	-.22	.37
23. L-L Information	.42	-.22	.07	.44	.22	-.08	.15	.50
24. Achievement in general	.78	.02	.07	.15	.10	.25	.15	.74
25. Achievement in French	.83	-.07	.10	.20	.09	.16	.00	.78
26. Achievement in English	.19	.26	.13	.12	.62	.05	-.08	.53
27. Marks in French *dictée*	.75	-.05	.01	.19	-.09	-.03	.02	.61
28. Marks in French *lecture*	.62	-.34	.06	.08	.42	-.05	-.20	.73
29. Marks in French *composition*	.71	-.04	.06	.07	.19	.21	-.27	.67
30. French skills of parents	-.13	-.42	-.16	.27	-.22	-.54	.11	.64
31. English skills of parents	-.38	.34	.11	.06	-.07	.14	-.06	.30
33. Attitude-to-English scale	-.10	.69	.02	-.13	.14	.21	.13	.58
34. Attitude-to-French scale	-.01	-.73	.09	.05	-.09	-.04	.01	.55
38. Parents' attitude to English Canadians (EC)	-.13	.67	.04	.09	-.19	.12	.11	.54
39. Parents' attitude to French Canadians (FC)	.03	-.49	-.33	.14	-.32	.10	-.09	.49
43. Identification of FC and Me	-.28	.35	.09	-.09	.36	-.36	-.19	.51
45. Identification of Me and EC	-.06	-.03	-.07	-.13	.13	-.42	-.29	.30
46. Voice Study	-.10	.38	.15	-.13	-.04	-.26	-.06	.27

achievement is the negative relation between Achievement in English and Attitude-to-French scale (−.42) which indicates that the more unfavorable attitudes to French the bilingual holds, the better he does in English. For the monolinguals on the other hand, attitudes play as important a role as intelligence. Factor V obtains its highest loadings from achievement in English. The high loading of the Identification of moi and English Canadians on this factor (−.58) indicates the importance of attitudes for English achievement for monolinguals. Correlations of −.51, −.52, and −.54 between Achievement in English and Identification of Me and English Canadians, of French Canadians and Me, and of French Canadians and English Canadians, respectively, suggest that a monolingual does better in English if he sees all these three as being similar, that is, French Canadians, English Canadians, and himself. Apparently it is necessary for him to identify with both groups in order to do well in English. This attempt at dual identification may well constitute a conflict for him and possibly hinder him from becoming bilingual. If he fails to identify with both, he does poorly in English.

It appears, then, that the attitude an individual holds toward the other language community plays a vitally important role in his learning the other group's language in school, as is particularly the case with our monolingual sample. If he views the other community with favor, he is more likely to do well in his attempts to learn the language, and vice versa. It also becomes evident that for those who have already practically mastered a second language, (e.g., our bilinguals) their attitudes to the second language community, of which they are in some way now a part, no longer play as important a role in their continued achievement in that language as do factors such as intelligence. The hypothesis that those with more favorable attitudes toward the English community would do better in learning English has received substantial support.

Bilingualism and School Grade

Previous studies had pointed out that bilinguals suffered from a language handicap and possibly because of it were behind in school. In the present study, where no handicap became evident, one should not expect bilinguals to be retarded in school. Indeed, the bilinguals as a group were significantly more advanced in school grade than were the monolinguals, and this, undoubtedly, can be attributed to their higher intelligence. For the bilinguals, school grade loads on the intelligence factors, especially the verbal intelligence factor (IV), suggesting that it is the verbal skills of the bilinguals that help them do well in school. Their bilingualism apparently gives them an advantage in those skills which depend on verbal fluency. For the monolinguals the picture is somewhat different. Grade in school loads about equally on Factor VI (intelligence) and Factor III (essentially an attitude factor). It is related to such variables as Space, Perception, Figure Manipulation, but not to Verbal Meaning or Vocabulary. Thus the monolinguals draw more on nonverbal than verbal abilities for their advancement in school grade, in contrast to the bilinguals. Socioeconomic class also seems to be a powerful determinant of how well monolinguals will do in school ($r = .46$). The implications of the correlates of achievement in school such as the contribution of socioeconomic class to school grade advancement for the monolinguals but not for the bilinguals, will not be fully considered in this thesis. In fact, many of the ramifications of the factor structures in general have not been fully explored. They constitute the start of the next phase of this research.

CONCLUSION

This study has found that bilinguals performed better than monolinguals on verbal and nonverbal intelligence tests. These results were not expected because they constitute a clear reversal of previously reported findings. How can we account for this difference in intelligence between the two groups? An attempt will be made here to integrate the explanations presented above into a description of the differences between the groups which may partially account for their differences in intellectual functioning.

The picture that emerges of the French-English bilingual in Montreal is that of a youngster whose wider experiences in two cultures have given him advantages which a monolingual does not enjoy. Intellectually his experience with two language systems seems to have left him with a mental flexibility, a superiority in concept formation, and a more diversified set of mental abilities, in the sense that the patterns of abilities developed by bilinguals were more heterogeneous. It is not possible to state from the present study whether the more intelligent child became bilingual or whether bilingualism aided his intellectual development, but there is no question about the fact that he is superior intellectually. In contrast, the monolingual appears to have a more unitary structure of intelligence which he must use for all types of intellectual tasks.

Because of superior intelligence, these bilingual children are also further ahead in school than the monolinguals and they achieve significantly better than their classmates in English study, as would be expected, and in school work in general. Their superior achievement in school seems to be dependent on a verbal facility. Those monolinguals who do poorly in their English study apparently fail to identify either with the English or the French cultural groups. In contrast, those monolinguals who do well in English, have closely identified themselves with both communities. Their failure to become bilingual may be attributed in part to the difficulties they may encounter in making a dual identification with both cultural groups, coupled with their acceptance of their own group (i.e., French Canadians) as being superior. The attitudes of the bilinguals are quite different. They hold more favorable attitudes towards the English than towards the French. Their clear identification with one group may contribute to their mastery of English. It is interesting to note that in the Voice Study, which attempts to tap stereotypes, the bilinguals evaluate the personalities of French and English speakers in a similar manner while the monolinguals evaluate the French more favorably than the English.

The pattern of attitudes that emerges for the two groups is distinctively different and these attitude differences might be expected to influence performance on intelligence tests, but this is not the case. There are no significant correlations between attitude and intelligence for either group. Nevertheless it is worthwhile examining the group differences in attitude patterns since they throw light on the possible reasons why some students become bilingual while others remain monolingual. This can best be done by comparing Factor III for the monolinguals with Factor II for the bilinguals. Factor III, for the monolinguals reflects a family-wide attitude to English Canadians, while Factor II for the bilinguals reflects a family-wide attitude to English Canadians versus French Canadians. The bilingual factor is bipolar in the sense that it has positive loadings of attitude variables favorable to English as well as negative loadings of attitude variables favorable to French. That is, the bilinguals, very likely through parental influence, are favorable toward the English community and at the same time unfavorable to the French.

Factor III for the monolinguals is a unitary factor. It indicates that the monolingual children of higher socioeconomic class, even though they hold positive attitudes to the English as do their parents, still have more favorable stereotypes of the French than of the English. This tendency to see the French as better may partly explain why the children have remained monolingual. Possibly children from these families of higher social class have developed positive attitudes to the English and yet feel a pressure to remain French. It is possible that some conservative nationalistic sentiment for the retaining of the French language exists among these children and prevents them from identifying sufficiently with the English community to be psychologically set to learn the language and thus they remain monolingual. And yet the higher social class families may admire and emulate the English Canadians as instrumentally valuable models in spheres of activity which contribute to maintaining higher social class standing, such as economic and social situations. Factor III also affords a second description of the monolingual family. In this case, the lower social class monolingual family has the following characteristics: the parents have little skill in English and hold negative attitudes to the English, although they do endorse favorable stereotypes of the English. The children are comparatively retarded in school grade. This pattern suggests that those French-Canadian families of lower socioeconomic class may become envious of the English Canadians and, perhaps through places of residence and type of work, culturally isolated and remain monolingual.

Thus a picture emerges of monolingual and bilingual children as representatives of two distinct groups, differing in intellectual structure, attitude patterns, achievement in school, and achievement in languages. The results of this study indicate the value of shifting emphasis from looking for favorable or unfavorable effects of bilingualism on intelligence to an inquiry into the basic nature of these effects. Perhaps further research may profit from this different emphasis.

SUMMARY

The effects of bilingualism on intellectual functioning are explored in this study. A group of monolingual and a group of bilingual ten-year-old children from six Montreal French schools were administered verbal and nonverbal intelligence tests, and measures of attitudes to the English and French communities. Contrary to previous findings this study found that bilinguals performed significantly better than monolinguals on both verbal and nonverbal intelligence tests. Several explanations are suggested as to why bilinguals have this general intellectual advantage. It is argued that they have a language asset, are more facile at concept formation, and have a greater mental flexibility. The results of factor analyses applied to the data supported the hypothesis that the structures of intellect for the two groups differ. The bilinguals appear to have a more diversified set of mental abilities than the monolinguals. The correlations of the attitude measures with other variables are also discussed.

Bibliography

Ahmed, M. A.-S. "Mental Manipulation." *Egypt. Yearbk. Psychol.*, 1954, **1**, 23–88.

Altus, Grace T. "WISC Patterns of a Selective Sample of Bilingual School Children." *J. genet. Psychol.*, 1953, **83**, 241–248.

Anastasi, Anne. *Psychological Testing.* 2nd ed. New York: The Macmillan Company, 1961.

Anisfeld, M., Bogo, N. and W. E. Lambert. "Evaluational Reactions to Accented English-Speech." McGill University, 1961. (mimeo)

Arsenian, S. "Bilingualism and Mental Development." *Teach. Coll. Contr. Educ.*, 1937, No. 712.

Arthur, G. "The Predictive Value of the Kuhlmann-Binet Scale for a Partially Americanized School Population." *J. appl. Psychol.*, 1937, **21**, 359–364.

Bere, M. *A Comparative Study of Mental Capacity of Children of Foreign Parentage.* New York: Teachers College, Columbia University, 1924.

Central Advisory Council for Education (Wales). *The Place of Welsh and English in the Schools of Wales.* London: Her Majesty's Stationery Office, 1953.

Christophersen, P. *Bilingualism.* London: Methuen, 1948.

Darcy, Natalie T. "The Effect of Bilingualism upon the Measurement of the Intelligence of Children of Preschool Age." *J. educ. Psychol.*, 1946, **37**, 21–44.

———. "A Review of the Literature on the Effects of Bilingualism upon the Measurement of Intelligence." *J. genet. Psychol.*, 1953, **82**, 21–57.

Darsie, M. L. "The Mental Capacity of American-Born Japanese Children." *Comp. Psychol. Monogr.*, 1926, **3**, 1–18.

Davies, M. and A. G. Hughes. An Investigation into the Comparative Intelligence and Attainments of Jewish and non-Jewish School Children." *Brit. J. Psychol.*, 1927, **18**, 134–146.

Dunn, L. M. *Peabody Picture Vocabulary Test*. Tennessee: American Guidance Service, 1959.

Evans, S. J. Address of the Conference of Headmasters of Grammar Schools, Wales, 1906. In Central Advisory Council for Education Wales), *The Place of Welsh and English in the Schools of Wales*. London: Her Majesty's Stationery Office, 1953.

Feingold, G. A. "Intelligence of the First Generation Immigrant Groups." *J. educ. Psychol.*, 1924, **15**, 65–82.

Ferguson, G. A. "On Learning and Human Ability." *Canad. J. Psychol.*, 1954, **8**, 95–112.

Gardner, R. C. Motivational Variables in Second-Language Acquisition. Unpublished doctoral dissertation, McGill University, 1960.

——— and W. E. Lambert. "Motivational Variables in Second-Language Acquisition." *Canad. J. Psychol.*, 1959, **13**, 266–272.

Graham, V. T. "The Intelligence of Italian and Jewish Children." *J. abnorm. soc. Psychol.*, 1925, **20**, 371–376.

Guilford, J. P. "The Structure of Intellect." *Psychol. Bull.* 1956, **53**, 267–293.

Hill, H. S. "The Effects of Bilingualism on the Measured Intelligence of Elementary School Children of Italian Parentage." *J. exp. Educ.*, 1936, **5**, 75–79.

Hirsch, N. D. "A Study of Natio-Racial Mental Differences." *Genet. Psychol. Monogr.*, 1926, **1**, 231–407.

James, C. B. E. "Bilingualism in Wales: An Aspect of Semantic Organization." *Educ. Res.*, 1960, **2**, 123–136.

Johnson, G. B. "Bilingualism as Measured by a Reaction-time Technique and the Relationship Between a Language and a Non-Language Intelligence Quotient." *J. genet. Psychol.*, 1953, **82**, 3–9.

Jones, W. R. "A Critical Study of Bilingualism and Nonverbal Intelligence." *Brit. J. educ. Psychol.*, 1960. **30**, 71–76.

——— and W. A. Stewart. "Bilingualism and Verbal Intelligence." *Brit. J. Psychol.*, 1951, **4**, 3–8.

Lambert, W. E. "Developmental Aspects of Second-Language Acquisition: I. Associational Fluency, Stimulus Provocativeness, and Word-Order Influence." *J. soc. Psychol.*, 1956, **43**, 83–89.

Lambert, W. E., Havelka, J. and C. Crosby. "The Influence of Language-Acquisition Contexts on Bilingualism." *J. abnorm. soc. Psychol.*, 1958, **56**, 239–244.

———, Havelka, J., and Gardner, R. C. "Linguistic Manifestations of Bilingualism." *Amer. J. Psychol.*, 1959, **72**, 77–82.

———, Hodgson, R. C., Gardner, R. C., and S. Fillenbaum. "Evaluational Reactions to Spoken Languages. *J. abnorm soc. Psychol.*, 1960, **60**, 44–51.

Langer, Susanne. *Philosophy in a New Key.* Cambridge Mass.: Harvard University Press, 1942.

Lavoie, G. and Laurendeau, Monique. *Tests collectifs d'intélligence générale.* Montreal, Canada: Institut de Recherches Psychologiques, 1960.

Lazowick, L. M. "On the Nature of Identification." *J. abnorm. soc. Psychol.*, 1955, **51**, 175–183.

Leopold, W. F. *Speech Development of a Bilingual Child.* Vol. 3. Evanston: Northwestern University Press, 1949.

Levinson, B. M. "A Comparison of the Performance of Bilingual and Monolingual Native Born Jewish Preschool Children of Traditional Parentage on Four Intelligence Tests." *J. clin. Psychol.*, 1959, **15**, 74–76.

Lewis, D. G. "Bilingualism and Non-Verbal Intelligence: A Further Study of Test Results." *Brit. J. educ. Psychol.*, 1959, **29**, 17–22.

McCarthy, Dorothea. "Language Development in Children." In L. Carmichael (Ed.), *Manual of Child Psychology.* New York: John Wiley & Sons, Inc., 1954.

Mead, M. "Group Intelligence and Linguistic Disability Among Italian Children." *Sch. Soc.*, 1927, **25**, 465–468.

Morrison, J. R. "Bilingualism: Some Psychological Aspects." *Advanc. Sci.*, 1958, **56**, 287–290.

O'Doherty, E. F. "Bilingualism: Educational Aspects." *Advanc. Sci.*, 1958, **56**, 282–286.

Osgood, C. E. Suci, G. J., and P. H. Tannenbaum. *The Measurement of Meaning.* Urbana: University of Illinois Press, 1957.

Pintner, R. "The Influence of Language Background on Intelligence Tests. *J. soc. Psychol.*, 1932, **3**, 235–240.

——— and S. Arsenian. "The Relation of Bilingualism to Verbal Intelligence and School Adjustment." *J. educ. Res.*, 1937, **31**, 255–263.

———— and R. Keller. "Intelligence Tests of Foreign Children." *J. educ. Psychol.*, 1922, **13**, 214–222.

Raven, J. C. *Coloured Progressive Matrices: Sets A, Ab, B.* London: Lewis, 1956.

Rigg, M. "Some Further Data on the Language Handicap." *J. educ. Psychol.*, 1928, **19**, 252–257.

Saer, D. J. "The Effects of Bilingualism on Intelligence." *Brit. J. Psychol.*, 1923, **14**, 25–38.

Saer, Hywela. "Experimental Inquiry into the Education of Bilingual Peoples." In, *Education in a Changing Commonwealth.* London: New Education Fellowship, 1931, pp. 116–121.

Seidl, J. C. G. The Effect of Bilingualism on the Measurement of Intelligence. Unpublished doctoral dissertation, Fordham University, 1937.

Smith, F. "Bilingualism and Mental Development." *Brit. J. Psychol.*, 1923, **13**, 270–282.

Spoerl, Dorothy, T. "The Academic and Verbal Adjustment of College-Age Bilingual Students." *J. genet. Psychol.*, 1944, **64**, 139–157.

Stark, W. A. "The Effect of Bilingualism on General Intelligence: An Investigation Carried out in Certain Dublin Primary Schools." *Brit. J. educ. Psychol.*, 1940, **10**, 78–79.

Thurstone, L. L. *Multiple Factor Analysis.* Chicago: University of Chicago Press, 1947.

———— and Thelma G. Thurstone. *Primary Mental Abilities: Ages 7 to 11.* Chicago: Science Research Associates, 1954.

Wang, S. L. "A Demonstration of the Language Difficulty Involved in Comparing Racial Groups by Means of Verbal Intelligence Tests." *J. appl. Psychol.*, 1926, **10**, 102–106.

Warner, W. L., Marchia Meeker, and K. Eells. *Social Class in America.* Chicago: Science Research Associates, 1949.

Weinreich, U. *Languages in Contact.* New York: Linguistic Circle of New York, 1953.

Wittenborn, J. R., and R. P. Larsen. "A Factorial Study of Achievement in College German." *J. educ. Psychol.*, 1944, **35**, 39–48.

THE LEARNING OF LANGUAGES

WILDER PENFIELD

There exists no more lucid explanation of the neurological basis of language than that which is given by Dr. Penfield in the following essay which is the eleventh and concluding chapter of Speech and Brain-Mechanisms, *by Wilder Penfield and Lamar Roberts. Dr. Penfield has been director of the Montreal Neurological Institute since its founding in 1934 and is chairman of the Department of Neurology and Neurosurgery of McGill University.*

From the neurologist and the physiologist the foreign language teacher has much to learn. Perhaps no stronger plea exists for teaching a foreign language in the elementary school than that set forth by this author. Even on a neurological basis the direct method is given preference over the translation method. A knowledge of the inner functioning of language will be not only helpful but certainly profitable to the teacher. This essay has had wide circulation and has been enthusiastically received.

A. FROM PHYSIOLOGY TO EDUCATION

In 1939 I was asked to give an address at Lower Canada College, and I decided to talk directly to the boys. Excerpts from that talk may serve as an amusing introduction here.

"I have long wondered," my talk began, "about secondary education from the safe distance of a neurological clinic. I have wondered why the curriculum was not adjusted to the evolution of functional capacity in the brain." . . .

Before the age of nine to twelve, a child is a specialist in learning to speak. At that age he can learn two or three languages as easily as one. It has been said that an Anglo-Saxon cannot learn other languages well. That is only because, as he grows up, he becomes a stiff and resistant individualist, like a tree—a sort of oak that cannot be bent in any graceful manner. But the Anglo-Saxon, if caught young enough, is as plastic and as good a linguist as the child of any other race.

When you have graduated and left Lower Canada College behind you, I hope that some of you will go into teaching as a profession, for there is no more important, no more challenging, and no more enjoyable profession that that of a teacher. But when you enter that profession, I beg you to rearrange the curriculum according to the changing mental capacities of the boys and girls you have to teach. . . . Remember that for the purposes of learning languages, the human brain becomes progressively stiff and rigid after the age of nine.

At the close of that somewhat naïve address the boys and their parents seemed most enthusiastic. What the teachers thought is not difficult to imagine. At all events, they smiled politely.

Again in 1953 I was called upon to address a lay audience. It was at a meeting of the American Academy of Arts and Sciences in Boston. By that time Dr. Roberts and I were in the midst of our clinical studies of speech disorders. Consequently, I chose as my subject: "A consideration of the neurophysiological mechanisms of speech and some educational consequences" (Penfield, 1953).

This aroused far more interest than I could have anticipated. The officers of the Modern Language Association of America heard of it, and, probably because it coincided with their own views, they had it reprinted. It was distributed then to the far-flung membership of that Association.

This dissemination resulted in at least one adverse criticism. A university president objected that early teaching of secondary languages was somehow in opposition to the teaching of those languages in institutions of higher learning. My intention, however, had been to promote more and better work in modern languages at the university level. But I consoled myself with the thought that there was, after all, nothing new in my proposals. Indeed, the ideas put forward were considerably older than modern education.

The world seems to have grown so much smaller and its peoples, all around the world, feel the need of direct communication. It is this need that emboldens us to add this chapter, which is primarily a scientific enquiry into *language learning,* and secondarily a plea for more consideration of the significance of neurophysiology in education.

It may well be convenient, for those who must plan the curriculum, to postpone the teaching of secondary languages until the second decade of childhood. But if the plan does not succeed, as they would have it, let them consider whether they have consulted the time table of the cerebral hemispheres. There is a biological clock of the brain as well as of the body glands of children.

Suppose a government, anxious about overpopulation, were to pass a law that marriage must wait until the age of forty. Perhaps there might be certain advantages for such a plan! Perhaps the plan might prove to be wise, too, if men and women were machines instead of the living, growing, changing creatures that they are. Such a law, you may well say, would be contrary to the unfolding nature of men and women. But, the same is true of a school curriculum in which the teaching of secondary language makes its first appearance at twelve or sixteen years of age.

For *bilingual countries* like Canada and Belgium, and for *multilingual countries* like India and the U.S.S.R., the learning of secondary languages is of the greatest importance. But unilingual lands have no less need of learning secondary languages. Ignorance deafens us so we cannot hear what our brothers are saying in other lands. Ignorance also blinds us so we cannot see them.

B. A GLANCE BACKWARD AND DOWNWARD

In the *history* of the human race we can only surmise how it was that man began to speak. Bees have a way of communicating ideas. So do birds and dogs and monkeys. They communicate ideas without words or names. The brain of the dog resembles the human brain in general organization. The brain of the chimpanzee is even more like ours. All the lobes are present. The pathways of muscular control are similar. Chimpanzee and dog have large areas of cerebral cortex, like our own, used for seeing, hearing, feeling. They have even larger areas for smelling.

More than that, animals have in their brains a mysterious store of useful instincts that I like to consider racial memories. These racial memories guide them at crucial times in life—teach them how to build a home and what to hunt. Man's brain is curiously lacking in these patterns of instinctive guidance for his behavior.

But to balance all that, man has the ability to learn. He is teachable. The infant possesses a *speech mechanism,* but it is only a potential mechanism. It is a clean slate, waiting for what that infant is to hear and see. Language must be taught first. And then, in time, language will serve as the vehicle for practically all forms of knowledge.

In the beginning, before he speaks, a child learns to know the meaning of the objects about him. Animals do the same. He understands certain concepts such as going out of doors, eating, etc., from experience. Animals do the same. He learns to understand the names for simple concepts, and animals follow him there, too, a little way.

When the child begins to speak, the animal is blocked and can no longer follow. This may be explained in part, perhaps, by the fact that man alone has an inborn control mechanism for vocalization in his cerebral cortex. Animals bark or mew or chatter by using neurological motor mechanisms in what may be called the old brain. Without the help of man's vocalization projection to the newer cortex, it is quite possible that vocalization could not be used in the complicated patterns which he employs for human speech. This must remain an hypothesis.

However, the neurological structures required for another and much more important mechanism are probably missing, too, in the subhuman brain. That is the mechanism employed by man for ideational speech. There is a very large increase in the extent of the temporo-parietal cortex that becomes obvious in passing from anthropoid ape to man. It seems likely that the posterior speech area of the human cortex constitutes a new appearance. It might seem that, by its addition, it had pushed the sensory and motor areas away and down into the fissures, and so, taken over this zone as the major ideational speech structure. One may assume that when these evolutionary enlargements of the brain made their appearance, in a far-off time, man began to talk. This, too, is hypothesis. . . .

The appearance of *writing* is certainly a much more recent event. This is even within the most distant limits of history. Collective civilization seems to have been made possible when man learned to cultivate grain in the valleys of the Nile and the Euphrates.

At the Iraq Museum in Baghdad is to be seen a most exciting series of clay tablets unearthed from ancient Sumerian cities where the Euphrates and Tigris rivers flowed into the Persian Gulf. These clay tablets are shaped like pieces of soap. At the time of writing, the tablet of soft clay was held in the palm of one hand while the scribe printed the cuneiform letters onto its surface, using a sharp stylus held in the other hand.

Many stages in the evolution of writing, beginning some 5,000 years ago, are to be seen in Baghdad.[1] One of the earliest tablets shows a pictograph of a bag of barley, and following it from left to right, suggesting that the scribe was holding the stylus in his right hand, is the single mark of the stylus that stood for the number ten (the number of a man's fingers). That is followed in turn by the marks to signify ones.

This was a record of sale at a time when speech must have been well advanced. It was a time when men were about to turn from the use of pictographs to writing. The development of their cuneiform writing from that time onward seems to have been relatively rapid.

C. THE DIRECT METHOD OF LANGUAGE LEARNING

The learning of language in the home takes place in familiar stages which are dependent upon the evolution of the child's brain. The mother helps, but initiative comes from the growing youngster. The learning of the mother tongue is normally an inevitable process. No parent could prevent it unless he placed his child in solitary confinement!

The learning of language by the direct method (the mother's method) is far more successful than the schooltime learning of secondary languages in the second decade of life (*language education*). The reasons for the success of the first method may be considered under two headings: 1) Physiological, and 2) Psychological.

---

[1] I was indebted to Seton Lloyd, who was curator of the Iraq Museum in 1943 at the time of my first visit, for the demonstration of these tablets. Somewhat similar tablets may be seen also in the University of Pennsylvania in Philadelphia, and in the British Museum in London.

1. *Neurophysiology.* The physiological reason for success in the home is that a child's brain has a specialized capacity for learning language—a capacity that decreases with the passage of years.

Evidence for this may be found in the experience of any immigrant family that arrives in a new country without previous knowledge of the local language. In two years the children learn a new language. They may come to speak it easily, with little accent, regardless of whether they go to school or simply play in the street. The same cannot be said of their parents. They seem to have lost the art of learning by a direct method. They may have recourse to special teaching by the scholastic or indirect method, but they cannot compete with their children. Their learning is indirect because they use the units of the mother tongue, which I shall describe below.

The brain of the child is plastic. The brain of the adult, however effective it may be in other directions, is usually inferior to that of the child as far as language is concerned. This is borne out still further by the remarkable relearning of a child after injury or disease destroys the speech areas in the dominant left cerebral hemisphere. Child and adult, alike, become speechless after such an injury, but the child will speak again, and does so, normally, after a period of months. The adult may or may not do so, depending on the severity of the injury.

Examples of completely successful transfer of speech mechanism from the left to the right hemisphere in children under three or four years of age are numerous. The upper age limit for this is not certain. But when the injury to the dominant hemisphere of an adult in his twenties or beyond is severe enough, he may never recover normal speech.

It must not be assumed, of course that speech is the only new skill that is more rapidly and perfectly acquired in childhood than it is later. Perhaps piano and violin playing and skiing come into similar categories.

2. *Psychology.* The second reason for the success of the direct method of teaching language in the home is the *psychological urge.* This must not be overlooked. For the child at home, the learning of language is a method of learning about life, a means of getting what he wants, a way of satisfying the unquenchable curiosity that burns in him almost from the beginning. He is hardly aware of

the fact that he is learning language, and it does not form his primary conscious goal.

The same may be true of a young child who is learning a new language in school, but it is only true if no other language is being spoken, for the time being, in the class room. The direct method is then employed in school, but the impetus for learning should still not be to collect words nor to acquire language. It should be to achieve success in games and problems, and success in learning about life and other delightful things.

It is interesting to speculate as to how such a man as William Shakespeare learned the English language. It seems quite unlikely that his mother could have taught him grammar or syntax, and one may doubt that such teaching in school was in any way responsible for the great gift of expression that was his, and the vast store of words in his memory. He must have learned English by the direct method at home, like other children. And, as he passed out of the primary stage of language learning into the second stage of *vocabulary expansion* in school, his rapid brain embraced thousands of new words in yearly succession.

The direct method of learning language can succeed at an older age—even after nine years—and adults can, of course, learn by it. The success of the Berlitz method is evidence of this. Some adults do quite well.

Take the case of Josef Konrad Korzeniowski, a Polish boy born in the Ukraine. He also became a master of the English language, second only to Shakespeare, perhaps. As a British subject and a celebrated author he was known as Joseph Conrad. English was for him a secondary, or rather, a tertiary language. Polish was his mother's tongue, but he spoke French as a child with his nursery governess, and he sailed away on a British ship at the age of fifteen years.

At sea he heard no other language but English, and so, at fifteen he began to learn this language by the "mother's method." He learned the "lingo" and the slang first, no doubt. The *psychology of language learning* in this sailing ship was like that in the home. There was no translating. English words were the immediate symbols through which he must come to understand life. They were the symbols that brought him food and success as a young sailor.

Thus, he learned the sort of language he would never have discovered, however hard he worked, with dictionary and grammar as his only guide. He learned the good, short, simple words and the speech that men use in the face of trial and danger.

"Goodbye brothers," he wrote, "you were a good crowd. As good a crowd as ever fisted with wild cries the beating canvas of a heavy foresail; or tossing aloft, invisible in the night, gave back yell for yell to a westerly gale."

I have been told by an Englishman, who knew Conrad after he had become a famous author in England, that he spoke English beautifully. He recalls, now, no obvious accent, either Polish or French. I suspect, however, that his accent at first and his early vocabulary must have resembled to some extent that of the sailors with whom he shipped. But once he had mastered the elements of that limited shipboard vocabulary in English by the direct method, he was ready to expand his English vocabulary in any and all directions.

There is some evidence to suggest that those who learn more than one language in early childhood find the learning of later additional languages easier. Theoretically it should be so, since they carry in their speech mechanism a larger variety of sound elements and speech units. I shall enlarge on this presently.

D. THE BIOLOGICAL TIMETABLE OF LANGUAGE LEARNING

The sequence of normal language learning has been studied exhaustively by Leopold (1939–1949) in his own children, who were brought up in a bilingual household, and by Gesell and Ilg in a large series of unilingual children, followed through succeeding years.[2]

During the infant's first year he cries at once. He coos later and then babbles. Babbling is verbal play "with front sounds and clear consonants." Around the time of the first birthday he usually says his first word. In the second year it is clear that the child learns to understand and later to speak. There is apt to be a lag of two to seven months from first hearing to utterance. From two to four

---

[2] See also *Bulletin No. 49*, August, 1956, issued by the Modern Language Association of America, 70 Fifth Avenue, New York 11, N.Y.

years the delightful lingo of baby talk disappears and is replaced by adult pronunciations. The skills of understanding and speaking are more or less perfected by the age of four. Reading and writing are not yet to be considered.

Leopold concludes that during the second year of life speech consists normally of one-word sentences. Gradually the child puts two words together, then three. There are many variations to these achievements, as any proud parent will testify. But by the time of the third birthday the three basic elements of simple sentences have made their appearance: subject, verb, object. The child uses some pronouns and employs plurals at this time, and is adding new words at the rate of about four hundred in six months.

Dr. Ilg would distinguish two types of child, which she calls "imitative" and "creative." Children in the first group learn more rapidly and accurately with less baby talk and jargon. Girls are more likely to be placed in this group of accurate learners than boys. The creative learner is slower and more apt to elaborate pronunciations and jargon of his own. Poets, she says, are prone to come from this group! It is obvious that individual differences are recognizable at almost any stage throughout childhood.

There seems to be little if any relationship between general intellectual capacity and the ability of a child to imitate an accent. Pronunciation is essentially an imitative process. Capacity for imitation is maximum between four and eight. It steadily decreases throughout later childhood.

According to Professor Leopold the child of six to eight years has formed his native speech habits completely. But they are not so firmly established as to interfere with his capacity to acquire a second language without translation. It would seem, however, that the first language is well set by the age of four or five. As I shall point out later, if the child is using a second language even before that time, the two may be set equally without interference.

Gesell and Ilg have concluded that at the age of eight the average child is "group-minded, expansive and receptive." At eight the child begins to hold on to patterns, and at nine, to fix these patterns. At the age of nine the child is said to become more analytical in language learning. He is apt to become analytical in regard to his general attitude as well.

E. BRAIN MECHANISMS OF LANGUAGE

Man's ability to talk is due to the development and employment of the specialized speech mechanisms of the dominant hemisphere, as described in the preceding chapter. Local injury of these areas in early childhood may produce a complete aphasia. This is followed by a period of silence, to be succeeded in time by complete relearning of language. The ability of an adult to relearn speech after injury is much inferior to that of a child.

With severe aphasia at any time, the individual's ability to convey meaning by gesture of head or hand is lost. He may use the muscles of neck and hand for other purposes, but he cannot nod assent in place of the word "yes," nor shake his head in place of the lost word "no." It must be assumed, then, that the characteristic gestures employed by anyone to convey meaning while speaking, or instead of speaking, must have neuronal units in the speech mechanism. This applies to meaningful gestures as it does to writing.

No statement of the evidence in regard to speech dominance and hand dominance need be made here. As far as our evidence can go, grave injury in infancy or childhood produces transfer of speech dominance to the opposite hemisphere, if the lesion occurs in the speech area. But hand dominance is not caused to change over unless there is injury to arm areas also. Thus the transfers are independent.

However, since injuries are apt to involve both areas rather than one, it can be understood that an individual who is left-handed because of early disease or brain injury is most likely to have speech function located in the right hemisphere. On the other hand, the "normally" left-handed individual who had no early brain injury may have speech dominance in either hemisphere. But he is still more apt to have it in the left hemisphere like other people.

It seems unlikely that speech correction or speech development can be aided by interference with the spontaneous tendency to use right or left hand in preference. It is also impossible for the observer to be certain (unless a radical sodium amytal aphasia test is carried out) whether, during the period of recovery from aphasia, the individual is making a transfer of speech function to the opposite hemisphere, as children sometimes do, or whether he is restoring function in the injured hemisphere, as adults are more likely to do.

Now to return to the normal process of language learning: The cerebral mechanisms involved in learning a language by the direct method may be pictured in hypothetical outline. . . .

1. *Acquisition of Speech Units.* Consider the second year of a child's life. The opinion of Leopold was quoted above, that at this age there is a lag of two to seven months from the first hearing of a word until its first meaningful utterance. During that time the child is faced with the necessity of making a neuronal record of the concept to be named and a neuronal record of the word. There is a third task, too. That is to establish an automatic reflex connection between the two.

For example, suppose that each time the mother takes the child out of doors, she says, "Go bye-bye." The child must learn to understand the meaning of the concept of going out of doors. To do that he must make a generalization from a number of particular experiences of going out in his carriage.

That concept must be recorded somewhere in the brain so he can get at it again when needed. It must be held there so he can alter it as time passes and new experiences come to him. One must assume that there are specialized areas in the brain where the patterns of passage of nerve impulse may be stored. The pattern of passage of electrical potentials through certain neurones (nerve cells) and over their connecting fibers forms a unit. In this case the unit becomes the concept (going out of doors) when nerve impulses pass through that pattern again.

Each passage of a stream of neuronal impulses leaves behind it a persisting facilitation, so that impulses may pass that way again with greater ease. This is, in general, the neuronal basis of memory. The pattern followed by those impulses may be referred to as a unit, for the purposes of our discussion. And I shall use the word "unit" to refer to the neuronal pattern that corresponds with the sound of a word. I shall use the word "unit," too, when referring to the neuronal pattern used in speaking the word.

It was pointed out . . . that memory of concepts, which does not depend on one hemisphere as speech does, is separate from the speech mechanism. Conceptual memory may be intact in the presence of severe aphasia when the left-sided speech mechanism is paralyzed. Therefore, a neurone-connection pattern must be established in what may be called the *concept mechanism*. In the case of the child, the idea of going out of doors is preserved as a *conceptual unit*.

In addition, then, to the idea of going out of doors, the child must remember the sound of the words "Go bye-bye." That means that a neurone-connection pattern is laid down in the speech areas of the left hemisphere. This we might call the *sound unit*. In addition to that, there must be an automatic connection from sound unit to conceptual unit, and from conceptual unit to sound unit.

When these two units are established with their interconnections, the baby is able to understand. An intelligent dog might achieve all of these things, too, as far as this process has gone. Now that the baby understands, he probably smiles or laughs at the phrase "Go bye-bye." The dog might well wag his tail under the same circumstances. Each would thus indicate his understanding without speech and add his approbation. It would be communication without words.

But the baby must now take the next step, and no animal can follow him there. He must speak. When he does do so, he will imitate the sound in a voluntary act, probably making one word of it—perhaps something like "bye-bye."

Having spoken, he will repeat that word often. Each time he hears his mother say it in the next few months, he will probably pronounce it better and so make for himself a more and more perfect verbal motor image. This *verbal unit* has its neuronal pattern located in the left hemisphere speech mechanism. Certainly, at all events, it is not in the areas of cortex concerned with voice control, although these motor areas of the cortex must be used in the voluntary formation of the sounds.

What the relationship may be between the word-sound unit and the verbal unit is not clear. The verbal unit seems to formulate for the child the set of the muscles to be used to pronounce the word. Some light may be thrown on this question by reconsidering the types of clinical aphasia.

It was pointed out . . . that there are definite differences in the types of aphasia produced by lesions in different portions of the speech cortex. In some cases there is more involvement of the sensory side of speech, and in others, more of the motor elements.

Thus, there is what clinicians have called *motor aphasia,* in which speaking is severely involved while understanding of speech is relatively, and comparatively, intact. There is also *sensory aphasia* in which the reverse is true. This strongly suggests that the motor units for words and phrases are separated somehow, spatially, from the sensory units. But it is also clear that they are both located in the general region of the cortico-thalamic speech areas of the left side, where they are closely interrelated in function.

Thus, when the child begins to understand, he is establishing general concept units in the brain and corresponding word-sound units. When he begins to speak he must establish word-formation units. During this early experimental period he uses his voluntary motor system to make a more and more accurate sound, thus correcting and reinforcing the image of how to speak the word. What I called an image is really a pattern of the motor complex required to produce the word. This image or motor pattern is a unit, too, and the neurones involved in the pattern unit are clearly located in the speech areas.

Between the motor-pattern unit and the motor-expression mechanism the connection is not automatic. If it were, the child would be an automaton, a machine, a robot. No. Between word pattern and word expression must come a conscious selection and decision. This means the employment of the *centrencephalic system.* That is the system of central organizing connections which makes available to conscious thinking the many different neuronal mechanisms within the brain.

When the child begins to write words and to read words, two new sets of units must be established. They are also located within the general structure of the dominant hemisphere speech mechanism.

Writing is carried out by one hand, which is called dominant. It is controlled through the motor-hand mechanism in the cortex of the opposite hemisphere. Writing must be considered voluntary in regard to each move, at the beginning. But in time it comes to be automatic. The image of the movement required to produce each word, taken together with the execution of the movement, becomes a skill that is eventually automatic but can be controlled voluntarily. It is so automatic that in time, a man can summon a word and discover that his hand has written it. He can go beyond that. He can summon to mind the concept, of which the word is a counterpart, and discover that his hand has written it. He can summon a series of concepts and find them recorded by that hand on the page before him. Writing, thus, takes on an automatic character like speaking and automobile driving.

The driver of a car makes each move under voluntary control while learning. Later on he thinks only of turning the automobile around the corner, and his hands "do the trick" automatically. Speaking becomes similarly automatic. A man may summon a word and his lips speak it. He may summon a series of concepts and the words are produced automatically.

But, nevertheless, the patterns of how the words are to be spoken and the patterns of the words to be written are each recorded in the speech mechanism, not in the motor mechanism of the right hand. If I should break my right arm and then train my left to do what I want it to do, my signature will soon be accepted by the experts at the bank who knew my name on cheques (all too well!) before the accident.

Let me recall the case of a patient who made his living by his handwriting. He suffered from writer's cramp, and so he had to shift from right hand to left hand, back and forth, because the cramp would come upon him after a few weeks or months. When I asked him about his signature on cheques, he replied, "Oh, the signature is in the mind."

Yes, he was correct in thinking that the signature was not in the motor mechanism. It is in the neurone unit within the brain. Probably that applies to all the words we write. It seems likely that we write according to the concept carried in the brain. The signature follows that neurone pattern. The written word is carried as a final pattern—a pattern of a motor complex. In the fully developed skill the unit pattern is only one station in the amazing automatic flow of electrical potentials from concept unit to muscle.

Returning to the act of speaking: We control voice and mouth by following the verbal motor units formed and fixed by early practice. It is difficult to make any certain statement on the question of accents by reference to the physiological evidence alone. One may say that children have a greater capacity for imitation than adults. That seems to be a fact, but it is not an explanation of what happens in later life.

We may reconsider the whole process more simply: During normal speech it may be said that two mechanisms are employed, and both are present only in the human brain. There is an ideational mechanism which makes available the acquired elements of speech, and a motor articulation mechanism that is inborn but may be utilized by the voluntary motor system.

(a) The ideational part of speech, whether spoken, heard, written, or read, depends upon the employment of a certain portion of one hemisphere alone—normally the left hemisphere. This localization of a function in one hemisphere is, in itself, something new in mammalian evolution. Other intellectual functions, such as perception, the recording of current experiences, and the storing of generalizations or concepts in memory, are made possible by the utilization of homologous areas of cerebral cortex on the two sides, together with the coordinating and integrating work of the higher brain stem.

It is thanks to the action of the ideational speech areas of the dominant cortex, and their connections with a small zone of gray matter below the cortex in the thalamus, that words may be "found" by the individual. Speech is made possible because of neurone patterns and reflexes that are formed there during the process of language learning.

The nerve cells and nerve branches of some parts of the brain, or perhaps the synapses which join the branch of one cell to the body of another cell, are altered by the passage of a stream of electrical potentials. That is what makes permanent patterns possible. This is the basis of all *memory*.

Thus, man is able to find, in his ideational speech mechanism, four sets of neurone patterns: the sound units of words employed when listening to speech, the verbal units followed for speaking, the visual units for reading, and the manual units for writing.[3]

This is, no doubt, an oversimplification. And yet it must be somehow true, since other areas of the cortex may be removed without

---

[3] It might be suggested that a word or a phrase is sometimes used in thinking without reference to sound of the word, its appearance when printed, or the movements of mouth or hand which make it. This implies that there is an abstract concept of a word. Butterfly is a word. The idea of the fluttering, living thing is a concept. Whether there is something else between the two is a matter for psychological discussion and need not detain us here.

producing aphasia, if only the speech areas of the dominant cortex and its subcortical connections are not interfered with. On the other hand, when they alone are involved, and the rest of the hemisphere is normal, the patient can no longer "find" words, though he "knows" what he wants to say. He can summon the concepts "to mind," but the previously automatic connection between concept unit and word unit is broken. This is *aphasia.*

(*b*) *Articulation,* on the other hand, depends upon the employment of special motor areas in the cortex of either hemisphere. There are areas devoted to vocalization—two in each cortex—and no other mammal yet studied possesses such areas in the motor cortex. There are areas also for other movements of mouth, tongue, and throat.

The streams of neurone impulses that produce voluntary movement arise in the circuits of integration in the brain stem—the *centrencephalic system.* They flow out to these cortical motor areas and from there down to the muscles of mouth and throat and diaphragm. But if the motor areas of cortex are damaged or removed on one side, those on the other side soon serve the purposes of speech movements quite satisfactorily.

Man has inherited the motor mechanisms which make speaking possible. But there is no inheritance of those things that he adds to his ideational speech mechanism while he is learning a language. The clean, blank speech slate which he brought with him into the world is soon filled with units, and after the first decade of life they can hardly be erased. They can be added to, but with increasing difficulty.

2. *Vocabulary Expansion.* When a child comes to the age of six he is ready to begin to expand his vocabulary rapidly, and as he passes the age of nine, the process is accelerated. He reads and talks and listens incessantly. If he is expanding his vocabulary in his native tongue, the process is simple, rapid, normal. He uses the speech units already written indelibly on the slate of his ideational speech mechanism.

He can pass from a vocabulary of 1,000 words to 10,000 perhaps, using the same language set. The sound, the pronunciation, and the spelling are all so similar. He can use his recorded units. The sentence construction does not alter. His eventual accent continues to resemble the accent of those he listened to first in home and school and playground.

If the child uses only one language until he becomes a young adult, he then approaches a second language by using the well-learned symbols of his mother tongue. This is correct for language expansion, but wrong for new-unit formation. Instead of imitating the sounds of the new language, he tries to employ his own verbal units—his mother-tongue units—and so, speaks with an accent, and even rearranges the new words into a construction that is wrong. Thus, all Swedes speak English with a Swedish accent, and the French, the Germans, and the Chinese each speak it with their own accents.

This is a common enough experience. Even though they travel over the world, the Cockney and the Scot and the Irishman betray their origin all through life by a "turn of the tongue" learned in childhood, to say nothing of the Canadian and the American.

1. *Language Learning by the Indirect Method.* The youth who approaches a second language for the first time in school, during the second or third decade of his life, faces a new problem. He has come, now, into the period of rapid vocabulary expansion, as well as the period of mathematical, historical, scientific, and philosophical studies. He employs the units which were fixed in his speech mechanism in childhood. Thus, he begins to translate, and there is set up a new neurophysiological process: *indirect language learning.*

It is not all a matter of age, for second languages are frequently taught by the indirect school method even to children before the age of nine. The teacher whose mother tongue was English, and who must explain French to little children using English to do so, is using the indirect method of teaching. She instructs them, not only because of her method, but also by her pronunciation, to speak French with units that belong to the English tongue. She teaches them to learn by the indirect method and to speak by it.

The teacher whose mother tongue was French and who enters the classroom and talks only in French, even though she makes no effort to do anything but play with them, allows the children to learn by the direct method and to acquire French speech units that can be used later, should they have the opportunity of expanding French vocabulary. They think in the new language from the beginning.

The indirect method of language teaching has been borrowed by educators from the methods that were developed for the teaching of Latin and Greek. These two languages, once the only link men had with the rich culture of the classical past, gradually ceased to be spoken and so became "dead languages."

Educators have often declared that the mental discipline involved is excellent, I agree with that. The same may be said, of course, in favor of the four-mile walk between home and the little red schoolhouse of yesterday.

Certainly there is a growing place in the educational scheme for the indirect method of teaching secondary languages in high school and university. It would achieve more if direct language learning could be used as an introduction to it. There is also an almost totally ignored opportunity for the use of the direct method of teaching secondary languages at an earlier age level.

My purpose here, it should be stated, at the close of this discussion of the indirect method, is merely to point out the differences in the brain physiology of the two methods. The planning of teaching methods and curricula is the task of the expert educator. If these discussions of the physiology and psychology of language learning have practical value for teaching, he will know best what practical application to make.

2. *Language Learning by the Direct Method.* The mechanism that is developed in the brain is the same whether one, two, or more languages are learned. French is not subserved by one area of brain and English and Chinese by others, in spite of the fact that cases have been published of adults who lost one language and preserved another as the result of "stroke" or other injury to the brain. Our conclusion is that these patients must have been inadequately studied, or else there were psychological reasons why one language was preferred in the recovery period. After thirty years of experience in the bilingual community of Montreal, I have never seen such an example. We have often been told, even by physicians, that this patient or that patient has lost his French, but not his English, or vice versa. But careful examination has proven invariably that such judgments were false.

A child who is exposed to two or three languages during the ideal period for language beginning, pronounces each with the accent of his teacher. If he hears one language at home, another at school, and a third, perhaps, with a governess in the nursery, he is not aware that he is learning three languages at all. He is aware of the fact that to get what he wants with the governess he must speak one way, and with his teacher he must speak in another way. He does not reason it out at all. There is no French, no German, no English. It is simpler than that.

Although the cortico-thalamic speech mechanism serves all three languages and there is no evidence of anatomical separation, nevertheless, there is a curiously effective automatic switch that allows each individual to turn from one language to another. What I have referred to as a "switch" would be called, by experimental physiologists, a conditioned reflex. When child or adult turns to an individual who speaks only English, he speaks English, and turning to a man who speaks French and hearing a word of French, the conditioning signal turns the switch over and only French words come to mind. During multiple language learning it would seem to be best for the learner that his environment should not vary too much. Teachers who teach language should speak only one language.

3. *Language Learning by the Mother's Method.* The best use of the direct method of teaching language is that employed in the home. The method of teaching children their mother's own language has been much the same in all lands and in all ages. It is extraordinarily efficient. It conforms to the changing capacities of the child's brain. The mother's method is the original direct method. It has also been used by servants and tutors in the home to teach one, two, or more secondary languages from the beginning of history. This makes it seem the more surprising that educators today do not generally employ the method in schools.

The mother's method is simple. It is familiar to everyone. Nonetheless, let us examine it. Even before the child understands, the mother talks to him. Before he speaks she watches for understanding. When he says his first words he has a delighted audience. Language is for him only a means to an end, never an end in itself. When he learns about words he is learning about life, learning to get what he wants, learning to share his own exciting ideas with others, learning to understand wonderful fairy tales and exciting facts about trains and trucks and animals and dolls. One secret of the success of this method is, of course, that it is employed while a child is forming the speech units in his eager little brain. A child who hears three languages instead of one, early enough, learns the units of all three without added effort and without confusion. I have watched this experiment in my own home, as many others must have done.

Our two younger children heard only German in the nursery from the ages of six months and eighteen months onward because they had a German governess. Even their parents talked German with them, to the best of their ability, when they entered the nursery. At the ages of three and four they entered a French nursery school. From their parents and others outside the school and outside the nursery they began to hear English gradually.

It was a conditioned reflex for those children, on entering the schoolroom, to utilize the language units of the French tongue; a conditioned reflex on meeting the governess, wherever they found her, to use the German units; from English playmates they learned English. There was no confusion.

After two years in the French nursery school they entered a regular English school. In retrospect, it would have been better to continue the French to the age of seven. The seven-year-old "hangs on" to things. In English school too many years elapsed before French and German were presented to them as regular secondary languages. But, nevertheless, they found the work easy and their accents were good. Hidden away in the brain of each were the speech units of all three languages, waiting to be employed in the expansion of a vocabulary which normally takes place in later school years.

Our two older children heard German first at eight and nine, when they played with German children for a few months in a small town in Germany. The governess who could speak no English entered the household then. They were never taught German until university level, but in the end they spoke it fluently with a perfect accent.

Of course, there is nothing new in all this. The experiment succeeded. But not all households can include a governess. If public education is to incorporate secondary languages into the curriculum, it should be planned according to the changing aptitudes of the human brain. When new languages are taken up for the first time in the second decade of life, it is difficult, though not impossible, to achieve a good result. It is difficult because it is unphysiological.

G. SCHOOLING

In this new day of nationalism and freedom, educators seek, quite rightly, to make education available to all. But unless the mother's method is introduced into the schools, the majority, even of those who are taught, will continue to fail to master any language but their mother tongue.

Bilingualism is not a handicap to a country. It has been a great benefit to mankind, as multilingualism has also. The language of Greece served the Romans very well as a second language for centuries, and both Greek and Latin were lamps in the great darkness of medieval Europe until the time of the Renaissance. Then, through these two secondary languages, the light of a bygone day flooded the minds of men, who woke, as though from sleep.

The time to begin what might be called a general schooling in secondary languages, in accordance with the demands of brain physiology, is between the ages of four and ten. The child sets off for school then, and he can still learn new languages directly without interposing the speech units of his mother tongue.

Suppose we discuss a hypothetical dayschool in the bilingual community that I know best—that of the city of Montreal and the province of Quebec. A million citizens in Montreal have French for their mother tongue, and less than half that number, English. Suppose the school is located in an English-speaking section of the city. Let the first years, from nursery school and kindergarten on to the grades for children of eight, perhaps, be conducted by teachers whose mother tongue is French.

The French teachers must speak only their native tongue in school, at work, and at organized play, with never a word of translation. Thus the little ones would begin their years of normal play, drawing, singing, and memorizing in French. They would be taught no language as such, but the teachers would "get on" from fairy tales to folk literature as rapidly as the child's mind is prepared for it. These children would have been hearing Mother

Goose stories and such things at home, and their play at the week-ends, as well as the home discipline and religious observance, would have been carried out in English.

Two or three years of this might well be enough. If so, they could be rotated then into a school or department conducted in another secondary language, if desired.

At the age of eight or ten they would graduate, perhaps, into a school conducted in the mother tongue. There they would carry on with all the subjects of a normal curriculum. This would include, in time, courses in the literature of those languages in which their earliest schooling had been presented. They would turn to those subjects effectively and without accent. They would be ready to expand their vocabularies using the language units of understanding and pronunciation learned earlier.

During higher education it will always be desirable that some students take up new languages at a later period, and there is a good deal of evidence that he who has learned more than one language as a little child has greater facility for the acquisition of additional languages in adult life.

There are alternatives to the one I have suggested, of course. One is the language teacher who enters the class for one period every day to speak his or her native tongue. This should begin at age five or six, when children are ready for games and singing if possible.[4] It would be most effective if there had been at least one preliminary year conducted entirely in the second language at kindergarten level.

Language, when it is learned by the normal physiological process, is not taught at all. It is learned as a byproduct of other pursuits. The learner should understand in the language, speak in the language, think in the language, even ignore the language. For the

[4] Dr. Robert Gauthier, director of French Education in the Province of Ontario, has introduced an interesting new method of teaching French to English children in English schools. The method was first described to him by Dr. Tan Gwan Leong, Curriculum Officer of Burma. In Gauthier's experiment the French teacher enters the English class for a period on certain days. He talks in French and the children answer in English, if they choose. This was carried out in fifth and seventh grades, beginning with the September opening of the term. At Christmas time half of the children were answering in French. When I visited the experiment, I thought the accent of the children was good, especially in the younger class.

direct learner, language is not a subject to be studied nor an object to be grasped. It is a means to other ends, a vehicle, and a way of life.

My plea to educators and parents is that they should give some thought to the nature of the brain of a child, for the brain is a living mechanism, not a machine. In case of breakdown, it can substitute one of its parts for the function of another. But it has its limitations. It is subject to inexorable change with the passage of time.

In the words of the unknown writer of Ecclesiastes, "To everything there is a season and a time to every purpose under heaven: A time to be born and a time to die. A time to plant and a time to pluck up that which is planted. . . . A time to weep and a time to laugh; a time to mourn, and a time to dance." Man's mind has its own peculiar calendar. There is a time to plant, a time to wait on increase, a time for the harvest of knowledge, and, at last, a time for wisdom.

PSYCHOLOGICAL APPROACHES TO THE STUDY OF LANGUAGE

WALLACE E. LAMBERT

The questions that relate to language learning and psychology are many and one of the persons best qualified to answer them is Wallace Lambert of McGill University. In the following essay, prepared for a Seminar on Language Teacher Training at the University of Washington, Professor Lambert looks into the various theories of learning as they relate to foreign language acquisition. The answers given are not based on theory alone but on findings backed by scientific experimentation. Any well-prepared foreign language teacher in the future will need a basic knowledge of psycholinguistics that he can apply to his own language teaching practices, procedures, and methods. In pointing this out, Professor Lambert has presented another discipline upon which the foreign language teacher should rely for better, faster, and more proficient teaching. Also considered is the bilingual and some of the many relevant problems of language learning that stem from bilingualism.

The assignment given me was to set forth and explain certain subject matter and research from the field of psychology which, if included in the training of language specialists, would enrich their understanding of the phenomena of language and increase their efficiency as trainers of teachers of foreign languages. Accordingly, my purpose here is to present various analytic schemes in psychology which could be of instructive value and practical use for those responsible for the training of language teachers. The term "analytic

Reprinted by permission of The Modern Language Journal from Vol. XLVIII, No. 2 (February, 1963) and No. 3 (March, 1963).

scheme" refers to a basic theory which has amassed sufficient supporters and generated enough reliable research to be considered as having permanent value in both accounting for empirical facts and orienting future research. The fact that a decision has been made to deal with *various* schemes of analysis indicates, first of all, that there is a selection being presented here. It is my own opinion that the contemporary developments in our field to be presented below are best suited for the assignment given me. For fear that I might overdo this assignment, I have dropped consideration of certain schemes which I also feel are appropriate. For example, language teachers and their trainers could profit from a careful study of current research in the psychology of personality. This area of specialization offers various means of selecting those who would be most effective as language teachers, a matter as important as it is neglected in educational research. In the second place, the fact that several schemes are to be dealt with highlights the fact that psychology is an extremely wide-ranging discipline with subspecialties concerning themselves with many different aspects of language.

My aim is to briefly introduce the basic ideas and implications of each scheme, as I see them, with a view to whetting appetites or enticing seminar members to turn to the more complete accounts which are referred to in the reading list presented in the bibliography.

1. THEORIES OF LEARNING OF RELEVANCE FOR LANGUAGE SPECIALISTS

Since its beginning as an independent discipline, psychology has always considered the phenomena of language and the language learning process as important matters falling within its field of specialization. But since World War II, a surge of interest in the cognitive aspects of behavior and the development of new methodologies have generated a widely felt hope that perhaps now psychologists can systematically study the phenomena of language rather than speculate about them. In fact, until the 1940s, "language" was typically categorized along with thinking and other "complex processes" and dodged by most lecturers and researchers in the field. Today many psychologists are starting to teach courses and carry out research on "verbal behavior," "psycholinguistics," or "language and thought." This new attitude stems from advances, perhaps normal ones, in many fields of specialization which feed into psychology, for example, advances in the neurology of brain functioning, in statistical and experimental procedures, in the design and operation of computers, and in methods of language teaching. As a response to these developments, psychologists are beginning to extend their principles and theories beyond the level of animal research (so very necessary for the establishment of basic principles in the first place) to the more complex behavior of man. Currently, all major theories of learning concern themselves with language and find a growing body of empirical data on the subject which they can use to test out their theories. The following discussion of two contemporary learning theories which are concerned in large part with language is presented with the belief that those responsible for language teaching can profit substantially from these psychological perspectives.

Psychologists are currently interested in two basic processes: the matter of meaning, the symbol-referent problem, and the matter of verbal behavior, how words are used in communication, either as units or as elements in larger response sequences.

In order to understand what psychologists think about these two major features of language, it is necessary to follow the arguments from their theoretical starting points. What follows is a very brief sketch of two contrasting learning theories. There are two because those dealing with meaning make use of one theory, while those concerned with verbal behavior make use of a second theory. There is nothing necessarily inconsistent in a discipline which has more than one scheme of analysis to integrate facts and explain events, especially when the facts and events are as complex as those of human cognitive behavior. When all the facts are some day in, two or more theories of learning may prove to be necessary, or as others very convincingly argue (Mowrer, 1960, chapters 3 and 4) a single set of principles may ultimately draw the two schemes together.

The contrast here is between what are called "classical" and "instrumental" forms of conditioning or learning. "Classical" refers to Pavlov's notions about the conditioned response. In this case, a stimulus with some "natural" or built-in evocative tendency (such as a hammer tap on the patellar tendon of the knee which evokes an involuntary muscular kicking response) can be replaced by an "unnatural" stimulus (such as the sound of a bell). The unnatural stimulus takes over the evocative capacity of the natural stimulus when the two stimuli are repeatedly paired as in the order bell–hammer tap, bell–hammer tap, etc., for a long series of presentations. Several notions are of importance in this statement. A stimulus which has a natural response sequel is a required ingredient; this is the "unconditioned" or uncontaminated element. The knee jerk is *not* a natural sequel to the hearing of a bell, and when a bell–knee jerk connection is finally made, the kick response is referred to as a "conditioned" response and the bell is called a "conditioned" stimulus. The time separating the conditioned and unconditioned stimuli is of major importance. The two stimuli must be nearly simultaneously presented, with the conditioned stimulus (the bell) coming a fraction of a second earlier than the unconditioned stimulus. It is not known how this transfer of evocative capacity takes place; psychology and neurology have had and will have a great deal of fun trying to understand the process. But the empirical facts are very dependable. Pavlov's dogs salivated (a conditioned response) to the sound of a bell (a conditioned stimulus) when bell and food were repeatedly paired. And Pavlov's dogs were not special in this respect. Literally thousands of experiments have re-established the same phenomenon with organisms at nearly every level of the phylogenetic scale.

The evocative capacity of the conditioned stimulus when on its own is ephemeral and it must be periodically "recharged" by being paired with the unconditioned stimulus. The repeated association of the two stimuli permits the transfer of evocative capacity and there must be periodical reassociation of the two if the transferred capacity is to be maintained. When fully charged the conditioned stimulus itself can be repeatedly paired with a second unnatural stimulus (for example, the flash of a light) and this second conditioned stimulus picks up the charge in the sense that it can also evoke the "conditioned" response. This is referred to as "second-order" conditioning. If a second conditioned stimulus which is *similar* in some sense to the first conditioned stimulus is introduced for the first time, it too will have an evocative capacity to call out the conditioned response. The conditioning is said to "generalize" to related stimuli, the degree of generalization depending on the degree of similarity between the original conditioned stimulus and the "similar" stimulus. If the original bell had a tone quality of

300 cps, generalization would likely take place to a tone of 325 or 275 cps.

Note in this argument that the conditioned stimulus (hearing a bell) functions as a signal or sign that something is to come, somewhat analogous to a symbol relating to its referent. The organism comprehends that the bell "stands for" the hammer tap and it is likely that a mental image of the hammer tap eventually occurs when the signal is received, as though some mental replica of the actual referent is evoked by the symbol because of some changes within the nervous system brought on by the continual pairing of stimuli. Here in compressed form is the psychological basis for the relation of symbol to referent. Charles Osgood (1953) has made this development especially clear. For Osgood, the meaning of a sign or symbol *is* the mental or neurological counterpart, in attenuated form, of the actual emotional and behavioral responses which have habitually been made to the referent for which the symbol stands. That is, linguistic symbols are originally learned in a context where they are repeatedly paired with their appropriate referents. An infant hears the word "dog" repeated several times while in the presence of an actual dog and in time whatever emotional and behavioral reactions are elicited by the presence of the actual dog are transferred to the symbol "dog." Symbols then come to evoke some miniature replica of the actual responses made to the referent, and these responses, referred to as "representational mediational responses" constitute the meaning of the symbol. They *represent* or stand for the full pattern of responses made to the referent, they *mediate* or link the responses made to the referent with those made to the symbol, and they are some form of nervous system *response,* hence their label, "representational mediational responses."

Osgood uses this scheme to explain how meanings are developed directly through classical learning principles or how meanings are "assigned" to us, ready-made so to speak, by "teachers" in our social environment. Because Osgood's conceptualization of meaning has the advantage of integrating a wide range of empirical facts, and because it has stimulated so much current research (Osgood, Suci, & Tannenbaum, 1957; Staats & Staats, 1957; Lambert & Jakobovits, 1960 for examples) it should be of particular value to those responsible for the teaching of languages. It will offer them a new and instructive orientation to meaning and it will suggest methods of studying the development, assignment and modification of meanings—matters of everyday concern to language teachers. Comparisons can be made of methods of teaching languages and their effectiveness in developing vivid and persistent meanings. The work of Staats and Staats (1957) indicates how favorable or unfavorable emotional components of meaning could be assigned to foreign language vocabularies as they are being studied by students. The work of Lambert and Jakobovits (1960) shows how meanings can be dissipated or "satiated" when continuous repetition of words takes place, as in vocabulary drill.

It would also be of value to compare Osgood's treatment of meaning with the recent thinking of O. H. Mowrer (1961, chapters 3 and 4, especially) and that of R. Brown (1958, especially chapter III). None of the richness of language is lost in the treatment given it by these psychologists. They express a genuine excitement in their study of language, but they also show a humility in the face of its complexity. They do not claim to have made much more than a start, but there is no question about their having "opened up" the study of language as very few before them have. This excitement, noted especially in the work of Osgood and Mowrer, contrasts with the vague treatment given the problem of meaning by most linguists, or the unconvincing arguments that meaning is some sort of "disposition to behave" or "response potential" (R. Brown, 1958, p. 103). It is clear that meaning at its very least is a response potential or disposition. Osgood and Mowrer want to indicate what meaning in its very complexity must be like.

B. F. Skinner of Harvard is the best-known modern exponent of a contrasting form of learning known as instrumental conditioning (Skinner, 1938, 1953). The distinctive characteristic of instrumental learning is the importance attributed to the receipt of a reinforcement of some sort when a particular response is made. Consider the case of an animal who, presumably in his exploration and random activity in a puzzle box, accidentally depresses a lever situated at one end of the box. The box is typically rigged so that on depression of the lever the animal immediately receives some desired outcome. For a cat in a puzzle box, the lever depression can open a door and release the animal; for a hungry white rat or pigeon, the lever pressing may deliver a pellet of wanted food. Getting out or getting wanted food are examples of "reinforcements" or rewards.

The crucial timing in this form of learning is that interval separating the organism's *response* (lever pushing) and the reception of *reinforcement* (food pellet). Note in this case, there is no pairing of an unnatural stimulus with a natural one in close temporal contiguity as was the case in classical conditioning. In fact, in this case attention is placed on the development of a brand new response which is brought under the management of other people in the environment (in this case the experimenter who controls the food-delivery mechanism) who control the doling out of reinforcements when the appropriate response is made. Once the properly timed reinforcement has been received, the response potential is raised and it will be noted that on further trials the organism will more quickly move closer to the lever and, with consistent reinforcement, will execute the new act with polished efficiency. When reinforcements are withheld, the lever-depression habit will gradually be "extinguished," that is, the animal will refrain from pressing the lever. Signals can be introduced to inform the animal when it is appropriate to respond. For example, a light can be flashed to indicate that the lever pressing will now lead to reinforcement. After practice, the animal will differentiate when it is worthwhile responding and when not. The basic plan can be complicated as when two animals learn to cooperate. Skinner (1953) describes how two pigeons can be taught to respond in coordination if food reinforcement is given both for a coordinated set of responses. Note that in this example, Skinner has moved his attention up to the intricate level of cooperative behavior and his experimentation suggests that simple forms of animals are docile enough to learn at least the rudiments of cooperative behavior.

Food is only one type of reinforcement which proves effective. Animals will also learn complicated patterns of response to escape from confinement or from fearful settings, or they will learn how to turn on a light when subjected to darkness. If the reinforcement is given with care, the animal will learn precise response sequences, but if the reinforcements are administered haphazardly, as when the timing is slow and irregular, the nature of the habit learned will also be vague and overgeneralized. The reinforcements need not be regular, however. If the reinforcements are presented only a certain proportion of times (some responses reinforced and others not) the habit is often more rapidly learned and better retained than when reinforcements are given consistently. When they are given, however, the reinforcements must be precisely timed. Animals will often learn "superstitions" or unnecessary elements of responding. For example, a pigeon may have stretched its neck just before pecking an electronically active button. The pecking response leads to food reinforcement, but for the animal the total sequence (neck stretch and then peck) is learned, so that neck stretching regularly precedes the pecking response, in much the same way as a baseball batter will spit in his hands, knock the dirt from his cleats, and twist his cap as he waits for a pitch.

In his major work on "verbal behavior," Skinner (1957) views the learning of language in essentially the same terms he uses to analyze the development of simple habits. Drawing on certain descriptive facts about the infant's extensive repertoire of sounds, Skinner argues that others in the baby's environment give reinforcements for the production of certain sound patterns and thereby restrict his range of sounds and make more probable certain oral productions. The parents or siblings must wait for the child to produce (presumably in his random verbalizations) something which is close enough to "belonging" so that they can realistically reinforce the attempt. For example, an infant's "baba" may be close enough to "mama" for a new mother to greatly surprise and please her, and her excitement may be transmitted to the infant in the form of affectionate and spirited attention. This attention is an example of reinforcement, and in this sense the child should be launched on a word-learning program. The reinforcements used are more social in nature than was the case with the animal studies mentioned above. It is argued that the infant and child will learn symbols for objects in his environment because he thereby gains a control over people and things. Saying "milk" or something close enough to be understood as "milk" gets him a wanted something. If his attempt is not recognizable, he suffers a frustrating delay in getting things. Following the pattern of instrumental learning, the word learner also learns to be a "demander" if he consistently gets what he asks for, i.e., if he is reinforced for demanding.

If the child's socializers hold off reinforcement until the verbal response is clear and appropriate, his use of words will be precise. However, others are often unable to check on the appropriateness of a response. When a child says he has a "stomach ache" (a very private feeling) he may actually have a pain in the intestinal region. The child may receive sympathy and some general pain reliever and thereby incidentally be reinforced for the idea that "stomach" runs from the throat region to the groin, with no differentiation being called for. On the other hand, the skill of the literary artist who can precisely describe very private emotional states is likely attributable to his having received appropriate reinforcements. Thus, infants, children, and adults may be precise or sloppy in their use of words depending upon the exactitude with which reinforcements have been administered to them for their verbal attempts.

It is characteristic of Skinner to leave matters such as semantics to others. His writings are marked by his zeal to be a "descriptive behaviorist," meaning that he wants to keep his attention on observable behavioral responses and relate them to observable environmental events, such as reinforcements. Any theorizing about internal mental or neurological processes is scorned by him and his large host of followers. Meaning is considered as such a mentalistic concept and he tries to explain language without reference to meaning. He is hampered in this attempt because his theory is limited (Osgood, 1958). Consequently it may appear as though he approaches psychological matters much as an engineer might, given the two notions that simple responses can be quantified and that certain reinforcements are effective when properly administered. It is difficult for those not aware of Skinner's desire to help psychology become a "science" to understand his hard-headed position. But in view of recent developments in cognitive and neurophysiological psychology, an imaginative person like Skinner must feel that being forced to be consistently the descriptive behaviorist is really being left with a very sticky wicket!

But the practical implications of this movement should be well understood by language specialists. Much important research has issued from his basic notions, much of it of direct relevance to the language learning of human subjects. For example, it has been clearly demonstrated that well-established verbal habits (some simple, Greenspoon, 1950, and others more complex, Barik & Lambert, 1960) can be modified under certain schedules of reinforcement. In these studies, subjects are typically reinforced by the experimenter saying "good" or "uh-huh" when, for example, the plural forms of nouns or particular pronouns are used in sentence construction. Because of the reinforcement, the tendency to use the reinforced forms is markedly increased. Barik and Lambert found that complex structures can be modified by verbal reinforcement. For example, a person who habitually forms his sentences in the fashion: "This is the (house) that (burned) last night" can be trained to shift to the form "This is the (house) that (I saw) burning last night." Apparently these modifications take place without the subject becoming aware of any relation between the experimenter's saying "good" and his own behavior, although this point is not certain as yet (Dulaney, 1960). These developments can be of immediate importance for language teachers who can be either effective or ineffective as social reinforcers of their students' attempts to develop appropriate verbal habits.

The most recent development in Skinner's thinking is evident in his interest in programmed learning and teaching machines (Skinner, 1958). Mechanical modes of instruction are old ideas in psychology. They didn't catch on in the 1930s, but are being enthusiastically entertained today, perhaps because Skinner is such a convincing proponent and because there has been a value shift toward mechanistic gadgets in this era. Skinner argues that teaching machines in certain respects are more effective than are teachers. The machines escape the problems of developing potentially unhealthy interpersonal dependencies between pupils and teachers. Furthermore, programed machine instruction is tailor-made to each student's learning pace; also, the machines control the timing between the pupil's response and his reinforcement (in this case, reinforcement is the feeling that he was correct and that he may now move on to the next step). Furthermore, since the machine teaches so effectively, the student feels he is clearly progressing in his task and is much better motivated than is the case in most classrooms. Experienced teachers who are not psychologists should study this new development, comprehending its origins. And they should study it soon before it's too late, in the sense that so much money will be invested in these potentially useful gadgets that educationists will be unable to objectively evaluate their value. Experimentation should be started to check on their long-term value. They may have a strong initial or novelty effect with teen-agers which diminishes rapidly. The programed materials should be tested in classroom settings *without* the machines themselves. The creation of good programs is an art and they can be of great help for most teachers who do not have the time to analyze course content into logical steps. On the other hand, programs should be carefully examined by specialists in human abilities (see section 3 below) to be more certain that the sequencing of steps is actually psychologically appropriate and maximally beneficial.

2. NEUROPHYSIOLOGICAL BASES OF THOUGHT AND LANGUAGE

As we have seen, Skinner's approach to psychology focuses attention on observable responses, including speech, and, in the manner of a skilled technician, indicates how response patterns can be developed, manipulated, and modified. The empirical research of those adopting this approach is impressive and usually of great practical value. Because the approach rejects the use of theory, it also contributes little to psychological theory and this bias may eventually limit its contribution to psychology. An important countermovement, developed particularly during the past fifteen years, is probing much deeper into the organism than those interested only in response patterns are able to do. This group is interested in inside mechanisms, those processes going on within the nervous system of people when they speak and comprehend others speaking. These processes have been alluded to by Osgood in his description of meaning. This is so because Osgood's own thinking has been guided by this movement. In fact, neurophysiological psychology is becoming one of the most popular areas of specialization for academically trained psychologists. The theories and research findings of this group should be of interest for teachers of language, at least for those who have seriously pondered the magical complexity and beauty of language, and for those who may be discouraged about psychology's role in the study of language because they have primarily encountered technician-type psychologists.

One of the chief catalysts in this new movement is Donald O. Hebb at McGill University (Hebb, 1949, 1958). After a brief career as a teacher of English and high-school principal, Hebb became thoroughly trained in both psychology and neurophysiology (evidence that dealing with high-school students can really shake a person up!). His aim in psychology has been to extend the significance of psychological concepts, especially those concerned with complex cognitive processes, by relating them to what is known about the neurology of the central nervous system. As a consequence of attempting to make this integration, he has liberalized some neurophysiological concepts and theories far beyond their actual level of empirical veridicality, at the same time as he forced most psychologists to become interested in the workings of man's nervous system and brain and stimulated many of them to search for neurophysiological correlates of psychological phenomena.

What are his basic ideas? First of all, he feels that the study of thinking should be psychology's major concern. Thought processes become the central theme of his own work. He is interested in how contacts with the environment leave their residues or traces within the nervous system, how, in other words, the nervous system stores up images and memories which can later be called into play often without the intervention of environmental stimulation. All the evidence in neurology and physiology made it clear that the brain is in a continuous state of activity, only slowing down somewhat in deep sleep. Other evidence suggested that nerve cells were distributed in such a way as to permit one cell to activate neighboring cells so that when an appropriately interconnected family of cells received one unit of stimulation, it would be passed on to the whole family. If, as seems to be a common case in certain centers of the brain, the family unit of cells were appropriately inter-meshed, a stimulation from one cell would lead on to another and, in a chainlike fashion, the stimulation would ultimately come back onto the *first* cell again. In such a fashion a stimulated network could store the imput signal and maintain its fidelity long after the environmental stimulation had ceased. Not only were there networks of cells found in the brain which might become reverberatory circuits, but it was also noted that the transition points from one cell to the next often involve a physical enlargement, a "terminal end bulb." These bulbs, it is argued, might facilitate transmission within a circuit; in fact it may be that the bulbs develop from regular and continuous contact between certain nerve cells. Once a circuit unit has become established, it would be possible for either outside stimulation to activate the whole unit or for some other *inside* stimulation coming from another point in the continuously active nervous system to activate a unit.

These reverberatory circuits Hebb calls "cell assemblies." It is apparent that such systems as these could[1] well be the neural

---

[1] The word "could" is used here because the cell assembly is not a verified entity; it is a theoretical construction. Neurophysiology has not yet advanced to the point where on-going processes can be precisely studied and

centers underlying the mediating processes described by Osgood. Representational mediation processes, considered by Osgood to constitute meaning, could have the biological form of assemblies of cells. Cell assemblies could become conditioned responses to verbal symbols so that they are activated when a symbol is recognized in either its auditory or visual forms. The activation of assemblies could revoke the complex of responses formerly made to the referent for which the symbol stands, as Osgood's theory demands.

Cell assemblies, according to Hebb, can have elements in common with other functionally distinct assemblies. For example, in a series such as ABCDX and ABCDY (where each letter stands for a cell assembly and the whole series makes up what he refers to as a "sequence" of assemblies) two different sequences can have certain assemblies in common. This postulate of the theory suggests that there may be a neural mechanism whereby root words can take on various endings and yet be recognized as derived from a common core. Synonyms, too, can be thought of as having certain assembly elements in common. Hebb argues that two originally distinct assemblies of cells which through time play functionally similar roles can become fused into a single neural system if no new element is introduced to reinstate their distinctiveness. Furthermore, two very similar networks of cell assemblies can develop more permanent distinctiveness if some elements are regularly found to play discriminable roles. In this fashion, Hebb describes how either fused or separated neural systems could develop. Such systems could, in turn, help explain how we can be precise in our use of synonyms and antonyms in language and how bilinguals manage to keep second-language equivalents functionally distinctive from first-language concepts. Recent theorizing about coordinate and compound bilingual systems have profited from Hebb's perspective (Ervin & Osgood, 1954; Lambert, Havelka, & Crosby, 1958; Lambert & Fillenbaum, 1959). A recent paper by P. Milner at McGill (1957) discusses a mechanism of neural inhibition which can also help to account for the bilingual's control over interlingual interference. Milner indicated that certain adjacent neural struc-

---

defined. Hebb has used evidence of a *static* sort, such as histological diagrams of interconnected nerve cells and end bulbs, and hypothesized about active states of nervous integration, keeping his theory in line with the facts that are known about active states from external sources such as electroencephalographic recordings of brain activity.

tures function in a reciprocal manner so that when structure X is activated the adjacent structure Y is automatically made inactive and unable to be stimulated. This mechanism may turn out to be an explanation of how bilinguals can keep their languages functionally segregated in usage, especially in the case of "coordinate" bilinguals (see section 4 below). That is, when the sequence of cell assemblies underlying the concept "house" is activated, the correlated neural assemblies underlying the concept *"maison"* may be automatically made inactive. Or when the neural mechanisms underlying a *total language system,* such as English, is activated, it may make the potentially competing system inactive.

Hebb (1958, pp. 58 ff.) is interested, as was K. S. Lashley before him (1951), in how complex sequences of responses can be so perfectly coordinated as is the case with the arpeggios of a skilled violinist or the rapid speech of native speakers of a language. Hebb argues that the appropriate serial ordering of such sequences is determined both by "sensory feedback" received when a single response is completed and by mediating processes or cell assemblies within the central nervous system. A sequence of cell assemblies could have some order built into it during the course of its development into a sequence. But Hebb feels this would not likely be sufficient. Take the case of the arpeggio. A violinist can perform up to sixteen finger movements a second. The precise timing of the different responses cannot be determined by feedback from each preceding movement because there is insufficient time. There are only about 50–60 milliseconds available before the next response, and the established reaction time for tactual stimulation is much slower, taking 140 milliseconds. But Hebb believes that possibly the feedback from the first response to the brain *could* regulate the fourth or fifth output in the long sequence and precise ordering could be achieved. In a similar fashion, Hebb argues that a speaker's sentence construction cannot be explained "as a series of CR's (conditioned responses) linked together by feedback alone," or as entirely controlled by cell assemblies since "there are strong indications that his thought processes (controlled by cell assemblies) run well ahead of his actual articulations" (1958, p. 60). Apparently some word ordering and grammatical sequencing must first be decided on, then rapidly scanned and found appropriate, and finally set in motion while active thought moves on ahead to the next phase. This whole chain of processes is remarkably fast and "automatic" in the native speaker, making a sharp contrast with the novice in a language who slows the process way down and makes evident to listeners that his thought and speech are running nearly in parallel.

For Hebb, *both* the mediating processes in the form of cell assemblies and sensory feedback must be necessary for the precise temporal sequencing required for normal speech. The background accompaniment of one's own speech testifies to the role of sensory feedback in speech. When the feedback of one's own speech is very slightly slowed down mechanically (B. S. Lee, 1950) one hesitates and is often unable to continue his normal speaking. Because of the inquisitiveness of men like Hebb and Lashley, we can look forward to continued research directed toward an understanding of how speech sequences occur.

Concepts, too, apparently have a neurological substructure. Hebb discusses how the concept of triangularity, for example, develops (for a secondary reference, see Osgood, 1953, p. 198 ff.). As a consequence of the interplay between visual stimulation of triangular figures and ocular-motor adjustments made to them, a sequence of cell assemblies is activated in those areas of the brain sensitive to visual stimulation (referred to technically as cortex region #17). Neurological findings have established that other areas of the cortex are concurrently active when cells are activated in area 17. For example, area-18 cells are concurrently made active when the cells in area 17 are stimulated by direct neural routes from the retina of the eye. It is argued that cell assemblies may be formed in area 18 and these may become electrochemically active whenever *various different* sequences fire in area 17, each area-17 response corresponding to a *particular* type of stimulation. Thus the correlated activity in area 18 is conceived of as the neural basis of a generalized concept, for example, of triangularity. Area 18 receives impulses from different assemblies in area 17 and also sends neural impulses *to* area 17 whenever a particular activity takes place in area 17, as though the conceptual system could indicate to the sensory receiving area that the new instance of stimulation is categorizable as belonging to a concept already established! Just as the visual system has its theoretically possible "conceptual" neural centers, so do other regions in the cortex very likely have such a capacity for conceptual development of other than visual information. These hypothetical centers concerned with the more generalized functions hold out a fascinating promise. They promise that someday we will be able to more comprehensively understand the mechanisms which make possible the development and use of thought and language.

3. LANGUAGE APTITUDE AND THE
THEORY OF HUMAN ABILITIES

One specialty in the field of psychology is concerned with the matter of individual differences in behavior. Practitioners of this specialty, often referred to as psychometricians, make use of a number of skills, including statistical competence and experience with the theory, construction and evaluation of psychological tests. Psychometricians have historically been called on to answer questions about the nature of intelligence and human abilities and they have developed some of psychology's most comprehensive conceptualizations of human capacities and behavior. Because of their training and interests, psychometricians have developed competence in educational matters and the problems of selection and placement of personnel in academic and applied settings. Several, through personal interest in the nature of language, have studied the nature of language aptitude, carefully constructing batteries of ingenious tests to measure individual differences in such a capacity. Because of their competence in statistical measurement and test construction, their products are typically about the closest to good science one can find in the social or biological sciences. Their contributions are often not fully appreciated because of naïvete on the part of those who ultimately use their theories and tests. Their theory-based tests have a remarkable predictive capacity when one considers the sources of error that typically accompany group testing. Each of the tests in a battery usually has a long and interesting history in itself, and is kept in a final battery because it adds a special predictive power to the total battery of tests.

We will be concerned here with the current work of one of these specialists, Dr. John B. Carroll of Harvard University who, with Stanley Sapon, developed an instrument of obvious value for those in the field of language, the Modern Language Aptitude Test (1958). In the following paragraphs, we will describe the test, indicating its usefulness in educational research and placement, and then discuss the setting of this test in a theory of human abilities developed by George A. Ferguson of McGill University. Certain papers by Carroll (1958, 1960) and Ferguson (1954, 1956) are suggested as important summaries of the relevant features of their thinking.

The learning of a foreign language is one of the most difficult of human skills to develop. Furthermore, language training is expensive. One could argue from these two facts alone that military, governmental, and educational institutions must select those who can most certainly profit from prolonged training, just as piano teachers and parents must select when they communicate the fact to the majority of piano students that they have little chance for excellence. But just as a thorough introduction to piano can have important personal value, so too can a series of well-taught introductory courses in foreign languages. Carroll turns his attention to the selection of those with great potential for languages, and in doing so his study of the components of language aptitude reveals for us the component skills that must be taught by teachers and learned by students. Future work will not only uncover other components, but it may also lead to a better understanding of the sequence or order in which these component skills should be learned and how best they can, if possible, be developed.

What are some of these components of language aptitude? The following extensive quotation gives a summary of Carroll's answer.

Our current thinking tends to consider language aptitude under the following headings:

1. *Phonetic coding.* One of the most important abilities required in learning a foreign language is the ability to "code" auditory phonetic material in such a way that this material can be recognized, identified and remembered over something longer than a few seconds. The "coding" is presumably a cognitive process which cannot be directly observed, but something of this sort may be inferred from the following case report: A woman who had received a low score on the Phonetic Script Test (of the Modern Language Aptitude Test) was presented with two spoken nonsense syllables /θej̆; θej̆/, and then ten seconds of mental arithmetic to do, after which she was asked to repeat the two syllables. She could not do this, although this task was known to be relatively easy for most people. Further, the woman could herself repeat the syllables accurately when allowed to do it immediately after original presentation. Thus, this ability is not the ability to make an echoic response to phonetic material, but the ability somehow to "code" or represent it in imagery so that it can be recognized or reproduced after an intervening period filled with other activity. This ability, it would seem, is measured chiefly by

the Phonetic Script Test, in which the individual has to learn how a series of speech sounds are represented by alphabetic characters; in order to do this, however, the sounds themselves have to be "coded" or "stored" long enough to be compared with other sounds, and the individual has to build up a considerable repertoire of responses. This ability may also be drawn upon, however, by paired-associates tests utilizing nonsense syllables and/or paralogs. To a slight extent, also, it may be involved in Test 1, Artificial Language Numbers, although in this test the individual has considerable opportunity to consolidate his learning of the nonsense materials. It is also measured by the Spelling Clues Test insofar as this represents phonetic-orthographic habits which the individual has learned. In learning a foreign language, a person low in this ability will have trouble not only in remembering phonetic materials (words, forms, etc.) but also in mimicking speech sounds. Apparently the process of making an echoic response involves some degree of "phonetic coding," or perhaps it would be better to say *phonemic* coding because the individual will impose upon his repetition of a heard utterance whatever system of phonemes he has acquired most strongly.

2. A second important variable in language aptitude is the ability to handle "grammar," i.e., the forms of language and their arrangements in natural utterances. This implies that the individual is sensitive to the functions of words in a variety of contexts. This may be a learned trait, but it is conceivable that variations in this ability may be observed even when the individual has no formal training in grammar. It is postulated that this trait is particularly well measured by the Words and Sentences subtest of the Modern Language Aptitude Battery.

3. A third important variable is that of rote memorization ability for foreign language materials. This ability is to be regarded as independent of and different from the phonetic coding variable described above; it has to do with the capacity to learn a large *number* of these associations in a relatively short time. Though a certain degree of phonetic coding ability is necessary, perhaps prerequisite, those who have requisite phonetic ability may still not be able to hear and remember the relationships. We may postulate that the *Paired Associates* test measures this ability fairly accurately; it is also tapped by the *Number Learning* test.

4. A fourth variable is what may be called "inductive language learning ability." This is the ability to infer linguistic forms, rules and patterns from new linguistic content itself with a minimum of supervision or guidance. It is not measured to any appreciable degree by the tests of the present final MLAT battery, but it had turned up in certain earlier studies (Carroll, 1958).

The above four factors do not include what is ordinarily called the *verbal* or *verbal knowledge* factor, which according to our results is not very important in predicting success. Vocabulary tests do not serve as particularly good predictors, at least in situations where other tests serve well, since the first stages of learning a language do not require one to acquire a large vocabulary. On the other hand, the present Spelling Clues test functions in part as a vocabulary test. (Carroll, 1960, pp. 46–48).

Carroll's evaluation of the test (summarized in his 1960 paper) indicates its great potential in educational research as well as for purposes of selection. The fact that the test is more valid in some settings than in others suggests that variables other than aptitude itself must also be involved in language learning efficiency. Carroll mentions that variables such as adequacy of presentation of the material, adequate opportunity to learn, individual differences in general intelligence, and motivation to learn may vary from situation to situation. In fact, in the final section of this paper we will discuss the role of certain other variables. It should be realized that Carroll expects that there will be modifications and improvements in the analysis of language aptitude.

What does Carroll mean by "aptitude?" He views aptitude as a "relatively invariant characteristic of the individual, not subject to easy modification by learning" (1960, p. 38). This stable personal characteristic manifests itself in the rapidity of progress or advancement made in language learning when the language is well taught in accordance with the basic intelligence of the learner.

Carroll, therefore, views language aptitude as a relatively stable personal characteristic, one which is made up of various component skills or abilities. It will be instructive to consider the nature of human abilities since they play such a fundamental role in more complex aptitudes.

L. L. Thurstone had defined an ability as "a trait which is defined by what an individual can do" (1947). A person is viewed as having as many abilities as there are activities he can perform. Ferguson (1954) views abilities themselves as relatively invariant features of behavior. These features manifest themselves as stable performance on particular psychological tests. Thus "intelligence" is made up of various groupings of abilities which become stabilized at a particular age level. Abilities are presumed to depend on overlearning. The stability of behavior reflects the fact that little change in behavior occurs as learning is continued. Basically, then, individuals vary in terms of the speed with which they reach this point of behavioral stability, and also in terms of the level of skill attained before the stability manifests itself. These individual differences, Ferguson argues, can be attributed to some complex byproduct of biologically transmitted capacity and the type and amount of "learning which occurs at particular stages of life" (1954, p. 99). Ferguson agrees with Hebb (1949) that the *sequencing* of what will be taught and learned at particular stages of the organism's development is of prime importance. "Early learning or its lack may have a permanent and generalized effect in the adult" (1954, p. 99). Ferguson later develops the important point that "a slow learner under given learning conditions may have a capacity for ultimate performances in excess of the fast learner under the same training conditions" (1954, p. 102). Likewise, people may have the abilities to learn rapidly in the earlier stages of learning, then perform so well in relation to others that they might not be prompted to acquire the necessary next-level abilities they will need for later stages of learning and later find themselves showing a stability of performance in the face of further training. This deceleration would not be due so much to a capacity difference as to a poor sequencing of learning abilities in their proper and necessary order.

The sequencing problem may be crucial as when "an individual will learn more readily activities which are facilitated by prior acquisitions, and will learn less readily those activities which are not facilitated or are perhaps inhibited by prior learning" (1954, p. 109). Ferguson also notes the likelihood that the transfer effects from previously acquired abilities are of greatest importance in the early stages of learning new activities. Ultimately, learning for the adult involves in large part a transfer and integration of appropriate components from previously acquired abilities (1956, pp. 128 ff.). Future research following from such a theory as Ferguson's may indicate how strategies of integration may be properly taught and properly learned.

Perhaps the most important notion which emerges from this treatment is a very novel idea for most people both in psychology or those outside the discipline; man's abilities are not permanently fixed by biological equipment.

This position is no longer tenable. Although it is conceded that biological factors fix certain boundaries, all the evidence seems to suggest that the range of variation that results from learning is, indeed, very great. If this is so, it immediately raises questions of value and social responsibility. It means that a society, through control of the environment and the educative process, can in some considerable degree determine the patterns of ability which emerge in its members (1956, p. 120).

The implications of this view of abilities for language teachers are immense. Over and above the general orientation derivable from the theory, its practical guides suggest that the learning of languages should be shifted to early age levels, or that experimentations on such a shift should be undertaken with very careful consideration given to ability requirements and their sequencing. It suggests that modern movements should be carefully studied to determine which students with what pattern of abilities will profit from such new approaches. For example, the generalized plan of commencing the teaching of second languages audio-lingually at all age levels probably has not taken into consideration age level changes in ability structures nor individual differences at any age level in visual and auditory preferences (see the UNESCO study, 1955, pp. 70 ff.). It may well be that the audio-lingual method is appropriate for second language learning at very early levels for certain children, but it may run counter to ability patterns developed over the years for older subjects.

The theory also suggests that the next steps in language aptitude research might profit from a consideration of which abilities, such as those isolated by Carroll, typically show themselves at which age levels. The sequencing of training in different skills could capitalize on normal age-level emergences of particular ability patterns. Factor analyses of those ability patterns which are considered basic to language aptitude could be carried out with children and adolescents of various age levels as a first step in this direction.

4. A PSYCHOLOGY OF BILINGUALISM

Psychologists are now becoming interested in systematically studying how one acquires a second language and how certain individuals are able to make efficient use of two or several languages. A group of graduate students and myself at McGill University have found the Montreal bicultural setting to be an outstanding field station for research on bilingualism. And yet we have found that actual bilinguals are often too complex as experimental subjects and we have accordingly been forced to restate certain bilingual problems in a more general form so that they can be investigated with experimental methods in a manner which only approximates the real bilingual case.

Our first step was to develop means of measuring individual variations in bilingual skill (Lambert, 1955). This work assumed that linguistic habits should be revealed in tests calling for speed of response, a commonly accepted measure of habit strength. It was hypothesized that students with different amounts of study experience in a second language should show a corresponding facility in responding with the second language when required to. It was found that students at three progressively more advanced stages of experience with French showed progressively more response speed to directions given them in French. This speed of response measure correlated highly with the spontaneously available vocabulary in French.

In a second study (Lambert, Havelka, & Gardner, 1959) a large number of tests were administered to students at various levels of skill in a second language, ranging up to bilinguality. The pattern of these tests suggested that one's degree of bilingualism is reflected in perception of words, facility in completing unfinished words, in finding imbedded words, in readiness to respond, and in speed of reading. These studies made it clear that some conceptualization of bilingualism was called for which stressed its individual properties. That is, one person can show equal facility in his two languages and yet be comparatively a limited person in both languages. Another person can be intellectually brilliant in both his languages and equally skilled in both. Thus, we distinguished between the degree of "balance" between the skill available in the two languages and interindividual comparisons of skill in either of the two languages. We have dealt with the concepts of "bilingual balance," where a person shows essentially similar skills in both languages, and "linguistic dominance," where there is a measurably greater facility in one of the individual's two languages. Questions then arise which pertain to how bilingual balance is best nurtured and what the psychological concomitants of balance are. Also, it has been intriguing to search out the motives and learning settings that promote dominance, especially cases where the *acquired* language becomes dominant over the first-learned language.

The next step was to study the "route" which leads to bilingualism (Lambert, 1956, I, II, III). Students at various levels of experience with a second language were given a series of tests which differed in the complexity of their content. The results indicate that students have to surmount various progressively more difficult levels of skill in order to approach nativelike performance in their second language. The easiest level to master involves the acquisition of vocabulary and grammatical skills. Then the student must become experienced to the extent that he can react automatically in the second language. Then he faces the problem of surmounting a "cultural" barrier where, for example, he thinks in terms of culturally appropriate concepts, such as those revealed in the type and form of free associations given in the second language. At this stage, too, he must acquire a nativelike accent in his second language. We have become interested in how the perfect accent is learned and we use a theory of "identification" with members of the other linguistic group to explain this process.

It is of psychological interest to understand how bilinguals can learn two symbols for each referent and yet manage to use each language system with a minimum of interlingual interferences. Consideration of this problem led us to examine the implications of theories of "coordinate" and "compound" bilingualism, proposed by linguists (Weinreich, 1953) and recently examined by psychologists (Ervin & Osgood, 1954). This theory states that bilinguals who have learned their two languages within one context will develop a "compound" bilingual system wherein the symbols of both languages function as interchangeable alternatives with essentially the same meanings. A "coordinate" system would be developed when the language acquisition contexts were culturally, temporally, or functionally segregated. This form of learning would promote bilinguals whose two sets of symbols would correspondingly be functionally more distinct and independent. We have tested these notions and have found that the learning contexts are apparently critical in determining the form of bilingualism which ultimately develops. Behavioral differences are measurable in terms of interlingual independence and degrees of similarity between meanings (Lambert, Havelka, & Crosby, 1958; Lambert, 1961). Coordinate bilinguals in contrast to compounds apparently can keep their two languages more functionally separated. They may be aided in this respect by the fact that they have more different connotative meanings for translated equivalents in their two languages. Furthermore, when the meaning of a symbol in one language is reduced through overuse, the other-language equivalent is *not* coreduced as is the case for compound bilinguals (Jakobovits & Lambert, 1961). We have also examined the implications of coordinate and compound systems among bilinguals who become aphasic (Lambert & Fillenbaum, 1959). Bilingual aphasics who learned their languages in a coordinate fashion are more likely to lose the use of only one of their two languages if they become aphasic, whereas compound bilinguals show a more general language deficit affecting their two languages when they become aphasic.

This line of research suggests that interlingual interference is reduced for coordinate bilinguals by the intrinsic distinctiveness of their two languages while compound bilinguals may have to rely more on cues emanating from the language-usage contexts in order to minimize the potential interference. That is, compound bilinguals may be more prone to switch from one language to another if the context in which communication takes place prompts them to switch. For example, another communicator's use of a word or phrase from language X might prompt the compound bilingual to switch to language X. Or the physical features of one member of a group might suggest that this person belongs to a particular linguistic group and be a sufficient cue for a compound to use a particular language. If the context provides various conflicting cues, the compound bilingual would be more likely to encounter interlingual confusions. The point here is that the coordinate bilingual would be less dependent on the cues stemming from the language-usage context because of the "built-in" distinctiveness of his two language systems. Future research will examine the validity of such notions as these.

Methods of teaching a second language take into account this matter of interlingual intereference. For example, the "direct" methods require students to relate a symbol directly with an environmental event rather than indirectly through the association of the equivalent symbol of the first language. The direct method, therefore, is analogous to coordinate training as the indirect method is to compound training. It was at this point we felt it wise to use closely controlled experimental methods to study the comparative merits of direct and indirect methods of training (Wimer & Lambert, 1959). For this purpose, we followed the tradition of experimental research on verbal learning, as covered in such work as McGeough (1942) and Underwood and Schulz (1960). Actually, the problem of direct and indirect methods is an old one and has been examined many times in the early 1900s by psychologists and educators. We improved on their procedures, we believed, and found that the direct method was relatively more efficient, at least for vocabulary learning, primarily because the task of associating new language words with referents (the direct procedure) afforded greater distinctiveness of elements to be learned than did the task of associating new language words with their equivalents in the first language. However, in a recent investigation of advanced students of a second language studying the language for a concentrated six-week period in a setting which was as "direct" as one could hope for, it was found that those students who kept their two languages functionally separated throughout the course did poorer in their course work than did those who permitted the semantic features of their two languages to interact (Lambert, Gardner, Barik, & Tunstall, 1962). Thus this study indicates that students studying under a direct method utilize the semantic features of *both* their languages and permit the two to interact and that this tendency toward linguistic *interdependency* apparently assists students on the question of direct methods of training.

A current study is examining the merits of learning two languages concurrently from an early age or learning one language well before the second is attempted, i.e., learning two languages consecutively (Lambert & Yeni-Komshian, 1962). This problem is often faced by educators and parents who fear that confusion will accompany the early introduction of a second language before competence is developed in the first. Lack of information on this point makes most parents cautious and children are often kept away from a second language until, inadvertently, it may be too late to learn it well. Our approach in this study is to approximate the real-life situation using artificial languages and restricting ourselves to the vocabulary acquisition phase of the process.

Finally, we have examined the question of the intellectual deficit which is supposed to plague bilinguals. Many studies in the educational and psychological literature have concluded that bilingual children show a lower average score on tests of intelligence when compared with monolingual children who are supposedly matched on all pertinent characteristics except bilingual experience. The findings are not convincing when one surveys the total range of studies undertaken. Miss Elizabeth Peal and I carried out a large study on this question with ten-year olds in Montreal (1962). We attempted to match very carefully the students who finally were categorized as bilingual or monolingual. For example, we painstakingly checked on the socioeconomic background of the two groups of students and made sure the bilinguals were really competent in both languages. Our results clearly show that the bilingual students are *far superior* to monolinguals on both verbal and nonverbal tests of intelligence. We concluded that the bilinguals may have an advantage in tests requiring "cognitive flexibility" due, perhaps, to their being bilingual. Miss Peal is presently examining this possibility more carefully. Because our results are in conflict with so many others on this point (although we have no doubt at all about the differences in intelligence just mentioned), we are not yet sure that this bilingual advantage is peculiar to bilinguals in Canada or to those who are actually "good" bilinguals. Our confidence in the generalizability of these findings for different settings will depend on more careful reexaminations in those settings where a bilingual deficit has been reported in the literature.

5. A SOCIAL PSYCHOLOGY OF SECOND-LANGUAGE LEARNING

When viewed from a social-psychological perspective, the process of learning a second language takes on a special significance. From this viewpoint, one anticipates that if the learner is appropriately oriented, he may find that by learning another social group's language he has made the crucial step in becoming an acculturated part of a second linguistic-cultural community. Advancing toward bi-culturality in this sense may be viewed as a broadening experience in some cases, or it can engender "anomie," a feeling of not comfortably belonging in one social group or the other. With a different orientation, a language learner may look on his learning task as making him better educated or more cultured, or as equipping him with a useful skill for his future occupation, with little regard for the culture or the people represented by the other language. In other circumstances, one might consider learning another group's language as a means of getting on the "inside" of a cultural community in order to exploit, manipulate, or control, with clearly personal ends in mind.

A series of studies carried out at McGill has been concerned with such topics, and various findings have increased our confidence in a social-psychological theory of language learning. This theory, in brief, holds that an individual successfully acquiring a second language gradually adopts various aspects of behavior which characterize members of another linguistic-cultural group. The learner's ethnocentric tendencies and his attitudes toward the other group are believed to determine his success in learning the new language. His motivation to learn is thought to be determined by his attitudes and by his orientation toward learning a second language. The orientation is "instrumental" in form if the purposes of language study reflect the more utilitarian value of linguistic achievement, such as getting ahead in one's occupation, and is "integrative" if the student is oriented to learn more about the other cultural community as if he desired to become a potential member of the other group. It is also argued that some may be anxious to learn another language as a means of being accepted in another cultural group because of dissatisfactions experienced in their own culture while other individuals may be equally as interested in another culture as they are in their own. However, the more proficient one becomes in a second language the more he may find that his place in his original membership group is modified at the same time as the other linguistic-cultural group becomes something more than a reference group for him. It may, in fact, become a second membership group for him. Depending upon the compatibility of the two cultures, he may experience feelings of chagrin or regret as he loses ties in one group, mixed with the fearful anticipation of entering a relatively new group. The concept of "anomie" first proposed by Durkheim (1897) and more recently extended by Srole (1951) and Williams (1952), refers to the feelings of social uncertainty or dissatisfaction which sometimes characterize not only the bilingual but also the serious student of a second language.

We are viewing the learning of a second language in much the same way as Mowrer interprets the child's learning of his first language. Mowrer's fascinating "autistic" theory (1960, see especially chapters 3 and 4) differs in an essential manner from Skinner's approach to the matter. For Mowrer, word learning in talking birds and children takes place when the *sounds* of the words have come to carry a reinforcement power in themselves so that the learner *wants* to produce words. The sounds become reinforcing agents through association with the users of words who are held in affection by the learner. Language learning is motivated by a basic desire to be like valued people in one's environment, first family members and then others in the linguistic community. The language learner has to identify with the language users to the extent that he wants to be like them linguistically, and undoubtedly in many other ways. It is not the case, as Skinner would require it, that the learner must emit words and have them immediately reinforced. All that is necessary, Mowrer makes clear, is for the word to be said by the bird *trainer* or the child's *mother* and have this sound followed by a reinforcing state for the learner (in the form of reception of food for the bird, of affectionate handling for the child). "The secondary (autistic) reinforcement provided by the sound of the word is alone sufficient to bring it (the word) into existence" (Mowrer, 1960, p. 107). In similar fashion we argue that the learner must want to identify with members of the other linguistic-cultural group and be willing to take on very subtle aspects of their behavior such as their language or even their style of speech. We also feel that there are various types of motivation which can underlie his willingness to be like the other group's members and we are interested in explicating each of these.

The first studies (Gardner & Lambert, 1959; Gardner, 1960) were carried out with English-speaking Montreal high-school students studying French who were examined for language learning aptitude and verbal intelligence as well as attitudes toward the French community and their intensity of motivation to learn French. Our measure of motivational intensity is conceptually similar to Jones' (1949, 1950) index of interest in learning a language which he found to be important for successful learning among Welsh students. A factor analysis indicated that aptitude and intelligence formed a factor which was independent of a second comprising indices of motivation, type of orientation toward language, and social attitudes toward French Canadians. A measure of achievement in French was reflected equally prominently in both factors. In this case, then, French achievement was dependent upon both aptitude and intelligence as well as a sympathetic orientation toward the other group. This orientation apparently sustained a strong motivation to learn the other group's language. In the Montreal setting, it was clear that students with an integrative orientation were the more successful in language learning in contrast to those instrumentally oriented. (We have not concentrated on the manipulative orientation mentioned earlier and we are aware that a certain degree of error in classifying students may occur until attention is given to this form of orientation.)

Gardner's 1960 study confirmed and extended these findings. Using a larger sample of English Canadians and incorporating various measures of French achievement, the same two independent factors were revealed, and again both were related to French achievement. But whereas aptitude and achievement were especially important for those French skills stressed in school training, the acquisition of French skills whose development depends on the active use of the language in communicational settings was determined solely by measures of an integrative motivation to learn French. Further evidence indicated that this integrative motive was the converse of an authoritarian ideological syndrome, opening the possibility that basic personality dispositions may be involved in language learning efficiency.

Information had been gathered about the students' parents' orientation toward the French community. These data supported the notion that the proper orientation toward the other group is developed within the family. Students with an integrative disposition to learn French had parents who also were integrative and sympathetic to the French community. The students' orientations were not related to parents' skill in French nor to the number of French acquaintances the parents had, indicating that the integrative motive is not due to having more experience with French at home but more likely stems from a family wide attitudinal disposition.

A study by Anisfeld and Lambert (1961) extended the experimental procedure to samples of Jewish high-school students studying Hebrew at parochial schools in Montreal. They were administered tests measuring their orientation toward learning Hebrew and their attitudes toward the Jewish culture and community, as well as tests of verbal intelligence and language aptitude. These tests were correlated with measures of achievement in the Hebrew language at the school year's end. The results support the generalization that both intellectual capacity and attitudinal orientation affect success in learning Hebrew. However, whereas intelligence and linguistic aptitude are relatively stable predictors of success, the attitudinal measures vary from one social class school district to another. The measure of a Jewish student's desire to become more acculturated into the Jewish tradition and culture was sensitive for children in a district of Montreal where sociopsychological analysis of the nature of the Jewish population's adjustment to the American Gentile culture suggested that these particular Jews were concerned with problems of integrating into the Jewish culture. In another district made up of Jews more recently arrived in North America who were clearly of a lower socioeconomic class level, the measure of desire for Jewish acculturation did not correlate with achievement in Hebrew whereas measures of pro-Semitic attitudes or pride in being Jewish did.

More recently, students undergoing an intensive course in French at McGill's French Summer School were examined for changes in attitude during the study period (Lambert, Gardner, Barik, & Tunstall, 1961). Most were American university students or secondary-school language teachers who referred themselves more to the European-French than the American-French community in their orientations to language learning. In this study, it became apparent that feelings of anomie were markedly increased during the course of study. As students progressed to the point that they "thought" in French, it was noted that their feelings of anomie also increased. At the same time, they tried to find means of using English even though they had pledged to use only French for the six-week period. The pattern suggests that American students experience anomie when they concentrate on and commence to master a second language and, as a consequence, develop stratagems to control or minimize such feelings.

The most recent study (Peal & Lambert, 1961) compares ten-year-old monolingual and bilingual students on measures of intelligence. Of relevance here is the very clear pattern that bilingual children have markedly more favorable attitudes towards the "other" language community in contrast to the monolingual children. Furthermore, the parents of bilingual children are believed by their children to hold the same strongly sympathetic attitudes in contrast to the parents of monolingual children, as though the linguistic skills in a second language, extending to the point of bilingualism, are controlled by family shared attitudes toward the other linguistic-cultural community.

These findings are consistent and reliable enough to be of more general interest. For example, methods of language training may be modified and strengthened by giving consideration to the social-psychological implications of language learning. Because of the possible practical as well as theoretical significance of this approach, it seemed appropriate to test its applicability in a cultural setting other than the bicultural Quebec scene. Our most recent study (Lambert, Gardner, Olton, & Tunstall, 1962) was therefore conducted in various regional settings in the United States, two of them also bicultural and a third more representative of "typical" urban American cities. The bicultural settings permitted an examination of attitudes working two ways: attitudinal dispositions of American students toward linguistic minority groups in their immediate environment and the general attitudes of members of the cultural minority group toward the general American culture about them. In this study, we were interested in comparing the importance in the language learning process of intellectual ability and language learning aptitude, on the one hand, and social attitudes toward the "other" language group and motivation to learn the language, on the other hand. Our attention was first directed to an examination of how these variables affect the language learning of American students who come from homes where only English is spoken. In order to compare the results of the U.S. investigation with earlier studies carried out with English-speaking students learning French in Montreal, we chose two samples of students from bicultural American communities in Louisiana and Maine. A third sample of American students was drawn from the public-school system of Hartford, Connecticut, which was considered representative of most large city-school systems along the Eastern coast of America. The Connecticut setting did not have a distinctive subcommunity of Franco-Americans in its immediate environment comparable to those in the Louisiana and Maine districts studied. Thus, the Hartford students would not be expected to have a clear linguistic cultural group in their immediate experience toward which favorable or unfavorable attitudes would have developed through direct contact.

A large battery of tests was administered to these students early in the year, and near the end of the year, tests of achievement in French were given, and grades in French were obtained from teachers. The tests were intercorrelated and factor analyzed. The resulting patterns of interrelations were studied and interpreted. The results indicate that, similar to the Montreal studies, two independent factors underlie the development of skill in learning a second language: an intellectual capacity and an appropriate attitudinal orientation toward the other language group coupled with a determined motivation to learn the language. The details of this major finding were discussed.

The second phase of the investigation was concerned with the role of aptitudinal, attitudinal, and motivational variables in the linguistic development of potentially bilingual Franco-American students—those coming from homes in which primarily French was spoken. Two samples of Franco-American high-school students were chosen from the Louisiana and Maine settings. The analysis indicated the manner in which social attitudes toward their own linguistic group and the American culture around them influence their progress in becoming bilingual, retaining the dominance of French or developing dominance of English. The manner in which the Franco-American student faces and resolves the cultural conflict he is likely to encounter in the American society was found to determine his linguistic development in French and English.

The third phase of the study focused on a comparison of Franco-American students from the Louisiana and Maine settings. The results make it very clear that whereas the Louisiana French culture is rapidly merging into the general American culture, the Maine community of Franco-Americans enjoys a comparatively dynamic and distinctive existence.

The fourth phase compared the Franco-American and American students in their various competences in French and in their attitudinal dispositions. The results reinforce the finding mentioned above of the cultural conflicts faced by Franco-American students. Furthermore, the Maine Franco-Americans show a decided superiority over the American students in their French skills whereas the Louisiana Franco-Americans show little or no advantage in French over American students.

The fifth phase of the study examined the stereotypes both American and Franco-American groups of students hold toward French people. The analysis makes it very clear that all groups except the Maine Franco-Americans hold unfavorable stereotypes of French people. The Maine Franco-Americans give evidence of a basic pride in their French heritage. The consequences of holding negative stereotypes toward the very people whose language one is supposed to learn became apparent in this analysis.

The sixth and final phase deals with the role of students' values in the language learning process. The results indicate that achievement in foreign language training is not a central goal for American students. Rather it is apparently incidental to the more challenging goal of trying to find and prepare one's way for the future. Intelligence coupled with a value placed on achievement are major determiners of success in most school work, including the study of language.

These findings not only supply needed information about the student learning languages, they also point the way to a large number of next steps to be taken in the fascinating study of language learning and bilingualism.

CONCLUDING STATEMENT

This paper presents certain points of view and research strategies used by psychologists in their study of language. The writing of the paper is a response to a request by those responsible for a graduate program of study for future trainers and administrators of high-school and college teachers of foreign languages who feel that the training can be enriched by an introduction to the psychological approaches to language behavior. What is presented here is a personal selection of various psychological schemes of analysis which I feel should be of both instructive and practical value for language specialists. My approach has been to explain how different branches of psychology view language and go about an investigation of it. An attempt has been made to introduce the central ideas of several approaches in a nontechnical manner so that nonpsychologists might be tempted to go to the original works which are given in a reading list. I consider the interest of those requesting this material as a compliment to the field of psychology. I also feel that it is a responsibility to try and predict the need of language specialists of the sort being trained at the University of Washington and then select and expose certain appropriate psychological schemes. One will only be able to judge whether this attempt has been worthwhile by observing if the seminar members are enticed to make way in their crowded program for reading and thinking about psychological approaches to language.

Bibliography

Anisfeld, M. and W. E. Lambert. "Social and Psychological Variables in Learning Hebrew." *Journal of Abnormal and Social Psychology*, 1961, **63**, 524–529.

Barik, H. C. and W. E. Lambert. "Conditioning of Complex Verbal Sequences." *Canadian Journal of Psychology*, 1960, **14**, 87–95.

Brown, R. W. *Words and Things*. New York: The Free Press, 1958.

Carroll, J. B. "A Factor Analysis of Two Foreign Language Aptitude Batteries." *The Journal of General Psychology*, 1958, **59**, 3–19.

———. "The Prediction of Success in Intensive Foreign Language Training." Cambridge, Mass.: Graduate School of Education, Harvard University, 1960 (Mimeo.).

——— and S. M. Sapon. *Modern Language Aptitude Test*. New York: Psychological Corporation, 1958.

Dulany, D. E. "Hypotheses and Habits in Verbal 'Operant Conditioning.'" *Journal of Abnormal and Social Psychology*, 1961, **63**, 251–263.

Durkheim, E. *Le suicide*. Paris: F. Alcan, 1897.

Ervin, Susan and C. E. Osgood. Second Language Learning and Bilingualism. In C. E. Osgood and F. Sebeck (Eds.). "Psycholinguistics." *Journal of Abnormal and Social Psychology*, Supplement, 1954, **49**, 139–146.

Ferguson, G. A. "On Learning and Human Ability." *Canadian Journal of Psychology*, 1954, **8**, 95–112.

———. "On Transfer and the Abilities of Man." *Canadian Journal of Psychology*, 1965, **10**, 121–131.

Gardner, R. C. and W. E. Lambert. Motivational Variables in Second-Language Acquisition. Unpublished doctoral dissertation, McGill University, 1960.

——— and W. E. Lambert. "Motivational Variables in Second-Language Acquisition." *Canadian Journal of Psychology*, 1959, **13**, 266–272.

Greenspoon, J. Referred to in Kreener, L. "Studies of the Conditioning of Verbal Behavior." *Psychological Bulletin,* 1958, **55,** 148–170.

Hebb, D. O. *Organization of Behavior.* New York: John Wiley & Sons, Inc., 1949.

————. *A Textbook of Psychology.* Philadelphia: W. B. Saunders Company, 1958.

Jakobovits, L. and W. E. Lambert. "Semantic Satiation Among Bilinguals." *Journal of Experimental Psychology,* 1961, **67,** 576–582.

Jonas, W. R. "Attitude Towards Welsh as a Second Language. A Preliminary Investigation." *British Journal of Educational Psychology,* 1949, **19,** 44–52.

————. "Attitude Towards Welsh as a Second Language. A Further Investigation." *British Journal of Educational Psychology,* 1950, **20,** 117–132.

Lambert, W. E. "Measurement of the Linguistic Dominance of Bilinguals." *Journal of Abnormal and Social Psychology,* 1955, **50,** 197–200.

————. "Developmental Aspects of Second-Language Acquisition." Parts I, II, & III. *Journal of Social Psychology,* 1956, **43,** 83–104.

————. Behavioral Evidence for Contrasting Forms of Bilingualism. Georgetown Round Table Conference, 1961, to appear in volume on proceedings in 1962.

———— and S. Fillenbaum. "A Pilot Study of Aphasia Among Bilinguals." *Canadian Journal of Psychology,* 1959, **13,** 28–34.

————, Gardner, R. C., Barik, H. C., and K. Tunstall. "Attitudinal and Cognitive Aspects of Intensive Study of a Second Language." To appear in *Journal of Abnormal and Social Psychology,* 1962.

————, Gardner, R. C., Olton, R., and K. Tunstall. "A Study of the Roles of Attitudes and Motivation in Second-Language Learning." Mimeographed, McGill University, 1962.

————, Havelka, J., and Cynthia Crosby. "The Influence of Language-Acquisition Contexts on Bilingualism." *Journal of Abnormal and Social Psychology,* 1958, **56,** 239–244.

————, Havelka, J., and R. C. Gardner. "Linguistic Manifestations of Bilingualism." *American Journal of Psychology,* 1959, **72,** 77–82.

———— and L. Jakobovits. "Verbal Satiation and Changes in the Intensity of Meaning." *Journal of Experimental Psychology,* 1960, **60,** 376–383.

———— and Grace Yeni-Komshian. "Concurrent and Consecutive Modes of Learning Two Languages." Research in progress, McGill University, 1962.

Lashley, K. S. "The Problem of Serial Order in Behavior." In L. A.

Jeffress (ed.), *Cerebral Mechanisms in Behavior*. New York: John Wiley & Sons, Inc., 1951, pp. 112–136.

Lee, B. S. "(On delayed auditory feedback)." *Journal of the Acoustical Society of America*, 1950, **22**, 639.

McGeoch, J. A. *The Psychology of Human Learning*. New York: Longmans, Green & Co., Inc., 1942.

Milner, P. M. "The Cell Assembly: Mark II." *Psychological Review*, 1957, **64**, 242–252.

Mowrer, O. H. *Learning Theory and the Symbolic Processes*. New York: John Wiley & Sons, Inc., 1960.

Osgood, C. E. *Method and Theory in Experimental Psychology*. New York: Oxford University Press, 1953.

————. "Language in the Objective Mode: The Question of Sufficiency." *Contemporary Psychology*, 1958, **3**, 209–212.

————, Suci, G. J., and P. H. Tannenbaum. *The Measurement of Meaning*. Urbana: University of Illinois Press, 1957.

Peal, Elizabeth and W. E. Lambert. The Relation of Bilingualism to Intelligence, *Psychological Monographs*, 1962.

Skinner, B. F. *The Behavior of Organisms*. New York: D. Appleton & Company, Inc., 1938.

————. *Science and Human Behavior*. New York: The Macmillan Company, 1953.

————. *Verbal Behavior*. New York: D. Appleton & Company, Inc., 1957.

————. "Teaching Machines." *Science*, 1958, **128**, 969–977.

Srole, L. Social Dysfunction, Personality and Social Distance Attitudes. Paper read before the American Sociological Society, 1951, Chicago, Illinois.

Staats, Carolyn K., and A. W. Staats. "Meaning Established by Classical Conditioning." *Journal of Experimental Psychology*, 1957, **54**, 74–80.

Thurstone, L. L. *Multiple Factor Analysis*. Chicago: University of Chicago Press, 1947.

Underwood, B. J. and R. W. Schulz. *Meaningfulness and Verbal Learning*. Philadelphia: J. B. Lippincott Company, 1960.

UNESCO, *L'enseignement des langues vivantes*. Paris, 1955, pp. 77 ff.

Weinreich, U. *Languages in Contact*. New York: Linguistic Circle of New York, 1953.

Wimer, Cynthia, and W. E. Lambert. "The Differential Effects of Word and Object Stimuli on the Learning of Paired Associates." *Journal of Experimental Psychology*, 1959, **57**, 31–36.

PART 2

The Foreign Language Teacher

THE TEACHER OF MODERN
FOREIGN LANGUAGES

THEODORE ANDERSSON

*With language teaching enjoying an unprecedented
period of prosperity, it should be the concern of the
profession to make this prosperity sound and well
grounded. High quality preparation is still one of
the most basic and thorny problems to be solved to
insure foreign language teaching of the highest
caliber. It is to this question that Theodore Andersson devotes the following essay. A long-time
proponent of longer sequences in foreign language
teaching, Professor Andersson also indicates desirable teaching practices and specifies the fields
and competencies of the foreign language teacher.
Professor Andersson writes from many years of
experience and dedicated leadership in the foreign
language teaching field.*

INTRODUCTION: IMPORTANCE OF EARLY EXPERIENCE,
SCHOOLING, AND TRAINING

The education of the future teacher of modern foreign languages
often begins with the first utterances he hears and learns to imitate.
This may be his native language, which he may someday teach as a
foreign language, or it may be a second language learned from
birth in a bicultural situation. Lucky are those children for whom
this first stage of language learning begins so early and continues
for several years, long enough to become a permanent acquisition.
A child in such a situation not only learns a language without special
effort, he also acquires the mental set, habits of behavior, and sense

Reprinted by permission of the Wesleyan University Press from Theodore
Andersson, *The Education of the Secondary School Teacher*, Middletown,
Conn.: Wesleyan University Press, 1962. Copyright © 1962 by Wesleyan Uni-
versity.

of values of those around him. This process of learning a language in the context of its culture is a part of what is known as enculturation.

It is estimated that in addition to the million and a half Americans living abroad and in direct contact with other cultures we have in the United States some twenty million speakers of languages other than English. These provide a considerable reservoir of potential language teachers. In New York City one American citizen in ten is a native speaker of Spanish of Puerto Rican background. One Texan out of six has a Spanish name and can usually speak Spanish. Louisiana alone has some 400,000 speakers of French. Speakers of French in New England and in Louisiana, of Spanish in New York area and in the Southwest, of German in the Midwest, of Italian in many large cities, of Chinese and Japanese on the West Coast and in Hawaii, and of Russian, Polish, and the Scandinavian languages in scattered places represent such vast linguistic and cultural resources that we should be able to find among them enough prospective language teachers to supply the entire country.

A second opportunity to begin the education of the future language teacher occurs when the child who knows only his native language goes to school. His first teacher of a foreign language is in a strategic position to plant in him the seed of a special interest in languages; and, with his first thought that he may one day like to teach, the pupil's observation of his teachers becomes more conscious and more critical. As teachers we too often fail to keep the possibility of a career in teaching attractively before our students. And in our teacher-training programs we often overlook the usefulness of these twelve to sixteen years of daily observation of teachers and school administrators.

The third aspect of the education of prospective teachers, the period of training, is our main concern in this chapter. This training may occur in a liberal arts college, in a school of education, in a teachers' college—now coming to be called a state college—or in a graduate school. We shall not describe existing programs, for they are changing and many of them are unsatisfactory. Too many have been organized to satisfy state certification requirements, which are in turn inadequate. Instead, we shall examine the desirable qualifications of a language teacher and use these as a basis for discussing an adequate teacher-training program. In order to suggest as concretely as possible what a teacher should be able to do, we shall start by describing two visits to language classes, the first near the beginning and the second toward the end of the secondary-school course. We shall then sketch briefly the six-year sequence of language study which these two classes presuppose. And finally we shall enumerate the elements of a teacher-training program designed to produce teachers competent to teach languages in the way that the times require.

A VISIT TO A SEVENTH-GRADE CLASS IN RUSSIAN

Let us first visit a seventh-grade class in a large city high school. Here a young woman is teaching a first-year class in Russian. The teacher's parents were both born in Russia, came to this country shortly after the Bolshevik Revolution, met, married, and raised their children here. By speaking Russian in the home, they enabled their children to learn this language as a mother tongue. At the same time the children learned English from their playmates and later in school. Our teacher inherited from her parents a deep-seated respect for the teaching profession and chose to become a teacher —of English. With the revival of foreign language teaching after the launching of Sputnik and the passage of the National Defense Education Act of 1958 (NDEA), school administrators began looking for qualified teachers of Russian. At this time our teacher, who was already licensed, decided to offer to teach her mother tongue.

Knowing little of modern theory and practice, she enrolled in an NDEA summer language institute. Here her experience was that of many a secondary-school teacher. At first she resisted all the talk about linguistic science, the primacy of speech over writing, and language as behavior. These concepts did not correspond to her own language-learning experience in school nor to that of her parents. She resolved to keep an open mind, however, and gradually she began to understand the new ideas and to find them acceptable. What finally won her over was the demonstration classes, conducted in the early stages entirely without writing and without grammar explanation. The children watched and listened to a native-speaking teacher, imitated his every utterance and gesture, gradually memorized by ear whole dialogues, created rearrangements of these, and acted them out with gusto. Fascinated by the speed with which the children learned, by their accurate pronunciation, and especially by their great satisfaction with this kind of learning, she decided that this was the way she was going to teach Russian.

And this is the way she is teaching today, some two months after the first class in early September. The class contains thirty pupils, an equal number of boys and girls. Fortunately modern electronic equipment and choral techniques have mitigated somewhat the difficulties of large classes. Today, for example, we find that fifteen of the pupils are working with such equipment at the rear of the room while the teacher is working directly with the others.

By plugging in a set of earphones and turning a button we may monitor any one of the fifteen pupils at the electronic stations. At the moment they are doing pattern practice. They listen to a model sentence in Russian spoken at normal speed by a native speaker. This sentence is taken from a dialogue concerning a situation in school. The teacher is conscious of the fact that the situation is more characteristic of an American school than of a Russian school, so she has questioned her parents about their school experience in Russia, and in fact she has persuaded them to record a dialogue on tape parallel to the one now being practiced but culturally more nearly authentic though perhaps a little out of date. This dialogue she will use on Friday, when she likes to vary the program. She will also make it available in the school library, where there are three magnetic tape channels and four tables with a total of twenty-four listening posts.

Let us return to our fifteen pupils wearing earphones and absorbed in what they are doing. This is their third contact with this dialogue, which they have by now memorized. Yesterday the teacher presented this material and showed the class how to practice. Last night the pupils learned the dialogue by listening to a disc taken home from school. On the disc two native speakers do the whole dialogue at natural speed while the pupil thinks of the meaning, reminding himself, if necessary, by looking at an English translation. Each pupil listens to the dialogue as many times as may be needed to understand but about three times on the average. Then the dialogue is broken into short but natural utterances, with pauses for repetition by the pupil, followed by a repetition by the speaker. This procedure is also followed several times, according to the pupil's need. And finally the pupil is assisted in memorizing the dialogue in the following way: the voice on the disc says the first sentence, then repeats, omitting the last word or two. The pupil accompanies the voice aloud and fills in the missing words from memory. The voice repeats the sentence, omitting a longer segment at the end, and again the pupil fills in the missing words. When only the first words in the sentence are left, a voice says, "Now say the whole sentence." The pupil tries. The voice repeats the sentence. The pupil imitates. The voice repeats again and the pupil imitates. And a third time the voice repeats and the pupil imitates. At this point the pupil stops the turntable and practices the sentence as many times as may be necessary for him to feel confident that he knows it. This same process is then repeated with each successive sentence in the dialogue.

At their listening posts the pupils are now busy practicing the various patterns involved. The voice on the tape gives a model in the foreign language: "Let's go to the library," *Pupil:* "Let's go to the library." *Voice:* "Gym." *Pupil:* "Let's go to the gym. *Voice:* "Post office." *Pupil:* "Let's go to the post office." Since the structure is kept constant and the vocabulary varied only within the limits of what has already been learned, the pupils are encouraged to make their utterances not only accurate in pronunciation, speed, intonation, and juncture (the way words are connected), but also to make them habitual, or automatic. Gradually the sounds, rhythm, intonation, and structure will become more familar and will lose their strangeness.

By listening to another form of replacement or substitution exercise we realize that not all is mere rote repetition, though much rote learning is essential to mastering a language. The voice on the tape says, with convincing naturalness, "There are two girls sitting at the table."

Pupil: "There are two girls sitting at the table."
Voice: "Desk."
Pupil: "There are two girls sitting at the desk."
Voice: "Standing."
Pupil: "There are two girls standing at the desk."
Voice: "Boys."
Pupil: "There are two boys standing at the desk."
Voice: "Three."

Pupil: "There are three boys standing at the desk."
Voice: "Were."
Pupil: "There were three boys standing at the desk."

Thus, while remaining conscious of the basic pattern, the pupil is led to vary the elements in it. Each repetition at natural speed and with faithful imitation serves to fix more firmly the fundamental structure of the language. The pupil thus becomes conscious of "correct" or appropriate usage, but there is no explanation of grammar, no talking *about* language. Gradually the pupils realize that at this stage the question "Why?" makes no sense, that the answer is always the same: "Because this is the way speakers of Russian say it."

This exercise has taken fifteen minutes. In the meantime, with the other half of the class, the teacher has been reviewing day before yesterday's lesson by means of pattern practices and question-and-answer drill. This is the fourth time over this unit. The response to pattern practice takes place first with everyone responding, then with boys responding, then girls, then with one row or file or group responding, then another. Instead of leaving fourteen pupils inactive while asking a question of one pupil, the teacher uses the chain system. She has one pupil ask another, who answers and in turn asks the next question of the third, and so forth. This proceeds simultaneously in each row or file, while the teacher listens, encourages, or corrects, as needed. After this the class is divided into pairs, the teacher taking on the fifteenth child, each pair going through the entire routine. Finally, the teacher calls on several pupils in turn to give a brief oral composition in the form of an original rearrangement of the structures and vocabulary that have been learned. The pupils get their greatest satisfaction from this kind of manipulation, which enables them to show that they can already "use" the language. The teacher takes note of mistakes, corrects them inconspicuously, and plans supplementary drills for use in class on the points involved. At the end of fifteen minutes the two groups change places. In this way two thirds of the class time is taken up.

The teacher uses the last fifteen minutes to introduce to the whole class the new unit, which the pupils will study at home from a disc for at least half an hour in the way that has already been described.

In class the teacher explains briefly in English the situation on which the new dialogue is based, models the dialogue, identifies the new structures, demonstrates the pattern practice, and begins the drill. She wastes no time "explaining" meaning or structure. Since the pupils must at all times know the meaning, they are provided with an English version containing a completely natural translation and as needed a literal explanation of an occasional word or phrase. The bell rings, the teacher goes to the door, says good-by in Russian to each pupil, and each one answers in Russian. As they scatter, we overhear snatches of dialogue in Russian, proudly spoken.

The reader will recognize the contrast between the procedure we have described and his own language-learning experience. In the class we have just witnessed the teacher talks less than 50 percent of the time and each pupil is engaged in listening and speaking more than half of the time. In addition, every time he listens he must make a prompt response, to that hearing and speaking are intimately connected. This routine is strictly adhered to Monday through Thursday, the teacher informs us. Fridays are used for a weekly test and for varied activities of a less formal nature. In testing listening comprehension the teacher uses only the structures and vocabulary that have been studied, though the words may be recombined in a new order. Different voices are used, but a normal conversational speed is maintained. Pupil response is tested by recording the pupil's oral reproduction of a few expressions, recording his response to various stimuli, such as questions, commands, incomplete sentences, and pictures, and recording an original one-minute oral composition given without notes. The test takes five minutes. As the first fifteen pupils record their tests on tape, the other fifteen have a brief recess outside the room. After five minutes they change places and the whole test is over in less than fifteen minutes. The teacher may either monitor the performance of the pupils or review their tape later.

The teacher uses the remaining time to broaden the interest of the pupils by extending their vicarious experience. For the purpose of giving her pupils some understanding of Russian ways of life, she uses films, filmstrips, recordings, books, magazines, newspapers, and pictures. The teacher makes her collection available to the pupils in the classroom or in the school library. In this early stage these materials are mostly in English or are pictorial. The pupils enjoy especially occasional visits of a Russian student from a nearby university or of a Russian *émigré* in the community, who reminisces about his youth in Russia. In addition, the teacher records the talks made by visitors, special interviews with Russian speakers, or radio programs in Russian. The teacher's resourcefulness and enthusiasm have of course a good deal to do with her pupils' interest. Already one of her boys has said that he would like one day to teach Russian.

A VISIT TO AN ELEVENTH–TWELFTH-GRADE CLASS IN FRENCH

The class we have just described is imaginary; it is a composite of elements observed or suggested in various schools. The class we are about to describe is authentic except in detail and has been observed by the writer.

This visit is to an independent boys' school, where a class in French literature is taking place in early May. It is a class called French V, which presupposes the *equivalent* of four years of French study before the beginning of this course. The head of the department has explained to us that not one of the twelve boys in the class has had a full four years of school French previously. Six of the boys started French in this school but by taking the "fast" sections on the first three levels were able to move into French V in their senior year. The other six are juniors who have had the advantage of living and studying in France or Switzerland for at least a year. Two of these were assigned to French III Special when they entered as sophomores and one to French IV. One will as a senior take advantage of an opportunity extended to outstanding students to take French VI as an individual reading course, choosing the works of Balzac as his project. He will confer with his teacher once a week for half an hour. In the course of the year he will read some twenty of Balzac's novels, will become familiar with the story of Balzac's life, and will gain some understanding of Balzac's world. He will become a skillful and perceptive reader and will learn to write quite effectively by doing each week a book report, which will be carefully criticized and corrected by his teacher. Near the end of his senior year he will take the Advanced Placement Test in

French administered by the College Entrance Examination Board, will receive the top grade, and in the university of his choice will receive six credits for a literature course and be given permission to take junior or senior courses in stylistics, civilization, or literature.

But we are anticipating. Let us return to our French V class. The teacher and the twelve pupils sit around a large circular table. The teacher is a man in his forties, a graduate of one of the Ivy League colleges, a major in French, and obviously adept at speaking French though his accent is not native. He himself began studying French in another independent school at the age of fourteen, became interested in it, and showed unusual aptitude. Immediately after completing his military service, he decided to become a teacher. He has had no formal preparation for teaching, but his sixteen years of contact with many teachers, a deep-seated love of teaching, a broad knowledge of and taste for the French language and literature, and four years spent living in France and traveling in other parts of Europe have combined to make him a skillful and dedicated teacher.

Today he is discussing with his class Jean Giono's novel *Le chant du monde,* published in 1934. The teacher takes the first few minutes to summarize in French the discussion that has taken place in the preceding classes, to clarify some points that have been left in doubt, and to set the stage for today's discussion. Before starting, however, he gives the boys a chance to ask in French about difficulties they may have had in vocabulary, construction, or meaning. Three or four boys ask about specific points. The teacher lets other boys answer if they can do so quickly. Otherwise he answers himself. The teacher then selects two boys to write in French on the board summaries of the day's reading. The boys work without notes but have obviously prepared to do this if called on. As we watch, we note with what accuracy they write. While the two work at the board, the teacher asks the class to summarize orally the reading of the day. He interrupts frequently with questions intended to probe more deeply the boys' understanding. Once this is finished, the teacher concentrates the discussion on one aspect of Giono's art, considering today the role of nature in Giono's novel, the pervasiveness, the vividness, and particularly the personification of nature. The boys enter eagerly into the discussion, talk easily, and appear intensely interested. The teacher tells us afterward that he had prepared for this book by having the French Club show two films based on Giono's works, namely, *La femme du boulanger* and *Regain,* thus giving the class a vivid visual impression of Giono's country and the personalities of his countrymen. About five minutes before the bell, the teacher ends the discussion in order to criticize and correct the two compositions on the board, with the participation of the other boys. He then assigns the next chapter for reading and dismisses the class.

In our conference with the teacher we learn that the course started with a reading of *Madame Bovary* in an unabridged edition. After this warming-up period the class turned to *La chanson de Roland.* From this point on the course became a survey of French literature. One of the standard anthologies was used but frequently assignments of whole works would be made. The readings included —and this is an authentic list—*Aucassin et Nicolette;* a *fabliau;* excerpts from *Le roman de Renart; La farce de Maître Pathelin;* selected poems from Charles d'Orléans and Villon; an episode from Rabelais; an essay from Montaigne; selected poems from Ronsard and Du Bellay; excerpts from Malherbe, Boileau, La Fontaine, Descartes, Pascal, Bossuet, La Rochefoucauld, La Bruyère, and Madame de Sévigné; Corneille's *Le Cid;* Molière's *Le bourgeois gentilhomme, Les femmes savantes,* and *Le malade imaginaire;* Racine's *Andromaque;* selections from Montesquieu's *Les lettres persanes;* Voltaire's *Candide;* Diderot's *Supplément au voyage de Bougainville;* selections from Rousseau's *Confessions* and *Discours;* Beaumarchais' *Le barbier de Seville* and *Le mariage de Figaro;* selections from Lamartine, Hugo, Vigny, and Musset; poems of Leconte de Lisle, Banville, Hérédia, Baudelaire, Verlaine, Rimbaud, Mallarmé, and Valéry; and Gide's *Le retour de l'enfant prodigue.* Unlike many a college survey course, this one did not stop at the end of the eighteenth century or even at the end of the nineteenth century but carried right into the middle of the twentieth, ending with Camus' *La chute,* published in 1956.

All of these twelve students will take the College Entrance Examination Board Advanced Placement Test in French, and it may be predicted on the basis of past records that approximately three of them will receive a grade of high honors, four a grade of honors, four a grade of creditable, and one a grade of pass. Most, and perhaps all, will receive credit for the first college course in literature.

At least seven of the twelve will be eligible to take junior or senior courses in French during their freshman year in college.

Not many schools in the past have offered a six-year course of language study, but such a program is sure to become increasingly common. The Connecticut State Department of Education Curriculum Bulletin Series No. V., *Foreign Languages, Grades 7–12* (Hartford, Connecticut, 1958), describes various ways in which such a sequence can be planned, and the bulletin issued in 1959 by the National Association of Secondary-School Principals, entitled *Modern Foreign Languages in the Comprehensive Secondary School,* also encourages school administrators to plan such a course of study.

THE SIX-YEAR SEQUENCE OF FOREIGN LANGUAGE STUDY, GRADES SEVEN TO TWELVE

We would do well at this point, in order to see the whole of the teacher's task, to sketch the main features of a course of study beginning in grade seven and continuing through grade twelve. The first stage is largely audiolingual because it emphasizes the training of the ear and the tongue, without the use of writing or print. Instead of discussion of grammar theory there is varied drill to help the pupil master the sound system and the structure of the language.

Stage two, in grade eight, continues to provide practice in hearing and speaking and continued exposure to culturally authentic materials. Here, however, reading and writing are commenced, both at the same time, provided they have not been begun in grade seven. The first objective is to learn to read and write the patterns that have already been learned by ear. Initially much of the reading is done aloud and should sound like natural talk and not a form of intoning. The spelling system is systematically analyzed and thoroughly learned by abundant writing exercises such as copying, written pattern practice, and dictation. In the second half of the year pupils should be able to read simple texts slightly beyond the limit of the vocabulary and syntax that have so far been learned. Likewise, once the spelling system is mastered, it will be possible to extend writing exercises to include dictation of somewhat more complex passages, the rewriting of passages with a change of person, time, and number. Controlled compositions, that is, compositions in which the pupil is told what to say though not how to say it, and brief original compositions by the student within the limits of the vocabulary and syntax that he has learned are also encouraged.

The third stage, in grade nine, continues and expands the earlier instruction in language and culture. To these objectives are added a brief summary of the grammatical structure of the language. By this time the pupil acquires a knowledge of basic grammatical terms. As he becomes increasingly familiar with structure and expands his vocabulary, his ear is trained progressively by the use of a variety of native speakers, by the inclusion of more rapid speech, dialogues, group conversation, telephone and radio discourse. To make the pupils more conscious of the way of life of other peoples, the teacher supplements culturally significant reading materials by pictures, filmstrips, films, recordings, and personal talks by nationals from the country concerned.

After the pupil has learned to read easily material he has first learned to understand and say and is ready to extend his reading horizons, the time has come for making use of edited or bilingual texts. At this point the chief obstacle to understanding a written text is lexical rather than structural. When he comes to a word or idiom with which he is unfamiliar, he should be able quickly to refer to the margin or the bottom of the page for the meaning. And a little later he should be taught how to use a bilingual text. The bilingual text, in which the original text is printed on the left and the English translation on the right, is as yet little used but may soon become an indispensable tool for learning to read, once the initial stage has been passed. The pupil must be trained to consult the English *only after* he has made a vigorous effort to understand the original text. The considerable amount of time saved by this procedure should enable the pupil to read much more and thus more quickly reach the point of enjoying his reading.

In the ninth grade the pupil's skill in writing should also increase considerably. In addition to dictations and controlled compositions, the pupil at this point writes summaries of his reading and continues to do original compositions on subjects within his linguistic grasp.

In grades ten, eleven, and twelve there is continued practice in hearing and understanding various types of speech, practice in speaking on more mature and complex subjects, reading, writing, culture, and literature. In these grades ear training might well include rapid, even familiar, speech, low-fidelity recordings, and broadcasts that have been partly jammed. Grammar at this point gives way to a careful analysis of the style of various worthwhile authors. The reading is substantial though appropriate to the age of the learners. It continues to reveal and illuminate cultural patterns and various aspects of contemporary civilization, and to provide historical perspective. For an appropriate guide to the study of literature, the *Advanced Placement Program: Course Descriptions* of the College Entrance Examination Board may be recommended.

The kind of language program we have sketched calls for highly qualified teachers, real professionals. Of course, not all teachers need to be able to teach at all levels. On the lower level they must be able to coordinate their teaching with that of the elementary school. They must in fact be ready to fit into the whole elementary school-to-college language program. In the future an increasing number of language programs are likely to begin long before the seventh grade. Already many school systems are experimenting with such programs, all the way from kindergarten to grade six, with satisfying results where conditions are favorable. Assuming favorable conditions, a program which begins in the fifth grade could in grades five and six accomplish approximately what is accomplished in the seventh grade in our hypothetical program, but better. Pupils who have had such a program in grades five and six might then very well move directly into the eighth-grade language program. Pupils who have started their foreign language instruction in grade three and continued it for four years might be expected to achieve, quantitatively, the equivalent of grades seven and eight. In the quality of their understanding and speaking they should be expected to do considerably better. They might therefore move straight into the grade-nine level of the language sequence. Children who have begun their language learning in kindergarten or grade one and continued through grade six would have acquired an even better grounding in understanding and speaking, but they would not have achieved significantly more in reading and writing than those beginning in grade three. Therefore they should normally not move into a language class higher than grade nine.

This kind of program, especially one beginning in kindergarten or grade one, would, if we had properly qualified teachers, supported by their school administrators and the community, help compete successfully with our European rivals, who for so long have had an advantage over us. Completely authentic mastery of the structure and sound system of a foreign language is normally acquired by a child only before age ten, provided the circumstances are highly favorable. Gaining familiarity with another way of life, especially if it must be done vicariously, requires a long exposure to the unfamiliar culture and the enlightened guidance of highly qualified teachers. And even the basic reading in history, civilization, and literature requires the six-year sequence we have described, as a minimum. Such a program would enable a student to do in college mature work in a second language as well as in English.

QUALIFICATIONS OF THE SECONDARY-SCHOOL TEACHER OF MODERN FOREIGN LANGUAGES

At this point we are faced with a dilemma. Teachers qualified to teach this kind of program should ideally have been educated in the same way themselves. But we know that most of today's teachers started their language learning at the age of fourteen or fifteen and were raised in the grammar-vocabulary-translation tradition. We know also that their training has been inadequate since liberal arts colleges have been negligent of their teacher-training function, teachers' colleges have neglected academic competence, and neither has collaborated closely with the other. We find no comfort in the certification procedures of state departments of education. A recent survey of certification practices conducted by the Modern Language Association of America reveals that not a single state *requires* of teachers eligible for certification even the basic ability to understand and speak a second language. The Russian teacher we watched has a certificate, the French teacher does not, and yet both are equally competent. This observation and many others lead us to conclude that there is no necessary relationship between certification and qualification.

On questioning the Russian teacher concerning her preparation, we found her critical of her courses both in education and in foreign languages. We have seen that her experience in the summer language institute opened her eyes and made her dissatisfied with the traditional type of work in foreign languages. Some of her courses in education were valuable, she felt, but others contained too many trivia and had no direct bearing on the teaching problem. They therefore tended to disenchant her. The French teacher we visited said that he enjoyed his courses in French literature, acquired from them a taste for reading and a critical sense, but regretted that he had had no apprenticeship in teaching until he took his first job.

The testimony of these teachers and of many others suggests that the teacher-preparation programs in many of our institutions, whether professionally or academically oriented, are inadequate for our present needs. State departments of education do little to remedy this situation. Instead of stating requirements in terms of proficiency, they are content with paper requirements, and even these are minimally stated in terms of twenty-four or eighteen or even twelve semester hours in the language concerned. There seems little hope for improvement without a completely new approach. A key to a more successful system of teacher preparation is certification based on demonstrated proficiency and readiness to teach, no matter how these qualifications may have been acquired.

Fortunately the beginning of such a program has been made in the field of languages. In 1955 the Steering Committee of the Foreign Language Program of the Modern Language Association (MLA) prepared a definition of the subject-matter competence of secondary-school teachers of modern foreign languages. This statement, which has been published in many places, was endorsed by eighteen national or regional language organizations and may therefore be taken to represent the present consensus of the language teaching profession. Competencies were defined on three levels, minimal, good, and superior. The Committee expressed regret that the present state of the profession made it necessary to publish minimal competencies.

It is one thing to define teacher qualifications; it is another to evaluate them. The MLA, under an NDEA grant, has developed some very effective tests to measure as objectively as possible these various competencies. As an initial step in their standardization, preliminary forms A and B of these tests were used at the beginning and the end of the summer language institutes in 1960. During the school year 1960–1961 they were revised on the basis of careful item analysis conducted by the Educational Testing Service and were made available to teacher-preparing institutions and school administrators.

THE TRAINING OF THE SECONDARY-SCHOOL
TEACHER OF MODERN FOREIGN LANGUAGES

We have considered how the qualified language teacher may be expected to perform in the classroom. This versatile performance requires that the teacher possess, in addition to the essential qualities of character, personality, and taste, certain knowledge and skills, which have been defined. These expected competencies appear formidable to most of our present teachers, who have had neither the advantage of learning a second language in its cultural context nor that of an early start and a long sequence of effective language learning in school and college. For such teachers in service who desire to improve we need an effective remedial program.

Such a remedial program has been provided by the NDEA, which subsidized twelve institutes in the summer of 1959, thirty-seven in the summer of 1960, fifty-five in 1961, and eighty in 1962, in addition to several year-long institutes. These institutes have amply fulfilled their purpose of explaining to the profession the new theories and of demonstrating the modern practices.

The main purpose of the present chapter, however, is to describe the kind of program suitable for a candidate who wishes to prepare for teaching a modern foreign language in the secondary school. As we list the desirable components of such a program, we must not forget the trainee's possible early exposure to another language and culture (enculturation), and his twelve to sixteen years of observation of teachers and schools.

Let us now consider the course of a prospective language teacher who enrolls in a teacher-training program at some moment between his freshman year in college and his first year in graduate school. Before such a candidate is accepted, the director and staff of the program should satisfy themselves that he has the necessary personal qualities, that he has a compelling desire to teach and a deep interest in the language and culture that he intends to teach, and that his basic mastery of this language is such that he can be expected by the end of the training course to qualify as at least "good" in all seven categories of the MLA qualifications.

Having been judged worthy of admission, the candidate should at the outset be assisted in appraising his strengths and weaknesses. This initial diagnosis will normally consist of a series of personal interviews and the taking of the MLA Foreign Language Proficiency Tests for Teachers and Advanced Students. Such interviews would reveal whether the candidate has had the advantage of childhood contact with another language and culture, when he first conceived the desire to teach, how much his formal education may have contributed to his vocational purpose, how conscious and critical he has been in observing his teachers and schools, how widely he has read on educational and related subjects, and whether he has any special interests or talents relevant to a teaching career. All of these factors make a difference and should be taken into account as the staff helps him plan his course.

The Proficiency Tests will help the staff to determine to what extent the candidate already has the qualifications defined by the MLA. The candidate receives credit for the knowledge and skills he possesses, and the director and staff prescribe a program to enable him to overcome his deficiencies. Such a program consists of courses, individual work, or a combination of the two. Thanks to the advent of the tape recorder, whole courses can be put on tape, and the independent type of student may prefer to work his way through such a course at his own speed, merely raising a question now and then in a seminar or a professor's office. Lists of readings and of other kinds of materials—recordings, films, filmstrips, slides, pictures—should be available. In fact everything possible should be done to free any student with the slightest spark of independence from the goosestep of our traditional practices. As soon as he feels ready, the student should be allowed to demonstrate his readiness by teaching in the classroom and by taking an alternate form of the MLA tests plus any other tests the director and staff may prescribe. Having given satisfactory evidence of his proficiency, he should be recommended by the institution to the state department of education and be granted a license to teach.

Providing each candidate with an opportunity to acquire the knowledge and skills outlined in the MLA statement of qualifications and in a form to suit his individual needs requires a program of great flexibility.

To be able to understand and speak another language with a near-native proficiency, a teacher must normally have been exposed to the foreign language before the age of ten. A teacher who has had such an advantage can usually model the language adequately for his pupils. We do not mean to imply, of course, that access to our language classrooms should be limited to native speakers of other languages. This *is* an ideal to be strived for, but there are many competent and inspiring teachers of modern foreign languages—like the French teacher we watched in the independent boys' school—whose teaching is excellent and whose services are needed. But a teacher should be able to recognize when his speech is not authentic and should be ready to supply authentic models on tape and discs. There is no room for compromise here. German is what the native speaker of German talks, not what a foreign imitator has learned belatedly and artificially in the classroom. Of those who have begun their language learning in high school and continued through college, only the most gifted approximate native mastery. A deficiency in understanding and speaking may be remediable, but it requires long hours of practice in listening to and imitating native speakers. A course in advanced oral composition should be available, but much practice in hearing and speaking can be provided in the language laboratory.

The literate skills (reading and writing) are the ones which have been traditionally stressed. Our teacher candidate may therefore not need much special training in reading, but he will probably need instruction and demonstration in how to teach reading. He will learn that without sufficient oral preparation silent reading is unsatisfactory. He will learn the technique of listening to a recorded reading while following a text with his eyes. He will examine studies that have been made of the "density" of reading texts (number of new words per page) and will learn how to adjust the density to pupils' progress. He will learn how to train pupils in the proper use of bilingual texts. And he may have the opportunity to explore the use of the tachistoscope in speeding up silent reading.

Teacher candidates will certainly need practice in writing. Writing is one thing that cannot be learned from tape; it requires a native teacher who is skillful in criticizing written exercises of all kinds. In addition to improving his own writing skill, the teacher candidate will need to learn how to teach writing. The teaching of writing has in the past been quite unsatisfactory in the secondary school, for two principal reasons. One is the fact that secondary-school teachers have been overwhelmed with classes both too numerous and too large and so have not been able to check carefully on assigned written work. The second reason is that we have not used properly the various forms of written exercises available to us. An adequate teacher-training program should provide a candidate with a course in advanced composition, if needed, and with instruction in the various techniques of teaching writing.

On the subject of grammar our teacher candidate will, if he has had the traditional instruction provided by teachers of English, Latin, and modern foreign languages, need to learn the newer concepts of linguistic science and the application of these concepts to the teaching of a second language. He must realize clearly that instead of studying grammar first and then language, as has so often been done in the past, pupils should first learn appropriate usage by direct imitation of authentic models. Only after having learned to use the basic structures of a language is one ready to learn how to analyze and describe the grammar of a foreign language. The procedure is similar to that used in learning one's mother tongue. By the age of five and a half the average child understands and speaks his mother tongue in perfect conformity to the cultural group within which he lives. In the primary grades of school he normally learns the basic elements of reading and writing and in the intermediate grades he learns, we hope, modern grammatical terms and concepts. His study of the structure of a foreign language should follow the same course and should provide him with the labels necessary to talk about language structure with an understanding of its classes, forms, and relations. This fundamental part of the teacher-training program can be provided in courses called "Introduction to Linguistics" and "The Application of Linguistics to Language Teaching." Mature students should naturally not be required to take these courses if they prefer to do the readings privately and take a rigorous examination on the subject.

Among the competencies of a modern foreign language teacher the most controversial is knowledge of culture. The word itself causes confusion. For our purposes it will be sufficient to distinguish two general meanings, one which has long been traditional, especially with humanists, and the other representing the newer point of view of social scientists. According to the latter, culture involves the regularly patterned way of life characteristic of a society, or people living, feeling, thinking, evaluating, acting together. According to the former, culture involves the things that people have produced, the things which we would be proud to have produced if we had been in their place, the outstanding achievements of a people, particularly in the arts. In the past, language teachers have been primarily concerned with the second of these definitions, and among the arts mainly with literature. The MLA qualifications statement suggests that in our day this exclusive concern with literature is no longer adequate. This is not to say that literature is not important. Literature is in fact the only art form directly related to language. It would be tragic if literary study did not continue to attract ever increasing numbers of foreign language teachers. What is needed, however, is a great broadening of interests in order to make room for some language teachers who will concern themselves with other aspects of culture, whether it be history, geography, economics, politics, or social institutions. Foreign language teachers have hitherto been either totally oblivious of culture in the social-science sense or have had a very superficial view of it.

Future modern language teachers therefore need first of all a clear idea of the culture concept. They will then gradually have to learn how to apply this concept, just as they are learning to apply the concepts of linguistic science, to their language teaching. The kind of understanding that is involved may be acquired in various ways. One of the best is by living among the people whose language one teaches, and particularly during one's early years. A person with such an experience comes closest to identifying himself with another culture. But feeling oneself to be part of another culture is not sufficient. One should become conscious of it, be able to talk about it, if one is to be successful in making younger learners in turn aware of it. We may say in summary then that the ideal teacher should be able to represent another culture and should be able to make his pupils sensitive to another way of life. This requires great delicacy and intelligence if one is to avoid superficiality.

Language reflects culture, both through the words which arbitrarily represent meaning and through the structures which combine words. The language learner can early be made aware how radically these differ from English and be led to understand that other nationals organize their experience in completely different ways, as revealed by their language. Fortunately the audio-visual materials which are coming into wider use can assist greatly in bringing other peoples right into our classrooms, where we can both see and hear them in characteristic activities. The number of films, filmstrips, and tape recordings of good quality that are now available is limited, but the few that we have suffice to show that young learners are stimulated by seeing the immediate connection between the language they are studying and the life of the people who speak this language. In the future, materials selected for our language teaching must meet as rigorous a test of cultural authenticity as of linguistic authenticity. Furthermore they must at every stage in the modern language course be appropriate to the age and experience of the learner. It is in the field of culture that the future language teacher finds his greatest challenge and his greatest opportunity. To acquire competence in this field our teacher candidate should have the choice of taking courses on the "Introduction to the Social Sciences" and "The Application of the Social Sciences to Language Teaching" or of reading the substance of such courses on his own in preparation for an examination.

Professional preparation to teach a language should remain, as it now generally does, in the hands of language specialists, although a complete program for learning to teach requires the collaboration of professional educators. Readiness to teach a modern foreign language presupposes an understanding of the nature of language, best interpreted by linguistic scientists; of the process by which a foreign language is learned, which psychologists are only just beginning to investigate; of the relation between language and culture, which cultural anthropologists, sociologists, and social psychologists can help us understand better; of the best available methods and materials for teaching in a modern manner; and of the tests available for evaluating various aspects of language learning in accordance with the objectives which have been established. Ideally, the desire and ability to conduct research and experimentation in the field of language learning and teaching should also be part of the language teacher's equipment. To help the prospective teacher with his professional preparation, a training program should offer a course on "The Teaching of Modern Foreign Languages," but again let us emphasize that the candidate who chooses to read and study by himself rather than take the course should be encouraged to do so.

The program we have described constitutes only a part, though a major part, of the training of the teacher of modern foreign languages. Another major part of his training falls in the area of what is commonly called professional education. It includes such elements as an understanding of human growth and learning, of the place of the school in our society, of current educational theories and practices, of evaluation and experimental design, and of an apprenticeship in teaching, in which professional and academic educators should share supervision. Unfortunately there are still lacking a satisfactory working definition of qualifications in the field of professional preparation and tests to measure as objectively as possible such qualifications. This lack is one of the chief obstacles to rapid progress in the field of teacher education. Let us hope that our colleagues in professional education will undertake without delay to fill this gap in our educational system.

SUMMARY AND CONCLUSION

Let us consider some of the implications of the principles and practices which we have outlined. In the preceding pages we have considered the training program to be only the culmination of the teacher's early language-learning experience and his exposure to a culture other than his own. Indeed we may safely affirm that a college or graduate-school program for the training of a language teacher has little chance of producing highly qualified teachers if entering students are not already equipped with at least the basic language skills of understanding, speaking, reading, and writing. The acquisition of these skills presupposes a long sequence of effective language learning, at the very least a six-year program beginning in grade seven and continuing through grade twelve. There are, to be sure, known cases of qualified teachers who did not begin their language study until senior high school or even college, but they are exceptional in their interest and aptitude. Under normal circumstances not even a six-year sequence is sufficient to guarantee a near-native command of a second language, for we have noted that the average person does not learn to speak a second language without accent and without constraint unless he is exposed to this language in its cultural context before the age of ten.

A respect for these basic principles concerning the nature of language and the process of language learning suggests the need that we reconsider the whole structure of teacher education. If we agree that the hard core of a language teacher's qualifications is mastery of language and cultural awareness, we are bound to accept certain implications. For one thing, we should recruit far more of our teacher candidates from among those of our citizens who have learned a second language in its cultural context. This in turn requires the preservation and constant replenishment of our linguistic and cultural resources. It should require only a moment's thought to realize that a United States citizen who is equipped to use two languages skillfully is more valuable to himself and to his country than one who is not. And yet, at the same time that our Congress appropriates millions of dollars to promote more and better language learning, our schools systematically suppress the knowledge of languages other than English in children who come to school so equipped. It would be easy to cultivate other languages if our citizens valued these languages and wanted to preserve them.

The technical problems are not difficult. Many children in bilingual communities still enter school able to understand and speak a language other than English. At this point they are ready to learn the elements of reading and writing that language, which now we withhold from them until grade nine or ten, by which time they have lost their desire. Let us by all means provide this opportunity to read, at the psychologically proper moment. While learning to read and write in their mother tongue, these children would learn everything else in English along with the English speaking children, except reading and writing in English, which could be delayed slightly until they were ready. One of our educational inconsistencies is that we are careful not to plunge our English speaking children into reading until we are sure they are "ready" even though they have lived in an English speaking environment for six years. With non-English speaking children we show no such scruples as we plunge them into the reading of English, a *foreign* language. In schools where some of the children speak English as a mother tongue and also another language there is an unusual opportunity

for effective language learning. While the children who speak another language are learning to read and write their mother tongue
and learning to understand and speak English, the English speaking children have the opportunity to learn to understand and speak
the second language of the community. As the children play together, they can teach each other a second language under something approaching ideal circumstances.

Not only do we fail to exploit our national supply of teachers of
other languages; we have also so far failed to develop on a large
scale the exchange of teachers with other countries. Here too is a
potential source of native-speaking teachers with the additional
advantage that they have been well educated and can represent
their culture authentically. Such exchanges would of course require
on both sides a thorough orientation in the prevailing school philosophy and practices.

In discussing the training part of our teacher-education program
we have emphasized the desirability of a flexible program conducted cooperatively by language educators, social scientists, and
professional educators. The collaboration of social scientists is
needed because the study of language—or linguistics—is a social
science as well as one of the humanities. The collaboration of professional educators is indispensable, for they are most intimately
concerned with educational theory and practice. The best basis for
a satisfactory collaboration is, we believe, the acceptance of the
principle that a teacher's qualifications when satisfactorily demonstrated should be recognized no matter how they may have been
acquired. The experience and education of teacher candidates vary
widely. But concerning what they should be able to do in the language classroom we have, as far as subject matter is concerned,
reached a workable consensus. What we now urgently need is a
similar working definition of what a teacher needs to know and be
able to do on the professional side. This is not nearly so difficult as
it seems. There are well defined fields of knowledge, such as the
place of the school in our society, the principles of human growth
and learning, evaluation and experimentation, and teaching apprenticeship. All of these have been the subjects of courses and
textbooks. By mobilizing its best thinkers the educational profession
could therefore conceivably agree on a definition of knowledge essential to the teacher. A demonstration in the classroom of readiness

to teach could be carried out in the presence of the supervising teacher and principal of the school and of a language educator and a professional educator from the teacher-training institution. A teacher whose basic knowledge has been validated by examination—whether or not he has taken specific courses—and whose readiness to teach has been demonstrated satisfactorily to such a committee as we have indicated above should, we believe, be recommended forthwith by the training institution and be granted a license to teach by the state department of education.

We have sketched the principal aspects of the education of the qualified secondary-school teacher of modern foreign languages. Is his education complete as he steps into his first regular classroom? Certainly not, but if his own teachers have been successful and he has in him the stuff of a teacher, he will think of his first class as the beginning rather than the end of his education. He will want to continue reading and speculating, and he will want constantly to improve his teaching by means of research and experimentation. And finally he will want to collaborate with other professional-minded teachers in improving unremittingly the quality of American education.

Bibliography

Balakian, Anna. "Certification Requirements for Modern Foreign Language Teachers in American Public Schools (1959–60)." *Publications of the Modern Language Association of America*, LXXVI, No. 2B, May, 1961.

Birkmaier, Emma. "Modern Languages." *Encyclopedia of Education Research*, 37th ed., Chester W. Harris, ed. New York: The Macmillan Company, 1960.

Brooks, Nelson. *Language and Language Learning: Theory and Practice.* New York: Harcourt, Brace & World, Inc., 1960.

Carroll, John B. "Research in Foreign Language Teaching." *Handbook of Research on Teaching*, N. L. Gage, ed. Chicago: Rand McNally & Company, 1961.

———. *The Study of Language: A Survey of Linguistics and Related Disciplines in America.* Cambridge, Mass.: Harvard University Press, 1953.

Chapin, Miriam. *How People Talk.* New York: The John Day Company, Inc., 1945.

Cleveland, Harlan, Gerard J. Mangone, and John Clarke Adams. *The*

Overseas Americans. New York: McGraw-Hill Book Company, 1960.

Cornelius, Edwin T. *How to Learn a Foreign Language.* New York: Thomas Y. Crowell Company, 1955.

Delattre, Pierre. "A Technique of Aural-Oral Approach." *The French Review,* January and February, 1947.

Desberg, Dan. "Structural Linguistics and High School Language." *The Classical Outlook,* November, 1959.

Dostert, Leon E. "Foreign Language Reading Skill." *Journal of Chemical Education,* March, 1955.

Duff, Charles. *How to Learn a Language.* Oxford: Blackwell, 1948.

Freeman, Stephen A. "A Report on the 1959 Summer Language Institutes." *Hispania,* March, 1960.

————. "A Report on the 1960 Summer Language Institutes." *Hispania,* March, 1961.

Gouin, François. *The Art of Teaching and Studying Languages.* London: George Philip and Son, 1912.

Hall, Edward T. *The Silent Language.* Garden City, N.Y.: Doubleday & Company, Inc., 1959.

Haugen, Einar. *Bilingualism in the Americas: A Bibliography and Research Guide.* American Dialect Society, Gainesville, Florida: University of Alabama Press, 1956.

Hutchinson, Joseph C. *Modern Foreign Languages in the High School: The Language Laboratory.* Washington: U.S. Office of Education, Bulletin No. 23, 1961.

Jespersen, Otto. *How to Teach a Foreign Language.* London: Allen and Unwin, 1956.

Johnston, Marjorie C. "Foreign Language Instruction." *Review of Educational Research,* April 1961.

————. ed. *Modern Foreign Languages in the High School.* Washington: U.S. Government Printing Office, 1958.

Lado, Robert. *Linguistics Across Cultures.* Ann Arbor: University of Michigan Press, 1957.

Langer, Susanne. Chapter on language in *Philosophy in a New Key.* New York: New American Library, 1948.

Marty, Fernand L. *Language Laboratory Learning.* Wellesley: Audio-Visual Publications, 1960.

Mathieu, Gustave. "Language Laboratories." *Review of Educational Research,* April, 1962.

Modern Language Association of America. *MLA Selective List of Materials.* New York: Modern Language Association of America, 1962.

————. Reports of Surveys and Studies in the Teaching of Modern Foreign Languages, New York: Modern Language Association of America, 1959–1961.

Moulton, William G. "Study Hints for Language Students." *Modern Language Journal,* October, 1952.

National Association of Secondary School Principals. "Foreign Languages in the Comprehensive Secondary School." NASSP *Bulletin,* June 1, 1959.

National Education Association and Modern Language Association. *Modern Foreign Languages and the Academically Talented Student.* Washington: National Education Association, 1960.

O'Connor, Patricia. *Modern Foreign Languages in the Secondary School: Pre-reading Instruction.* Washington: U.S. Government Printing Office, 1960.

Parker, William R. *The National Interest and Foreign Languages.* 3rd ed. Washington: U.S. Government Printing Office, 1961.

Penfield, Wilder and Lamar Robers, *Speech and Brain Mechanisms.* Princeton, N.J.: Princeton University Press, 1959.

Politzer, Robert L. "On the Relation of Linguistics to Language Teaching." *Modern Language Journal,* February, 1958.

Stack, Edward M. *The Language Laboratory and Modern Language Teaching.* New York: Oxford Book Co., 1960.

Starr, Wilmarth H. "Foreign Language Teaching and Intercultural Understanding." *School and Society,* March 19, 1955.

UNESCO. *The Teaching of Modern Languages.* Paris: UNESCO, 1955.

U.S. Office of Education. *Source Materials for Secondary School Teachers of Foreign Languages.* Washington: U.S. Office of Education, 1962, Circular No. 27001A.

―――. *Useful References for Teachers of Foreign Languages.* Washington: U.S. Office of Education Circular No. 509.

QUALIFICATIONS FOR SECONDARY SCHOOL TEACHERS OF MODERN FOREIGN LANGUAGES[1]

The Modern Language Association is vitally interested in seeing that foreign language teachers are prepared in the best possible way. The following qualifications endorsed by them, and many other organizations, represent a milestone in teacher-preparation history and indicate desirable language knowledge and skills. It is to be hoped that not only will additional teaching qualifications be determined in the future, but that those presented here will be required in certifying teachers. Teacher preparation is the basis for a good foreign language program. It is the teacher who kindles or kills the interest of the students, who imparts exact or wrong notions. A well-prepared foreign language teacher is the best insurance of good foreign language teaching.

It is vitally important that teachers of modern foreign languages be adequately prepared for a task which more and more Americans are declaring essential to the national welfare. Though a majority of the language teachers in our schools are well trained, many have been poorly or inadequately prepared, often through no fault of their own. The members of the Steering Committee of the Modern

Reprinted by permission of the Modern Language Association of America from *PMLA*, 1954.

[1] The following statement was prepared by the Steering Committee of the Foreign Language Program of the Modern Language Association of America, and was subsequently endorsed for publication by the MLA Executive Council, by the Modern Language Committee of the Secondary Education Board, by the Committee on the Language Program of the American Council of Learned Societies, and by the executive boards or councils of the following national and regional organizations: National Federation of Modern Language Teachers Associations, American Association of Teachers of French, American Associa-

Language Association, therefore, present this statement of what they consider the minimal, good, and superior qualifications of a secondary-school teacher of a modern foreign language.

The group regrets that the minimum here stated *cannot yet* include real proficiency in the foreign tongue or more than a superficial knowledge of the foreign culture. It must be clearly understood that teaching by persons who cannot meet this minimal standard will not produce results which our profession can endorse as making the distinctive contribution of language learning to American life in the second half of the twentieth century.

The lowest level of preparation is not recommended. It is here stated only as a point of departure which carries with it the responsibility for continued study and self-improvement, through graduate and in-service training, toward the levels of good and superior preparation.

Those who subscribe to this statement hope that the teacher of foreign languages (1) will have the personal qualities which make an effective teacher; (2) has received a well-balanced education, including a knowledge of our own American culture; and (3) has received the appropriate training in professional education, psychology, and secondary-school methods. It is not our purpose to define further these criteria. We are concerned here with the specific criteria for a teacher of modern foreign languages.

1. AURAL UNDERSTANDING

Minimal. The ability to get the sense of what an educated native says when he is enunciating carefully and speaking simply on a general subject.

---

tion of Teachers of German, American Association of Teachers of Italian, American Association of Teachers of Spanish and Portuguese, American Association of Teachers of Slavic and East European Languages, Central States Modern Language Teachers Association, Middle States Association of Modern Language Teachers, New England Modern Language Association, Northeast Conference on the Teaching of Foreign Languages, Northwest Conference on Foreign Language Teaching, Philological Association of the Pacific Coast, Rocky Mountain Modern Language Association, South Atlantic Modern Language Association, and South-Central Modern Language Association.

Good. The ability to understand conversation at average tempo, lectures, and news broadcasts.

Superior. The ability to follow closely and with ease all types of standard speech, such as rapid or group conversation, plays, and movies.

Test. These abilities can be tested by dictations, by the *Listening Comprehension Tests* of the College Entrance Examination Board —thus far developed for French, German, and Spanish—or by similar tests for these and other languages, with an extension in range and difficulty for the superior level.

2. SPEAKING

Minimal. The ability to talk on prepared topics (*e.g.*, for classroom situations) without obvious faltering, and to use the common expressions needed for getting around in the foreign country, speaking with a pronunciation readily understandable to a native.

Good. The ability to talk with a native without making glaring mistakes, and with a command of vocabulary and syntax sufficient to express one's thoughts in sustained conversation. This implies speech at normal speed with good pronunciation and intonation.

Superior. The ability to approximate native speech in vocabulary, intonation, and pronunciation (*e.g.*, the ability to exchange ideas and to be at ease in social situations).

Test. For the present, this ability has to be tested by interview or by a recorded set of questions with a blank disc or tape for recording answers.

3. READING

Minimal. The ability to grasp directly (i.e., without translating) the meaning of simple, nontechnical prose, except for an occasional word.

Good. The ability to read with immediate comprehension prose and verse of average difficulty and mature content.

Superior. The ability to read, almost as easily as in English, material of considerable difficulty, such as essays and literary criticism.

Test. These abilities can be tested by a graded series of timed reading passages, with comprehension questions and multiple-choice or free-response answers.

4. WRITING

Minimal. The ability to write correctly sentences or paragraphs such as would be developed orally for classroom situations, and the ability to write a short, simple letter.

Good. The ability to write a simple "free composition" with clarity and correctness in vocabulary, idiom, and syntax.

Superior. The ability to write on a variety of subjects with idiomatic naturalness, ease of expression, and some feeling for the style of the language.

Test. These abilities can be tested by multiple-choice syntax items, dictations, translation of English sentences or paragraphs, and a controlled letter or free composition.

5. LANGUAGE ANALYSIS

Minimal. A working command of the sound patterns and grammar patterns of the foreign language, and a knowledge of its main differences from English.

Good. A basic knowledge of the historical development and present characteristics of the language, and an awareness of the difference between the language as spoken and as written.

Superior. Ability to apply knowledge of descriptive, comparative, and historical linguistics to the language teaching situation.

Test. Such information and insight can be tested for levels 1 and 2 by multiple-choice and free-response items on pronunciation, intonation patterns, and syntax; for levels 2 and 3, items on philology and descriptive linguistics.

6. CULTURE

Minimal. An awareness of language as an essential element among the learned and shared experiences that combine to form a particular culture, and a rudimentary knowledge of the geography, history, literature, art, social customs, and contemporary civilization of the foreign people.

Good. Firsthand knowledge of some literary masterpieces, an understanding of the principal ways in which the foreign culture resembles and differs from our own, and possession of an organized body of information on the foreign people and their civilization.

Superior. An enlightened understanding of the foreign people and their culture, achieved through personal contact, preferably by travel and residence abroad; through study of systematic descriptions of the foreign culture; and through study of literature and the arts.

Test. Such information and insight can be tested by multiple-choice literary and cultural acquaintance tests for levels 1 and 2; for level 3, written comments on passages of prose or poetry that discuss or reveal significant aspects of the foreign culture.

7. PROFESSIONAL PREPARATION[2]

Minimal. Some knowledge of effective methods and techniques of language teaching.

Good. The ability to apply knowledge of methods and techniques to the teaching situation (*e.g.,* audio-visual techniques) and to relate one's teaching of the language to other areas of the curriculum.

Superior. A mastery of recognized teaching methods, and the ability to experiment with and evaluate new methods and techniques.

Test. Such knowledge and ability can be tested by multiple-choice answers to questions on pedagogy and language-teaching methods, plus written comment on language teaching situations.

[2] Note the final paragraph of the prefatory statement.

THE FOREIGN LANGUAGE TEACHER AND LINGUISTICS

DWIGHT L. BOLINGER

In his work paper for a seminar on Language Teacher Training held at the University of Washington, Professor Bolinger considers the role of linguistics in foreign language teaching and outlines the linguistic competence which the teacher should have. Certainly, the well-prepared teacher, and particularly the educator of teachers, should have linguistic training in the areas discussed. Of particular interest is the recommendation of a comparative linguistic study between the native and the target languages. Also to be noted is the exhortation for an open and inquisitive mind in matters relative to language and language teaching.

INTRODUCTION

Let me begin by saying what I believe the program should *not* include. I take it that we do not have here merely another area program under another name, where the students pluck courses from every imaginable discipline—history, sociology, literature, art, music, language—with the sole amalgam being the fact that all are simultaneously manifested by members of one speech community at some particular latitude and longitude. If this assumption is correct, then certain things will have to be excluded to avoid the risk of dilettantism. I assume that the title of the program means what it says, that its aim is to teach the teachers and supervisors of foreign *language;* my conclusions and exclusions follow from this assumption.

The traditional allied fields in foreign "language" departments have always been literature and language, with the literature in most cases receiving the major attention. It is inconceivable that the Ph.D.'s under this plan should receive less training on the language side than they did before. From the language department's point of view, then, comparing it with the traditional state of affairs, the new Ph.D.'s will be getting less literature—quite possibly none at all—as part of their training explicitly under the plan. This needs to be stated frankly in the conference, if not outside it.

The issue as I see it is simply this, and I cannot conceive of one whose interests are *language* in all its aspects disagreeing in any fundamental way: Language is the handmaiden of *all* disciplines, and should no more be wedded to *belles lettres* than to metaphysics, symbolic logic, history, political science, theology, or home economics. One can explain the historical reasons for the concurrence of literature and language, in the erstwhile restriction of language study to the study of ancient documents. This relic of classical antiquity no longer weighs on us. Our attitudes toward language have changed. If they had not, these work papers would not have been solicited. Part of the change has been the realization that while *belles lettres* and language overlap, neither one includes all of the other. Language teachers deserve to be trained as language teachers. Literature teachers deserve to be trained as literature teachers. The two are not the same, and this program is addressed to language.

In place of the traditional allied fields of literature and language, I see here the allied fields of language and aids-to-the-teaching-of-language. It is a language and area program with a different area.

By the "language" part of the program I understand concentration in one language (possibly more) sufficient to bring a respectable command of it. I do not think that you want your Ph.D.'s only to know "about" a few languages. They cannot appreciate the full range of difficulties that learners of a language must face unless they have faced them themselves. We accept it as almost axiomatic nowadays that it is better for undergraduate students to learn one language thoroughly than to learn two superficially. The same is true of your graduate students. They should themselves be qualified to do exactly what they are to train others to do: teach a class in a particular foreign language; in fact, if they are to be models to the models, they must be especially well qualified.

The area field includes the discipline inclusive of language, linguistics; the disciplines closest to teaching, psychology and programmed learning; and the inclusive, plus one included, discipline of culture, anthropology and literature. Since linguistics is only one of several, I adjust my recommendations accordingly.

I take it that the program is to be mainly a realignment of old courses (some of which may be revised) plus a very few new ones. I shall therefore try to visualize what the course offerings might be, in terms of a modification of what is probably being offered now, rather than in terms of innovations from top to bottom.

1. *Major Language.* This should include, probably, all the properly linguistic courses in the major language that offer graduate credit: the synchronic structure of its standard form (courses in phonology, morphology, and syntax), its antecedents and development (historical grammar), and its variants (dialectology). In addition there should either be a new course having to do with a structural comparison of the language with English (assuming that the program is to serve those who will be teaching native speakers of English), or, if courses already being offered in the structure of English (or whatever is the native language) are adequate, these could be used instead. I do not believe that this part of the program should be set up in a vacuum on the supposition that the individual can make his own applications later; structural comparison—and I mean its practice, not just its theory—is the main contribution of linguistics to the whole plan, and needs to be based on concrete intentions: candidate A to teach language R to native speakers of language T.

These courses in and around the target language should presuppose, as they normally do, a certain prior level of achievement in the language. Inasmuch as we are recommending proficiency rather than credits as a general policy, it might be a good idea to start the reform in our own household: in place of, or in addition to, the equivalent of an undergraduate major in the language, a demonstration of fluency and literacy in its use.

Of the two solutions—structural comparison and existing courses in English structure—I urge the former as a better way to shed light on the pedagogical problem that each point of conflict between native and target language poses. The student must be reminded that he is not comparing two languages to satisfy his curiosity about them, but as a way of finding out what are the points that need to be taught and how best to teach them. A special course can then embody principles and methods. It is better to take up the problem of the conflict between Spanish /r/ and English /r/, and the problem of how best to resolve that conflict, in the same course, than to divide the two and risk the possibility of getting one presented and not the other, and the certainty of not having them presented as two sides of a single question—which they are, as far as the program is concerned. This course could be made one of the most fruitful of all if taught with the point of view that plenty remains to be done, even in the most-taught languages, in settling on the points of conflict. In fact, this kind of comparison is the most illuminating where the two structures themselves are concerned, since it reveals facts about them that we do not suspect until we are compelled to bridge them. But I return to the importance of learning the *what* of the dissimilarity and the *how* of teaching it at the same time. Each point has its trick; we cannot generalize about all of them. Dissimilarities are usually qualified in some way, and the trick is to find the qualification. We can discover and describe the difference between Spanish /r/ and English /r/; the trick is the qualification that English does have a flapped sound, in some environments, like that of Spanish /r/—I use Donald Bowen's *totter they* for *tarde*. There are similar tricks —similar exceptions to absolute difference between two languages —in most points of conflict; they need to be exploited, and can best be exploited if we keep the what and how together.

Even with the course in structural comparison, it might be well to include something from the courses already offered in the structure of the native language. If there happens to be a course in the teaching of English as a foreign language, especially if aimed at native speakers of the language which is here to be the target language, it might well be integrated into the program.

2. *Allied Field, Aids-to-the-Teaching-of-Language.* My concern here is only with the offerings in linguistics. I assume that there will be prescribed courses in psychology, anthropology, and certain aspects of culture, and if courses in the major language comprise about half of those taken, this means that requirements in general linguistics will have to be pretty limited—perhaps only six semester hours or so. How this is handled will depend on how much of a

general nature can be included in the courses in the major language, but I shall describe the points that need to be taught, and leave their distribution to administrative convenience. What follows could, for example, be divided between two courses, one an introduction to linguistics (to take advantage of present offerings and avoid duplication) and the other an application of linguistics to the teaching of language, though I am inclined to favor keeping most of the applied matters in the structural comparison course already mentioned, to maintain as practical and untheoretical an orientation as possible.

As the program is not intended to train specialists in linguistics but specialists who will in turn train and supervise nonspecialized teachers of foreign languages, it should be planned to train linguistically in breadth but not in depth, except that a small amount of training in depth in some selected subfield should be included *as a sample* of "doing" over and above "knowing about." I take it that the question of subject matter from the field has to do with the broader objective, and that of forms of research mainly with the narrower one. This does not exclude research in the application of linguistics to the teaching of foreign languages, and I shall include, for the latter, some suggestions about topics that involve linguistics.

The broad training, as I conceive it, consists of an unlearning stage and a learning stage. The first is therapeutic: the student is taught to recognize popular misconceptions about language. The following need to be touched upon:

1. The relative positions of precept and description: grammar as a way of making people behave, and grammar as a way of telling how people behave. Suggested topic: a study of any of the numerous attempts to bring linguistic behavior in line. For Spanish, this might include the successes and failures of the campaigns for /v/, or *usted* or *tú* versus *vos;* or the more general question of Hispanic attitudes toward authority.

2. Notions about the structure of language: e.g., "Languages are words put together to form sentences." It is hard to put in a nutshell the kind of concept we want to replace one like this, without falling into the same kind of fallacy; but I hazard "Languages are

a reciprocal activity between preformed sentences learned as wholes, and recurrent partials of those sentences built up into new wholes; the rules of the activity are more central to language than are the coordinates of the activity." I do not mean that the instructor stands up and makes this pronouncement, but that he identifies the false notions and offers examples to counter them, leaving the mature concept to the accumulated evidence of the entire course. Suggested topics: theories of the nature of language; examples of holophrasis in English; bondage and freedom; concepts of the sentence.

3. Notions about the kinship of languages, e.g., "All languages are alike," the fallacy of equivalent codes. In its most familiar yet most complex manifestation, this is exemplified in the incommensurate coding of experience: *brush—Burste, Pinsel; soil, earth, ground, floor—suelo, tierra, piso;* holes in the semantic spectrum like the one left by the abandonment of *to err* and only recently filled again by *to goof.* Our course should not neglect the lexicon as linguistics courses tend to do nowadays, but obviously nonequivalence needs to be demonstrated in other areas too. Included here should be the most striking deviations from English form that we can lay our hands on: phonemic tone, differently organized pronominal and number systems, infixation, etc. As false notions stem to some extent from the categories of a generalized Latin grammar, we can sharpen the appreciation of them by calling attention to covert classes in English of which native speakers are likely to be unaware: mass, count, and plural; animate-inanimate; theme-rheme order; covert negation; etc.

4. Language and logic. "Logic" in this connection needs first to be broken down into "what is natural and reasonable" and "what is internally consistent," and the first of these thrown back into the examples of the preceding paragraph. For the second, topics such as the inconsistent hyperurbanisms noted by J. N. Hook ("Today's Collegiate English," *Word Study,* XXVI, No. 3, Feb., 1951, pp. 1–2) are good medicine.

The learning stage is of course the longer one. I conceive of it in turn as divided into two phases, an "appreciation" phase and a technical phase. More important than any body of knowledge in leading to empathy with other peoples is sympathy toward them. The obvious linguistic path to understanding is dialect geography, and since it is the easiest of the linguistic fields for the beginner to understand, I would introduce it first. Practically any class nowadays contains speakers from different areas. Their differences can be quickly exploited to show variation in language by noting regional pronunciations and regional usages: potentially leveled contrasts like *cot-caught;* deviations in the paradigms like *dived-dove;* lexical preferences like *kerosene, coal oil;* avoidances resulting from dialect conflicts, like *had swum;* uncertainties resulting from mixture, like *greased-greazed;* specializations like *bust, passel,* and *gal.* Any Atlas list will serve to prime the instructor for this, and the result —showing differences in a context of similarity, where the student expects everyone to be the same—has more impact than comparing two separately compartmentalized languages, and teaches the student to appreciate the universality of differences in human behavior.

Technically, the student should be familiar enough with each of the following to know where and how to look for further information if he needs it:

1. *The structural hierarchy of language: nesting of sentences within discourses, of morphs within sentences, etc.* This includes an understanding of each level in the hierarchy: distinctive features, phonemes, morphemes, constructions, and the intonational matrix. Here is where the most substantial amount of time will have to be spent; it is also the area about whose inclusion there can be no disagreement.

2. *The physiological basis of speech.* This is important not only for the mechanics of speech production, which every teacher must be able to explain and put to use as a model, but also for its implications. Older teachers need to be retrained out of an obnoxious mentalism that makes them regard slow learners as stupid, on the assumption that they don't "get the idea" when the problem is really one of "performing the act."

3. *The physical basis of speech.* This is least important in itself, but most important to show the kinship of linguistics to the physical sciences. Also I find spectrography and speech synthesis to be immensely appealing to our generation of science-fiction readers. It is worth including to whet the appetite.

4. *Linguistic change.* Some venture into diachrony is called for to enrich the appreciation of diversity. Examples of the fragmentation of Latin will serve, although less needs to be done here since

the ideas have been pretty well popularized. I would look for some phenomena in flux in English at the present time (e.g., the *-ed* adjectival suffix or the progressive disuse of the pluperfect subjunctive) to make the issue livelier.

5. *Language and writing.* Some notion of different systems of writing (what they include, what they leave out, what they add) will aid in understanding the derivative nature of writing.

6. *Meaning.* This must be included if only to end by excluding it. The question is too insistent in students' minds to ignore it. Perhaps the best way to present it would be to take an example from one subfield of linguistics to show the steps taken to circumvent it; e.g., the juncture signals in phonological syntax. In any case, the dichotomy of differential versus referential meaning needs to be explained, and, for the latter, the trichotomy of sign-meaning-denotatum. If the university has a properly taught course in semantics, this assignment could be farmed out.

7. *Schools and doctrines.* Our students must learn to keep their minds open and seek for themselves. To this end they should be made aware of differences of opinion as well as of the cooperative accomplishments of groupings of linguists. This segment of our field will help toward an appreciation of American contributions to the study of language.

The sampling, in-depth research topics are potentially infinite, but should have one main objective: to show the student how to draw on his own resources to arrive at new knowledge. This means being confronted with a problem, gathering data from native speakers, organizing, generalizing, and testing. The first problems of this type should be predigested ones that the instructor can guide. A microlanguage is set up which the student is asked to phonemicise. Or, more in the line of the kind of original findings a teacher is likely to make, a set of data is presented from which an inference is to be drawn.

A couple of examples from English:

Where did they go?
What would you do?
Why didn't somebody say something?
Which house does the lady want?
How come you didn't eat anything?

Interrogative-word questions invert the auxiliary and the subject; exception, *how come.*

I thought as much.	It will happen, I hope.
I supposed as much.	It will happen, I suppose.
I feared as much.	etc.
I guessed as much.	
I worry as much.	It will happen, I worry.

As much patterns with quotative verbs that may follow their quoted objects.

After these, each student should attempt a full-scale problem that will require the whole series of steps to be gone through, as it should be at least once by each student: if the research topic is to be used for the dissertation, it should involve the major language; if only as a term paper (in case the dissertation topic is from another field, as it might well be), it could be in the native language and on some topic involving a point of structure, a trait of bilinguals, a particular case of dialect mixture, or anything from any of the subfields that have been touched upon. The possibilities here are endless.

Particular research topics in the application of linguistics to language teaching could include the following. (These are general areas which could serve as group or cumulative projects, with individual topics to be assigned). First, secondary sources:

1. A survey of findings from the NDEA linguistics projects. There is a mine of information here that should be brought together and rationalized.

2. A critique of textbooks and official courses of study to see whether they meet standards of linguistic accuracy.

3. A critique of pedagogical writing. Is it linguistically ignorant, linguistically superficial (purveying clichés), or linguistically sound, however limited?

Second, original sources:

1. Research in objectives and their linguistic implementation. If we prize nativelike phonetic accuracy above everything else, we are not going to use the same linguistic tools in the classroom as if we gave preference to fluency and intelligibility without worrying about a foreign accent. Similarly if our preference is for well-constructed sentences. Applied linguistics is not an absolute, but depends on ends.

2. Classroom experiments to put linguistic assumptions to the test. For example, is it better to explain a point in the native language of the learners or in the target language? Is it better to avoid reading and writing altogether for a time, and if so, for how long? Is it better to use respelling in a language with a good but not perfect orthography? How effective is laboratory drill by comparison with drill under the direction of informants? Questions like these should be answerable through fairly straightforward experiments, though the answers will vary for different ages and for teachers with different styles. Teachers should know how to find out such things for themselves, and teachers of teachers how to encourage them to do it.

3. Comparative grammars. These, of which we are already getting a few, show points of interference between two languages one of which is to be learned by native speakers of the other. An individual topic might be to study composition written in English by native speakers of Spanish, errors to be collected, classified, and analyzed.

CONCLUSION

It may seem strange coming from a linguist, but I should like to caution against overstating the importance of linguistics to the training of language teachers. I think that to a certain extent linguistics has been used as a club over traditional teachers in order to get them to adopt new ways on which linguistics generally touched but sometimes only obliquely. The traditional teacher did not know linguistics—he had to admit that he didn't. So here was the prescription for his retraining, and compounded along with the linguistics went a good deal of pedagogical theory that could have been conceived if linguistic science had never been invented. I give some examples of claims of the audio-lingual method that have been presented as if linguistic science originated them or were their chief support:

1. That hearing-speaking-reading-writing is the best sequence in learning a foreign language. This is a tenet borrowed from the old direct method [see Marjorie C. Johnston "Methods of Teaching" in *A Handbook on the Teaching of Spanish and Portuguese* (Boston: D. C. Heath, 1945), p. 185]. In fact, a good deal of the direct method seems to have climbed aboard the linguistics bandwagon.

It would be just as scientific, and just as much (or as little) in accord with what one can deduce from or prove by linguistic science, that the best sequence is a passive-to-active one, with hearing-reading and speaking-writing coupled as indicated. Linguistics has determined, let us say, that the language in question has a reasonably phonemic orthography. Machines are then devised that will make for guided reading in the laboratory: the visual and auditory stimuli are presented simultaneously so that spellings— even the irregular ones—are correctly associated from the start and the student has no opportunity to relate them to anything but the target language. It then becomes possible to present writing simultaneously with speaking. I am not advocating this as a method— only experiment can show whether it would work or not; I merely offer it as something just as consistent with linguistics as the four-step sequence now so heavily advertised.

In broader terms, what I foresee in experiments of this kind is finding a way around our big problem at present, which is that we have no way of *preventing* students from making mistakes. We can correct them *after* they have made mistakes, but cannot head off the errors. Exponents of the audio-lingual method are fond of comparing the teacher's role with that of a physical-education instructor. If a novice swimmer makes a wrong stroke, his teacher can lay hold of the errant muscle and guide it. All that we can do with a speech muscle is to coax it indirectly.

2. That only situational equivalences will do if equivalences are to be offered at all between the native and target languages. In practice—that is, in the insistence on no "intermediary English"— this is another offspring of the direct method, but the new twist comes from linguistic evidence of nonequivalence between languages. The difficulty with this evidence is that it is interpreted in a swing-of-the-pendulum fashion. Nonequivalence is relative, just as equivalence is relative. If we can imagine two languages that formerly were confronted and of which speakers of one had to break their heads in learning the other, wherein there were absolutely no points of similarity, and then imagine linguists discovering other languages which shared features and ranges of meaning with the original native language, we might suppose a resulting state of mind in which all the attention was on these marvelous equivalences. Linguistic science neither confirms nor refutes the

avoidance of translation. That depends on proofs from other fields.

3. That normative grammar has no place in the FL classroom. That "grammar" to the linguist has to mean something different from what it means for the prescriptivist is obvious from the divergence of their interests. But what is important here is not the supposed fact (which is untrue) but an attitude. Teachers of any foreign language with a dialectal spread are well advised to teach a normalized version of it, which implies normative decisions at the outset. (What is not implied is the set of normative prejudices in the culture, to which mainly just lip service is given anyway. But these are few and not a real problem.) The question of normative grammar is one of morale. If students or teachers dislike grammar it is because they associate it with normative grammar. We can overcome this for them by showing them that it is respectable to use grammar not to make people behave but to tell how they behave.

So linguistics does not prove that normative grammar should be shut out of the classroom. It does prove, however, that there is a wider sense of "grammar" which calls for more attention day in and day out.

PART 3

Practical Aspects of Language Teaching

FOREIGN LANGUAGES IN THE ELEMENTARY SCHOOL

Many of the basic reasons adduced in favor of FLES have already been encountered in this book. In the present chapter a working committee of the Northeast Conference on the Teaching of Foreign Languages[1] considers the whole field from a pragmatic viewpoint and gives some forthright answers to many of the practical problems involved in organizing such a program. The people on the committee represent experience, and hence, speak in a far-different tone from the theoreticians. The particular importance of FLES lies in the utilization of the child's special language gift, lost in later life. From a curriculum viewpoint it makes possible a longer language sequence and thus ensures a more proficient end product. This essay and the following three represent a consideration of the foreign language program.

INTRODUCTION

The longer a student studies a foreign language, the more proficient he becomes in it. It therefore seems logical to begin the study of a foreign language in the elementary school. Much has been said and written about FLES, some of it negative and some of it positive. It is the purpose of this report to describe the practices which actually exist in some excellent and productive FLES programs in this country. Although there is room for differences of opinion on questions of detail, this committee feels that the program herein described does constitute an ideal program to which Ameri-

Reprinted by permission of the Northeast Conference on the Teaching of Foreign Languages, Inc., from *Foreign Language Teaching: Ideals and Practices*, Working Committee I, 1964.

[1] Working Committee I: Conrad J. Schmitt, Marjorie P. Bowen, Janice S. Calkin, Gladys Lipton, Protase E. Woodford, and Seymour O. Simches.

can communities can confidently aspire. It goes without saying that there are obstacles at every turn, which, if not foreseen and not met head on, can be deeply frustrating. The report highlights these problems by discussing them in the form of answers to the questions most frequently asked of language specialists by teachers, administrators, and parents.

1. DEFINITION AND RATIONALE OF FLES

1.1. What Is FLES?

FLES is an abbreviation for Foreign Language in the Elementary School. The foreign language experience of children must not, however, end in grade six, the last year of elementary school. FLES envisages continued instruction from an early elementary grade (see below) through grade twelve in the senior high school. The elementary program must be completely coordinated with both junior and senior high school programs. Such continuity and coordination are essential characteristics of a successful program.

1.2. Why FLES?

Much time and practice are required for attaining the four language skills: listening comprehension, speaking, reading, and writing. As indicated above, the longer a student pursues the study of a foreign language, the more proficient he becomes in it. There are other factors, which, taken together, lend further support to the idea of beginning foreign language study at an early age:

1.2.1. Many young children seem to be able to imitate and reproduce unfamiliar sounds more readily than older children or adults can. Although facility in imitation and production of speech is not well understood, experience seems to indicate that, on the average, the earlier a student begins the study of a foreign language the better his pronunciation will be.[2] Further, most young children have had less exposure to certain constraints imposed by the society in which they live and are therefore less inhibited. They enjoy

---

[2] Cf. the inferences of W. Penfield and L. Roberts, *Speech and Brain Mechanisms* (Princeton, N.J.: Princeton University Press, 1959) chap XI. But see also J. B. Carroll, "Foreign Languages for Children: What Research Says," *National Elementary Principal,* Vol. 39 (1960), pp. 12–15.

playing with language and are generally quite willing to experiment with making strange sounds.

1.2.2. Younger children are less analytical in their approach to learning than adolescents are (especially adolescent boys)[3] and therefore learn to speak more easily, since analysis interferes with spontaneous acquisition of spoken language. In addition, young children are more receptive to drill, which is so necessary for acquiring language habits.

1.2.3. A person who has begun the study of a foreign language early in life and continued it long enough to attain real proficiency should have fewer inhibitions concerning the study of other foreign languages.

1.2.4. If a child is exposed to the customs of a foreign culture at an age when he has fewer prejudices, and is hence more receptive to the idea of cultural difference, he will have a better chance of developing an understanding of that culture and a sympathetic attitude toward it.

1.3. What is an ideal FLES program? It is one in which:

1.3.1. The language is introduced in grade three. This is perhaps an arbitrary recommendation, but we want to begin as early as possible, in order to take maximum advantage of the factors mentioned above. To begin later loses time, to begin earlier may detract from time best devoted to native language skills.

1.3.2. The FLES class is taught by a special teacher qualified in the foreign language and capable of teaching young children. The teacher's role cannot be overemphasized. He must serve as an excellent model for the pupils to imitate. He must motivate and stimulate the children constantly. He must correct errors immediately.

1.3.3. Classes meet daily for a period of fifteen minutes in grades three through five with a slightly longer period in grade six. Because language learning is cumulative, daily exposure is of the utmost importance, particularly in the early stages.

1.3.4. The program provides an orderly sequence of instruction which continues through the junior and senior high school. The

[3] W. B. Waetjen and J. D. Grambs, "Sex Differences: A Case of Educational Evasion?", *Teachers College Record,* Fall, 1963.

seventh- and eighth-grade classes meet either three times a week for forty-five minutes, or daily for thirty minutes.

1.3.5. Provision is made for periodic evaluation of student achievement, even though much evaluation must be subjective, especially in the early stages.

1.3.6. The program is under the direction of a Foreign Language Coordinator who is responsible for continuity from grade three through grade twelve. In large city systems the coordinator needs assistants to help supervise the program.

1.3.7. The ultimate goal of the above-described practices is proficiency in the use of the foreign language. Whereas proficiency should be achieved in all four skills by the end of the program, administrators, teachers, and parents should not expect this goal to be accomplished by the end of grade six. Fluency will steadily improve if instruction is continued in an orderly sequence into the senior high school.

2. PLANNING FOR FLES

2.1. How is an ideal program initiated?

2.1.1. Many FLES programs have started through community interest. Community interest is important, but *before a program is initiated it must have the support of the school administration and be placed under the direction of a qualified foreign language specialist.*

2.1.2. Careful thought must be given to the selection of the foreign language. Two major considerations are the availability of capable well-qualified foreign language teachers and provision for continuity in the secondary schools.

2.1.3. One must decide, somewhat arbitrarily to be sure (see 1.3.1. above), in which grade the foreign language will be introduced. During the first year of the program the language should be begun in one grade only, rather than in several grades simultaneously. Since course content and materials must then be chosen or developed for only one grade at a time, these tasks are thereby greatly simplified.

2.1.4. When the program is first initiated, there should be a meeting with elementary classroom teachers and administrators to explain the objectives and the methods of the program. It is equally wise to inform parents very carefully of these same objectives and methods in order to forestall criticism based on their own experience with language learning.

2.1.5. Adequate budgetary provisions must be made for continuing the program.

3. ADMINISTRATION

3.1. What teaching load should the FLES teacher carry?

The teaching load of a FLES teacher must be established in accordance with the time allotted for each class and the number of schools served by the teacher. A reasonable assignment would be eleven or twelve sections of fifteen minutes each. If the teacher serves more than one building, he should be assigned fewer sections in order to compensate for necessary travel time.

3.2. How can coordination with the secondary school be achieved?

Students with a FLES background should not be placed in classes with students who have not had elementary instruction. This means that a separate "track" must be established for FLES graduates. The materials used must take into account the FLES graduate's previous preparation. Below is an outline of an ideal dual-track program. The dual track begins with grade nine. C stands for continuing classes, in which all students have had Spanish since grade three. B represents classes made up of students beginning Spanish in grade nine.

Elementary School

Grades 3–6   15 minutes instruction daily.
Grades 7–8   45 minutes instruction three times each week.

Secondary School

45 minutes instruction five times each week.

	Track I	Track II
Grade 9	Spanish I C	Spanish I B
Grade 10	Spanish II C	Spanish II B
Grade 11	Spanish III C	Spanish III B
Grade 12	Spanish IV C	Spanish IV B

3.3. When and on what basis should one select the students who will continue with the foreign language?

We recommend that they be selected at the end of grade six. This does not mean, however, that only the gifted or academically talented pupils should be allowed to continue. Many of the slower pupils also benefit from language study. Selection should not be based on mere academic ability, but rather on demonstrated performance in the foreign language.

3.4. What is the relationship of the FLES teacher to the entire elementary-school program?

3.4.1. The FLES teacher should be considered an integral part of the elementary-school staff. It is important that he develop good rapport with the regular elementary classroom teachers and keep them informed of the goals he is trying to attain. The attitude of the regular classroom teacher toward the program affects the attitude of the pupils in his class.

3.4.2. The FLES teacher should also help in preparing assembly programs that deal with the country of the target language. Once or twice during the year he should set up bulletin boards or display cases like those prepared for other areas of the elementary school curriculum.

3.5. What is the relationship between the language coordinator and the FLES teachers?

3.5.1. As already stated, the coordinator should be responsible for the entire program for grades three through twelve. In order to advise the teachers as to the best methods to be used, he should take over classes at each level to keep abreast of the teaching problems involved.

3.5.2. In return, the teachers should cooperate and follow the suggestions of the coordinator, since it is he who is fully aware of what is taking place at each level. Of necessity, teachers will have to change their approach to teaching as the pupils come to them with more preparation.

3.5.3. Teachers within the language department should be encouraged to observe one another and to share each other's problems and techniques. Because language learning is rigorously cumulative, teachers should also observe what is being done at the levels that they do not teach.

4. MATERIALS

4.1. What type of materials should be used in the FLES classroom?

4.1.1. Considerable progress has been made recently in the development of effective teaching materials for FLES classes. Needless to say, the materials used should be adapted to the age, interests, and experience of the child.

4.1.2. Each unit of instruction should take advantage of different forms of presentation. Although the dialogue still plays an important role in elementary school instruction because of its dramatic appeal, it is only one of the means through which the language is presented. Since much conversation consists of "talking about" situations, pupils should immediately begin learning to narrate in the target language. They must learn to control the structures used in the memorized dialogue in such a way that they may manipulate them according to the requirements of other real-life situations. In order to be able to make the necessary changes in form and word order, they must practice these changes in structure drills, gradually coming to avoid dependence on parrotlike repetition of previously memorized language. The items so drilled must be simple enough for the students to handle them readily, especially in the early stages of instruction. This calls for careful design of the dialogues on which the drills are based.

4.1.3. All parts of a FLES unit must be interrelated. There should first be a careful presentation of new vocabulary to be used in the unit. Once the new vocabulary has been presented, the child should answer a series of questions to show that he has learned it. He should also ask the questions himself, in order to learn the use of the interrogative words.

4.1.4. As soon as the new vocabulary has been presented, the structure drill should be mastered. Since the teacher cannot explain grammatical points to an eight-year-old child in technical terms, it is the drill itself that must convey the grammatical structures. The drill must make use of carefully delineated sound patterns in which the student can actually hear the changes that take place.

For example, in a Spanish drill dealing with the definite article, only "o" and "a" nouns should be presented at first, so that the child can hear that "*el*" accompanies words ending in "o," while "*la*" accompanies words ending in "a." The same is true when agreement is presented. If only regular "o" and "a" nouns and adjectives are used, the pupils will actually become aware of what they are doing. The simultaneous introduction of nouns or adjectives ending in "e" or a consonant would turn the drill into a mere exercise in memorization, rather than into one that teaches a linguistic principle. The same is true of a drill on agreement in French adjectives whose final sound does not change, such as "*jeune*" and "*laide*," can be presented first, whereas adjectives such as "*verte*," "*vert*," "*grise*," and "*gris*" should be presented later. Now the pupil learns that differences in the final sound of adjectives can depend on whether a "*le*" noun or a "*la*" noun is used. He can hear the difference and consequently he needs no further explanation.

4.1.5. According to Politzer, "the student must not only learn a construction—he must also realize how this construction is 'made up,' how it 'comes apart,' how some building stones can be replaced by others."[4]

4.1.6. The dialogue should contain points of structure that have already been drilled or will be drilled in the unit. It should not be too long, and it should exclude grammatical constructions not ordinarily used by children. Certain necessary but grammatically complex words such as *je voudrais, quisiera,* or *ich möchte,* can be treated simply as lexical items.

4.1.7. Once the dialogue has been memorized, the child can retell the dialogue in his own terms because it has been carefully correlated with the structural points currently being drilled. The child should be able to change the first and second persons to the third and to recall vocabulary and situations of previous units. Next, the child should be asked to describe a situation that is slightly different from that of the dialogue.

4.1.8. FLES materials should be organized in such a way that one lesson builds on another and one level is neatly articulated with the next. Materials learned in Unit III can easily be recalled in

---

[4] R. L. Politzer, *Teaching French: An Introduction to Applied Linguistics* (New York: Ginn and Company, 1930), p. 6

Unit V. The pupil can also make up a narrative that combines several units, rather than merely the unit that is being studied.

5. METHODS

5.1. What methods should be used in the elementary classroom?

5.1.1. The first 2½ years (beginning in grade three) should be devoted to teaching the listening-speaking skills with no attention given to the teaching of reading and writing. This necessitates much repetition and drill at a normal rate of speed. A great variety of activity is necessary to prevent boredom, and the major responsibility for this rests on the teacher.

5.1.2. Each class period should present a balance between choral repetition and individual response. When pattern drills are presented, the teacher should not have to spoon-feed the response to the child. When presenting first-conjugation verbs, for example, the teacher should drill several model verbs while the class repeats in unison. Once the pupils seem to have grasped the point, individuals should be called upon to answer questions by basing their answers on the models that have just been drilled. This should be followed by questions containing other regular first-conjugation verbs that have not yet been drilled. If pupils understand the principle, they will be able to handle new verbs without difficulty. If the teacher finds that the pupils are still making errors, rather than prompt them he should return to the drill of the model verbs until the principle is understood. Then, if a pupil makes an error or does not respond at all, the teacher should go on to the next pupil; and, having elicited the correct answer, he should return to the pupil who made the error and have him try again. Then he should ask the child a similar question to see if he now understands the point.

5.1.3. When children present a dialogue they should be encouraged to act it out realistically and to perform all the actions called for.

5.1.4. The teacher should circulate around the room to hear whether the pupils are pronouncing correctly. If a pupil mispronounces a word, the teacher should merely supply him with the correct pronunciation and have him repeat.

5.1.5. Activities in the elementary classroom should be changed frequently. Each fifteen-minute period should include some structure drill, some dialogue, some question-answer drill, and some narrative practice.

5.2. What is the role of audio-visual aids in the FLES program?

5.2.1. Audio-visual aids play an important part in FLES programs, but extreme care must be taken in their selection and application. Pictures should be used to present new vocabulary in each unit, and there should also be a picture or series of pictures presenting the situation in the dialogue. Once the dialogue has been memorized, the children can discuss the picture. The pictures should illustrate exactly what the child is repeating.

5.2.2. Because the time available for each class session is severely limited, there is no time to set up elaborate equipment. This curtails the effectiveness of many mechanized teaching aids. A simple tape recorder can be very useful, however.

5.3. What is the role of television in FLES classes?

Television can sometimes be used as a teaching aid, but it can *not* replace a good foreign language teacher. To be effective, any televised lesson must be "followed up" by a teacher who has specialized in the foreign language.

5.4. Should reading be presented in the elementary school?

5.4.1. Yes. When a program begins in grade three, reading should be introduced in the second semester of grade five. The reading program should be carefully developed. At first, pupils should read only material that they have already learned audio-lingually. Next, the written symbols for the sounds of the target language should be introduced. Consistent (regular) sound-letter correspondences should be presented first. As the written symbol for each sound is presented, pupils should receive a list of previously learned words that contain the particular sound. Special drills are advisable to handle the problem of interference from Roman letters and to account for writing systems, such as the French, in which sounds have many written representations, and letters represent many different sounds. Next, the pupils should read narratives which draw on all the material learned in the previous 2½ years.

5.4.2. It is important to note that the audio-lingual skills should not be neglected when the reading skills are introduced. There should be a balance between reading and further development of the audio-lingual skills, each skill now reinforcing the others. This will be explained in detail in the section dealing with the junior high school level.

5.5. What is the role of writing?

Writing should be introduced in a limited way in grade six. Pupils should copy dialogues that they have already learned to read. They should also learn to write from dictation the common spellings of the sounds of the target language, such as *ca, que, qui, co, cu* in Spanish or *ez, er, é* in French, preferably in words taken from previously learned material that contains these sounds.

6. FLES GRADUATES IN THE JUNIOR HIGH SCHOOL

6.1. What type of course should be offered to FLES graduates in the junior high school?

As previously stated, students who have had four years of language background in the elementary school should be placed into continuing classes in the junior high school and not into classes with students beginning at that level. The major emphasis should be on the spoken language even though reading and writing will begin to assume more importance.

6.2. How should grammar be taught in the junior high school?

Grammar should be presented through pattern drills. Each drill should give the student ample opportunity to practice the particular structural point of the unit. After the students have gone through the pattern practices, they should receive a series of questions, the responses to which will cause them to use the new structure without being cued. After the drill has been completed, an explanation should be given so that students will understand what they are doing. The explanation should be brief, since students learn better by doing something than by talking about it. Analysis should be rigorously subordinated to the formation of habits.

6.3. What is the role of reading in the junior high-school program?

6.3.1 Reading plays an important role in the junior high-school curriculum, chiefly in reinforcing the oral skills. Students should not be made to read language they cannot speak. As a result, the language used in the first readers should be simple and should contain only structures that the students can use. Before the students actually read, they should be familiar with the material orally.

6.3.2. Pictures or slides can be used to illustrate the reading material. The teacher can pick out several basic sentences that outline the plot and have the students repeat them. After sufficient oral presentation, students may open their books. The teacher should read each sentence and have the class repeat in unison imitating his pronunciation and intonation. Next, individuals are called upon to read. After each sentence or group of sentences the teacher should stop and ask many questions, both to check comprehension and to stimulate conversation. For example, if students were to read, *"Juan va al cine con sus amigos el viernes por la noche a las nueve"* they could be asked the following questions dealing with the same sentence:

1. *¿Quién va al cine?*
2. *¿A dónde va Juan?*
3. *¿Con quiénes va al cine?*
4. *¿Cuándo va al cine?*

Jean va au cinéma avec ses amis vendredi soir à neuf heures.

1. *Qui va au cinéma?*
2. *Où va Jean?*
3. *Avec qui va-t-il au cinéma?*
4. *Quand va-t-il au cinéma?*
5. *A quelle heure va-t-il au cinéma?*

Hans geht Freitag abend um neun Uhr mit seinen Freunden ins Kino!

1. *Wer geht ins Kino?*
2. *Wohin geht Hans?*
3. *Mit wem geht er ins Kino?*
4. *Wann geht er ins Kino?*
5. *Um wieviel Uhr geht er ins Kino?*

6.3.3. After the above questions have been asked, they can be repeated again in the second person to elicit a first person response. Once the entire passage has been read in the manner suggested above, more general questions should be asked. In better groups, students should be called upon to give a résumé. For slower groups this is quite difficult and might best be delayed until grade nine.

6.4. What is the role of writing in the junior high school?

6.4.1. The writing skill should be developed in the junior high school, and many types of written exercises should be given. Students should copy assigned sentences from reading passages for subsequent dictation, and they should also be asked to write answers to questions based on the reading material. Students in grades seven and eight should write guided compositions by answering a series of questions, the answers to which make a unified paragraph. Students in grade nine should write their own paragraphs without the aid of guide questions, by reviewing material that they have read.

6.4.2. Another extremely important area of written work is exercises based on the pattern drills. In many cases experience has shown that students do not transfer what they have learned orally to the written form without a great deal of controlled practice in writing.

7. FLES GRADUATES IN THE SENIOR HIGH SCHOOL

7.1. What type of course should be offered to FLES graduates in the senior high school?

As in the junior high school, FLES graduates in the senior high school should be placed in continuing classes and not in classes with students who have begun the foreign language at some point on the secondary level. The methods used should follow audio-lingual principles, even though much more discussion will be based upon material that the students have read.

7.2. What administrative problems are involved in the continuing high-school program?

7.2.1. Because there will be students in the secondary school who lack a FLES background, a dual track must be set up. One track should be for classes with FLES background and the other for students beginning language study at the secondary level. This latter track will also accommodate FLES graduates who wish to begin a second language while continuing the language begun in the elementary school.

7.2.2. When FLES graduates reach high school, enrollment in

the language department will increase noticeably. As a result, a system should be devised to group students according to language ability. More students should be encouraged to continue four years of language study in high school. Third- and fourth-year classes should not be limited to the "intellectual elite." Courses should be considered in terms of levels of achievement. A fourth-year group composed of slower students will not be able to achieve as much as a fast group. In turn, the top groups will be able to progress at a faster pace than the other groups and will permit the more talented to profit fully from their language experience.

7.3. What is the role of reading in the senior high-school continuing program?

Reading is extremely important in the continuing program. Much of the class discussion will be based upon material that has been read previously. Fast groups will not need the great amount of oral presentation necessary in the junior high school prior to reading; but slow groups will have to continue this activity. Needless to say, the discussion of all material read outside of class should be carried on in the target language. Fast groups should not need the detailed type of questions suggested in the junior high school program, but rather they should be expected to develop answers to general questions about material they have read. On the other hand, slower students will find it easier to answer detailed questions. All students, both fast and slow, should be asked to give résumés of what they have read. These résumés should be extemporaneous rather than prepared outside of class or memorized. The résumé given by the faster students will naturally be more complete and detailed than that given by the slower ones.

7.4. What type of material should be read in the senior high school?

There are many types of material that can be read in the senior high school, among which are civilization books that are more detailed than those used in the junior high school. In the sophomore year, students could be introduced to short stories written by well-known authors, because the short story serves as a good introduction to other literary genres. In the second semester of the sophomore year students should be introduced to poetry, drama, and the novel. In the third and fourth years, students should be able to read and discuss all types of literature, and works should be selected for their appeal to young people. Students should also read current newspaper and magazine articles. In the third and fourth years, fast groups should be encouraged to do outside reading. In slower groups most reading should be under the teacher's supervision.

7.5. How should literature be presented in the senior high school?

Literature serves a useful purpose in the continuing high school language class, but it should be remembered at all times that *the major objective of the language program is to teach the language skills.* In the high-school program the main objective in reading literature is not stylistics or literary trends. The concern of the high-school teacher is to have the student read and understand what he is reading, to discuss what he has read, and to write about what he has read, understood, and discussed. Students should *not* be given lectures on literary trends, comparisons of style of one author with another, or the influences of other authors on the author being read. Students should discuss what the author has said and should express their own personal viewpoints concerning the author's ideas. Literature should serve as a vehicle for achieving proficiency in the four language skills.

7.6. What is the role of grammar in the senior high-school program?

The sophomore year should introduce pattern drills dealing with intricate structural points that have not been presented in the junior high school. All important structural points of the language should have been presented by the end of the sophomore year.

7.7. What is the role of writing in the senior high-school program?

There are many writing activities that should take place in the senior high school. In the sophomore year, students should continue to write exercises based on pattern drills in order to practice new structural points, and they should also write answers to questions about their reading material. They should likewise write short compositions about the material they have read. In the third and fourth years, students should be assigned one composition per week, and they can also prepare written reports on cultural topics.

7.8. What other activities should be included in the senior high-school program?

To achieve a proper balance between the types of vocabulary presented in literary works and in conversation, students should be given situation dialogues containing vocabulary that could be used at an airport, railroad station, restaurant, etc. Since students are already able to speak the language at this point, they need not always memorize these dialogues but should study them for the sake of learning new vocabulary and different ways of expressing the same idea. Once they have learned the vocabulary, they can make up their own dialogues.

8. SUMMARY

This report has outlined the practices of an ideal FLES program. These practices should not be considered too idealistic or too unrealistic to be realized. Nor must they be regarded as limited to wealthy suburban communities. They are already in use in various programs around the country.

The main elements that we have stressed in the ideal FLES program are (*a*) the use of qualified foreign language teachers, (*b*) continuity of the curriculum into the junior and senior high school, (*c*) the maintenance of a separate track of FLES graduates in the junior and senior high schools, (*d*) the presence of a well-qualified foreign language supervisor in the community to develop and supervise the FLES curriculum at all levels, and (*e*) a cooperative and interested school administration.

If a FLES program does indeed have these elements, it will be successful. The success of any program can be evaluated according to just one criterion: its output of Americans who really know a foreign language.

FOREIGN LANGUAGES IN THE SECONDARY SCHOOL[1]

The following committee report of the Northeast Conference takes a close and practical look at present-day teaching of foreign language in the secondary school. Although high school is the traditional place for teaching foreign language, much of the teaching had deteriorated. It was reduced to reading, translation, and to the so-called learning of literature, to the detriment of understanding and speaking skills. This report considers each of the four skills, endeavoring to place them in perspective —what they mean and how they should be taught. For the secondary-school teacher it furnishes a wealth of material for thought and discussion.

INTRODUCTION

The introduction to the reports of the Northeast Conference for 1963 stated that "a determined quest for excellence is beginning to dominate practically every segment of American education. This quest for excellence is characterized by a search for ever more precise formulations of what is to be learned and how it is best learned by American students."

It is the purpose of this report to describe in some detail what constitutes "excellence" in a secondary-school foreign language program. It will profit from insights recently contributed by enlightened thinking about the nature of language and the way it is learned, and from experience in classrooms where many of those insights have been tested in recent years.

The secondary-school program under consideration here is one in

Reprinted by permission of the Northeast Conference on the Teaching of Foreign Languages, Inc., from *Foreign Language Teaching: Ideals and Practices,* Working Committee II, 1964.

[1] Working Committee II: Milton R. Hahn, Colette Garimaldi, Jack B. Krail, James F. McArthur, Arnold Tauber, Joseph Tursi, Russell Webster, and M. Jeannette Atkins.

which the study of a foreign language may begin in grade seven, eight, nine, ten, or eleven and continue without interruption for a period of from two to six years. It should be stated at the outset that the degree of "excellence" sought cannot possibly be attained in a two-year program. The minimum ought to be at least four consecutive years of study in any one language. However, it is important that all programs be directed toward the same objectives and make as much progress toward them as possible in whatever time is available. Hopefully the recognition of the importance and validity of these objectives will demonstrate the compelling need for longer sequences of study.

The languages referred to will be the modern foreign languages most often taught in the secondary schools of the United States: French, German, Italian, Russian, and Spanish. Since the goals of the classical languages are different, in part, from those of the modern languages, Latin and Greek cannot be dealt with adequately in this report, although many of its recommendations will apply. The committee believes that the place of the classical languages in the total school program is an important one and it endorses the resolution adopted by the 1959 Northeast Conference with respect to Latin.

The learning of Latin and the learning of a contemporary language that can replace the mother tongue are different disciplines, which for the most part have different objectives, different procedures, different outcomes.

Latin is not for everybody. Nor can its study profitably be begun as early as that of a contemporary language. Where both modern foreign languages and Latin are available—and this should be the case everywhere—the contemporary language should be started early, certainly not later than at the beginning of junior high school. A good Latin course can then be pursued in the senior high school by those of proved interest and ability.

The broad base upon which Latin enrollment now lies is its presentation as a subject of general learning in our secondary schools. After two years of study at this level, enrollment dwindles so much that far too few students pursue the study of Latin at the upper levels. Latin would be in a much stronger position if it could first be offered principally to students at the level of Grade ten who have already proved by their performance in a contemporary language course their capacity for language learning. Such students would be encouraged to continue their work in the contemporary language and to pursue the study of Latin until their graduation from high school. From such a group would come more students with better preparation for the study of Latin and contemporary languages at the college and graduate level.

The case for Latin is far stronger if it is not put on the basis of learning English vocabulary or structure or of acquiring mental discipline. Instead, Latin should be studied for what it is, linguistically and culturally, with the beneficent influence upon English vocabulary and structure and upon the understanding of contemporary civilization a by-product rather than a prime objective.[2]

Even as we begin to describe what should be learned in an ideal secondary school foreign language program and to offer some ideas on how it may be learned, we are aware of two essential prerequisites, namely, a variety of instructional materials planned and prepared with specific goals and purposes in mind, and well-trained, competent teachers who know how to use them. Instructional materials are steadily improving in quality and quantity, while adequate teacher preparation remains a serious problem. While neither area is specifically dealt with in this report, there are strong implications for both in the program described here and in the report on the college program.

What should be the primary all-important goal of a secondary-school modern foreign language program in the second half of the twentieth century? In the opinion of this committee, it should be to teach as much *language* as possible to all students who pursue foreign language study. By language we mean the four skills of communication: listening comprehension, speaking, reading, and writing.

The statement of this objective in these terms does not rule out other much discussed and eminently desirable objectives such as the development of cultural sensitivity and awareness of humanistic values. What it does do is to make all other objectives dependent on and subordinate to that chief purpose, the learning of language. This position must not be construed as in any way denying the value of such secondary objectives. The clear, unambiguous ad-

[2] F. D. Eddy (ed.), *The Language Learner, Reports of the Working Committees, 1959 Northeast Conference on the Teaching of Foreign Languages,* pp. 57–58.

mission that the fundamental secondary school objective must be the teaching of the four skills can only serve to define more clearly the relation of the secondary-school program to the college program and to make it possible to achieve both the cultural and humanistic aims more efficiently and effiectively as a result of increased language competence.

1. THE AUDIO-LINGUAL SKILLS

Hundreds of printed pages have been devoted to this subject in recent years. It is safe to say that most teachers today recognize that listening and speaking competence can come only through extensive practice in hearing and producing authentic speech. While actual classroom procedures vary, most teachers try to develop these skills first by extensive pattern practice through which the new sound system is learned in common grammatical structures as are found in the everyday speech of educated people, later by extensive manipulation of these patterns in such a way that the learner comes to understand and say things he has not memorized by rote. As we have used these procedures in the classroom, certain problems have developed. It is likely that, from the very beginning, insufficient time is devoted to listening to new material. Equally important, it is evident that special techniques are necessary to achieve steady progress from imitation and manipulation toward actual communication. But the crux of the matter is this: we know that two years is not enough for learning to understand and speak a foreign language, yet by the end of two years, or even earlier, many teachers no longer regard these skills as central. There are a number of reasons for this state of affairs, which this report will discuss, but, in keeping with our definition of the central purpose of the ideal secondary school language program, this committee must insist that *listening and speaking progress be based on a planned sequence maintained throughout the entire program.* Such a sequence will be related to the reading program in many ways (see below), but it must have its own identity.

As controls built into the materials are ever so gradually reduced, listening and speaking practice will be based on material designed not only to introduce new vocabulary and new constructions, but also to provide practice in comprehending and producing longer and longer stretches of natural speech. Not all communication consists of dialogue material in which each person speaks a short sentence in turn; probably not much of it consists of responses to questions based on reading. People produce many sentences in sequence, and the learner must eventually be able to understand the native speaker when he does so, and produce such sequences himself. Such stretches of speech must be presented in the common *styles* used by educated speakers. One may be able to tell informally what just happened on the way to the office, but not be equipped to say a few words at a formal dinner. The possibilities are endless, and techniques will vary; but again, we insist, *a planned sequence must provide for consistent progress in understanding and speaking throughout the entire program.*

1.1. The Language Laboratory

As in the case of audio-lingual techniques, many pages have set forth the merits and deficiencies of the language laboratory. Surely we have now come far enough along the road of audio-lingual teaching to acknowledge that a properly chosen and equipped installation provided with the necessary materials can considerably extend the contribution of the best teachers and compensate for some of the deficiencies of the less well prepared.[3] A language laboratory can greatly increase the amount of controlled listening and speaking practice. Instead of being controlled by the teacher, practice is controlled by properly chosen tape and disk recordings, under circumstances which provide many more opportunities for responding than is usually possible in the classroom. It is unfortunate that these obvious merits should have been recently obscured by the scarcely startling discovery that there are schools which do not seem to use the language laboratory effectively. The committee acknowledges that, although most desirable, it may not be practical in every instance to develop the best possible laboratory program before purchasing equipment. It recommends, therefore:

a. that no laboratory be considered to be actually "in use" until the work of the laboratory is completely integrated with the work

---

[3] For a detailed discussion, see A. S. Hayes, *Language Laboratory Facilities,* OE-21024, Bulletin 1963, No. 37, U.S. Department of Health, Education and Welfare, esp. chap. II.

of the classroom. Lab for lab's sake is seldom profitable and may be even harmful.

b. that schools *add* to available laboratory practice time by suitable adjustment of class schedules. All too often, this possibility is dismissed without investigation.

2. READING

Throughout the history of language teaching no one has ever questioned the inclusion of reading as an essential objective. Indeed, for a long period, reading was considered to be the only attainable objective; for years no secondary-school programs purported to teach anything else, except incidentally. This was the era when the modern language program followed by most high-school students was a two-year sequence in grades eleven and twelve. The reading skill acquired in that kind of program was significantly different from the one recommended in this report, with respect to both the end result and the methods used to attain it. The result desired was reading in the sense of being able to translate from the foreign language into English. Obviously, the way to acquire this skill was by extensive practice in translating. The student's reading skill was evaluated most often by exercises in translation. In the program recommended here, reading in the sense of translation is not an objective at all. Translation is a special skill which requires special training. It has no place in a secondary-school program.

For the purposes of this discussion, reading has two definitions: (1) to pronounce phrases and sentences aloud with normal intonation, in response to the stimulus of sequences of printed or written letters (the expert native reader does this in a consistent way, whether or not he knows "the meaning of the words") and (2) to follow printed or written sequences rapidly for comprehension, usually silently, while the eye scans whole groups of words or sentences at a time.

It is clear that the first definition refers to a basic skill which at first demands control of the sound-letter correspondences of the language. This does not take place automatically. Extensive practice is required. When reading is first introduced, provision should be made for an orderly presentation of sound-letter correspondences with special attention given to the interference problems caused by the student's tendency to respond to Roman letters as if they represented English sounds. Even in the case of languages like Spanish and German where the sound-letter correspondences are reasonably regular, established pronunciation habits will show less deterioration during the initial stages of becoming literate, if practice with the proper drills is provided. In the case of French, where most sounds have a number of written representations, the difficulties are proportionately greater and more time and practice are required. In Russian, even after the new sound-letter correspondences have been established, there are certain kinds of interference problems which require special treatment.[4]

The second definition of reading, reading for comprehension, is the one with which a considerable portion of the high school program is concerned. Like the other three skills it is necessarily developed in a step-by-step sequential program which excludes the kind of translation more aptly called "decoding." The steps or stages of such a program were described in detail in the report on "Reading for Meaning" presented to the 1963 Northeast Conference by Professor George Scherer and his committee.[5] To summarize briefly, it is a program in which the student learns to read as much as possible by direct association between the printed foreign language and its meaning. The spoken foreign language remains the natural intermediary between sight and comprehension, in time reducing to "inner speech" as it does for the expert native reader. The introduction of new words is carefully spaced to minimize reading "stoppages," and marginal glosses are provided; the new words are repeated as soon and as often as possible; structure used in reading selections is kept on a level with what the student has learned or is learning to control; he is encouraged to use contextual clues and inference as much as possible; cognates and derivational systems are fully exploited. At every stage he is given many varied opportunities

[4] See the introduction to the *Reading-Writing Spelling Manuals* (French, German, Spanish, Russian) *A-LM Level One* (New York: Harcourt, Brace, 1961–1962).

[5] G. A. C. Scherer *et al*, "Reading for Meaning," in W. F. Bottiglia (ed.) *Language Learning: The Intermediate Phase, Reports of the Working Committee, 1963 Northeast Conference on the Teaching of Foreign Languages,* pp. 23–60.

to test his comprehension by means of oral questions, résumés, and the like. At the end of a four-level program organized and presented in such a manner, it is reasonable to believe that the average student will have reached the stage Professor Scherer calls "liberated reading"—he will be able to read a foreign language book of normal difficulty with comprehension and pleasure.

Partly because reading was considered the only attainable objective of a foreign language program for so long and partly because all the important foreign language tests—from the College Entrance Examination Board Achievement Tests to the language examinations required in graduate programs in other fields—have been so largely concerned with reading, even the high-school language teacher who is sincerely committed to a program designed to develop all four language skills tends to be more preoccupied with reading than with the other skills. He inevitably asks two questions about reading which he seldom asks about listening, speaking, or writing, though they ought to be just as pertinent with respect to those skills. Those two questions are: How much should my students read? What should they read?

It is neither desirable nor possible for any single committee to prescribe a certain number of pages of reading for any or all levels of a secondary school program. It *is* possible, however, to note some important factors that should be considered before determining the amount of material to be read.

First, the primary objective of a reading program is reading for meaning in the language. At least through the first two levels it is desirable for the student to read a relatively small number of pages with complete comprehension and have an opportunity to discuss in detail what he has read, using the vocabulary and structure of the selections as often as possible.

Second, the development of reading skill depends as much on the student's control of structure as it does on the extent of his vocabulary. Unfamiliar grammatical constructions can and often do cause more serious reading stoppages than new lexical items. Thus, it is probably more productive in the long run for the student to spend more of his time in the beginning and intermediate stages gaining audio-lingual control of the basic structure than it is for him to read extensively. The amount of reading should increase as mastery of vocabulary and structure do, but not disproportionately so.

Particularly in a long sequence it would be desirable to increase the amount of reading by what we may call confirmation readings. These would be additional reading selections that use only the basic structure learned at a given point and introduce new lexical items very slowly, 1–100 or 1–150. Such selections could be assigned for rapid reading at home without the student's needing to skip or skim. They would help to confirm and reinforce what has already been learned and would have the psychological value of giving the student a feeling of reading power.

Unfortunately such readings do not exist at this time and too many teachers, influenced by the great prestige and tradition of the reading objective, push students too soon into reading that is too difficult. Until appropriate confirmation readers are prepared, it would seem wise to reduce the amount of reading but to improve the quality of performance with attendant active use of the other three skills.

The question of *what* the student should read in the secondary-school program brings us face to face with the place of literary studies, such as literary history, analysis, and criticism. *It is the contention of this committee that premature preoccupation with these areas constitutes the most discouraging obstacle to the successful teaching of the language skills in high school.* Such premature preoccupation with literary pursuits is a sure road back to the horrors of decoding, a road which leads, ultimately, to utter distaste for further language study. It is wishful thinking to suppose that "literary values" will be communicated to any but a trivial percentage of students, unless they already control the language. This committee believes, therefore, that a prerequisite for the *genuine* study of literature is, or ought to be, language proficiency. Even in a long sequence, the time allotted to foreign language study is necessarily limited. If the student is to be expected to reach the point where he can use *all* the skills, especially that of speaking, with reasonable facility, he needs to be immersed in those activities every bit of the time available.

This point of view by no means excludes literature from the secondary-school program. Literary selections should be used to further the development of the reading skill, but only those which the student's command of the language permits him to understand in every sense. Discussion of literary texts is obviously limited by the student's ability to express himself in the language both orally and in writing. In high school classes literature has too often been cheapened, reduced to bare bones and less, because the language skills have not been developed sufficiently. Insistence on firm linguistic control is the surest way to make it possible for students to benefit from literary study.

In selecting reading material, the language used must receive careful and critical consideration. We are developing listening and speaking ability on the basis of current, authentic, usually informal language. Clearly, reading material must offer written varieties of this contemporary language, including nonfiction and articles from current magazines and newspapers as well as novels, plays, short stories, and poetry. It will always be a challenge to combine linguistic requirements with due consideration for the maturity, interests, and hence motivation of the American high-school student. It seems obvious that he will be more strongly motivated by carefully chosen material which treats the contemporary scene than by the writings of earlier periods. The tradition which insists on the uncritical perpetuation of the works of nineteenth-century writers, for example, is thus open to serious question.

Above all, we must never lose sight of the place of reading in the ideal secondary-school program. Properly developed and used, it can maintain and strengthen its own vital role, while contributing to the development of the other skills. But these other skills must not be sacrificed by excessive concern with reading, which is one part, but only one, of a program dedicated to the development of listening comprehension and speaking, reading, and writing ability.

3. WRITING

The article "Writing as Expression" appeared as one of the reports of the Working Committees of the 1963 Northeast Conference. It sets forth in considerable detail the role of writing in an audio-lingual foreign language program. It is fitting here to present its major points by way of review.

The English word "write" has two meanings. It means to spell, in the sense of making the proper choice of letters in the proper sequence in response to both oral and written stimuli. It also means to put down on paper what one wishes to express, using a style and a vocabulary appropriate to the material or the occasion—informal or formal, literary or technical. It is the second kind of writing, writing as expression, that must be one of the long-range objectives of any modern-language program. It should be obvious, however, that one can hope to attain this objective only by proceeding deliberately through a series of steps which lead toward the ultimate goal.

There is reason to attempt to suggest and describe some of the more promising procedures, because we have so far fallen quite short of accomplishing the stated objective in any effective way. This lack of success in teaching students to write a foreign language is surely not because writing has been neglected or omitted as listening comprehension and speaking were for many years. On the contrary, writing has always been one of the aspects of the program to which a rather large segment of time has been devoted and it should not be regarded as unimportant because consideration is now being given to listening and speaking skills. Rather, its relation to the total program should be re-examined for the purpose of improving this aspect as well as all the others.

In the kind of program commonly referred to as "traditional," in which reading and the study of literature were recognized as both the most realistic and the most important objectives of either a classical or a modern foreign language course, there was inevitably great emphasis on the rules of grammar and extensive use of translation, from the foreign language to native language and from native language to foreign language. This translation was done both orally and as an exercise in writing. It is doubtful that many teachers believed that these written translation exercises could be classified as "writing as expression." To attain that objective, students were given, more or less frequently, depending on the strength and endurance of the teacher who corrected the papers, assignments called "free composition." The shift to an audiolingual approach . . . is still proceeding, and there are many unsolved problems. In our approach to writing many factors have prevented us from reconsidering our procedures in terms of the recognized goals. We have been preoccupied with other matters. It is hardly surprising that even teachers otherwise audio-lingually oriented should have resorted to the established devices of translation and free composition whenever the obvious need to do something about writing arose.

Written translation traditionally proceeds from the native language to the foreign language. The structures, the vocabulary, and the style of the native language are, then, the points of departure for the student. They are constantly before him. He seeks "equivalents" in the foreign language, and having found some, or some approximations, eagerly returns to familiar ground for his next cue. Not only does the native language remain the source of all inspiration, but the resulting foreign language is unlikely to bear much resemblance to authentic native writing. Worse yet, the student does not know this, and is likely to remain largely unaware of the atrocities he has perpetrated. He has "solved" a problem and, unfortunately, many of us will accept such "solutions," if the verb endings are correct. At best, this procedure helps to fix inflectional endings and rudimentary word order, although even the latter is apt to suffer because of the powerful influence of the native language. What this procedure does not do is move the student in any way toward written self-expression in the foreign language.

Since the ultimate writing goal in modern-language programs is free composition, it is again hardly surprising that teachers have traditionally approached it by assigning a topic or subject on which the student is expected to express something in writing from the first week of class. Since the student has only extremely limited foreign-language resources, it is natural for him to seek some firm ground from which to proceed. Confronted with such an assignment, he will dutifully write out a suitable English version and proceed to translate it. He now finds himself faced with the same problem that he would have had if he had been assigned a passage to translate; only in this case the student, not the teacher, has provided the English. But the effect is even worse, because the controls that the teacher or the textbook may have exercised in order not to extend the student completely beyond his depth are now absent. The result can only be the invention of foreign-language word sequences totally unacceptable to any native speaker.

It is clear that the student cannot proceed from listening and speaking to reading and writing without firm mechanical control of the way the sounds of the language he is learning are represented on paper. In the process of establishing these sound-letter correspondences, copying exercises and frequent dictation of largely familiar material are indispensable. As the student becomes increasingly able to respond in writing to both oral and written stimuli, he is given other types of writing practice which afford him the opportunity for a limited kind of self-expression. He often works first with parts of sentences, as in sentence-completion exercises, then with controlled sentence construction, then with making minimal changes such as those involving tense, person, or number in a paragraph, and finally with an elementary kind of controlled paragraph construction. . . . Obviously, all writing exercises are based on material which has either been practiced orally or read, preferably both. They allow the student to use structure and vocabulary that he has already learned.[6]

The 1963 Report provides copious examples of various drill types which can lead eventually to writing as expression.[7] The student proceeds gradually through parts of sentences, then sentences, finally to the paragraph, with a reduction of controls so gradual that he is never placed in the position of having to invent language. At more advanced levels, as progress in understanding and speaking moves toward comprehension and production of longer sequences, this new skill can also be reflected in the ability to write such sequences.

The committee endorses this 1963 Report and, as in the case of reading, suggests that writing is clearly one—but only one—of the four skills to be developed. The great danger is too much and too early concern with free composition, which provides no consistent progress toward good writing and serves only to undermine progress achieved in better controlled parts of the program.

4. OBSTACLES

There are some major deterrents to the general acceptance of the goals outlined in this report. They are the College Entrance Examination Board Achievement Tests, the Advanced Placement Program, and most college foreign language programs.

4.1. The CEEB Achievement Test.

In the booklet entitled *A Description of the College Board Achievement Tests* (1963) in the section on foreign languages we read: "Because language teachers are by no means in full agreement on the relative emphasis that should be placed on the various language skills, the College Board examiners strive for balance rather than for a particular viewpoint in the tests. Different parts of the test are designed to measure familiarity with both the spoken and the written language."

---

[6] M. Prochoroff, *et al.*, "Writing as Expression," in *Language Learning: The Intermediate Phase, op. cit.*, pp. 63–67.

[7] *Op. cit.*, pp. 67–80.

The booklet then proceeds to illustrate and explain some of the types of questions used, making it clear that these types may vary from year to year and that no attempt has been made to illustrate every possible type. The types illustrated are: Situation Questions, Usage Questions, Vocabulary Questions, and Reading Comprehension Questions.

Of the four skills, the development of which this report recommends as the primary goal of a secondary school program, only one, reading, is tested by the CEEB. It is true that there is an optional listening comprehension test, but the fact that it has remained optional for several years indicates that it is not yet regarded as essential.

The only bow in the direction of the speaking skill is in the Situation Question where the student is asked to select one from four or five remarks most likely to be made in connection with, or in response to, a situation described. The booklet itself says "Obviously this type of question tests your ability to read. . . ." It surely does not test speaking ability in any way.

Since all the questions are multiple-choice questions, the student's ability to write is not tested.

The College Board officials often state that they have no desire to influence the secondary school curriculum through the tests they prepare. Nevertheless they do exercise this kind of influence and will continue to do so as long as their tests are required by so many colleges and universities, especially those of the greatest prestige. Just as long as the CEEB continues to test reading alone of the four skills, it will be difficult to convince school administrators, boards of education, and parents, to say nothing of language teachers, that the other skills should be given appropriate consideration in the school program. That the CEEB is aware of this influence and some of its effects, is made evident by the fact that in another of their publications, *College Board Scores, Their Use and Interpretation,* there is a section "What about evaluation of instruction?" It says among other things:

A few schools use the scores to a limited extent as a means of evaluating their own instruction. That is, they compare the mean performance of their own candidates with the mean performance of some appropriate norm group. If the school mean is above the norm, the school officials infer that they are doing an effective job of college preparation; if it is below the norm, these same officials become concerned about the adequacy of their instruction.

There is a real question whether such use of scores is legitimate. The current College Board tests have been designed primarily to identify the college candidate who has the mental equipment to succeed in college. The tests would have been designed differently if their main purpose were to evaluate secondary school instruction. It is doubtful whether any test suitable for inclusion in a national selection program can also be entirely suitable for evaluating the work of an individual school.

It is probably dangerous to use Achievement Test scores for the evaluation of instruction. Even with the rather elaborate statistical controls employed in the studies of two of the Achievement Tests reported, it has not been possible to separate clearly elements of *instruction* from elements of aptitude and self-motivation.

In general, then, the tests are designed to evaluate *studenₜs* from a wide variety of schools, *not* to evaluate the *instruction* in any given school.

This seems to make the official position of the CEEB clear enough and it should be repeated as often as possible to department chairmen and other school officials who are responsible for decisions about curricula.

It is also true that high school teachers and administrators tend to attach more importance to individual achievement test scores than college admissions officers do. Achievement test scores are just one, and by no means the most important, of the criteria reviewed by the college admissions department when deciding on the acceptance or rejection of a candidate.

While language teachers may not be in *full* agreement on the *relative* emphasis that should be placed on the various language skills, it is the opinion of this committee that there is, and has been for some time, general agreement that the development of four skills is the only pedagogically justifiable goal for secondary school foreign language programs. We recommend that the CEEB:

1. make the listening comprehension test mandatory;
2. include a test of speaking ability;
3. include a test of writing ability.

Clearly, these recommendations also apply to any testing program of similar prestige and influence, e.g., the New York State Regents Examinations.

4.2 The Advanced Placement Program

The Advanced Placement Program of the CEEB, which prepares and administers examinations for admission to college with advanced standing and credit at the discretion of the admitting institution, has been growing in size and influence for several years. It has been referred to by its director as "the cutting edge of curriculum change" in both secondary and college education. Unfortunately, the influence of these examinations has had an inhibiting effect on the kind of foreign language program recommended as ideal in this report. The Advanced Placement foreign language tests are heavily weighted in the direction of literature as opposed to language. Only in French are all the questions answered in the language.

A thorough examination of the Advanced Placement examinations was the purpose of an article in the *French Review*, May, 1963, "The Relation of Language to Literature in the Advanced Placement Program" by Professor Robert J. Nelson of the University of Pennsylvania. Professor Nelson believes that the present stress on literature in these tests is forcing teachers to teach in a way which precludes proper attention to the development of the audio-lingual skills which have received such emphasis since World War II. He points out the ironic contradiction in this situation, noting that the teacher cannot really teach literature until the student can *speak* French (or whatever the language may be).

He believes that, as long as the examinations continue to follow the present pattern, "the influence of the AP program in modern foreign languages will be counter to the best interests of sound foreign language training." He suggests that "AP courses should limit the amount of literature to one-third, with the remaining two-thirds devoted to language skills and, among these, the active skills in particular." He further suggests a two-part test. Part one would test all four skills, while part two would be a test on literature. The four-skill language test would be required of all AP students. The literature test would be optional. Students who receive a high grade (4 or 5) in both language and literature tests would be placed in any course they chose. Students with a high grade in language, but who either did not elect to take the literature test or failed it, would be placed in an appropriate literature course. In the case of a high grade in literature and a low grade in language, the student would be placed in an advanced language course. This last possibility, Professor Nelson acknowledges, will be with us until permission to take the literature test *depends* on a four-skill language test grade of 3, 4, or 5.

This committee is in general agreement with the point of view expressed in Professor Nelson's article.

4.3 College Programs

It is regrettable that far too many college foreign language programs admit students to courses in literature when they do not control the language well enough to benefit from them. The inevitable result is that many of these courses are conducted in English. Many secondary-school teachers are aware of the complaints voiced by their former students who return from college and report that their college teachers do not use the foreign language.

The report on the college program will discuss this problem in some detail. In the opinion of this commitee, the ideal secondary-school foreign language program outlined in this report would receive a powerful impetus if colleges and universities would demand real language proficiency of all students who enter their courses in literature.

5. PROGRAM EVALUATION

It has not been easy to test four-skill performance, yet meaningful evaluation is absolutely essential if we are to demonstrate the strengths and discover the weaknesses of any foreign language program. Successful teaching stands helplessly before inquiring administrator and irresponsible critic alike, unable to offer any reasonable proof that it is doing what it says it is. Fortunately for our profession, the instrument which makes evaluation possible is now at hand—the Modern Language Association Cooperative Classroom Tests. Developed under a contract between the U.S. Office of Education and the Modern Language Association, directed by Professor Nelson Brooks of Yale University, and administered by Educational Testing Service, these tests measure proficiency in each of the four skills. They have been prepared in five languages—French, German, Italian, Russian, and Spanish—with two forms at two levels, lower and middle, for each language. They may be ordered from the Cooperative Test Division, Educational Testing Service, Princeton, New Jersey.

The committee urges the widest possible use of this testing program as an effective answer to a frustrating problem.

6. SUMMARY

The major recommendation of this report is a planned sequence of four-skill development throughout a program comprising at least four years of study, preferably six. The report discusses each of the four skills within this context. While such a recommendation may seem obvious, there exists a strong tendency to neglect or even abandon the audio-lingual skills, even after good beginnings have been made. This tendency, toward premature extensive reading and premature concern with literary studies, fostered by various pressures, undermines rather than strengthens the ideal secondary-school program. Some pressures are illusory; others can be reduced. When it is possible to state that the entire secondary-school program is clearly and unambiguously dedicated to the planned development of listening comprehension, speaking, reading, and writing *without the kind of disproportionate emphasis on any one skill which operates to the detriment of the others,* a kind of ideal program will be in operation which will produce a high level of proficiency in interpersonal communication and intercultural performance on the contemporary scene, while at the same time furnishing the essential prerequisites for the subsequent more efficient and effective achievement of humanistic aims.

OBJECTIVES OF FOREIGN LANGUAGE TEACHING

One of the most important steps in any foreign language program is determining the objectives. In the essay which follows the immediate objectives are treated at some length as well as the manner in which they may be realized. The question of subject-matter content is also treated. It is interesting to contrast this chapter with the foregoing one by a committee of the Northeast Conference. Also of interest is the mention of travel abroad for high-school students, an activity which unquestionably motivates their learning and widens their intellectual horizons. This article is part of a report of a conference sponsored jointly by the NEA Project on the Academically Talented Student and the MLA Foreign Language Program. It was compiled on the basis of conclusions reached by members of the conference. Since it represents the conclusions of specialists in the field, it merits serious consideration.

The objectives of modern foreign language instruction for the academically talented and for all who would obtain real competence in language are proficiency in language skills accompanied by familiarity with the outstanding traits of the foreign culture.

PROFICIENCY IN FOUR SKILLS

The four skills to be developed in foreign language study are listening comprehension, speaking, reading, and writing.

Reprinted by permission of the National Education Association from Wilmarth H. Starr, Mary P. Thompson, and Donald D. Walsh (eds.), *Modern Foreign Languages and the Academically Talented Student,* 1960.

Listening Comprehension

The student should understand the foreign language as it is spoken by native speakers in situations similar to his own experience. For example, he should be able to understand conversations based on everyday situations, questions about his usual activities in and out of school, accounts of similar activities of his peers in other countries, stories, brief descriptions of historical and current events, discussions about famous people, past and present, and the reading aloud of carefully selected passages from plays, books, and periodicals suited to his age level.

Speaking

The student should speak the foreign language in everyday situations with reasonable fluency and correctness, and with pronunciation acceptable to a native speaker of the language. In addition to participating in simple dialogues based on daily life situations and answering questions about his usual activities, he should be able to ask similar questions, to retell simple stories, to describe historical and current events with which he is familiar, and to discuss aspects of the foreign civilization and the literary merits of the materials that he has studied.

Reading

The student should read the foreign language easily and without conscious translation. He should be able to read books and periodicals appropriate to his age level (biography, history, geography, science, novels, short stories, poetry, other nonfiction). He should read rapidly for the sense of the story and more deliberately for fuller understanding.

Writing

The student should be able to write descriptions, reports, and informal letters with clarity and correctness. For example, he should be able to communicate in writing anything he can say: write simple dialogues and compositions dealing with his own experiences or with other topics that interest him and are based on materials previously learned.

Mastery of the skills must be accompanied by familiarity with the culture the language represents, as well as a larger view of life resulting from the realization that there are many cultures and value systems, some far different from our own, operative in the world today.

Language Expresses a Way of Life

The student should come to realize that language is the essential expression of a people's behavior and outlook, the medium in which and by which they think about and react to life. As community life becomes more and more complicated, our skill in using language and its written symbols must become progressively sharper. Each linguistic group's conscious thoughts, feelings, attitudes, and values are expressed through, and shaped by, the language of the group, and they can be completely understood only in that language. One can learn a great deal about what speakers of a foreign language do, and approximately what they say and think and feel by reading about them in English; but one does not begin to understand precisely how persons in other cultures think and feel until he comprehends and uses effectively the language in which they express their thoughts and feelings.

Many Value Systems

The student should know that there are many cultures and many value systems in the contemporary world and should learn to act accordingly. He will thus accept the fact that other peoples attach to their different way of life the same importance he attaches to his and he will arrive at a more realistic approach to life and, consequently, a more profound appreciation of other culture systems and of his own. The fact that it is a matter of serious importance to people of other cultures that we try to speak their language is of great significance in the development of a student's intercultural understanding.

Understanding and Appreciation

The student should acquire understanding and appreciation of another people's way of life, institutions, literature, and civilization.

Learning a foreign language involves the student in the culture of which the language is an expression and frees him from the ethnic-centered attitudes of his community and from the prejudices that he must overcome if he is to be a responsible citizen of the world.

MEANS OF ACQUIRING THE SKILLS

The process of acquiring these second-language skills at any age level is in many respects like learning one's native language in infancy and childhood: hearing and speaking come first, followed by reading and writing.

Listening and Speaking

The first or audio-lingual stage is by far the most important; it not only produces the most immediately satisfying and useful skills (hearing and speaking) but it lays an indispensable foundation for the other two (reading and writing). In this first stage, only the ear and tongue are trained, without use of the written language. This exclusively audio-lingual stage may vary in length from two or three years at the elementary-school level to a very short period in college. Some of the basic activities during this stage are:

1. Dialogue learning: hearing and repeating the phrases of a simple dialogue until the latter is "overlearned," i.e., completely mastered to the point of automatic response to the dialogue situation, the kind of immediate response that occurs in greetings or comments on the weather.

2. Dialogue adaptation: practice with the phrases and sentences of the current basic dialogue and previously learned items of vocabulary and structure, allowing the student increasing freedom and control in the use of these elements. Two steps in this process are: question and answer (the student, in answer to simple questions, uses and reuses his basic dialogue material, at first with little or no change, later with some variation); and directed dialogue (the student, told to ask or answer a question or to make a statement, still using his basic material, moves farther along toward the free use of new elements in combination with those already learned).

3. Structure drills: isolating certain speech patterns (structure patterns or grammar points) and drilling them by various techniques until the student has them under complete and automatic

control. Once this control is achieved, a simple statement of the grammatical principle involved may be made. There are many kinds of drill: repetition, substitution, restatement, expansion, response. A simple substitution drill for the present tense of "to be" follows this pattern:

Model Voice	Student's First Response	Model Voice Confirming or Correcting	Student's Second Response
I'm at home.	I'm at home.	I'm at home.	I'm at home
He ———	He's at home.	He's at home.	He's at home.
You ———	You're at home.	You're at home.	You're at home.

4. Practice of dialogue and drills: leading to the progressive development of skill in handling larger units of speech and thought. For example, with the present tense of "to be," positive, negative, and interrogative, and "at home," "when," and "today," the student can be guided by various techniques (an actual or pictured situation; brief directions in English, spoken or written; a few words in the foreign language by way of suggestion; a question in the foreign language) into saying a sequence of sentences such as the following:

Are you at home?—No, I'm not at home.
When are they at home?—They're at home today.
Is she at home today?—No, she's not at home today.

The end product of such exercises is student manipulation of dialogues and oral compositions, at first rather short and closely guided by the teacher, ultimately quite long, relatively free, and spontaneous. This step is close to, sometimes identical with, the ultimate objective of this part of the learning procedure—the free use of the foreign language in meaningful conversation within the limits of the student's control of structure and vocabulary.

5. Language laboratory aids: The effectiveness of the memorization and drill activities described above is multiplied many times by the use of good recorded materials and a language laboratory properly integrated with class procedure.

These audio-lingual skills must be kept active all through the student's foreign language learning experience, for speech is the most essential aspect of living language. The pupil who has begun learning through the spoken language will find that this introduction facilitates his reading and writing.

Reading

At the first stage, the student will read only what he has already learned to understand and say. The priority of hearing and speaking should continue until the student's audio-lingual skills are well established. How soon students reach the stage of safe initial exposure to written material will depend on their age, their language skill, and the language they are learning. The more mature student is more impatient to see the written equivalents of what he has learned to understand and say. The linguistically apt student can more quickly master the sounds and, therefore, advance more rapidly toward the reading stage. There are certain basic "rules" to be observed during this stage.

1. All reading should be directly in the foreign language. It is of the utmost importance that the student read only what he has already thoroughly learned through ears and tongue. This material he can read and understand without recourse to English equivalents. If a student's early reading is carefully controlled, he can read directly in the foreign language and thereby make more rapid progress than by translating into English.

The first introduction to reading is of crucial importance in conditioning the student against translation, a stumbling matching of words that has little to do with reading. Systematic translation into English is to be avoided except as a literary exercise for advanced students who have already learned to read in the foreign language with appreciable skill.

2. Discussion of material which has been read inside or outside of class should be in the foreign language. The most elementary exercise to test reading comprehension is one that calls for a repetition of most of the words of the question. The teacher asks (in the foreign language): *Where did George go after school?* The student replies (in the foreign language): *George went home after school.* More advanced exercises are free responses to questions (with encouragement of full rather than minimal answers), paraphrases (changing from the first person to the third person, from present to past or future), résumés, and interpretation, which may advance to the level of literary discussion in the foreign language.

3. The texts to be read should be graded in linguistic difficulty and suited to the intellectual maturity of the student. Two dangers must be avoided in the second of these areas: the one extreme, that of giving the adolescent beginner reading material that, because it is linguistically easy, is so childish in content that it offends his relative maturity; the other, that of expecting the adolescent student to understand in the foreign language cultural and intellectual values that may be beyond his scope in English.

4. In addition to the class reading, provision should be made for extensive and individual reading. The class reading, which can well be intensive, can either be material assigned for preparation outside of class or new material, and the text can be analyzed and explained in the foreign language in several ways: questions and answers, paraphrases, synonym and antonym drill, word families, expansions, restatements. In addition to this intensive reading in class, there should be extensive reading of a story or novel at a rate that will preclude translation. Testing of this extensive reading should be less detailed than for intensive reading.

Beyond this extensive reading by the class in common, provision should be made for individual readings, adjusted to the reading skill and the interests of each student. These individual readings will be of special value to the academically talented, whether in special classes or not, and also to those with pronounced interests (Rolland's *Jean Christophe* for the student of French and of music, Azuela's *Los de abajo* for the student of Spanish and of twentieth-century history, Albert Schweitzer's *Leben und Denken* for the student of German and of science).

Writing

Writing is the fourth of the skills, the most difficult to acquire, and the one for which fewest students will have a direct and immediate need. At the first stage the student will write only what he has already learned to understand, speak, and read. There are several established techniques for learning to write in a foreign language. The most elementary and helpful is straight copying of a foreign text. After this follows dictation, variations on a model (changing from masculine to feminine, from singular to plural, from present to past or future, from direct to indirect discourse, from third to first person), summarizing (reducing a page to a paragraph), guided composition (expanding an outline, continuing a discussion whose beginning is given, describing a picture), writing a composition on an assigned topic, and, eventually, free composition.

Grammar

The elementary-school pupil learns grammar inductively, without realizing it, and this is proper for his age group. He is not yet ready to profit from grammatical explanation and analysis. The adolescent student, especially the intellectually alert, wants to know the reason why, and he can profit from an abstract statement and a generalization. With adolescents the able teacher will avoid two extremes: one is to give the rules instead of the language, which is to substitute the scaffolding for the building; the other is to refuse the student any generalizations, which is to equate him with the infant making his first contact with language.

MEANS OF ACQUIRING AN UNDERSTANDING OF THE CULTURE

Concentration on authenticity of models and participation in other activities such as correspondence and travel abroad are necessary if students are to become familiar with the outstanding traits of the culture of the people whose language they are learning.

Authenticity of Language

1. The spoken language in the classroom and all recorded materials should be authentic in pronunciation, intonation, accent, and idiom. Without such models it is almost impossible to transmit the feelings and thoughts of the people whose language is being studied.

2. Brief expositions in the foreign language of different aspects of everyday life in the foreign country are invaluable. In addition to dealing with such matters as the use of the telephone or the making of appointments, subjects selected should, whenever possible, make use of current events and scholastic activities in such other disciplines as history and English. Structure and content of all such expositions should be adapted to the foreign language skills and to the interests of the students.

3. When recordings (discs or tapes) are made, the voices, if

possible, should be those of native speakers properly coached and directed. In addition, commercial recordings of native singers and actors may be, for many students, a source of authentic cultural experience.

4. Visual materials should also be authentic representations of the native culture. Films, filmstrips, and other visual materials must depict accurately foreign life, customs, and institutions. All material must be meaningful and purposeful, avoiding the stereotyped, the bizarre, and the picturesque images commonly presented to the tourist and the idly curious.

Authenticity of Reading Matter

1. Authenticity is equally important in reading material to ensure the student's awareness of the similarities as well as the significant differences between his culture and the one being studied.

2. In addition to works of literary value, which are in themselves authentic expressions of culture, some readings should be chosen on the economic and social life of the country. Others may concern people of the student's age group, to encourage him to compare his habits and attitudes with theirs.

3. Periodicals are valid sources of information about the foreign culture. Through them the student is introduced to topics of immediate interest to the people whose language he is studying. He will, by this means, also become familiar with some of the attitudes that others have toward his own people and his own culture. Some of this reading can well be correlated with work in other classes, particularly art, music, and social science.

Correspondence

Able students should be encouraged to correspond with foreign students. Letter writing between students of two countries, whether or not each writes in the language of the other, is an activity steadily recommended by teachers and eagerly undertaken by students. Such correspondence provides writing practice related to everyday situations, with an enlightening exchange of opinions and attitudes in the framework of two cultures. Such correspondence has been known to motivate travel abroad and to lead to continuing friendships.

Resource Persons

A chief difficulty in teaching foreign languages in many parts of this country is that of providing the American student with sufficient contact with native speakers and representatives of the culture being studied. To remedy this, native speakers of the language who live in the area may be brought, from time to time, into the classroom. At first only cultivated speakers of the standard language should be invited and the class meeting should be carefully planned.

As a result of the native speaker's presence, the student is made more aware that the language being studied is a living language. Questions and answers invariably bring into play divergent points of view that are significant in relating the cultures to each other. Further valuable experience is gained by the student in adapting his listening awareness to individual speech differences, always evident even between speakers of similar educational and social background.

Before he speaks to a class of beginning students, the native speaker should be coached to use, as much as possible, the words and phrases the students have learned. At later stages, special benefit may be derived from contact with speakers representing greater differences in speaking habits and a greater variety of national and regional accents. In a similar fashion the student's understanding of a foreign culture will increase in depth as he becomes aware of the individual differences within the over-all cultural pattern. Whenever possible, it is desirable to invite to the classroom foreign students brought to this country under the sponsorship of such groups as the American Field Service and the Experiment in International Living. The interchange of ideas between groups of approximately the same age has all the advantages of contact with native speakers plus the benefits of the sympathetic understanding normally generated between young people with similar interests.

Travel Abroad

No foreign language classroom experience, however aptly presented, can equal, in its effect upon the student's comprehension of the characteristics of a foreign culture, the impact of travel and residence abroad. The better the student has been prepared for this experience, the more valid his impressions are likely to be. In like manner, the student poorly prepared linguistically and culturally is prone to disappointments, misconceptions, and false impressions that may damage the intercultural understanding for which language learning can be, under proper circumstances, the principal resource.

The academically talented student who has become reasonably fluent in a foreign language should be encouraged by all the resources at our command to expect travel or residence abroad as the natural and rewarding outcome of his language studies. The language teacher should have information at hand concerning the many exchange plans, travel scholarships, and foreign study opportunities which are available. Publications of the Institute of International Education and of UNESCO are available for this purpose.

Other Disciplines

Primarily in the area of understanding a foreign culture, and particularly for the academically talented student, important cultural values and refinements of knowledge may be found in such related fields as art, music, history, geography, and science. Exploration of this kind of material illuminates the complexity of the culture and civilization of the country whose language he is studying. In these activities, particularly where they are reinforced by his own interests, the academically talented student will find inexhaustible resources for individual enrichment. The scope of language courses is often limited to the linguistic and literary materials at hand, and they seldom explore the country's fine arts resources, its history, and creative spirit. Moreover, the academically talented student will discover that his foreign language study provides new insights into and additional interest in the related disciplines of fine arts, humanities, and social sciences.

The alert teacher will be aware of these opportunities and will encourage the academically talented student toward independent study, guiding his skills, knowledge, and interests toward the thorough integration and synthesis which results from the study of related fields.

ARTICULATION IN THE TEACHING
OF FOREIGN LANGUAGES

DONALD D. WALSH

*No discussion of the foreign language program
would be complete without a consideration of the
articulation of program and practices between elementary, junior high, high school, and college. To
this problem Donald Walsh, former director of the
Foreign Language Program for the Modern Language Association, addresses himself. His words
have a special importance for curriculum directors,
but concern teachers and principals as well. The
notion that one teaches a foreign language at a
given grade, or in a given school, without close
consideration of what precedes and follows is totally obsolete, but the problem remains crucial. It
indicates the need for a foreign language supervisor
within every school system to help with the task
of articulation. Neither can the college professor
any longer afford to disregard the teaching that
goes on prior to the time the student enters college.*

With increasing emphasis on longer sequences of foreign language study, from kindergarten to graduate school, adequate articulation of foreign language courses is one of the first desiderata of
modern curricular reform. The present situation is alarming. In
most school systems there are not sequences but mere fragments of
foreign language learning, in which the student is the victim of
interrupted study and conflicting methods that dull all but the
keenest enthusiasm for language learning.

The study of a first foreign language should begin very early,
no later than grade three. This is the ideal time to begin—when

Reprinted by permission of the author and the College Entrance Examination Board from *Curricular Change in the Foreign Languages,* 1963.

the vocal organs are still pliable and capable of imitating any sound in any language and when the child is uninhibited, and eager to experiment with language and to welcome the endless drilling that is needed to instill automatic language habits. This *is* the perfect age for language learning—everyone who has seen an elementary school foreign language class in action will agree—but even if it were *not* the perfect age, even if it were a very unpropitious age, we would still have to urge that foreign language study begin no later than grade three in order to get the job accomplished by the end of grade twelve.

One of the most absurd delusions in American education is that a student can learn a foreign language in two high-school years, attending only five classes a week totaling three or four hours and spending as little or even less time on preparation. Two years of study in grades nine and ten and two years of forgetting in grades eleven and twelve leave the student with precious little language knowledge as he enters college. Whether or not he takes a placement test, it will soon be apparent how little he has retained, and he will either have to repeat the elementary work, with consequent loss of interest, or shift to another language, abandoning any hope of mastering the first one and probably dropping the study of the new language as soon as he has satisfied the piffling foreign language degree requirement. It is this sad and prevalent experience that has produced the monolingual American adult, monolingual not because he can't learn a foreign language but because he has never had a proper chance to learn one.

Learning a new language, acquiring a second set of language habits, is a long, slow process, but it is not a painful process if it is begun early under expert guidance and if the elementary school learning is an integral part of a planned sequence. Two factors in American education have prevented the widespread introduction of foreign language study into the elementary schools, and the two factors are closely related. Most of the leading theorists in elementary education in the United States are (or have been until recently) in favor of the self-contained classroom, taught by a grade teacher who has majored in education and who therefore has no specialty except teaching children. As a result, most institutions that prepare future elementary school teachers have not given them any opportunity to specialize in a subject-matter field. Foreign-language study at this level is therefore hampered by the opposition of the theorists and by an acute shortage of elementary school teachers who have had any contact with a foreign language. One of the great advantages of the FLES program (Foreign Languages in Elementary Schools) is that young children are wonderfully good at imitating speech. If the teacher has a native or near-native accent, the children's accent will be equally good. But if the teacher speaks fractured French, the children will imitate her with frightening fidelity.

The Modern Language Association Foreign Language Program Advisory and Liaison Committee, meeting in New York in 1961, five years after its first Policy Statement on FLES, viewed with alarm the many FLES programs instituted without adequate teaching staff or provision for continuity and articulation. The committee issued a Second Statement of Policy, from which I quote:

Redefinition. We must sharpen our definition of FLES. It is not an end in itself but the elementary-school (K-6) part of a language-learning program that should extend unbroken through grade 12. It has 15- or 20-minute sessions at least three times a week as an integral part of the school day. It concerns itself primarily with learning the four skills, beginning with listening and speaking. Other values (improved understanding of language in general, intercultural understanding, broadened horizons), though important, are secondary.

FLES *in Sequence.* We believe that FLES, as here defined, is an essential part of the long sequence, ten years or more, needed to approach mastery of a second language in school. There is good evidence that the learning of a second language considerably quickens and eases the learning of a third language, even when there is little or no relation between the languages learned. Since children imitate skillfully and with few inhibitions in the early school years, the primary grades (K-3) are the ideal place to begin language learning, and the experience is in itself exciting and rewarding.

Priority. If a school system cannot provide both a FLES program and a six-year secondary-school foreign-language sequence (grades 7–12), it should work *first* toward establishing the grade 7–12 sequence. Unless there is a solid junior and senior high school program of foreign-language learning with due stress on the listening and speaking skills and fully articulated with the previous instruction, FLES learnings wither on the vine.

Articulation. It requires: (1) a foreign-language program in grades

7 and 8 for graduates of FLES, who should never be placed with beginners at *any* grade level; (2) a carefully planned coordination of the FLES and secondary-school programs; (3) a frequent interchange of visits and information among the foreign-language teachers at all levels; (4) an over-all coordination by a single foreign-language supervisor or by a committee of administrators. These cooperative efforts should result in a common core of language learning that will make articulation smooth and effective.

The Teacher. Ideally he should be an expert in the foreign language he teaches, with near-native accent and fluency, and also skillful in teaching young children. Few teachers are currently expert in both areas. If a teacher's foreign-language accent is not good, he should make every effort to improve it, and meanwhile he should rely on discs or tapes to supply authentic model voices for his pupils. But since language is communication, and a child cannot communicate with a phonograph or a tape recorder, no FLES learning can be wholly successful without the regular presence in the classroom of a live model who is also an expert teacher. The shortage of such doubly skilled teachers is the most serious obstacle to the success of FLES. To relieve this shortage every institution that trains future elementary-school teachers should offer a major in one or more foreign languages.

Cautions. A FLES program should be instituted only: (1) if it is an integral and serious part of the school day; (2) if it is an integral and serious part of the total foreign-language program in the school system; (3) if there is close articulation with later foreign-language learning; (4) if there are available FL specialists or elementary-school teachers with an adequate command of the foreign language; (5) if there is a planned syllabus and a sequence of appropriate teaching materials; (6) if the program has the support of the administration; (7) if the high-school teachers of the foreign language in the local school system recognize the same long-range objectives and practise some of the same teaching techniques as the FLES teacher.

One apparent solution to the great community demand for FLES instruction, even where there are no available teachers, is the use of televised and filmed foreign language lessons, given by a teacher who is a good model and involving a variable amount of follow-up work by the classroom teacher. The success of these substitute programs is directly related to the seriousness with which the classroom teachers undertake the follow-up work and to the skill with which they are trained (by special television broadcasts) for their daily tasks.

If we think of stages of language learning as levels, following the suggestion of Nelson Brooks,[1] we hope that students who have successfully completed a four-to-six-year course in FLES will have a language achievement comparable to level I, which will also represent the achievement of students who have had two years of foreign language study in grades seven and eight or one year of study in high school or one semester in college. These achievements are comparable only roughly because of the different ages and degrees of sophistication of the students and because the younger the students, the better their ability to acquire native accent and fluency.

We believe that all children should be given the opportunity to study a foreign language in the grades and that they should continue such study at least through grade six. At this point, if a child seems to have made little language progress, and if he appears to be a slow learner in most fields, it may be decided that he should not go on with his foreign language study in junior high school.

What happens, not in theory but in practice, to the pupil who does go on to junior high school foreign language study after three to six years of FLES? The worst thing that can happen to him is to make him start all over with ninth-grade beginners. The next worst is to put him with tenth-grade students who began their foreign language in grade nine. Their social maturity is greater and their linguistic command is weaker than that of the younger students. The student who has had a successful FLES experience deserves something better than this. He should have a separate track or stream or series of courses that will build on *his* foundation, instead of being thrown in with other students who have had other kinds of preparation. Having reached a level I achievement by the time he enters junior high school, he should expect to complete level II in grades seven and eight and be ready for level III in grade nine and therefore complete level VI by grade twelve.

These multiple tracks admittedly complicate the junior high school curriculum, but the move toward consolidated high schools will make the complications more bearable. The little red school-

---

[1] See "The Change from Traditional to Modern in Language Teaching," *Curricular Change in the Foreign Languages.* Princeton, N.J.: College Entrance Examination Board, 1963, pp. 46–52.

house, that symbol of the golden age of American education, is fortunately disappearing from the contemporary scene and with its disappearance will pass the curricular restrictions that we all deplore.

Administrators at all educational levels and throughout a single geographical area should agree on which foreign languages should be offered at each level, so that the FLES offerings will not put unbearably complex demands on the junior and senior high schools, or so that the junior high school will not decide to institute instruction in a neglected language that the senior high school wishes to continue to neglect. But with planned articulation, there is no reason why, in a large city system, a neglected language (Arabic, Chinese, Japanese, Italian, German, Portuguese, for example) could not be offered in the elementary and junior high school, with French or Spanish, to give some students a rare opportunity to become specialists in a neglected foreign language by the time they reach college.

Articulation must occur not only between schools but within schools. The grade two course must do more than repeat or parallel what was learned in kindergarten and grade one. It must build on what has already been learned. Between any language course and the course in the next higher grade there must be articulation in materials covered and in the use of these materials. There must be an interchange of ideas, coordination, common direction. And this requires a common philosophy of language learning throughout the school system. Without this unified set of objectives, no system of tracks will produce a meaningful sequence of language learning. There is simply no point at which the product of a course with audio-lingual stress can merge with the product of an analytical grammar-translation course without bruising both products. But if there is a common philosophy and comparable content in levels I and II at whatever grade levels they are studied, there is no reason why two tracks or streams cannot merge at level IV or even at level III. And this merger will greatly lessen the administrator's headaches.

Articulation has two dimensions: it is horizontal as well as vertical. Teachers must know what is happening in language courses that parallel the ones they are teaching as well as in courses that precede and follow them. They should make a practice of visiting the classes of their colleagues in their own school and in other schools and in other communities. Just as a picture is worth a thousand words, a demonstration of a master teacher in action is worth a thousand pages of methodology.

With America on the move, pupils are constantly transferring from one school system to another, and there is increasing need for some degree of uniformity in our elementary and secondary school curriculums. And there is a need for a reliable set of tests to measure the achievement of an incoming student so that he may be correctly placed in his language classes. The Modern Language Association, by contract with the United States Office of Education, has produced tests of this sort in the four language skills and in the five languages most commonly taught in the United States (French, German, Italian, Russian, and Spanish). The tests, produced by twenty committees of foreign language teachers under the general direction of Nelson Brooks of Yale, were widely pretested in the spring of 1962 and the spring of 1963. Norms are being established as a result of this pretesting and will be available to schools and colleges early in 1964 through the Cooperative Test Division of Educational Testing Service, Princeton, N.J.

If we do achieve an early start to foreign language study and if we do achieve effective articulation at grade seven and at grade ten, what then? More opportunities, and more problems. For we must be prepared to teach the courses at levels IV, V, and VI that will be required to meet the needs of the students whose FLES training makes them eager to do advanced work. So much foreign language instruction has been confined to the first two levels that few teachers are really equipped to teach these advanced courses effectively. Those who are entrusted with this responsibility should be urged to apply for admission to NDEA Language Institutes and to seek invitations to attend the College Board Advanced Placement Program's foreign languages conferences.

One of the articulation points most charged with emotion and beclouded with rumor is the transition from school to college. At the 1958 Northeast Conference on the Teaching of Foreign Languages, I was chairman of a session called "Ghosts in the Classroom." One of the "ghosts" whose reality we tried to examine was the belief that secondary-school students beautifully trained to speak and understand the spoken language enter college with enormous linguistic enthusiasm, enroll in intermediate French or Spanish or Whatever, and thereupon discover that not a word of the language is spoken in class, even by professors who are native French or Spanish or Whatever but attempt to communicate with their students in Echt-English. We concluded that, though the sweeping condemnation was unfair to many colleges, there was enough truth in it to make it sobering. Most of the blame rests immediately on past generations of teachers and early forms of the College Entrance Examination Board tests. They both reflected what the colleges then demanded of incoming students: a high degree of reading skill and a moderate degree of writing skill, with no mention of and no chance to exhibit any skill in listening or speaking.

An autobiographical note may be in order at this point. I graduated from Harvard many decades ago with a major in Romance languages that included quite respectable demands for competence in Spanish and French. My first teaching job was at one of the most prestigious private boarding schools in New England, and I was eager to teach my students to speak and understand French and Spanish. But this wildly radical desire was promptly squelched, for all the language instruction was geared to what was examinable on the College Board tests, and, alas, at that time, it was mostly translation into and out of English. I didn't last long at this school, and I am immodest enough to think that my leaving it was its loss and my gain, for I moved to another school that shared my belief that language is organized sound, not printed words on a page, and that language learning must begin (but *not* end) with the spoken word.

End of autobiographical note. Back to articulation between school and college. If we foreign language teachers, at school and college levels, could learn to think of ourselves not as opponents or rivals but as partners in the common task of teaching languages to Americans, we might more frequently and more successfully break through the college-admissions curtain. The schoolteacher, for example, might write to the head of the Whatever Department at a given college to ask him to see that John Smith's freshman teacher pay him some special attention, because he has developed such skill in and enthusiasm for speaking Whatever that it would be a tragedy to put him in a course conducted in English. Or he could write about George Jones, whose literary appreciation considerably exceeds his powers of self-expression in Whatever and hope that George would not, as a consequence, be reduced to reading Basic Whatever forever. Conversely, or reversely, the college teacher, noting that graduates of a given school entering his college with two credits (grades nine and ten) in Whatever and taking a placement test were almost uniformly assigned to the second-semester course (or even the first-semester course) instead of the expectable third, might write to the foreign language chairman in the school pointing this out and perhaps thus indirectly strengthening the school's foreign language content and lengthening its sequence.

Let us return to the college course in Whatever that is conducted in English. The explanation is either that the professor doesn't know enough Whatever to conduct the class in it or that he thinks his students wouldn't know enough Whatever to understand him if he tried. If it's the former reason, we can't do much about it, since the professor probably has tenure. We'll just wait it out. But if it's the latter reason, we can ask how recently the professor has tested his students on their linguistic capacities. Did he last try out a class and find it wanting in 1940? or 1950? or even 1960? If so, we urge him to keep trying, to submit each new batch of students to the test. Any year now he is going to find a class of students eager and able to use the foreign language actively, not merely to ask their way to the bathroom, but to discuss literature on a genuinely collegiate level. Until we get this kind of recognition of what is going on in some secondary-school language learning, we will be inarticulate at this crucial point in foreign language education. I would go further than to urge the professor to try out his opening lecture in the foreign language. I would plead with him to use the foreign language for the first month, to see to what extent a heterogeneous group of students could begin to catch on to what he is saying and be so excited by their success that they would have a memorable and rewarding year in language *and* literature. They might even decide to major in Whatever, and some of them might even want to teach it.

Among the most admirable attempts to improve articulation at any educational point are the Advanced Placement Examinations (an unsolicited testimonial). If they have been less than completely successful in modern foreign languages, the fault lies not in the examinations but in the extreme diversity of college freshman courses that they are intended to replace. Since there is little hope of achieving uniformity in the content of these freshman courses, we urge the colleges and (in this) their servants the College Board to agree upon a type of examination that would test the candidate not on which literary works he has read or read about but on the degree of his literary perception of prose or poetry, judged by his analysis of unfamiliar literary works. A shift to this type of Advanced Placement Examinations would solve a present dilemma: if the test is to have specific literary content (show, by references to four novels [poems, short stories] that virtue succeeds [fails] in the end), one must either limit the literary references that the candidate may use, which prescribes the content of his Advanced Placement course (very authoritarian), or one must assume that the examiner is able to evaluate any candidate's references to any literary work in the language, and omniscience is in short supply, even among College Board readers.

The next point of articulation is between the college and the graduate school of arts and sciences. Most of these graduate schools require the applicant to present credits in at least one foreign language for admission. But few of his graduate-school teachers ever require that he make any use of this knowledge in his graduate study or research. This failure to follow through makes the requirement a fraud. The solution is not to abolish the requirement but to implement it in as many graduate courses as possible.

At the end of our articulation points is the language examination for the doctorate. The Association of Graduate Schools is developing a series of examinations (in cooperation with Educational Testing Service) that will, we hope, bring order out of chaos. The series will allow, for example, a graduate student in biology presenting French (or German) as one of his foreign languages to prove his knowledge of this language as a research tool by reading and interpreting passages from Pasteur (or Mendel). An equally important step is the determination of the best time for demonstrating language proficiency. If the proficiency is to be useful in research that leads to the doctorate, it should clearly be demonstrated at the beginning or soon after the beginning of the graduate program, not, as is now the distressing custom, on the eve of the awarding of the degree.

The lengthening of the span of foreign language instruction (from predental to predoctoral) has complicated life for the administrator, who may view with nostalgia the good old days when the foreign language program consisted of two years of one foreign language in grades ten and eleven with no articulation worries except to provide for two sections of French I or German I or Spanish I in grade ten and one section of French II or German II or Spanish II in grade eleven. The job is infinitely more complex and demanding today, and, if foreign language teachers are to cope with all its complexities, they need the wholehearted and understanding support of school and college administrators from kindergarten to graduate school.

PLANNING FOR LANGUAGE LABORATORY FACILITIES

JOSEPH C. HUTCHINSON

One of the great contributions of technology to better language teaching has come in the guise of the laboratory. Like the textbook and audio-visuals it is only a tool and is no better than the use to which it is put. Joseph Hutchinson examines the use of the lab, the steps for its installation, and cautions against misconceptions concerning its purpose and use. The understanding of this tool, and skill in its manipulation are now basic to any modern foreign language teacher. The language laboratory cannot do wonders by itself, but it is an invaluable aid to the competent foreign language instructor.

RATIONALE OF THE LANGUAGE LABORATORY

It would be entirely unrealistic to approach such a complex subject as the teaching-learning process in foreign languages through only one of the many interrelating factors that must be considered. Decisions on equipment to help implement a foreign language program cannot be made properly until the program itself has been carefully planned, for the language laboratory is not an end in itself.

Planning must take into consideration first of all the students and their specific range of needs, age levels, interests, and special abilities. Next, the objectives of the course, both short-range and long-range, must be considered. The question must be raised here as to whether the listening and speaking skills are to be given emphasis. If not, there may be no need for equipment other than occasional audiovisual aids for enrichment purposes.

Reprinted by permission of the author from *Bulletin 1961,* No. 23, U.S. Department of Health, Education and Welfare, Office of Education.

Objectives cannot be decided upon adequately without some understanding about the nature of language and language learning. For example, language as talk compared to language as writing, and language learning as the formation and performance of habits compared to language learning as problem solving.

Another step to be considered is the method to be used in carrying out the objectives of the course. Will there be an initial period of exclusively audio-lingual training, and will frequent and regular guided practice with authentic speech models be used to facilitate overlearning? Or will emphasis on grammar-translation activities retard the listening-speaking-reading-writing progression?

A further major consideration is the choice of adequate materials to be used in instruction. Are they based on authentic speech patterns? Do they provide for gradual mastery of the most common structures and vocabulary in context through pattern practice? Are basic text materials and recorded practice materials the same for both class and laboratory use?

A final consideration of equal importance is the readiness of the teacher, by attitude and training, to use any electromechanical equipment as a teaching tool. First of all, if the teacher is not ready to teach according to the aims, methods, and materials that have been decided upon and do it without equipment, how can he be expected to do it with equipment? An inservice training program that gives teachers a basic orientation in the newer methods and materials, as well as ample opportunity to coordinate these with the use of simple equipment, is the least that can be done to prepare the way for purchasing any kind of language laboratory system.

Before considering what type of equipment may be needed, it would be profitable to examine carefully what it can contribute to the foreign language program and what it cannot contribute. One cannot expect language laboratory facilities, or any other teaching aid, to be a panacea for instructional problems or to do the whole job of teaching. A well-qualified teacher with adequate materials can achieve good results without the aid of equipment, although even the best qualified teacher, with the best prepared materials, can use his energies to better advantage if the machine takes over the purely repetitive types of drills.

The following are things the language laboratory facilities can do:

1. Provide for active simultaneous participation of all students

in a class in listening and listening-speaking practice in or out of class.

2. Provide a variety of authentic native voices as consistent and untiring models for student practice.

3. Provide for individual differences through guided practice in individualized group, small group, or individual study situations with facilities for student self-instruction and self-evaluation at his own learning rate.

4. Free the teacher from the tedious task of presenting repetitive drill material, thus allowing him to perform a dual role simultaneously.

5. Afford the teacher an opportunity and convenient facilities for evaluating and correcting the performance of individual students without interrupting the work of others.

6. Provide intimate contact with the language, equal hearing conditions for all students, and facilities for simultaneous grouping of different activities through the use of headphones.

7. Provide a reassuring sense of privacy, reduce distractions, and encourage concentration through the use of headphones and partitions.

8. Provide facilities for group testing of the listening and speaking skills.

9. Provide for special coordination of audio and visual materials in sequential learning series or in isolated presentations.

10. Provide aid to some teachers, who for various reasons do not have adequate control of the spoken language, in improving their own audio-lingual proficiency.

Language laboratory equipment, like other educational media, has potential dangers as well as exciting and useful possibilities. It is easily subject to overuse, misuse, and unrelated use, yet it has strong capabilities for enhancing instruction and contributing to more effective learning of the listening-speaking skills. It is up to the teacher, with the support of administrators, to get the best out of it. Equipment does not necessarily make it feasible to raise the student-teacher ratio, nor does it make the teacher's task less time-consuming. Equipment does not necessarily make teaching or learning easier, but it can make them more interesting and more productive. Hundreds of dedicated secondary school foreign language teachers have already been struggling with the pitfalls and enjoying the rewards which often mark the initial period of language laboratory use.

The language laboratory makes its greatest contribution as an integral part of a program in which audio-lingual instruction forms the basis for the progressive and continuous development of all the language skills. The language laboratory is at its weakest (1) when used as an adjunct to a traditional grammar-translation type of program, (2) when it is expected to fulfill requirements other than its basic function of helping develop and maintain the listening and speaking skills, (3) when used only for enrichment or peripheral activities, (4) when it is expected to perform the miracle of teaching the listening and speaking skills alone without the coordination and integration of classroom activities and materials, (5) when the teacher is expected to prepare all the recorded practice materials, (6) when it is used to further unsound pedagogical practices, and (7) when it allows the machine to interfere with teacher-student rapport. But, chiefly, it is at its weakest without the humanizing influence of the teacher over the machine.

There are areas of controversy and lack of agreement among members of the profession concerning the relative importance of various aspects of the language laboratory. Not all agree that there is value in having students record and replay their own practice responses for comparison with the model utterances of the recorded lesson. The advantages and disadvantages of installing sound-treated booths or partitions are still being discussed. There is disagreement about the advantages and disadvantages of teacher-student inter-communication facilities. There is also some uncertainty as to the exact specifications needed for audio quality in equipment, although a consensus is rapidly forming to protect both students and teachers from some of the inferior equipment on the market.

Research on these and other aspects of language learning equipment is imperative. Many of these problems are intricately involved with the complexities of the psychology of learning (especially the peculiar problems of language learning), psychoacoustics, and electronics. Research projects on some of these problems are already underway, but more will be needed, especially a highly controlled kind of research with properly planned experimental design. One of the greatest needs at present is for adequate standardized tests for the listening and speaking skills. This difficult field has been explored to some extent, and such testing instruments are already being developed.

In spite of lack of agreement on some things and lack of certain kinds of experimental evidence, large numbers of teachers and students derive genuine benefits from the use of language learning equipment. In the foreign language teaching profession there is general acceptance of many new basic concepts such as the listening-speaking-reading-writing progression of learning. Superior teaching is still an art which gains much of its strength through intuitive and empirical procedures. However, the fields of linguistics, psychology, and other allied disciplines have already contributed much, and hopefully will contribute more research to identify those elements in the applied field of language teaching and learning that are most productive.

THE LANGUAGE LABORATORY IN THE SECONDARY-SCHOOL PROGRAM

It cannot be emphasized too strongly that any plan for using language laboratory facilities must first include a reappraisal of the school's foreign language curriculum. Such facilities by their mere presence do not guarantee the improvement of instruction. Their proper role is that of a useful tool which can help implement the work that needs to be done, provided the tool is used skillfully as an integral and planned part of the program. Too much emphasis on the "hardware" aspects of such facilities can lead to the dangerous position of owning a language laboratory as a status symbol. One must also anticipate what will take place after the initial enthusiasm based on novelty begins to wear off. The installation of language laboratory facilities is only one of several ways to improve a foreign language program.

Learning that leads to mastery of the four basic language skills (understanding, speaking, reading, and writing) requires a fairly long apprenticeship that must be reinforced by sequential continuity. In a school situation, such learning cannot be accomplished in a span of two years. To develop language skills and to provide for the increasing student interest in foreign languages, numerous schools are extending the sequence of courses offered. In many cases, schools are planning to offer four-year, six-year, ten-year, and even twelve-year sequences of foreign language instruction. In this connection it should be stressed that long-range educational objectives include much more than mastery of skills. Foreign language study also contributes many important intellectual, humanistic, cultural, and general educational values.

In the past, schools often neglected the development of the active listening and speaking skills. Now that schools are planning to devote considerable attention to training in the spoken language, the installation of language laboratory facilities should be considered.

Once decisions are made to provide training in the various language skills, much cooperative planning and work by teachers, supervisors, and administrators are needed before consideration should be given to a specific type of commercial language laboratory installation.[1]

An inservice training program is of primary importance at this stage of planning. This can sometimes be carried out completely on the local level as a cooperative study group using local resources whenever they are available and adequate. Many teachers have already attended NDEA institutes and other workshops and seminars at colleges and universities. Such teachers can provide valuable leadership in planning and conducting workshop sessions. Even when local resources are available, it would be advisable to seek assistance and guidance from the foreign language supervisor or consultant in the State department of education. These professional leaders have much to offer in the form of resources and consultative services, sometimes including financial assistance for inservice training programs. Many have sponsored special programs of this type in various parts of their states.

Another source of consultative aid in workshops can be found in colleges and universities. A few universities have realeased staff members from part of their normal duties in order to make them available to schools for helping with inservice programs or for assisting in planning language laboratory facilities.

An inservice training program for these purposes cannot be ex-

---

[1] Alfred S. Hayes, *Step-by-Step Procedures for Language Laboratory Planning: Some Suggestions for Schools and Colleges* (New York: MLA Foreign Language Program Research Center, 1960), 16 p. Processed.

pected to be very effective if it tries to cover methods, materials, and equipment in the space of a few hours. Several sessions will more than likely be needed in order to be productive in results. In addition to becoming acquainted with new methods and materials through talks and discussions, teachers will need actual demonstrations of the techniques used in applying them. The same applies to equipment. This orientation is most easily achieved initially with a simple basic piece of equipment such as a tape recorder. Later on, more complex equipment may be used when available in a nearby school.

To be successful a workshop must provide ample opportunity for the participants to practice the application of what is presented, whether it be methods, materials, or equipment. It is especially important for teachers to learn early how to manipulate any equipment that may be used in instruction at a later date. Unless confidence is gained in these operations, away from the tensions of the classroom, teachers may experience embarrassing situations before mastering the equipment for effective teaching.

One should not expect commercial equipment representatives to train teachers in pedagogical matters. Their function in demonstrating the operation of equipment, either before or after actual installation, is very useful and often necessary. In fact, once an installation has been made, all teachers who will use the equipment should receive thorough training by the installers in the physical and operational functions of the equipment. On some occasions, it has been reported that administrators were so curious and interested in these briefing sessions that the teachers themselves were lost in the background and later had to learn for themselves how to operate the system.

Teachers should not feel hesitant to admit a lack of knowledge about the new methods, materials, and media, since few people are real experts as yet. But a teacher should try to have an open mind, display a willingness to learn, and try to keep abreast of the many new developments rapidly taking place in the profession. Membership and participation in professional language organizations and study of the current professional journals can do much to enhance a teacher's effectiveness, not only as an individual teacher, but also as a member of a profession.

METHODS AND MATERIALS FOR THE LABORATORY

The key to the newer approaches to foreign language learning is found in the methods and materials rather than in equipment. The function of equipment is merely to help implement instruction which the teacher presents in a particular form (materials) and manner (method).

Once inservice training is underway, much study and evaluation will be needed in the process of selection and preparation of materials. Most logically, one would begin with the materials of the first level of instruction and gradually devote attention and effort to the next level above in sequence, especially if radical changes are to be made. Adequate and complete materials in printed and recorded form for integrated class and laboratory use with the audio-lingual approach are not readily available for all levels during this transitional period, but adequate materials for the beginning level are starting to appear and more should be forthcoming in the near future. The revision of the *Materials List for Foreign Language Teachers* is now being made by the Modern Language Association. In addition, a carefully prepared list of evaluative criteria for guidance in selecting materials has been prepared by the MLA.

Teachers should not be expected to prepare their own basic instructional materials. The teacher is not usually equipped to prepare what is equivalent to a textbook, nor does he have the time. Yet a large number of teachers have attempted to do this out of desperation when proper materials were not available. A few cooperative groups of teachers in large school systems have been successful in sharing the burdens imposed by such a procedure. Some have adapted existing materials to the newer concepts,[2] while only a few have been able to create new materials.

In planning ahead, teachers can at least get a gradual start by getting acquainted with samples of the new types of materials and by beginning to use them in instructional situations including use with a portable tape recorder. One of the wisest things a school

[2] Patricia O'Connor. *Modern Foreign Languages in High School: Pre-reading Instruction.* U.S. Department Health, Education and Welfare, Office of Education Bulletin 1960, No. 9: OE 27000 (Washington: United States Government Printing Office, 1960), 50 p.

could do during this transitional period is to see that a portable tape recorder is provided every foreign language teacher for use in the classroom and outside the school.

In order to present some of the interrelating features of the newer methods and materials, the following outline and commentary attempts to show that sequences of progressions and levels are constantly involved in different combinations and with changing emphases. Whenever there is a time differential between some of these steps it may be a few seconds or minutes for one item while for another it may mean months. The main purpose here is to show that sequences and sequences within sequences are involved. In addition, even though emphasis may change from one sequence to the next, the preceding steps are usually maintained throughout. Overlearning is implied as a prerequisite of one step to the next in those items concerned with development of skills.

Listen → Listen-Speak → Listen-Speak-Read-Write

Listen. Ear training must precede mouth training. The acoustic image of the model must be established or internalized as a part of speaking readiness. This involves listening for aural discrimination (distinguishing between contrasting sounds in the foreign language and distinguishing between correct and incorrect versions of these sounds) as well as listening for comprehension or meaning. The format of this material in recorded form would normally be that of uninterrupted natural speech, special exercises contrasting various sounds, or even the basic materials used later for mimicry-memorization.

Listen-speak. The overt responses by the student to spaced model utterances can begin after sufficient listening practice has established sound discrimination and comprehension. The length of utterances for imitation is critical, for the auditory memory span is surprisingly short in early training. Utterances of twelve to fifteen syllables should be given in partials, or built up from the end so that each partial utterance forms a meaningful segment and retains its natural intonation pattern. Partials should preferably be no longer than five or six syllables.

The combination of partials with silent spaces and final complete utterances with silent spaces gives the student several successive opportunities with each utterance before proceeding to the next.

The length of the pause or silent space on the recorded program should preferably be equal to the preceding utterance plus an additional second or two for reaction time. The space should hardly ever exceed twice the length of the preceding utterance. The level of difficulty of listening and speaking practice should increase as these skills are maintained throughout the foreign language program.

Reading and writing. Practice in these should normally be imitative at first, that is, reading and writing practice only with material that has been mastered through listening and speaking practice.

Audio-Lingual →	Recycling →	Direct Reading →
Initial Time Lag	of Time Lag	and Writing

Initial audiolingual time-lag. This period is devoted exclusively to the listening and speaking skills before any reading or writing activities are begun. The amount of time involved in such a prereading period can vary from several weeks to several months, depending upon many other factors.[3]

Recycling of time-lag. Once the students are exposed to reading and writing, there is usually a period in which each new unit of material is mastered orally before the students are given access to the written version. Such a cycle may be completed during a few days but the process of recycling would normally continue throughout the first year.

Direct reading and writing. Once the students have control over the sound and the basic structures of the language through audiolingual practice, direct reading and writing of new material may begin with continued reinforcement by maintaining audiolingual practice.

Dialog →	Pattern Drills →	Creation of New Utterances →

Dialog. Dialog or situation-oriented material for mimicry-memorization practice contains the basic material for each unit. These model utterances (usually ten to fifteen at first) should contain authentic speech patterns based on high frequency or the most common structures and vocabulary of the spoken language. They are more useful when based on meaningful and authentic life situations

[3] *Ibid.* p. 8–9.

of interest to the age level of the students. Meaning or comprehension can be presented in several ways, but translation, except as an occasional teaching device, should not be used as an exercise for students. The use of the word *dialog* assumes that the conversational forms of the language are used, proceeding from two or more persons talking about themselves to talking about other people and things. Narrative and description may be gradually added.

Pattern drills. After mastery of the dialog sentences, one structure at a time can be presented for practice in various kinds of pattern drills in order to achieve automatic control of the structure. Models for these drills are usually based on sentences from the dialog and may begin branching out through directed dialog and other such procedures. These drills should be for learning first. Testing can follow later.

Creation of new utterances. After mastery of a number of related utterances and situations, the student may gradually be encouraged to recombine these into new utterances and situations within the limits of structures and vocabulary under his control.

$$\text{Imitate} \longrightarrow \text{Manipulate} \longrightarrow \text{Create}$$

Imitate. This is the mimicry-memorization practice, usually with the model sentences of the dialog, which follows listening practice. Imitation of the model should include numerous repetitions to the point of automatic response by memorization. It is also during this phase that pronunciation of the models should be perfected.

Manipulate. This is the pattern practice in which controlled variables of a specific structure are practiced to the point of mastery. This should proceed stey-by-step from simple or known elements to more complex or unknown elements of a specific structure. These may be based on a situational context and do not consist of mere questions and answers or conjugations of sentences. The recorded practice material may present the problem, followed by a space for the student's response, but confirmation should follow next in the form of the correct response. When the student is asked to imitate the correct response, it is usually preferable for the program to repeat it again so that the student's last impression of the utterance is that of the correct model. This presentation of challenge with a built-in reward provides an immediate reinforcement that is important in learning. The challenge should not be beyond the student's reach, however.

Create. As the audiolingual skills are developing and as control over segments of conversational interchange is gained, controlled conversation practice with the teacher and with other students should gradually become more free and creative. This is one area where only the teacher can give creative guidance, for equipment can contribute nothing at this point.

Sound	Form and Order	Vocabulary
Form and Order and Vocabulary	Sound and Vocabulary	Sound, Form, and Order

Sound. The pronunciation, rhythm, and intonation of language should normally receive initial emphasis in listening and in speaking practice even though the models also contain examples of structure and vocabulary. Natural and authentic native speech should be used as the models. Complete utterances in a meaningful context offer a more productive vehicle for the materials. Special materials for aural discrimination training would not necessarily appear in this form.

Form and order. This includes the grammatical structures of the language as they are incorporated in pattern drills. The various forms of words and the order in which they occur in normal utterances receive increasing emphasis along with the sound of the language. The number of variables practiced at one time should be carefully controlled. Explanation and analysis of grammar may be necessary at brief, carefully chosen intervals, but automatic response habits should minimize the need for this. Progression in the learning of structure is not linear in the sense of learning all about one grammatical item and then proceeding to learn all about the next one. Only conversational forms should be used during the audiolingual period and perhaps for the entire first year. At any rate, purely literary forms should be withheld until the basic reading and writing skills have been established.

Vocabulary. Vocabulary should be learned as an integral part of the practice material rather than in isolated lists. The choice of items should be very limited during the early stages of training and should be based on the most common words used in the spoken language of everyday life. Vocabulary can be explanded gradually as it is used with known structures. Once the basic structures and sound patterns are mastered, the free expansion of vocabulary can be almost unlimited.

Present   →   Drill   →   Maintain

Present. New material should generally be presented by the teacher in class. The teacher in person can control the rate of introduction of new material according to the immediate situation. He can provide the proper setting for comprehension in a variety of ways, including natural gestures, facial expressions, and visual materials. Much later in the course, when sound and basic structures are well established, new material can be presented effectively by a recorded program source.

Drill. Once the new material has been well presented and drilled through classroom procedures, the machine can then present the models or problems for the numerous repetitions needed for over-learning. This drill for the formation of automatic habits can also be guided by the teacher as he works along with the machine. Drill is one of the major functions of the language laboratory.

Maintain. Audiolingual skills must be maintained through constant review and practice. Frequent recurrence of old material should be interwoven throughout the course. Both learning tests and achievement tests are a part of this process. The language laboratory can play a large part in providing this kind of practice and facilities for testing.

Evaluating and Selecting Equipment

After reappraising its foreign language program and studying the specific needs and resources for supporting equipment, the teachers and administrative staff of a school can begin a careful study of specific equipment. One should not consider a year as too much time to spend in planning, if it is decided that language laboratory facilities are needed. Such a large variety of equipment is now available from approximately fifty different companies that the evaluation and selection of equipment can be a difficult procedure for many schools.

Valuable advice and information can be obtained from careful study of the *Purchase Guide* and its *Supplement*.[4] In addition to these, most State departments of education have formulated standards and guidelines for schools participating in title III programs.

Visiting other schools which already have language laboratory facilities can be a very revealing experience, and much valuable information can be gathered from such visits. Frank discussion with teachers and administrators of other schools about their experience with the equipment can often prevent mistakes and can also confirm judgments that may have already been made. Before attempting to copy what another school has done, one should consider that each situation may call for a different combination to suit the specific requirements of the school. For example, colleges and some private secondary schools usually face a different set of problems from those of a public secondary school where students are present only during a scheduled part of the day.

Pedagogical, administrative, and technical factors must all be considered in the planning. Each feature of equipment should be examined in relation to what it contributes to the instructional program. One should consider whether a commercially produced language laboratory system is appropriate or whether simpler combinations of equipment would be adequate.

Whatever decision is made, the number of students and the number of courses which the equipment will serve must be considered. A further consideration should be given to scheduling of facilities according to groups and according to time. Will the equipment be used during regular class periods by the entire class under the instructional supervision of the teacher, or will it be used by individual students in special periods during or outside the school day? Can provisions be made to accommodate the largest foreign language class or will the students in the same class have to rotate in groups? Will scheduling the equipment for 100 percent usage during each session cause major problems whenever a few of the student stations are not functioning because of temporary electromechanical difficulties? Will laboratory sessions in addition to regular class periods be needed? Will the equipment provide facilities

[4] Council of Chief State School Officers, *et al.*, *Purchase Guide for Programs in Science, Mathematics, and Modern Foreign Languages; Supplement to Purchase Guide for Programs in Science, Mathematics, and Modern Foreign Languages* (Boston: Ginn and Co., 1959, 1961), 336 p.; 60 p.

for regular and frequent machine drill sessions or will it defeat its own purpose by affording beginning students only one laboratory session per week?

Some of these questions lead to a consideration of whether centralized or decentralized facilities will be more appropriate. Many secondary schools have decided against separate laboratory rooms in favor of the electronic classroom arrangement. Administrative factors have often led to this decision, but in many cases the decision was made for pedagogical reasons. In some schools, it is difficult to distinguish between the two types, since an electronic classroom in some cases may have more elaborate equipment than some separate laboratories.

Decisions on whether to provide for individual or group use should be based primarily on pedagogical factors. The question of whether to include booths of a specific type or no booths is not easy to answer. Will the room be used exclusively for laboratory work or for a variety of activities? Using a room with fixed student partitions for regular class activities can cause a frustrating situation for both teacher and pupils. Should student recording facilities be included? If so, what kind, and how many? These questions can only be answered in relation to all the factors involved. For example, is the expense justified if other students are deprived of having any laboratory facilities? Will there be adequate facilities for testing the speaking skills without student recording facilities?

The question of whether to provide a teacher console and the number of features to be incorporated in it can pose many problems. Is an intercommunication system really needed? Will it be simple enough to operate effectively? How many different program sources are needed? Are the controls all within easy reach of the teacher? Is there sufficient writing space for the teacher? Will the teacher be able to maintain eye contact with the pupils, and will the pupils also be able to see projected visual materials? Are extra features needed if there is no plan to use them?

A few more of the numerous questions which must be considered include:

1. Are adequate storage facilities available for the materials and simple accessories?

2. How much minor remodeling and extra electrical power wiring will be required for installation? For future expansion?

3. How much preventive maintenance will be required, and who will do it?

4. What accessories, supplies, and spare parts will be needed?

5. Who will service the machines and when?

6. What kind of warranty is included, and what does it cover?

7. How much money should be budgeted for maintenance, repair, and replacement?

8. What is the relation of the actual audio quality to the claimed specifications?

9. Do the specifications contain all the pertinent technical information that is necessary to make them valid?

10. Will a sworn affidavit that the installed equipment actually meets the specifications protect the school?

11. What procedures are established to permit the school to reject an unsatisfactory installation or equipment that does not meet the required specifications?

12. Is the audio quality of the system weakened by inferior headphones or microphones?

13. Will the equipment hold up under constant heavy use?

14. Is it safe to subcontract language laboratory facilities as part of a new building contract?

15. Will the installation be completed by the date specified in the contract or should a penalty clause be added?

16. Will the equipment be compatible with other facilities in future expansion?

17. Will the supplier leave a sample of his equipment to be tested by the school?

Reliable answers to these and many more questions are not usually found in a single source. An unbiased technical consultant can provide some of them. Professional language experts as well as audiovisual personnel in schools and colleges can be helpful. Planning for language laboratory facilities is not generally a simple job for one person to undertake. It requires the cooperative efforts of many people if it is to be done well.

FL PROGRAM POLICY

The most appropriate conclusion for this anthology is to present the Modern Language Association Foreign Language Program Policy. It touches various aspects of foreign language teaching and presents the pertinent summarized thinking of the MLA and various sister organizations. This statement gives the profession a crystallization of thinking and policy on matters relative to the basic points of foreign language teaching.

Broad policies governing the general conduct of the Foreign Language Program were laid down during the spring of 1952 by the Executive Council of the Modern Language Association, which at the same time appointed the MLA Executive Secretary to be director of the Program, with discretionary powers to determine future policy. In December 1952 the Council appointed a Steering Committee[1] to advise the director.

Since the FL Program during its first two years was essentially an investigation, no further policies were enunciated in this period. In 1955 the Steering Committee was enlarged by the inclusion of representatives of the American Associations of Teachers of French, German, Italian, Slavic and East European Languages, and Spanish and Portuguese. At the first meeting of this enlarged Committee, on February 12–13, 1955, an important statement on "Qualifications for Secondary School Teachers of Modern Foreign Languages" was formulated. This statement was subsequently endorsed for publication by eighteen national and regional language organizations.

At its meeting on April 28–29, 1956, the Steering Committee ad-

Reprinted by permission of The Modern Language Association of America from *PMLA*, September, 1956.

[1] The Steering Committee: Theodore Andersson, Josephine Bruno, Stephen A. Freeman, Renée J. Fulton, Claude P. Lemieux, Albert H. Marckwardt, Bayard Q. Morgan, Werner Neuse, Howard Lee Nostrand, William R. Parker, and Donald D. Walsh.

dressed itself to the formulation of additional policy statements. These and two earlier statements are published on the following pages in the hope that they will be discussed by foreign language teachers at local, state, regional, and national meetings.

VALUES OF FOREIGN LANGUAGE STUDY

The study of a foreign language, like that of most other basic disciplines, is both a progressive *experience* and a progressive acquisition of a *skill.* At no point can the experience be considered complete, or the skill perfect. Many pupils study a foreign language only two years; longer time is of course needed to approach mastery. At *any* point, however, the progress made in a language, when properly taught, will have positive value and lay a foundation upon which further progress can be built. It is evident therefore that the expectancy of values to be derived from language study must be relative to the amount of time and effort devoted to it.

The study of a foreign language, skillfully taught under proper conditions, provides a *new experience,* progressively enlarging the pupil's horizon through the introduction to a new medium of communication and a new culture pattern, and progressively adding to his sense of pleasurable achievement. This experience involves:

1. The acquisition of a set of *skills,* which can become real mastery for professional use when practiced long enough. The international contacts and responsibilities of the United States make the possession of these skills by more and more Americans a matter of national urgency. These skills include:

a. The increasing ability to *understand* a foreign language when spoken, making possible greater profit and enjoyment in such steadily expanding activities as foreign travel, business abroad, foreign language movies and broadcasts.

b. The increasing ability to *speak* a foreign language in direct communication with people of another culture, either for business or for pleasure.

c. The ability to *read* the foreign language with progressively greater ease and enjoyment, making possible the broadening effects of direct acquaintance with the recorded thoughts of another people, or making possible study for vocational or professional (e.g., scientific or journalistic) purposes.

2. A new understanding of *language,* progressively revealing to the pupil the *structure* of language and giving him a new perspective on English, as well as an increased vocabulary and greater effectiveness in expression.

3. A gradually expanding and deepening knowledge of a foreign country—its geography, history, social organization, literature, and culture—and, as a consequence, a better perspective on American culture and a more enlightened Americanism through adjustment to the concept of differences between cultures.

Progress in any one of these experiences is relative to the emphasis given it in the instructional program and to the interests and aptitude of the learner. Language *skills*, like all practical skills, may never be perfected, and may be later forgotten, yet the enlarging and enriching results of the *cultural experience* endure throughout life.

ON FOREIGN LANGUAGE TEACHING

The elementary language course at all levels, from elementary school through college, should concentrate at the beginning upon the learner's *hearing and speaking* the foreign tongue. Optimum results can be achieved by giving as much individual or controlled group oral practice as possible, and by setting the upper limit of class size at twenty. Throughout later stages, in lectures and in class discussions of literature and civilization, students should be provided with frequent opportunities for *maintaining* the hearing and speaking skills thus early acquired.

These recommendations are made with awareness of important differences among languages, among teaching situations and objectives, and among both learners and teachers. We recognize also that progress requires continuing experimentation and therefore an attendant variety of practices.

Learning to *read* a foreign language, the third phase of the hearing-speaking-reading-writing progression in the active and passive acquiring of language skills, is a necessary step in the total process. In teaching this skill, the goal should be reading with understanding and without conscious translation. Translation should be used only rarely as a device in teaching reading, but may come at a later stage as a meaningful literary or linguistic exercise provided that high standards are insisted on. Repeated systematic grammar review is wasteful in a reading class, but explanation of recurring, complex syntactical patterns is essential.

Writing is the fourth stage in the early acquirement of language skills; the student should write only what he is first capable of saying correctly. Topics should be assigned and carefully defined in such a way that the student may utilize to the maximum the vocabulary and speech patterns he has acquired. On an upper level of accomplishment, writing may include original composition, consideration of stylistics, analysis of literary texts, and translation of passages of literary English.

FLS AND INTERNATIONAL UNDERSTANDING

American education is seriously concerned with the achievement of international understanding and cooperation. Foreign language learning has three contributions, two of which are unique, to make to the cultivation of better understanding among peoples of different linguistic background.

1. *Direct Intercultural Communication.* Only language learning permits direct intercultural communication through speech or writing. Some direct communication takes place through music, art, and other means, and interest and good will can be shown in many ways, but willingness to learn another language is perhaps the best token, in a multilingual world, that we *care* about international understanding. We must learn to use the other fellow's language if we would understand him because he will not find self-evident or satisfying the twist that English will inevitably give to partially shared ideals, aspirations, and concepts. If we insist on the exclusive use of English, we isolate ourselves from people of other cultures and miss altogether a wealth of important human contacts. At the same time we demonstrate that we expect others to describe things as *we* see them, not as they do.

It must be admitted, however, that, having studied the Orient in college and acquired fair proficiency in French, we may later find ourselve vacationing in Latin America or sent to Germany on business. Of what value is language learning to international understanding unless, by good luck, we have chosen the particular language we shall later need? A knowledge of one foreign language will normally make easier the learning of a second, but that is beside the point; we must remember, as well, a second unique contribution of language learning to international understanding.

2. *Experience of a Foreign Culture.* Through mimicry and speech-pattern assimilation, language learning brings the beginnings of direct comprehension, without translation, of foreign utterance and writing, and the beginnings of automatic vocal response in conversational situations. From this point on, the learner *experiences* the foreign culture (i.e., the total pattern of behavior) by actually participating in an integral part of it. He has crossed an intellectual border, from a state of monolingualism to the realization that one can learn to make, without conscious effort, *foreign* responses to foreign stimuli. When the language student progresses to the point of being able to read foreign literature with understanding, his awareness of the new cultural medium is further enriched by the insights of creative writers, and his sympathies are involved by the skill of great art directly experienced.

Only language learning affords this intimate perception of a culture. It thus makes a crucial contribution toward the potential understanding of many cultures unlike our own, for a single experience with cultural relativity makes easier the transition to another mode of thought and, if need be, to many others. The antipathies that develop as psychological reactions to "foreign-ness" are much more likely to appear in monolingual persons than in those who have experienced direct comprehension and response in a foreign communication system.

3. *Information About a Foreign Culture.* The moment that language learning moves beyond the initial stage of listening and speaking it makes use of the printed word in the development of additional skills. The modern textbook "reader" in language classes usually has cultural content selected to give students an increasing knowledge of significant differences between the foreign peoples and Americans—in behavior, attitudes, and historical background. The language teacher, whose training (including foreign travel and acquaintance with the people and their literature) has given him personal experience in international understanding, is able to bring additional life and meaning to even the best of textbooks with his own knowledge and insight.

Foreign language teaching obviously has no monopoly on imparting information; indeed, information *about* a foreign culture derived from a language teacher or a language textbook may be somewhat more costly of time than information obtained, say, in a social studies class or through a translation. This third contribution of language learning to international understanding would be inefficient, therefore, were it not for the two other contributions which it *uniquely* makes.

THE PROBLEM OF TIME

Most public statements about the values of language learning, whether made by language teachers or by other persons, stress values that are achieved only with mastery of a foreign language or very considerable proficiency in speaking and reading it. No harm is done by such statements unless they imply or assume—as too often they do—that mastery or real proficiency can be achieved in two years of high school or one year of college instruction.

In the educational system of *no other nation on earth* is such an assumption made. It is not made because it is irresponsible. It is made in the United States only because language instruction here, unlike language instruction elsewhere, is frequently limited to two years of high school or one year of college instruction. The inevitable result has been disillusion for both pupils and public. With more and more people now advocating foreign language study in the national interest, both the public and educational administrators need to realize the amount of curricular time necessary for the acquisition of real proficiency in a second language. Here is the truth about the factor of time.

1. *Vocabulary.* Given adequately prepared teachers, classes of reasonable size, and proper aims, methods, and materials, in two high school years or one college year of instruction it is possible to inculcate an "active" (speaking-writing) vocabulary of between 500 and 1,000 words, and a "recognition" (hearing-reading) vocabulary of approximately 1,500 to 2,500. "Language," of course, is more than a body of isolated words than can thus be counted, but these figures give us a basis for significant comparison. A typical modern "reader" for seven-year-olds in an American elementary school contains between 500 and 600 English words. "Basic English" consists of 850 words. A responsible estimate (1941) gives an American child of six an

average "recognition" vocabulary of 16,900 basic words or 23,700 total (basic plus derivative) words. The youth of eighteen has a recognition vocabulary of 47,300 basic words or 80,300 total words. Another study (1945) based on children's writing shows that the composite active, i.e., written, vocabulary of American first-graders amounts to 5,099 words and that the corresponding figure for eighth-graders is 17,930 words.

A moment's reflection will make it clear that the limited vocabulary taught in a beginning foreign language course is, of pedagogical necessity, carefully chosen for its usefulness in connection with graded readers and in illustrating a variety of grammatical and idiomatic points about the new language. Usually it is *not* chosen with a view to tourist or business needs, as would be the vocabulary taught, say, in a commercial language course.

The president of the Berlitz School of Languages estimates that "a good working knowledge" of a spoken foreign language takes about 100 hours of *individual instruction.* The wartime Intensive Language Program, with its very small classes, involved 612 or more hours of concentrated instruction. On the other hand, a typical one-year beginning language course in college involves between 90 and 120 hours of instruction in classes of twenty or more students. One must consider the problems faced by the instructor of such a course.

2. *Knowledge and Skills.* Properly directed, language learning is a richly varied experience; but when time is severely limited, the language teacher is compelled either (*a*) to attempt all the possible things and therefore do them superficially, or (*b*) to neglect some because of the desperate effort to do justice to others. Either decision leads to disappointment for many students. Let any reasonable person think for a moment about the problem in its simplest terms: How, in ninety hours of classroom time, to teach the following:

a. Listening comprehension of a new tongue.

b. Speaking ability involving the making of new sounds in unfamiliar structures.

c. Reading ability involving the rapid acquisition of a "passive" vocabulary considerably in excess of that used in speaking.

d. Writing ability.

e. Knowledge of structural differences between the foreign tongue and one's own, explained through grammatical terminology that in many cases will be as foreign to the student as the new language.

ƒ. Knowledge of the foreign culture.

g. Comprehension of the subject matter of any texts used.

What emerges from the usual one-year college or two-year high-school attempt to achieve all these basic, widely acknowledged objectives? We get a student who can read, say, a little very simple French, or talk Spanish within a very limited conversational range. Make no mistake about it, he has no "mastery" of a second language, and both the vocational and cultural advantages of genuine proficiency are still beyond his reach. He has merely had what in many other nations would be the beginning of seven or nine years of uninterrupted instruction, leading to eventual proficiency.

We believe that, while even limited instruction in a foreign language has educational value as a "Copernican step," it does not produce results commensurate with national needs on the one hand or the normal and natural expectations of parents and students on the other hand. Accepting blame, as a profession, for some beclouding of this issue in the past, we urge that educational administrators, wherever and whenever possible, institute in our schools and colleges sequences of language instruction that will guarantee to those students with aptitude and interest the mastery they want and need to achieve.

AUDIO-VISUAL AIDS

Professional alertness demands that language teachers consider unremittingly how technological advances in their field may help them improve their individual proficiency. New types of equipment, which at first disturb our customary procedures and serve us awkwardly in the early stages, have a way of becoming indispensable later. As more people learn to master the new machines, they add to their total teaching effectiveness.

It is a matter of national urgency as well as of professional pride that teachers of foreign languages, along with their colleagues in other fields, seek all possible means of improving their efficiency, individually and collectively. The possibility that audial and visual aids to language teaching—especially, instruction by radio and television and use of language laboratories—can enable the highly skilled language teacher, with the help of assistants, to teach a greater number of students without loss of effectiveness, deserves investigation.

The general satisfaction experienced by the more than 100 colleges and universities which have already installed and experimented with language laboratories leads us to conclude that the language laboratory has already been accepted by many as a highly desirable aid to language teaching.

We therefore recommend:

1. That language instructors through experimentation familiarize themselves with and develop the possibilities of using audio-visual equipment.

2. That objective evaluation techniques be developed and applied.

3. That state, regional, and national organizations of language teachers make increased efforts to study these experiments and to communicate their findings to the widest possible audiences.

4. That adequate training in the use of A-V techniques be included hereafter in the preparation of FL teachers;

5. That language instructors in individual institutions seek administrative support for language laboratory equipment, including visual aids, as an already widely accepted adjunct to teaching.

FLS IN THE ELEMENTARY SCHOOLS

After more than three years of studying a variety of reports on the teaching of foreign languages in the public elementary schools, we express our approval of this popular movement in American education.

In our judgment the movement deserves the support of parents and educational administrators because:

1. It recognizes the evidence concerning the process of language learning, introducing study of a second language to children at an age when they are naturally curious about language, when they have fewest inhibitions, and when they imitate most easily new sounds and sound patterns.

2. It recognizes the fact that the greatest natural barriers to international understanding are the unreasoning reactions to "foreign-

ness" which are often acquired in childhood but which may be offset by experiences with foreign speech and behavior; and

3. It recognizes the fact that real proficiency in the use of a foreign language requires progressive learning over an extended period.

It is our further judgment that the public should be warned against faddish aspects of this movement. No new venture in American education can long prosper without the wholehearted support of parents, teachers, and educational administrators in a given community. Proponents of foreign language study in the elementary schools should not, therefore, initiate programs until

1. A majority of the parents concerned approve at least an experimental program.

2. Local school boards and administrators are convinced that necessary preparations have been made.

Necessary preparations include:

1. Recruitment of an adequate number of interested teachers who have both skill in guiding children and the necessary language qualifications.

2. Availability of material appropriate to each age level, with new approaches and a carefully planned syllabus for each grade.

3. Adequate provisions for appraisal.

The success of existing programs thus initiated, prepared for, and appraised convinces us of the urgent need of providing, for children who have the ability and desire, the opportunity for continuous progress in language study into and through junior and senior high school.

THE UNUSUAL LANGUAGES

Although it is a commonplace that the United States now occupies a position of world leadership, it is still not sufficiently recognized that in order to meet, on a basis of mutual understanding and co-operation, not only the diplomats and military men but also the common people of the other nations of the globe, the United States does not yet have nearly enough persons adequately trained in the languages of those nations. We urge, therefore, that constructive measures be taken as rapidly as possible to encourage in our colleges and universities the study of the more significant world languages; for example, those of the people of India, of the Near East, of Japan and China, of Indonesia, of Central Africa. Even the study of Russian has been and is seriously deficient, compared with our national need in view of the present struggle of ideologies.

Language study in our schools is still limited too exclusively to the Western European countries. Adequately trained teachers and instructional materials for other languages are scarce or nonexistent. The Committee on the Language Program of the American Council of Learned Societies, therefore, with the aid of Ford Foundation grants is now developing a body of trained linguists, a corpus of descriptive analyses of many of the less-known languages, and materials for instruction in the form of manuals, recordings, and dictionaries. This tooling process is slow, but it is indispensable and merits wider recognition and encouragement.

In order to develop effective instruction, we urge the establishment of *centers of instruction* in colleges and universities in various parts of the country, each one specializing in a single group of languages spoken by millions of people but practically unknown to us. It would be desirable also to make available in each center instruction in the geography, history, economics, and politics of the language area studied. It is essential and urgent *educational planning*, regional and national, that we call for; we believe it is possible and desirable to develop such centers throughout the United States. Without such progress in language competence, the United States can hardly measure up to its present world responsibilities.

THE FL PROGRAM AND THE CLASSICAL LANGUAGES

The steering committee for the Foreign Language Program of the Modern Language Association of America believes that the obvious relevance of modern language study to modern life should not blind educators or the American public to the importance of our having more citizens who know *ancient* languages. It is not only that our Western civilization is more intelligible to those who can directly read its origins and development in our heritage from Greece and Rome; there is also the urgently *modern* fact that our children and grandchildren are going to have to understand this Western heritage in relation to the cultural traditions of the East.

Accumulating evidence shows that a first foreign language can most readily be learned in childhood and learned primarily as spoken language. Unless Latin is taught in this way, we believe that study of an ancient language is best postponed until secondary school age, and that an ancient language can be learned most efficiently if a modern foreign language has first been approached as speech. Hence we recommend that the study of Latin as a second foreign language be vigorously promoted in our secondary schools, and we further recommend that administrators, counsellors, and teachers of modern languages in our colleges and universities take practical steps to encourage more students to learn ancient Greek, Hebrew, classical Arabic, Chinese, and Sanskrit.

Latin is the parent language of French, Italian, Spanish, and Portuguese. It has also, with Greek, furnished nearly the whole of our English intellectual vocabulary. Its literature is the key to many basic concepts that we have modified to create what we tend to think of as our uniquely modern political, esthetic, and intellectual life. Ignorance of this cultural heritage is a dubious preparation for cultural advance. Ignorance of one's linguistic heritage is, moreover, a dubious basis for informed and effective use of either English or a modern Romance language. We view the decline of Latin in American education as an unfortunate result of radical and short-sighted efforts to "modernize" the curriculum and make education "practical."

The curriculum of the future, if it is designed to meet problems of the future, will recognize that the classical languages—Eastern as well as Western—have a claim to the attention of educated men and women who would, through language study, know the significant past at first hand. This is an essential contribution of the Humanities, which the modern languages—whose own past is steadily lengthening—share in, but cannot monopolize.

COLLEGE FL DEGREE REQUIREMENTS

We believe, as do the faculties of 706 liberal arts colleges in the United States, that some experience with and some degree of skill in using a foreign language are a truly *indispensable* element in liberal education. We further believe that our country's foreseeable international responsibilities make it imperative for more Americans to acquire a more functional knowledge of modern foreign languages. In a world in which the skill is in growing demand, ability to use a modern foreign language more than justifies its continued prominence in curricula offering many other rewarding educational experiences, for the cultural benefits of language study are as great as ever. We therefore affirm:

1. That no curriculum leading to the B.A. degree is educationally defensible unless it requires of all students reasonable proficiency in the use of *at least one* foreign language.

2. That by "reasonable proficiency" we mean, in the case of modern foreign languages, certain abilities, no matter how or when acquired: (*a*) the ability to get the sense of what an educated native says when he is speaking simply on a general subject, (*b*) the ability to use the common expressions needed for getting around in the foreign country, speaking with a pronunciation readily understandable to a native, (*c*) the ability to grasp directly the meaning of simple, non-technical writing, except for an occasional word, and (*d*) the ability to write a short, simple letter. We spell out these skills because we believe that the increasingly important educational justification of a language requirement is not served by statement of the requirement solely in terms of courses or credit hours.

Pledging ourselves to strive for continued improvement of language teaching in our colleges, we urge the colleges to make certain that their language requirement, as affecting the modern languages, is rewarding to the student and meaningful for the nation. Finally, we urge any institutions which have hitherto either decreased or abandoned their foreign language degree requirement to reconsider their educational programs in the light of changed conditions and critical needs.

ON LEARNING FOREIGN
LANGUAGES: ADVICE TO THE
LANGUAGE LEARNER[1]

About 3,500 languages are spoken in the world today, and more than 140 of them have over a million speakers each. Since the United States is involved in some way with almost every other country, members of your generation will need to learn all the major languages and even some of the minor ones. The trouble is that no one can predict today which of these many languages you will need to know ten or twenty years from now. Maybe some day you will have to learn a language that you have not even heard of yet. Your present foreign language course, therefore, serves a double purpose, teaching you the language you are now studying and also teaching you techniques of foreign language study so that you can apply them to later study of other languages.

Learning Your Own Language. All over the world children learn to understand and speak their own language before they go to school. They acquire this wonderful skill by constant practice, by listening and talking all the time to themselves, to their family and friends. At first the child only repeats words and phrases that he has heard and learned. But, he finds that he has to put new sentences together to get what he wants. He tries the new sentences out on people. They accept some of his sentences but reject others because they are funny or because they don't make sense. The child keeps on trying until he works out a system for producing acceptable, understandable sentences. He assembles in his mind a simple model of the language, his own grammar of his language.

Languages Are Different. The new language you are learning will be easier if you do not expect it to behave like English. It will have different sounds, and its words will have different kinds of meaning fitted together in un-English ways. Even though every living language has been learned by every child who speaks it, you will

[1] This statement grew out of a conference on the application of linguistics to language learning held at the offices of the Modern Language Association in 1964. It was printed in tentative form in the 1965 Directory issue of *PMLA*. It was then revised in the light of comments from many teachers and linguists. Donald D. Walsh.

not find it child's play to learn this new language. Learning it will require a lot of hard work, but any intelligent student can accomplish it, especially with a good teacher and a good textbook.

Language and Writing. In all languages writing has always followed speech, often by many thousands of years. Most of the languages of the world have not yet been put into written form by their speakers. Most writing systems are just ways of putting on paper what someone has said, either aloud or to himself. For example, all the written languages of Western Europe use the Roman alphabet, but each one uses these letters to represent its own sounds. When you study the written form of any of these languages you will have to learn to overcome the interference from English, which will tempt you to pronounce letters in another language as they are pronounced in English. They almost never are.

Learning a Foreign Language. Learning a foreign language is not something that you just think and talk about, like rules and theories. It is something that you *do*, a physical *activity*, a little like learning to play the piano or the violin, except that it is easier. Learning any skill requires a great deal of practice. And since using a language means using sounds, you must do much of your practicing aloud. Learning a language means learning a whole new pattern of habits. You must work hard to prevent your English habits from getting in your way. Many of your English language habits will be bad habits for your new language.

There are three techniques in language learning: imitation, analogy, and analysis. You must use them all.

Learning by Imitation. In learning a language you must practice imitating a model who is speaking at normal speed. You need also to hear a variety of voices, on records and tapes. Watch your teacher carefully, listen carefully to your teacher and the other models, and practice imitating them aloud. Concentrate first on the spoken form of sentences and conversations, not on the written forms that you will find printed in your book. Repeat what you hear as closely as you can, so that your pronunciation will improve with practice. Listen to the pitch levels of each phrase. Don't learn words singly but learn phrases.

Learning by Analogy. A significant moment in a child's learning his own language is the first time he says something like "Mary goed home." This mistake is a creative mistake, for it shows that the child is beginning to understand how language works. By thinking of "sew, sewed" or "show, showed," which he learned through imitation, he has created by analogy a new pair, "go, goed," that he had probably never heard, and in so doing he has shown that he can learn by analogy, even though this attempt is not a complete success. Until you can make and understand new utterances, building upon patterns learned earlier by imitation, your knowledge of the language is even more limited than the child's when he says "Mary goed home." Learning how to create by analogy is the purpose of pattern drills and other exercises. Each of these drills begins with a model phrase and asks you to produce new phrases by analogy from the model. A child has to grope his way toward language control through many trial-and-error analogies, but a student using a good textbook will have step-by-step practice arranged to keep his errors to a minimum.

Learning by Analysis. Young children learn sounds more accurately and with more enthusiasm than their elders. As you grow older, you begin to lose this capacity for easy imitation. But to make up for this loss, you have the advantage of being able to reason; you can analyze language. You can see how your new language is put together, how it works, how it differs from English. Information of this sort, given in grammatical explanations or rules, can help you to learn the language faster. But language analysis (learning *about* the language) is not the same as learning to *use* the language. Explanations are only an aid to learning; they are not the language itself, just as knowing the rules of the road does not make you automatically a good driver. That takes practice.

The Need for Practice. Unless you are learning your new language in a country where everyone speaks it, you will not get as many opportunities to practice speaking it as you got when you were learning English. So you will learn more rapidly if you make your opportunities for practice intensive and enthusiastic. You will find many conversations and drills in your textbook. Practice them as intensely as you can, in class and out. Whenever someone else is reciting, practice silently right along with him. When you do your homework, practice out loud. Practice with tapes and records. Repeat after them, and speak up just as if you were talking all the way across a big room. And practice your newly learned phrases on your fellow students.

Memorizing. You will have to learn a great many patterns and phrases as you study a language. Don't be afraid of stretching your memory. The more you use it the better it gets. You can involve almost all your senses as you learn a language, by using your ears, mouth, eyes, fingers. Use your imagination. Pretend that you are an actor whose lines you are learning. Break up your memorizing sessions into several intense, short periods (fifteen to twenty minutes) instead of a single long stretch of time. Be sure to practice out loud when you memorize. And of course make sure that you know the meaning of each phrase that you learn, so that you can combine and vary phrases to express what you want to say.

Reading and Writing. You can learn the difficult skills of reading and writing more easily if you have learned to *speak* the language. You must practice speaking it right from the start and continue to practice speaking throughout all your study of the language. Even if you are not interested in the spoken language, you can not learn to read it without using *some* kind of pronunciation, even if it is only a silent one that you invent. So it makes sense to learn the normal pronunciation. Reading foreign articles and books for information and enjoyment is one of the principal reasons for studying a foreign language; your enjoyment will increase if you know what the language sounds like to the writers and readers of its literature.

Writing Systems. Writing systems are incomplete because they seldom indicate rhythm, pitch, or stress. They often seem senseless —even in English—because there may be no apparent reason why any letter or combination of letters represents a sound. Consider, for example, the various spellings of a single English sound: *see,* k*ey,* sh*e,* rec*ei*ve, bel*ie*ve, t*ea,* or the various sounds represented by the letters *ea* in m*ea*t, cr*ea*te, gr*ea*t, h*ea*rt, S*ea*ttle. Speech and writing, though related, are different systems. Speech came first in the development of language, comes first for every native learner, and it should come first for you, too.

How to Read in a Foreign Language. At first, you should read only what you have practiced saying, and you should read it aloud. When you begin to read silently and you come to words and phrases that are new to you, use the following techniques: (1) Read the passage through for general sense first, without stopping to puzzle over unfamiliar words or constructions. Then go back for a second, more careful reading. When you come to an unknown word, read on at least to the next punctuation mark before you look it up. Try to get the meaning from the sentence without having to look for it in the vocabulary. (2) When you decide that you must look up a word, (a) underline the word with your pencil, (b) take a good look at the phrase that contains it, and pronounce the phrase aloud, (c) repeat the phrase over and over, aloud if possible, concentrating all your attention on its sound and spelling while you are looking for the key word in the vocabulary, (d) when you find it put a dot before the word in its column, (e) turn back to your page, find the last underlined word, and go on reading. Never write the English translation on the page. Doing so puts the emphasis on the English equivalent and not on the foreign word which is the word that you must learn. When you finish your assignment, reread it and see how many of the phrases containing underlined words you still understand. Look up the words you have not yet learned and put another dot in front of them in the vocabulary. Look through the vocabulary once a week and make a special effort to learn the words with several dots. These are your "hard" words. Learn them now or you will be spending hours looking them up month after month, year after year. And go back over you reading material to check your understanding of the sentences that have underlined words or phrases.

Prepare for the Future. We said earlier that you have no sure way of knowing now which foreign languages will eventually be of most value to you. But if you learn one foreign language well in school, the skills that you acquire will be helpful in learning your next foreign language, whenever and wherever you learn it. You may then have to work with inadequate materials or with no materials at all and with a model who has had little or no training as a teacher. But if, in learning your first foreign language, you have also learned how to study languages in general, you will be able to apply this skill to the study of any other language at any time or place.

GENERAL BIBLIOGRAPHY

Allen, Harold B. *Teaching English as a Second Language.* New York: McGraw-Hill Book Company. 1965.

Andersson, Theodore Murdock. *The Teaching of Foreign Languages in the Elementary School.* Boston: D. C. Heath and Company, 1962.

Bagster-Collins, Elijah William. *Studies in Modern Language Teaching.* New York: The Macmillan Company, 1930.

Belasco, Simon (ed.). *Anthology for Use with a Guide for Teachers in NDEA Language Institutes.* Boston: D. C. Heath and Company, 1961.

———. *Applied Linguistics: A Guide for Teachers,* 5 vols. Boston: D. C. Heath and Company, 1961.

Beliaev, Boris Vasil'evich. *The Psychology of Teaching Foreign Languages,* trans. by R. F. Hingley. New York: Pergamon Press, 1964.

Bloch, Bernard and George L. Trager. *Outline of Linguistic Analysis.* Baltimore: Linguistic Society of America, 1942.

Bloomfield, Leonard. *Language.* New York: Holt, Rinehart & Winston, Inc., 1933.

———. *Outline Guide for the Practical Study of Foreign Languages.* Baltimore: Linguistic Society of America, 1942.

Boas, Franz. *Race, Language, and Culture.* New York: The Macmillan Company, 1940.

Britton, Karl. *Communication: A Philosophical Study of Language.* New York: Harcourt, Brace, & World, Inc., 1939.

Brooks, Nelson. *Language and Language Learning,* 2nd ed. New York: Harcourt, Brace, & World, Inc., 1964.

Carnap, Rudolf. *The Logical Syntax of Language,* trans. by Amethe Smeaton (Countess von Zeppelin). New York: Harcourt, Brace, & World, Inc., 1937.

Carroll, John Bissell. *Language and Thought.* Englewood Cliffs, N.J.: Prentice-Hall, Inc., 1964.

———. *Research on Teaching Foreign Languages.* Cambridge, Mass.: Harvard University Press, 1960.

———. *The Study of Language: A Survey of Linguistics and Related Disciplines in America.* Cambridge, Mass.: Harvard University Press, 1953.

Cassirer, Ernst. *An Essay on Man.* New Haven: Yale University Press, 1944.

Chomsky, Noam. *Syntactic Structures.* 's Gravenhage (The Hague) Netherlands: Mouton, 1964.

Cole, Robert Danforth. *Modern Foreign Languages and Their Teaching.* New York: Appleton-Century-Crofts, Inc. 1937.

Coleman, Algernon. *The Teaching of Modern Foreign Languages in the United States.* New York: The Macmillan Company, 1929.

Conference on Modern Foreign Languages in the High School, Washington, D.C., 1957. *Modern Foreign Languages in the High School.* Washington, D.C.: Office of Education, 1958.

Conference on the Interrelations of Language and Other Aspects of Culture, Chicago, 1954. *Language in Culture.* Chicago: University of Chicago Press, 1954.

Cornelius, Edwin T., Jr. *Language Teaching.* New York: Thomas Y. Crowell Company, 1953.

Council of Chief State School Officers. *Purchase Guide for Programs in Science, Mathematics, and Foreign Languages.* Boston: Ginn and Company, 1959.

Diekhoff, John Siemon. *NDEA and Modern Foreign Languages.* New York: Modern Language Association of America, 1965.

Eriksson, Marguerite *et al., Foreign Languages in the Elementary School.* Englewood Cliffs, N.J.: Prentice-Hall, Inc., 1964.

Ferguson, Charles A. and W. A. Stewart (eds.). *Linguistic Reading Lists for Teachers of Modern Languages: French, German, Italian, Russian, Spanish.* Washington, D.C.: Center for Applied Linguistics, 1963.

Finocchiaro, Mary Bonomo. *English as a Second Language: From Theory to Practice.* New York: Regents Publishing Company, 1964.

————. *Teaching Children Foreign Languages.* New York: McGraw-Hill Book Company, 1964.

Fodor, Jerry A. and Jerrold J. Katz. *The Structure of Language: Readings in the Philosophy of Language.* Englewood Cliffs, N.J.: Prentice-Hall, Inc., 1964.

Fries, Charles Carpenter. *Teaching and Learning English as a Foreign Language.* Ann Arbor: University of Michigan Press, 1960 (c1945).

Georgetown University, Washintgon, D.C., Institute of Languages and Linguistics. *Monograph Series on Languages and Linguistics.* September, 1951–1966, No. 1–16, Washington, D.C., 1951–1966.

Gleason, Henry A., Jr. *An Introduction to Descriptive Linguistics,* rev. ed. New York: Holt, Rinehart, and Winston, Inc., 1961.

Gullette, Cameron Charles *et al. Teaching a Modern Foreign Language: A Brief Manual of Methods and Practices.* New York: F. S. Crofts & Co., 1942.

Hall, Edward T. *The Silent Language.* Garden City, N.Y.: Doubleday & Co., Inc., 1959.

Hall, Robert Anderson, Jr. *Linguistics and Your Language*, 2nd rev. ed. of *Leave Your Language Alone!* Garden City, N.Y.: Doubleday & Co., 1960 (c1950).

Halliday, Michael Alexander Kirkwood *et al. The Linguistic Sciences and Language Teaching.* Bloomington, Ind.: Indiana University Press, 1965.

Handschin, Charles Hart. *Methods of Teaching Modern Languages.* New York: World Publishing Company, 1923.

Haugen, Einar Ingvold. *Bilingualism in the Americas: A Bibliography and Research Guide.* Gainsville, Fla.: American Dialect Society, 1956. Obtainable from University of Alabama Press.

Hayakawa, Samuel Ichiye. *Language in Thought and Action.* New York: Harcourt, Brace, & World, Inc., 1964.

———— (ed.). *Our Language and Our World: Selections from Etc.: A Review of General Semantics, 1953–1958.* New York: Harper & Row Publishers, Inc., 1959.

Hjelmslev, Louis. *Prolegomena to a Theory of Language,* trans. by Francis J. Whitfield. Madison, Wisc.: University of Wisconsin Press, 1961.

Holton, James S. *et al. Sound Language Teaching: The State of the Art Today.* New York: University Publishers, 1961.

Huebener, Theodore. *How to Teach Foreign Languages Effectively,* rev. ed. New York: New York University Press, 1965.

Hutchinson, Joseph C. *Modern Foreign Languages in the High School: The Language Laboratory.* Washington, D.C.: Office of Education, 1961.

Jespersen, Otto. *How to Teach a Foreign Language,* trans. by Sophia Yhlen-Olsen Bertelsen. London: G. Allen and Unwin, 1956. First published in 1904.

————. *Language: Its Nature, Development, and Origin.* New York: The Macmillan Company, 1949.

Korzybski, Alfred. *Science and Sanity: An Introduction to Non-Aristotelian Systems and General Semantics,* 4th ed. Lakeville, Conn.: The International Non-Aristotelian Library Publishing Company, 1962. Distributed by Institute of General Semantics.

Lado, Robert. *Language Teaching: A Scientific Approach.* New York: McGraw-Hill Book Company, 1964.

————. *Language Testing.* London: Longmans, Green & Co., Ltd., 1961.

————. *Linguistics Across Cultures; Applied Linguistics for Language Teachers.* Ann Arbor, Mich.: University of Michigan Press, 1957.

Lambert, Wallace E. *A Study of the Roles of Attitudes and Motivation in Second Language Learning; Final Technical Report.* Montreal: McGill University Press, 1961.

Landar, Herbert Jay. *Language and Culture.* Fairlawn, N.J.: Oxford University Press, 1966.

Lehmann, Winfred Philipp. *Historical Linguistics; An Introduction* New York: Holt, Rinehart, and Winston, Inc., 1962.

Leopold, Werner F. *Speech Development of a Bilingual Child; A Linguist's Record,* 4 vols. Evanston, Ill.: Northwestern University Press, 1939–1949.

Lewis, Morris Michael. *Infant Speech; A Study of the Beginnings of Language,* 2nd ed. London: Routledge and Paul, 1951.

Libbish, B. (ed.). *Advances in the Teaching of Modern Languages.* New York: The Macmillan Company, 1964.

MacRae, Margit W. *Teaching Spanish in the Grades.* Boston: Houghton Mifflin Company, 1957.

Malinowski, Bronislaw. *Coral Gardens and Their Magic,* 2 vols. Bloomington, Ind.: Indiana University Press, 1965.

Martinet, Andre. *A Functional View of Language.* Oxford, England: The Clarendon Press, 1962.

Marty, Fernand L. *Language Laboratory Learning.* Wellesley, Mass.: Audio-Visual Publications, 1960.

Meras, Edmond Albert. *A Language Teacher's Guide,* 2nd ed. New York: Harper & Row Publishers, Inc., 1962.

Miller, George Armitage. *Language and Communication.* New York: McGraw-Hill Book Company, 1951.

Modern Language Association of America. *MLA Selective List of Materials for Use by Teachers of Modern Foreign Languages in Elementary and Secondary Schools.* New York: Modern Language Association Foreign Language Program Research Center, 1962.

————. *Reports of Surveys and Studies in the Teaching of Modern Foreign Languages.* Washington, D.C.: Modern Language Association Foreign Language Program Research Center, 1961.

————. Committee of Twelve. *Report.* Boston: D. C. Heath and Company, 1910.

Morris, Charles William. *Signs, Language, and Behavior.* New York: G. Braziller, 1955 (c1946).

National Education Association of the United States, Academically Talented Student Project. *Modern Foreign Languages and the Academically Talented Student.* Washington, D.C., 1960.

————. Department of Audiovisual Instruction, *Language Laboratory and Language Learning.* Washington, D.C., 1964, monograph 2.

Newmark, Maxim (ed.). *Twentieth Century Modern Language Teach-*

ing; Sources and Readings. New York: The Philosophical Library, 1948.

Northeast Conference on the Teaching of Foreign Languages. *Report of the Working Committees.* New Haven: Yale University Press, 1954–1966.

Nostrand, Howard Lee *et al. Research on Language Teaching; An Annotated International Bibliography for 1945–64,* rev. ed. Seattle: University of Washington Press, 1966.

Ohannessian, Sirarpi. *Interim Bibliography on the Teaching of English to Speakers of Other Languages.* Washington, D.C.: Modern Language Association of America, Center for Applied Linguistics, 1960.

Osgood, Charles Egerton and Thomas A. Sebeok (eds.). *Psycholinguistics; A Survey of Theory and Research Problems* with A. Richard Diebold, *A Survey of Psycholinguistic Research, 1954–1964.* Bloomington, Ind.: Indiana University Press, 1965.

Palmer, Harold Edward. *The Principles of Language-Study.* London: Oxford University Press, 1964 (c1921).

Parker, William Riley. *The National Interest and Foreign Languages; A Discussion Guide,* 3rd ed. Washington, D.C.: United States Government Printing Office, 1961.

Piaget, Jean. *The Language and Thought of the Child,* 3rd ed., trans. by Marjorie Gabain. New York: Humanities Press, 1959.

Politzer, Robert Louis. *Teaching French; An Introduction to Applied Linguistics.* 2nd ed. New York: Blaisdell Publishing Company, 1965.

——— and Charles N. Staubach. *Teaching Spanish; A Linguistic Orientation.* Boston: Ginn and Company, 1961.

Rivers, Wilga M. *The Psychologist and the Foreign-Language Teacher.* Chicago: University of Chicago Press, 1964.

Sapir, Edward. *Culture, Language, and Personality.* Berkeley: University of California Press, 1961 (c1949).

———. *Language; An Introduction to the Study of Speech.* New York: Harcourt, Brace, & World, Inc., 1949.

Saporta, Sol (ed.). *Psycholinguistics.* New York: Holt, Rinehart, and Winston, Inc., 1961.

Staats, Arthur W. and Carolyn K. Staats. *Complex Human Behavior; A Systematic Extension of Learning Principles.* New York: Holt, Rinehart, and Winston, Inc., 1963.

Stack, Edward MacGregor. *Language Laboratory and Modern Language Teaching.* Fairlawn, N.J.: Oxford University Press, 1965.

Sweet, Henry. *The Practical Study of Languages; A Guide for Teachers and Learners.* London: Oxford University Press, 1964.

Thorpe, James Ernest (ed.). *The Aims and Methods of Scholarship in*

Modern Languages and Literatures. New York: Modern Language Association of America, 1963.

United Nations Educational, Scientific, and Cultural Organization. *The Teaching of Modern Languages*. Paris, 1955.

United States Office of Education. *Language Laboratory Facilities*. Washington, D.C.: United States Government Printing Office, 1963.

——. *Modern Foreign Languages in the Elementary School; Teaching Techniques*. Washington, D.C., 1960.

——. *Modern Foreign Languages in the Secondary School; Pre-Reading Instruction*. Washington, D.C., 1959.

——. *Source Materials for Secondary School Teachers of Foreign Language*. Washington, D.C., 1962.

——. National Defense Language Development Program, *Research and Studies*. Washington, D.C.: United States Government Printing Office, 1960–1963.

Walsh, Donald Devenish (comp.). *What's What; A List of Useful Terms for the Teacher of Modern Languages*, 2nd ed. New York: Modern Language Association of America, 1964.

Weinreich, Uriel. *Languages in Contact; Findings and Problems*. New York: Linguistic Circle of New York, Columbia University, 1953.

Whatmough, Joshua. *Language; A Modern Synthesis*. New York: St. Martin's Press, 1956.

Whorf, Benjamin Lee, *Language, Thought, and Reality; Selected Writings*. Cambridge: Technology Press of Massachusetts Institute of Technology, 1959 (c1956).

INDEX

Abilities, theories of, 230–35
Accent, 96, 208
Advanced Placement Program, 330–31, 352–53
African languages, 88, 381
Ahmed, M. A. S., 172
Air Force Academy, 59n
Alphabets, textbook presentation of, 93
Altus, Grace T., 148
Amala, 8
American Assembly, 117n
American Association of Teachers of French, 85, 371
American Association of Teachers of German, 85, 371
American Association of Teachers of Italian, 85, 371
American Association of Teachers of Slavic and East European Languages, 85, 371
American Association of Teachers of Spanish and Portuguese, 86, 371
American Council of Learned Societies, 124
American education
second culture as imperative in, 112–42
standards in, 67–71
Anastasi, Anne, 171
Andersson, Theodore, "The Teacher of Modern Foreign Languages," 253–77
Animals
brain structure in, 194–95
communication among, 4–6
instrument conditioning of, 220–22
symbolic behavior in, 10–15
teaching of words to, 16n, 18n
Anisfeld, M., 243
Anomie, 241
Anthropology Curriculum Study Project, 124
Apes, 25, 26n
communication among, 4–6
symbolic behavior in, 10–15
teaching of words to, 16n, 18n
Aphasia, 201, 203–4, 207
in bilinguals, 238
Arsenian, S., 150, 151–52, 154, 155
Aristotle's *Rhetoric,* 51
Articulation, 95
brain mechanism in, 207
Asiatic languages, 88, 381
Aspiration, 95
Association of Graduate Schools, 353
Audio-visual materials, 80–81, 256, 378–79
in FLES program, 308
in understanding other cultures, 126–27, 134, 138, 340–41

395